Media and Politics in Japan

Edited by

Susan J. Pharr and Ellis S. Krauss

University of Hawai'i Press
Honolulu

01 00 99 98 97 96   5 4 3 2 1

Library of Congress Cataloging-in-Publication Data

Media and politics in Japan / edited by Susan J. Pharr and Ellis S. Krauss
     p.   cm.
    Includes bibliographical references and index.
    Contents: Media and politics in Japan : historical and contemporary perspectives / Susan J. Pharr — Media as trickster in Japan: a comparative perspective / Susan J. Pharr — Mass media as business organizations : a U.S.-Japan comparison / D. Eleanor Westney — Portraying the state in Japan : NHK television news and politics / Ellis S. Krauss — Japan's press and the politics of scandal / Maggie Farley — Television and political turmoil : Japan's summer of 1993 / Kristin Kyoko Altman — Media and policy change in Japan / John Creighton Campbell — Media and political protest : the bullet train movements / David Earl Groth — Media coverage of U.S.-Japan relations / Ellis S. Krauss — Media exposure and the quality of political participation in Japan / Scott C. Flanagan — Media in electoral campaigning in Japan and the United States / Hiroshi Akuto — Media agenda setting in a local election : the Japanese case / Toshio Takeshita and Ikuo Takeuchi — The mass media and Japanese politics: effects and consequences / Ellis S. Krauss.
    ISBN 0-8248-1698-6 (alk. paper) ISBN 0-8248-1761-3 (pbk.)
    1. Mass media—Political aspects—Japan. 2. Japan—Politics and government—1945– I. Pharr, Susan J. II. Krauss, Ellis S.
P95.82.J3M43 1996
302.23'0952—dc20   95-8730
                                                                                                            CIP

Designed by Paula Newcomb

Media and Politics in Japan

CONTRIBUTORS

HIROSHI AKUTO

KRISTIN KYOKO ALTMAN

JOHN CREIGHTON CAMPBELL

MAGGIE FARLEY

SCOTT C. FLANAGAN

DAVID EARL GROTH

ELLIS S. KRAUSS

SUSAN J. PHARR

TOSHIO TAKESHITA

IKUO TAKEUCHI

D. ELEANOR WESTNEY

This book grew out of a workshop series sponsored by the Joint Committee on Japanese Studies of the Social Science Research Council and the American Council of Learned Societies.

To Robert and Martha
with love and gratitude

CONTENTS

TABLES

PREFACE

THIS book resulted from an international collaborative venture that has a long history. The project from which it grew was sparked by a discussion of the Joint Committee on Japanese Studies (JCJS) of the American Council of Learned Societies and the Social Science Research Council (SSRC) in the early 1980s. Reflecting on what key areas of research had been neglected in the social science literature on Japan, the committee asked why the media as a force in social and political life had received so little attention. No country in the industrial world is as media-saturated as Japan. Its five national dailies—each with a circulation of over 2 million—translate into the highest per-capita newspaper circulation in the world. Some 90 percent of adults read newspapers daily, and the average person watches more than three hours of television a day. Given the rising importance of the media in all the industrial societies, Japan thus presents itself as a laboratory for exploring the role the media play today in democracies. Japan is an especially useful testing ground, JCJS members held, because the great bulk of research on the role of the media in politics and society has focused on the United States. Japan offers a setting for testing and rethinking theories derived from American experience.

The JCJS agreed to make funding available for a planning meeting if scholars came forward to take up the challenge. But organizing a project on the media in Japan proved to be more difficult than the committee had thought. Most collaborative research ventures of the kind encouraged by the SSRC bring together scholars who are already working independently on related topics or themes and who are thus ready and willing to join in a common endeavor. In the case of work on the Japanese media, however, the situation was entirely different. Remarkably, despite the widely acknowledged importance of the topic, relatively few scholars outside Japan have conducted research on the contemporary Japanese media's role in politics. In Japan itself, despite the existence of key media research centers at the University of Tokyo, Keiō University, and elsewhere, relatively little research has focused on the broad effects of the media on political life in a comparative framework.

Susan Pharr agreed to organize the project, and there followed a long period of recruitment that continued, indeed, until the book assumed its final shape. Of the American authors whose work is represented in this volume, none had a lengthy track record of academic research on the media in Japanese politics at the time of the first planning meeting, held in Cambridge, Massachusetts, in May 1984. Partly as a result of this project, Ellis Krauss was stimulated to expand his preliminary research on NHK into a larger research program. He came to play a leading role in the project and later joined Susan Pharr as an editor of this volume.

John Campbell, University of Michigan, and Scott Flanagan, Florida State University, joined Pharr and Krauss at the first planning session. Also at the session were Michael Reich of Harvard University, Fukashi Horie of Keiō University, and Ted Bestor representing the SSRC. Frank Schwartz, then a graduate student at Harvard, served very ably as rapporteur. David Paletz, a political scientist at Duke University who has studied the media in a comparative political-science framework, was unable to attend, but he made valuable suggestions concerning scholars working on related topics with a focus on other parts of the world who might be enlisted at some stage as discussants.

At the session, it was agreed that the project should be binational, in order to draw on and learn from the base of media research in Japan. Pharr subsequently contacted Hiroshi Akuto, University of Tokyo, who became, with her, co-organizer of the project. It was also agreed that Akuto would edit any Japanese-language publication resulting from the project. Further recruitment then proceeded on both sides of the Pacific. Akuto successfully sought a grant from the Japan Society for the Promotion of Science (JSPS) to support travel and research-related activities of the Japanese participants. Pharr received funding from the SSRC for the first workshop, and from the Japan–United States Friendship Commission for the second and follow-up activities.

The first workshop was held at the Nissan Institute, Oxford University, 11–14 July 1985. Arthur Stockwin, director of the institute and Nissan Professor of Modern Japanese Studies, served as host. The Nissan Institute provided a congenial setting for a workshop that included Michio Muramatsu, Kyoto University; Hirohisa Suzuki, University of Tokyo; Olga Linne, University of Leicester; and Colin Seymour-Ure, University of Kent; Ted Bestor, representing the SSRC; and Morio Watanabe, then of the University of Wisconsin, serving as rapporteur. At the workshop, the project participants presented preliminary drafts of their papers or research plans. Because most of the participants were new to comparative research on the media in politics, Olga Linne and Colin Seymour-Ure, both of whom have studied the media in other advanced industrial nations, made very valuable contributions to the meeting. Michio Muramatsu, though he is not a media specialist, played an important role in the discussion because of his deep knowledge of politics and political behavior in Japan.

The relative scarcity of data on the media in Japanese electoral politics spurred the Japanese team to conduct an election study in Japan for the project. Sponsored by JSPS and carried out in February 1986, the survey (described in the chapters by Hiroshi Akuto and by Toshio Takeshita and Ikuo Takeuchi) included questions submitted by Ellis Krauss and Scott Flanagan. It enriched the data base for the project and represented a form of American and Japanese collaboration that has not been common in binational projects sponsored by the joint committee.

The second workshop was held in Hawai'i, 5–9 January 1987. All the people whose work appears in this volume (except journalists Maggie Farley and Kristin Kyoko Altman) presented drafts at the workshop. Hirohisa Suzuki and Kiyoshi Midōka, both of University of Tokyo, also made presentations that proved highly useful in the exchange. Patricia Steinhoff of the University of Hawai'i, at that time a member of the JCJS, joined the sessions as a discussant. Majid Tehranian, also of the University of Hawai'i, was an able general discussant for the workshop. Stefan Tanaka of the SSRC served as staff.

From the second workshop emerged a fascinating series of drafts at various stages of research and preparation. But the picture of the media's role in politics was still incomplete. To round it out, a contribution on the media's highly visible role in political scandals was required. In the late 1980s and early 1990s, scandals were convulsing Japanese politics, ultimately triggering the fall of the Liberal Democratic Party in the summer of 1993. Maggie Farley, a professional journalist with much experience in Japan, was invited to contribute a chapter to this volume based on her 1992 master's thesis at Harvard. Kristin Kyoko Altman, a political reporter and anchor for TV Asahi, agreed to prepare a chapter on the intriguing and portentous role of television in the watershed events of the summer of 1993. Krauss contributed a new chapter on another topic of growing interest today: the media's role in trade tensions between the United States and Japan.

Conceived a decade ago to fill a lacuna in the literature on Japan as well as to contribute to comparative research on the media's role in politics, this project has achieved what it set out to accomplish.

Remarkably enough, this book stands alone as the first major collaborative research volume in English to deal with the media's role in contemporary Japanese politics in comparative perspective. The project has also sought to play an active part in spurring further research. In addition to the collaborative activities discussed so far, the project has led to panels at meetings of the American Political Science Association, the Association for Asian Studies, and the International Political Science Association, and to numerous meetings in Cambridge, Tokyo, New York, Pittsburgh, and elsewhere among the many scholars who have participated at various stages. Works by Gregory Kasza (*The State and the Mass Media in Japan, 1918–1945* [Berkeley: University of California Press, 1988]), Ofer Feldman (*Politics and the News Media in Japan* [Ann Arbor: University of Michigan Press, 1993]), and others that have appeared since the project began, or that are now under way, offer promising signs that scholarship on the Japanese media's role in politics and society in comparative perspective is thriving today.

According to the usual practice of books on Japan that seek a wider audience, Western name order is used for Japanese names throughout this volume.

A book so long in the making incurs many debts. We would like to express appreciation to the Joint Committee on Japanese Studies for providing both the inspiration for the volume and the resources for the project in its early stages, and to the Japan–United States Friendship Commission for its generous financial support. We are also grateful to the Japan Society for the Promotion of Science for providing funding for the Japanese participants in the project. We would like to single out Ted Bestor, Stefan Tanaka, and Mary Byrne McDonnell of the SSRC and Lyn Sloan of the Friendship Committee for particular thanks; we have a debt to them as well as to numerous other people in those organizations.

We also extend thanks to the many scholars mentioned in this account who, though not contributors to this volume, took part in the planning meeting, workshops, or related panels at professional meetings, or who participated in some other way. This project brought many of the contributors, including the editors of this volume, into a new area of research, and we all benefited greatly as a result. None of those mentioned bears responsibility for the final volume, but each helped to make it possible.

In closing, the editors of this English-language volume wish to express particular thanks to Hiroshi Akuto and other members of the

Japanese team for their warm hospitality in Tokyo to both of us over the years of the project, and to the Nissan Institute and Arthur Stockwin for providing such a pleasant and stimulating setting for the first workshop. We also extend our thanks to the Center for Strategic and International Studies, formerly headed by Amos Jordan and now by David Abshire, where the workshops were planned and organized; to Harvard's Reischauer Institute of Japanese Studies, directed formerly by Akira Iriye and now by Helen Hardacre, where the final work on the volume was completed; and to the Japan Council and its Japan Iron and Steel Federation endowment fund, Faculty of Arts and Sciences Dean Peter Koehler, and Political Science Department Chair B. Guy Peters, University of Pittsburgh; to Margot Chamberlain, who ably oversaw the many drafts and changes that come with an editing project; to John McVey and George Scialabba for their editing; and to Kim Reimann, Saori Horikawa, and Christina Davis for their valuable research and other assistance; to Mary Mortensen, who prepared the index; and to Patricia Crosby and Cheri Dunn of University of Hawai'i Press. On a personal note, Ellis Krauss is grateful to Martha Leche for her unflagging support and tolerance during the later stages of this project. Susan Pharr would like to thank her husband, Robert Cameron Mitchell, for his help and unstinting support throughout.

SUSAN J. PHARR
ELLIS S. KRAUSS

PART I

The Mass Media and Japan

Introduction

Media and Politics in Japan: Historical and Contemporary Perspectives

SUSAN J. PHARR

FEW questions are as intrinsically fascinating and of obvious importance for understanding the present and the future of industrial democracies as those that concern the role of the media in society and politics. At the U.S. political conventions in the summer of 1992, media representatives far outnumbered the presumed "real" players, the delegates. Lingering television images of town halls, memories of billionaire Ross Perot on camera with graphs in hand, and news of a media-stung Democratic president's 1994 moves to reshuffle his team of spokespersons and spin-doctors once again: these are vivid reminders of the omnipresence of the media in politics today and of their centrality to politicians and the public alike.

The role of the media in the political upheavals in Japan in the summer of 1993 offered similar reminders. Prime Minister Kiichi Miyazawa's fall, sealed by a no-confidence vote in Japan's parliament, or Diet, on June 18, began on May 31 with some ill-advised remarks in a television interview.[1] As new conservative parties rose to challenge the long-standing dominance of Japan's Liberal Democratic Party (LDP), which had held power since 1955, their leaders raced from one talk show to the next positioning themselves for the July 18 lower house election. No sooner had election results confirmed the demise of the LDP's solid majority than leading politicians from all of Japan's parties rubbed shoulders on two- and three-hour television specials discussing coalition formulas. In the political rumble of summer 1993, *tarento* (literally, "talents")—media celebrities turned candidates—trumped Japan's aging generation of conservative leaders who were more skilled at backroom deal making than talking on camera.

3

In industrial societies today, some politicians—no matter how intelligent their grasp, how astute their political judgments, or how incisive their issue positions—cannot be packaged successfully, while others can. This has led numerous scholars and other observers to conclude that the media are recasting political leadership itself, at least in the case of national political elites. Meanwhile, media-borne scandals—whether over nannies in America or stashed gold bars in Japan—thin the ranks of those who would serve the public.

As the bureaucracies of the advanced industrial societies "note, register, inventory, tax, stamp, measure, enumerate, license, assess, authorize" (to quote the French anarchist Proudhon) by way of policies that reach into ever increasing domains of human behavior, the media become powerful screening devices for vast flows of information. Only a tiny fraction of the work of the state in the United States, Japan, or elsewhere becomes exposed to public scrutiny, and many of the struggles within bureaucracies and among and between interest groups represent efforts to capture or deflect media attention or to turn it to advantage. Not only do politics and bureaucracy feel the media's presence and power; so, too, does the public. Despite a vast amount of research, mystery surrounds the simple act of voting in a media age: from what confluence of forces and factors do voters make their decisions on candidates, and how do the media confound the process? A broader issue for the 1990s and beyond is whether the media—especially television and new electronic media technologies—foster political community or, instead, breed apathy and alienation.

If media saturation is well advanced in most industrial societies, Japan is no exception. The case can be made—and indeed has been made in works by scholars such as Ezra Vogel—that Japan leads the world in the information revolution and in the breadth of coverage and sophistication of the media.[2] The circulation of Japan's largest daily newspaper, *Yomiuri Shimbun,* is greater than that of the *New York Times, Washington Post, Wall Street Journal, Christian Science Monitor,* and *New York Daily News* combined.[3] Over 72 million newspapers are published each day in a country where 90 percent of the public, according to one study, reads newspapers on a daily basis.[4] Japan's per-capita newspaper circulation (581 copies per 1,000 persons) is the highest in the world, more than twice that for the United States (250 copies per 1,000 persons).[5] The penetration and influence of the print media are even greater than these figures suggest, since five newspapers *(Yomiuri, Asahi, Mainichi, Sankei,* and *Nihon Keizai)* are national papers, each with a circulation of more than 2 million. In addition there are the local and regional newspapers, some of which have circulations exceeding those of many leading U.S. newspapers; daily mass-circulation party newspapers, such as the Japan Communist Party's *Akahata* (Red Flag); and magazines that range from book-length "comprehensive magazines" *(sōgō zasshi)* to the ubiquitous comic books *(manga)* read by young and old alike on the trains. NHK (Nihon Hōsō Kyōkai), Japan's public broadcasting organization, is the second largest broadcasting corporation in the world (after Great Britain's BBC) but increasingly it is losing audience to the "big five" commercial stations, each of which has organizational and financial links to Japan's five major dailies. In Japan there are far more television sets than homes, and the average Japanese spends three hours and twenty-three minutes daily watching television.[6] Radio and extensive mini-media published by various citizens' groups round out the picture. Table Intro.1 provides an overview of Japan's media.

The media have a vast following in Japan, and they enjoy great prestige. While Gallup and Harris surveys in the United States have found that less than 20 percent of Americans polled express high confidence in television and the newspapers, both media enjoy far greater credibility in Japan. Reversing an earlier trend, today newspapers in Japan have higher credibility ratings than television news, but a solid majority of Japanese trust both.[7] Indeed, surveys on the public's views of NHK indicate that NHK is trusted more than any other major institution in Japan, including the Diet, the courts, or the government in general.[8] (NHK and its news coverage are explored in chapter 3.) One Japanese study found that only some 20 percent of those surveyed saw any kind of partisan bias in the newspapers, television, or magazines.[9] Meanwhile, Japanese media coverage of domestic and international political events and phenomena—as measured by number of reporters posted abroad, amount of broadcasting time and column inches devoted to political news, and numerous other indicators—may be more extensive than that of any nation on earth.[10]

Most political gurus and academic media specialists today agree that the information revolution generally and the growth of the media more specifically have had a profound impact on politics, culture, and society in advanced industrial democracies. They often disagree, however—as do social scientists generally—over the actual nature of the media's role. There are three major interpretations of the role of the media in relation to state and society in democracies. The first approach sees the media as *spectators*—more or less neutral

Table Intro.1   Japan's Mass Media

MEDIA TYPE	DESCRIPTION	DIFFUSION
Newspapers	"Big 5" national dailies: *Yomiuri* (14.4 m), *Asahi* (12.8 m), *Mainichi* (6.0 m), *Nikkei* (4.6 m), *Sankei* (2.9 m)	combined daily circulation more than 50 m
	Local and regional newspapers, including *Hokkaidō* (2.0 m), *Tokyo* (1.1 m), *Chūnichi* (3.1 m)	
	Party press, including national daily *Akahata* ("Red Flag"), published by Japan Communist Party	
TV	Public broadcasting: NHK	60 m sets; subscriber fees paid by 90% of all households; 5.8 m households receiving cable
	"Big 5" commercial channels, including Nippon TV *(Yomiuri)*, TBS *(Mainichi)*, Fuji-TV *(Sankei)*, Asahi-TV *(Asahi)*, TV Tokyo *(Nikkei)*	
	New media, including two NHK satellite broadcasting channels, cable television	
Radio	Public broadcasting: NHK	more than 150 m sets
	Commercial channels	
Magazines	High-brow monthly "comprehensive magazines" *(sōgō zasshi)*, including *Chūō Kōron, Sekai, Bungei Shunjū, Shokun* (200–300 pp. volume combining news; fiction; cultural, social, economic, and political commentary and analysis; reviews)	4.24 b combined circulation
	Popular weekly and monthly magazines, including weekly news magazines such as *Shūkan Asahi (Asahi)* and *Shūkan Yomiuri,* scandal magazines such as *Focus,* and *manga* (comic books, including adult comic books)	
Mini-media	Published by citizens' groups, including newsletters, magazines, brochures, and handouts	

Source: Newspaper circulation figures, which are as of November 1993, are those given in Nihon Shimbun Kyōkai, *The Japanese Press 1994* (Tokyo: Nihon Shimbun Kyōkai, 1994). Data for television and radio are from Foreign Press Center, *Japan's Mass Media* (Tokyo: Foreign Press Center, March 1990), p. 48. For television and magazines, tie-ins with "big five" newspapers are indicated in parentheses. Figure for combined magazine circulation is for 1988, ibid., p. 64. Figure for cable television subscribers is for 1989, ibid., p. 62.

conduits for the flow of information among the various "real" players in politics. The general public and the overwhelming majority of media specialists reject such a view, but most social science research must accept it (witness the remarkably little systematic attention the media receive in mainstream political science scholarship). Furthermore, the difficulties that researchers in media studies have had in documenting major media effects on politics make it hard to overturn such a view. A second approach sees the media as a major independent force in politics—a "fourth branch of government"[11]—that works as a *watchdog* on behalf of society to protect the public interest. A third approach holds that the media ultimately are *servants of the state,* which forge a consensus on social and political values and generate support for a regime.

Each of these contradictory interpretations, which are discussed in more detail in chapter 1, has been applied to Japan's media in their relation to state and society. Most social science research on Japan has paid relatively little attention to the media's role, lending support to the view of the media as spectators to political life. On the face of it, this interpretation seems to make sense in Japan because of the severe legal limits on the media's role in political campaigning—which, after all, is at the heart of political life in democracies—and because of the norms of neutrality that have been stringently maintained in Japan by television (at least until recently) and by newspapers. For all the talk-show sparring by politicians in the summer of 1993, severe limits on media use in campaigning have created a political landscape in Japan very different from the one in the United States. Japan's Election Law prohibits political candidates from buying space in newspapers or magazines or time on television and radio. For each candidate, the government pays for a total of four television appearances of five and a half minutes each, which may include an additional thirty seconds of biographical material, and five newspaper ads of a specified size to appear in newspapers of the candidate's choosing. Following revision of the Election Law in 1975, political parties, as distinct from candidates, have been able to buy time and space freely, but the ads cannot mention the candidacy of particular party members. Industry codes as well as the law dictate strict neutrality in campaign coverage. For the evening news, television stations edit scrupulously to make sure that candidates receive equal exposure; if equal footage of a candidate's rivals is lacking that day, viewers may see only a candidate's back.[12] Though the Japanese themselves rate their newspapers along a liberal-conservative continuum (see chapter 10), newspapers do not endorse candidates or parties editorially, and they bend over backward to adhere to a norm of impartiality in their campaign coverage.[13]

Some of these prohibitions are not enforced. For example, though the law bars newspapers from publishing opinion poll results comparing the candidates' popularity, the leading dailies all conduct such polls and forecast the election results. This triggers an "announcement effect" *(anaunsu kōka)* that influences voters' views.[14] Opinion journalism is on the rise, at least on television, and news anchors now pepper reports with their personal views.[15] In the 1990s parties and candidates have edged forward into the electronic age, hiring media consultants and experimenting with party-focused documentaries that stay within the law. In the 1990s, too, television debates among candidates are fast becoming an institution. But the limited coverage led Gerald Curtis to conclude in his 1988 study of Japanese politics: "Nowhere else where comparable technologies are available have the print and electronic media had as minimal an impact on election campaign styles as in Japan."[16] Little wonder that political hopefuls in 1993 vied for exposure on talk shows and television specials; that summer's turmoil had bequeathed them an "electronic loophole."[17]

Limitations on media use in political campaigning and norms constraining media partisanship, then, offer grounds for seeing the Japanese media as "spectators." But alternative interpretations also find support. Numerous observers of Japanese politics and society, including Japanese media professionals themselves, have hailed the media as "watchdogs" pure and simple. According to many, in a country that at least until recently had weak opposition parties, the media have served as the functional equivalent of a viable opposition, offering a continuing critique of those in power.[18] Whether covering environmental pollution cases in the late 1960s or "money politics" in the 1990s, the media have sought to protect the public by exposing the powerful, or so this interpretation goes. (Chapters 4 and 7 explore the media's performance as social critic.)

The diametrically opposed interpretation that casts the media as servants of the Japanese state finds equally strong support. As shown in chapter 2, media conglomerates dominate in Japan as elsewhere in the industrial democracies; indeed, their power ostensibly is greater in Japan because the major commercial television channels are owned by the big newspapers. National dailies, each with a circulation in the millions, have a financial base well beyond that achieved by any U.S. newspapers, only a few of which (such as the *New York Times*, *USA Today*, and *Wall Street Journal*) even attempt a national reach. Given the ties between media conglomerates and political and economic elites in Japan, and the former's high stakes in the state of the economy, there is a reasonable basis for believing that a bias exists favoring the status quo. Furthermore, media organizational factors are thought to compromise media independence, lending further support to the "servant" thesis. A leading example is the media's reliance on *kisha* (reporters') clubs, which are attached to ministries, key politicians, business organizations, and so on, and which foster cozy, "insider" ties between journalists and their sources.

This book provides a basis for examining all three interpretations in the context of Japan's experience. But before taking up this task, it is first important to review briefly the historical legacy that operates behind the Japanese media. For unlike the media in the United States, Great Britain, France, and other Western democracies, media in Japan today emerged from a recent past characterized by censorship and struggle against numerous forms of government control. Only since 1952 have the Japanese media operated within a framework of legal guarantees of a type in place, generally for a much longer time, in the other advanced industrial democracies.

From State Sponsorship to State Control to Censorship

Before Japan's opening with the Meiji Restoration in 1868, Japan had little in the way of newspapers, in the modern sense of the term. Though regulations were sometimes defied and not always enforced, the long Tokugawa era (1603–1868) had had strict censorship of printed materials.[19] The first Japanese-language paper was the *Kanban Batabia Shimbun,* issued in 1862 by the Office for the Study of the Western Writings of the Tokugawa Shogunate. Its appearance presaged an era lasting through 1873 in which newspapers began to appear with direct government sponsorship and encouragement. Like the *Yokohama Mainichi Shimbun,* Japan's first daily, which was backed by the Kanagawa prefectual governor, these early newspapers were, in a very literal sense, servants of the state: they were intended for the most part as "useful organs in furthering understanding and acceptance of new government policies."[20]

The advent of the Popular Rights Movement in 1874 transformed the role of the press and created a different legacy. After Taisuke Itagaki's call for the immediate founding of popular assemblies appeared in the press, most newspapers fell in with the proposal and began to function like a political opposition.[21] Formerly a part of the ruling clique, Itagaki had high prestige, legitimating the shift; furthermore, his use of newspapers to defy the government and appeal to the public awakened the press to its potential.[22] Circulations soared, affirming that the role of watchdog was good business; several of today's leading newspapers—including *Yomiuri Shimbun,* established in Tokyo in 1874, and *Asahi Shimbun,* founded in 1879 in Osaka—began publication in this era. As is characteristic of the media today, the press during this period saw itself taking a critical stance with regard to the government in power; unlike the situation today, however, newspapers did not back away from partisanship. After the imperial edict of 1881 that provided for the establishment of a national assembly by 1890, political parties soon formed; the leading newspapers took sides in the fray, lining up behind one or another of the opposition parties. According to Masaichi Midoro, in 1882 some sixty-four newspapers backed the two main opposition parties, while only twenty-one supported the government's party.[23]

The press continued to flourish after the 1889 constitution had been adopted. By the early twentieth century, however, newspapers had shed their ties with particular political parties, though they retained both a critical orientation toward the government and their basic populism. Several factors explain the change: rising independence-fostering prosperity of the newspapers as their circulations increased; after 1909, the emergence of party governments, which gradually made insiders of the former outsiders, and thus left their newspaper backers without a raison d'être; and recognition by an increasingly commercial media that an independent popular and anti-government stance was good for business. Press laws passed in 1883 and 1909 set constraints on the media's role. Indeed, censorship provisions, which extended to magazines and literature, put all the media under the shadow of possible police suppression through the end of the Pacific War. Newspapers, by then well established as major media organizations, settled into their role until the end of the Allied Occupation: providing "neutral" news coverage while criticizing the government within the constraints set by prevailing censorship laws and by the predisposition of officials at any given time to enforce them.[24]

This role in no way constrained the growth of the media. Over the interwar period, the major newspapers grew in prestige and professionalism and changed in ownership from "one-man operations" to a "corporate format."[25] Japan's three leading national dailies of today—*Yomiuri, Asahi,* and *Mainichi*—all became well established during this era, even as censorship laws tightened. The *Osaka Mainichi Shimbun* had a circulation of 1.5 million in 1930, and the number of journals more than tripled between 1918 and 1932, when the figure stood at 11,118.[26] Like the British Broadcasting Corporation in England, radio, which first broadcast in 1925, became a state monopoly. NHK, after its founding in August 1926, established itself as a major prewar media institution under the communications ministry as the number of radios in Japan increased to 1.4 million.[27] Most of Japan's key media institutions of the 1990s were thus fully in place in the period of military ascendancy and strict censorship from the 1930s through the end of World War II.

A central issue for interpreting pre-1945 developments is the precise relationship between the media and the state from 1868 until the end of World War II. Speaking of the newspapers, Shūichi Katō summarizes the government's changing posture toward the media over that long era: "It encouraged their founding; then imposed strict censorship and police control; then adopted a more liberal attitude, if not *de jure*, at least *de facto*; then in the era of military domination, exerted direct control over all means of expressing opinion."[28] Gregory Kasza generally concurs, contrasting lighter government control over the 1918–1932 period with the draconian measures of 1937–1945. Richard Mitchell, while acknowledging and tracking the major changes in censorship laws and their enforcement over the entire period, stresses the "continuity in state policies," as does Jay Rubin in his work on prewar writers and their varied responses to censorship.[29] Certainly at no time were restrictions on the press lifted, even in the heyday of Taishō democracy, though the degree of enforcement in any given era, the severity of the punishments for violation, and the strategies used by the press to evade censorship all varied. Despite censorship laws, for example, *Tokyo Asahi Shimbun* mounted an editorial attack on the government over the Peace Preservation Law of 1926, "accusing the cabinet of betraying democracy."[30] By 1944 Taketora Ogata, vice president of *Asahi,* had become a cabinet minister, reflecting the virtual merger of media and state in wartime Japan. Even in the late 1930s, the press struggled to resist state control. Challenging the views of media specialists today, who see large media organizations in industrial societies as those most susceptible to serving the powers that be, Kasza found that the "large, dominant media organs [were] best able to resist state power."[31]

Examining Japan's prewar legacy in relation to various interpretations of the media's role today, what stands out are dual traditions. Given the powerful roles exercised by the state with regard to the media over the era from 1868 to 1945, the "servant" tradition is obviously strong. Certainly the Meiji state, in encouraging the estab-

lishment of newspapers, saw them as an instrument of state policy—
a view that the military after 1937 echoed much more strongly. Censorship laws, even at the height of Taishō democracy, reflected the
government's determination to keep the media in a subject role, and
after 1918 the commercial newspapers often bent to accommodate
their would-be censors, whether by toning down editorials or by
wooing government officials.[32] But the persistent efforts of the press
to resist censorship measures, even in the face of possible fines and
jail terms for writers and editors, also established a strong legacy for
a "watchdog" role in the postwar era. After the brief interlude during the Popular Rights Movement when the press opted for partisan
roles, newspapers adopted the nonpartisan but antigovernment and
populist stance that they see themselves maintaining today.

The Allied Occupation (1945–1952) carried forward both legacies. Like the early Meiji government, it actively fostered the media
and encouraged newspapers to reestablish themselves. Clearly, it saw
the media as vehicles to convey its own policies of democratization
and, later, revitalization of the capitalist state. Ironically, given the
zeal with which it abolished the Japanese military's censorship appa-
ratus, the Occupation did not hesitate to institute measures of its
own to thwart criticism of its policies, officials, and troops. Journalist Kazuo Kawai, who worked under those restrictions, charges that
the Occupation put in place "a considerably tighter check than had
been exercised by the Japanese military at the height of their wartime
control," a claim that many would dispute.[33] But at the same time
the Occupation, with the reforms it introduced, obviously gave
strong support to the watchdog legacy as well, setting the stage for
the Japanese media's emergence in 1952 for the first time into an
environment with basic freedoms in place and no censorship laws of
any kind in force.

The following chapters seek to unravel the role the media have
come to play in Japanese society and politics today. After 1952, with
the economic recovery and growth of the early postwar decades, the
mass media expanded rapidly in an increasingly educated and prosperous information society. The big newspapers, already major corporations in the prewar era, became multimedia conglomerates, as
described by Eleanor Westney in chapter 2.

With a guarantee of freedom of the press embedded in the 1947
constitution, the Japanese media operate in an environment free from
all overt forms of control. But in Japan, as elsewhere in the advanced
industrial democracies, norms and conventions of reporting some-

times constrain what the public is allowed to know. Best known is the stringent set of informal controls over news about the emperor and his household. A well-known recent example was the "voluntary restraint agreement," visited upon major media organizations in July 1991 by the Imperial Household Agency, to refrain from reporting news about the Japanese crown prince's search for a bride. At that time, Shōichi Fujimori, grand steward of the agency, attended a meeting of the Editorial Affairs Committee of the Japan Newspaper Publishers and Editors Association (Nihon Shimbun Kyōkai, or NSK), in which he appealed to the media to show restraint on the grounds that "a marriage involves a lot of private factors such as a meeting between two people and cultivating understanding between the two" and that such a process should be "conducted in a quiet and restrained atmosphere."[34] Though word of the crown prince's imminent engagement to Masako Owada, a Harvard graduate and Foreign Ministry official, had spread to many media people in December 1992, they initially abided by the restraint agreement. Only after the *Washington Post* broke the story on January 6, 1993, did NSK, after an emergency meeting that same evening, terminate the agreement, triggering a Japanese media blitz.[35] Similar forms of self-restraint operate, as in the virtual taboo on reporting news relating to *burakumin,* the 2 million or so Japanese who are descendants of a former outcast group.[36] Other examples include the practice, in place until recently, of not reporting "below the belt" activities of Japanese politicians and, far more broadly, the role of reporters' clubs in disciplining fellow journalists for violating collective agreements over what is acceptable to publish (see chapter 4).

Beyond these more obvious forms of self-restraint, the real issue is the larger role of the media in Japanese politics and society in comparative perspective. Coming out of the prewar legacy of repression, overt censorship, and preemptive self-policing, do the media in Japan operate primarily to serve the state, despite legal guarantees? Or are they what they portray themselves to be, neutral and nonpartisan watchdogs of the public interest? These are puzzling questions that, independent of the Japanese case, are central in any consideration of the role of the media in advanced industrial societies.

Chapter 1 explores these questions about the role of the media. Drawing on the literature of symbolic anthropology, it rejects the idea that the media are servants of state or antistate forces, instead offering an alternative interpretation of the media's role—media as trickster—that provides a framework for interpreting seemingly contradictory elements. In chapter 2, Eleanor Westney provides a look at the Japanese media as big business organizations and, indeed, as multimedia conglomerates. She lays out evidence that is basic to any claim that the interests of the media and the state are closely congruent. In chapter 3 Ellis Krauss traces how NHK, Japan's huge public broadcasting company, reports the news; he demonstrates how organizational factors in NHK shape the type of news the Japanese public receives.

The book then turns to look at how the media operate in politics and policy. In chapter 4 Maggie Farley, a journalist with long experience in Japan, examines the role the media, including the foreign media, have played in the major political corruption scandals and other affairs that have rocked Japanese politics in recent years and that helped trigger the downfall of the ruling LDP in the summer of 1993. Chapter 5, by Kristin Altman, a political reporter and anchor for Asahi-TV, looks at commercial television's role in the 1993 political upheavals. Altman makes a strong case for television as watchdog of the public interest. In chapter 6 John Campbell explores the relationship of the media to Japan's powerful elite bureaucracy, focusing on the role of the media in agenda setting and on bureaucracy's complex relationship with media sources. In chapter 7 David Groth illuminates the dual nature of the media in relation to protest movements. On the one hand, they serve as a resource, while on the other, they may undermine the credibility and leadership of such movements in the eyes of the watching public. Groth highlights the role of the nonmainstream media—including materials distributed by movements themselves—in communicating their message. In chapter 8 Ellis Krauss examines yet another political arena where the media operate: foreign news reporting. He explores how the Japanese and U.S. media portray each other's country.

The next three chapters probe how the media affect the political behavior of ordinary people. In chapter 9 Scott Flanagan offers an analysis of how media exposure may affect political participation in Japan. Hiroshi Akuto, in chapter 10, compares the Japanese media's role and effect in electoral campaigning with those of the U.S. media, based on electoral data. In chapter 11, drawing on the same data set, Toshio Takeshita and Ikuo Takeuchi explore how the media operate in comparison with other factors in shaping the Japanese public's views about which issues matter. Finally, in chapter 12 Ellis Krauss draws on evidence presented throughout the book to review once more the question posed at the outset, and to suggest where future research on the role of the media in advanced industrial nations may fruitfully head.

Notes

1. The interviewer, journalist Sōichirō Tahara, pressed Miyazawa, over his earlier objections before the program, on the political reform issue. Although his own party was balking at the issue, Miyazawa put his political life on the line on camera by pledging to deliver without fail. He angered his party when he made the pledge and his opponents when he failed to keep it, leading to the no-confidence vote. Sōichirō Tahara, *Shūkan Bunshun*, 1 July 1993. See also this volume, chapter 5.

2. Ezra F. Vogel, *Japan as Number One* (Cambridge: Harvard University Press, 1979).

3. The monthly average circulation figure for *Yomiuri* reported in 1993 was 9.9 million. Nihon Shimbun Kyōkai (Japan Newspaper Publishers and Editors Association), *The Japanese Press 1994* (Tokyo: Nihon Shimbun Kyōkai, 1994), p. 108.

4. Foreign Press Center, *Japan's Mass Media* (Tokyo: Foreign Press Center, March 1990), p. 13. The October 1993 figure of 72 million represents total daily circulation, including morning and evening editions. Circulation declined slightly in the recessionary 1991–1992 period for the first time since 1983; by 1993, the figures once again showed growth. In Japan as in the United States, however, newspaper publishers voice concerns about the threat of declining circulations in the television age. Nihon Shimbun Kyōkai, *The Japanese Press 1994*, p. 15.

5. Nihon Shimbun Kyōkai, *The Japanese Press 1994*, p. 87. The figure for former East Germany is higher at 593, but is based on 1988 data that predate reunification.

6. Foreign Press Center, *Japan's Mass Media*, p. 48. The figure is for the daily average over the course of a week, and it comes from a 1989 survey by NHK of Japanese people seven years old or older. The same survey found that Japanese also listened to the radio for an average of forty minutes daily.

7. Nihon Shimbun Kyōkai, *The Japanese Press 1992*, (Tokyo: Nihon Shimbun Kyōkai, 1992), pp. 32, 36–37. The Nationwide Newspaper Credibility Survey conducted in 1991 by the Research Institute of Japan Newspaper Publishers and Editors Association found, by averaging the ratings in eight questions, that 73 percent of the public gave newspapers affirmative evaluations on credibility; the rate for television was 56 percent.

8. NHK Hōsō Yoron Chōsajo (NHK Broadcasting Public Opinion Research Institute), ed., *Zusetsu sengo yoron-shi* (Explanatory Tables on Japanese Public Opinion after World War II) (Tokyo: Nihon Hōsō Shuppan Kyōkai, 1982).

9. Scott C. Flanagan, Ichirō Miyake, Shinsaku Kōhei, Bradley Richardson, and Jōji Watanuki, *The Japanese Voter* (New Haven: Yale University Press, 1991), p. 304.

10. Terebi Hōdō Kenkyūkai, ed., *Terebi nyūsu no kenkyū* (A Study of Television News) (Tokyo: NHK Publishers, 1980), p. 11; Bradley M. Rich-

ardson, *The Political Culture of Japan* (Berkeley: University of California Press, 1974).

11. Douglas Cater, *The Fourth Branch of Government* (Cambridge, Mass.: Riverside Press, 1959).

12. See Gerald L. Curtis, *The Japanese Way of Politics* (New York: Columbia University Press, 1988), pp. 166–169. Also see *New York Times,* 18 July 1993, p. 8, for a summary of recent changes and practices.

13. See Shūichi Katō, "Nihon no shimbun, gaikoku no shimbun" (Newspapers in Japan, Newspapers Abroad), *Asahi Jānaru,* July 1962. Kato criticizes Japanese newspapers for adhering to norms of "objectivity" and "neutrality" that stifle debate; such norms, he argues, are a far cry from the practice in other democracies where many newspapers (such as *Figaro* in France) openly adopt a political stance.

14. See Ofer Feldman, *Politics and the News Media in Japan* (Ann Arbor: University of Michigan Press, 1993), pp. 14, 23.

15. Hiroshi Akuto, "U.S.–Japan Communication Gap and the Role of TV News," paper presented at the Twentieth Anniversary International Symposium on Communication between Diverse Cultures through Broadcasting, Tokyo, June 1994, p. 90. In Akuto's study, 28 percent of Japanese news programs he analyzed included expressions of personal opinion by the anchors; in a comparable set of U.S. data, no anchors expressed personal opinions.

16. Curtis, *Japanese Way of Politics,* p. 167.

17. *New York Times,* 18 July 1993, p. 8.

18. See this volume, chapter 12, for more discussion of this view.

19. See Richard H. Mitchell, *Censorship in Imperial Japan* (Princeton, N.J.: Princeton University Press, 1983), pp. 3–12; and Gregory Kent Ornatowski, "Press, Politics, and Profits: The Asahi Shimbun and the Prewar Japanese Newspaper," diss., Harvard University, May 1985. English-language sources on the prewar media include Shūichi Katō, "The Mass Media," in *Political Modernization in Japan and Turkey,* ed. Robert E. Ward and Dankwart A. Rustow (Princeton, N.J.: Princeton University Press, 1964), pp. 236–254; Gregory J. Kasza, *The State and the Mass Media in Japan, 1918–1945* (Berkeley: University of California Press, 1988); James L. Huffman, *Politics of the Meiji Press: The Life of Fukuchi Gen'ichirō* (Honolulu: University Press of Hawai'i, 1980); and Jay Rubin, *Injurious to Public Morals: Writers and the Meiji State* (Seattle: University of Washington Press, 1984).

20. Ornatowski, "Press, Politics, and Profits," p. 7. Mitchell (*Censorship in Imperial Japan,* p. 30), writing about the early 1870s, concurs: "The government regarded newspaper publishing as a semi-government business."

21. Ornatowski, "Press, Politics, and Profits."

22. See Mitchell, *Censorship in Imperial Japan,* p. 44.

23. Masaichi Midoro, *Meiji Taishō shi I: genron hen* (Meiji and Taishō History I: Public Expression) (Tokyo: Asahi Shimbunsha, 1930), cited in Kasza, *State and Mass Media in Japan,* p. 5.

24. See Kasza, *State and Mass Media in Japan,* pp. 16–17; Mitchell, *Cen-*

sorship in Imperial Japan, pp. 180–181; Katō, "Mass Media," p. 242; and Rubin, *Injurious to Public Morals.*

25. Kasza, *State and Mass Media in Japan,* p. 28.
26. Ibid.
27. Ibid., p. 88.
28. Katō, "Mass Media," p. 237.
29. Mitchell, *Censorship in Imperial Japan,* p. xii.
30. Kasza, *State and Mass Media in Japan,* p. 44.
31. Ibid., p. 267.
32. Ornatowski, "Press, Politics, and Profits."
33. Kazuo Kawai, *Japan's American Interlude* (Chicago: University of Chicago Press, 1960), p. 214.
34. Nihon Shimbun Kyōkai, *The Japanese Press 1994,* p. 77.
35. Nihon Shimbun Kyōkai, *The Japanese Press 1993,* p. 16.
36. Interviews conducted in Tokyo, Osaka, and Cambridge, Massachusetts, with journalists working for major national dailies. According to one journalist in a 1992 interview, the taboo is in place partly because *burakumin* themselves are sensitive to what the media have to say about them; partly because the newspapers fear the radical protest tactics of the *burakumin* liberation movement, which can include confrontational denunciation *(kyūdan)* sessions; and partly because Japanese people "don't like to think about things like that." See Susan J. Pharr, *Losing Face: Status Politics in Japan* (Berkeley: University of California Press, 1990), for more on *burakumin.* Feldman, *Politics and the News Media in Japan,* p. 199, provides a useful discussion of right-wing attacks on Japanese newspapers over perceived missteps in reporting on the emperor.

1

Media as Trickster in Japan:
A Comparative Perspective

SUSAN J. PHARR

No institution in advanced industrial societies is more elusive as to its role and its effects on politics than the media. Numerous books on modern political systems make no more than passing reference to the media, listing the major daily newspapers and their circulations, per-capita television viewing time, and so on, and then moving on to consider the "real" institutions of government and the policies that emerge from them. The great bulk of political science research in the 1990s—whatever its focus or methodological approach—hardly acknowledges that the media exist as a distinct force in political and social life.

In contrast with this neglect of the media in the general literature of political science, there has emerged over the last thirty years an extensive literature on the media as such. Claims have been made that the media amount to a "fourth branch of government," that they increasingly shape the contours of social reality, and that they are transforming the nature of political leadership, as politics becomes a matter of who can best shape and sell, through the media, a compelling, evocative persona.[1] The results of surveys similarly confound those interpreters of political systems who would ignore the role of the media. One study in Japan reported an astonishing and much cited finding: when a broad range of actors in politics—bureaucrats, party officials, business elites, union leaders, media elites, leaders of feminist and other social movements, and so on—were asked to rank each other according to power and influence, all actors, except the media themselves, ranked the media first. Nor was Japan an exceptional case. The same study reported similar results for Sweden and the United States.[2]

Just as the media's power and significance are assessed quite differently, depending on who is doing the research, the nature of that power has also proved elusive. A survey of the bodies of literature discussed so far suggests that there are at least three major interpretations of the media's role in relation to the state and to society in advanced industrial societies, according to whose interests the media are thought to serve. In the first, the media are cast in the role of *spectator.* This approach sees the media as more or less passive transmitters of information among the various "real" players in politics, and thus as serving no particular interests at all. Though the media are seen as an important resource, they are essentially neutral conduits for information and ideas in political battles of which they are largely observers. From the late 1940s to the early 1960s, most of the literature on the media saw them as having minimal effects on politics and the public.[3] By the early 1970s the view that the media play an independent role—for example, in agenda setting—had been widely accepted by scholars in media studies. However, the difficulties of verifying major independent media effects on politics continue.[4] Further, because much of the general literature of political science ignores the media, it too, by implication, casts them in the minimalist role implied in the "spectator" approach.

A second view sees the media as *watchdog.* According to this perspective—which is typically the one adopted by the media themselves in explaining their role—the media are an independent critical force on behalf of the public. Thus Shanto Iyengar, Mark Peters, and Donald Kinder showed that the media set the public's agenda and have a "priming" effect by altering the standards people use in evaluating public officials.[5] Doris Graber went further to hold that the media in their watchdog role are a major force for political change; in the United States after the Watergate affair, for example, Graber found that the media through investigative reporting stirred public reactions and demands for reform, aroused political elites who were in a position to remedy political and social ills, and proposed remedies themselves.[6] Obviously, not all who adopt such a view accept the media's motives at face value, or see the effects as wholly beneficial. Some see commercialism and populism going hand in hand and point out that taking on the powers that be swells media audiences. Indeed, an outpouring of popular criticism of the media in the mid-1990s has charged, in effect, that the mass media take their watchdog role too far, invading the personal lives of politicians, demeaning them publicly, and eroding public confidence in leadership.[7] Even such critics tend to agree on the essence of this view, however, which sees the media as an independent critical force.

A third approach, in contrast, sees the media as *servants* of the state. Directly challenging the finding of those who see the media as independent critics, these writers step back from the political fray and ask whose interests in the end are served by the media. This approach portrays the media as instruments of the state for forging a consensus on social values and for generating support for prevailing political arrangements. Such a view sees the media as denying legitimacy to, or trivializing, issues that fall outside a domain of concern that is set by the state and maintained and regulated by it, partly through the state's influence over the process of information dissemination. In an extreme version of this view, Ralph Miliband argues that in spite of their seeming diversity, the media, on behalf of the ruling class whose interests they share and serve, reject radical political alternatives and treat the norms and values of the capitalist order as natural and legitimate.[8] In the same vein, Todd Gitlin argues that the media have become core systems for the production and distribution of ideology. He has attempted to show how the U.S. media "unmade the New Left" through such techniques as trivializing the issues it raised, emphasizing its internal dissension, and undercounting and disparaging its base of support.[9] Looking at the links between the media and the public, writers such as Murray Edelman portray the media as manipulators of symbols par excellence, which define the debate and provide the quiescent masses with a basis for belief in political leaders and in the legitimacy of the state itself.[10] A key issue among those who see the media overall as servants of the state is how much autonomy the media exercise. Writers such as Miliband tend to emphasize the subject role of the media, while Peter Dreier and others argue that media institutions do not simply transmit passively capitalist class and state propaganda but instead have a degree of autonomy resting on their staff and organizational base, sources of revenue, and ideology.[11]

Obviously there are numerous writers, including some of those already cited, whose work does not fit easily into a single approach. Increasingly, much work that is more or less part of the "media as watchdog" school views the media as overstepping bounds in pursuit of its own commercial interests, with deleterious effects, even while professing to serve the public.[12] Thus David Paletz and Robert Entman see the media as influencing the decisions and actions of politicians and officials, reducing their power to control events, but at the same time limiting the public's ability to comprehend and respond intelligently to political events and issues.[13] Nonetheless, the differences among these schools of thought are highly significant.

Altogether, writers treating the elusive role of the media present an

array of contradictory interpretations of the media's broader consequences for state and society and for political change. The contradictory nature of the debate carries into the literature on Japan. Each
major school of interpretation has adherents among those who have
focused on the role of the media in politics in Japan. Paralleling the
first approach, many observers of Japan portray the media as a spectator, or neutral force, in Japanese politics. Mirroring the general
trend in political science research, most ignore the media and thus
implicitly assign them such a role. Some scholars who give explicit
attention to the media's role in Japan would agree. Scott Flanagan,
for example, sees the national press as so eager to appear nonpartisan that it goes "beyond neutrality," even censoring newsworthy stories that might appear to favor one party over another.[14] Some
observers for this and related reasons argue that the media in Japan,
at least in certain areas of political life, may be less significant actors
than they are in many other advanced industrial nations. In support
of this view they cite the restrictions set up in the Election Law on
media use by electoral candidates, which drastically limit the media's
impact—for example, on election campaign styles.[15]

A view of the media as watchdog is also well represented in the literature on Japan. According to this view, the Japanese press, for
example, "conceives its mission as involving systematic and continuous criticism of the government in power," with little in the way of
"praise or confidence concerning governmental performance, capacity, or plans."[16] Early examples of a powerful independent role exercised by the media include the setting of a mood that was hostile to
Prime Minister Nobusuke Kishi in the period of the struggle against
the United States–Japan Mutual Security Treaty in 1959–1960, the
fanning of Okinawa reversion sentiment in Japan in the late 1960s,
and promotion of a national resistance to textile quotas in 1969–
1971. Environmental pollution control, old people's problems, and
political corruption are more recent issues in which many observers
see a major media watchdog role.[17] Some trace such a role to the particular history of the press in Japan, established as it was by former
samurai in the Meiji period who were outside the ruling group. The
press' base in Japan's metropolitan areas and its strong links to a left-
wing intellectual tradition are thought to contribute to a "prevailing
leftist slant" in the newspapers.[18] So widely accepted is the role of the
media as a powerful, independent critical force in Japanese politics
that much media research in Japan has been concerned with locating
where the major newspapers and broadcasting companies stand
ideologically, as a way of assessing how critical that role may be.[19]

Several writers have argued that during the long era of single-party dominance, the watchdog role of the Japanese media was, in effect, a functional equivalent of the role of opposition parties in industrial democracies with stronger political oppositions.

Meanwhile, the diametrically opposed view of the media as servants of the Japanese state has many defenders. Tokyo University professor Jun'ichi Kyōgoku once dismissed Japan's newspapers as little more than "trade journals for the political establishment."[20] Nathaniel Thayer has emphasized the crucial role of the media in controlling the quality and quantity of information flowing from bureaucracy to the public; in his view, adroit Japanese bureaucrats shape the content of news through their use of briefings and their personal relationships with reporters in Japan's remarkable reporters' *(kisha)* clubs.[21] According to Dutch journalist Karel van Wolferen, the Japanese press today is among the "servants of the system," frequently engaging in self-censorship and "never really 'tak[ing] on'" the powers that be.[22] Such a view is part of a "revisionist" interpretation of Japan that tends to portray Japan, despite a legal framework similar to that of other industrial countries, as unique, undemocratic, and elite-run; as Ellis Krauss points out in chapter 8, since the late 1980s the revisionist perspective, with its tendency to dismiss the Japanese media as subservient, more or less has dominated mainstream U.S. media coverage of Japan.

The media are portrayed as serving the interests of the state in numerous ways. For example, according to some writers, Japanese officials see the press as important allies in negotiations with the United States, particularly on trade issues, and boost their own position in bilateral negotiations by leaking information or interpretations to the Japanese media. This practice is facilitated by the extent to which Japanese reporters in Washington rely on Japanese official sources.[23]

Numerous accounts portray multiple and often conflicting roles of the media in their relationships with other political actors and the state. Thayer, for example, even as he described the media as passive conveyers of leaks from Japanese bureaucrats, elsewhere portrayed them as independent critics of the government more generally when it comes to their ideological allegiances.[24] Edwin Reischauer, while remarking on the independent and critical role of the press and its "leftist slant," also stressed its overall neutrality.[25]

The literature of political science and media studies, as well as analyses of how the media function in modern Japan, suggest how extraordinarily complex and varied media roles are. The contradictory nature of the interpretations poses a formidable problem in the attempt to ask and answer broader questions about the relationship of the media both to society and to the state in all democratic countries today. Do the media stand apart from the state, or are they pawns? Do they stir their audiences to try to control political events and reform institutions, or do the media reduce the public to passivity and submission to the powers that be?

Looking ahead, the chapters in this volume do not resolve these issues. Instead, they provide a full range of evidence for those on the various sides of these ongoing debates. The media, after all, include a wide range of actors in a variety of relationships to institutions, so it is not surprising that collectively they adopt no single consistent stance in relation to state and society. Critics of Japan today point to the press club system, the single-conglomerate ownership of both newspapers and television stations, the powerful role of the Japan Newspaper Publishers and Editors Association, and a recent historical legacy of state control of the media to buttress a view of the Japanese media as subservient to the powers that be. But such a position ignores the mainstream media's track record in forcing issues such as environmental pollution onto the agenda, pressing for political change (as in the summer of 1993), and criticizing public officials (for example, for their handling of the Kobe earthquake in January 1995). And it ignores, too, the role of the antimainstream press, from the Japan Communist Party's mass-circulation newspaper *Akahata* to Japan's many critical or rumor-mongering magazines, in challenging official versions of reality.

The debate over the role of the media in relation to state and society in Japan, as well as elsewhere, will continue in scholarly exploration of the specific conditions under which specific media actors adopt a given stance, or induce particular effects; this volume hopefully furthers such an effort. But to broaden the inquiry, it is useful to step back from the debate and think more broadly about the role of the media, viewed collectively, in relation to state and society.

Reconciling the Contradictions: The Media as Trickster

Symbolic anthropology offers a compelling framework for thinking about the various contradictions in the media's role and suggests a fourth view that can accommodate and reconcile them: the view of the media as trickster. Ethnographic accounts of life in agrarian societies have long focused on trickster figures.[26] In the literature of symbolic anthropology, the trickster is a metaphor for a whole range of stranger-outsiders whose numbers historically have included artisans, artists, minstrels, monkey performers, healers and diviners, clowns, and village idiots, along with many others.[27] A chief characteristic of the trickster figure is its unfixed social position; from this position of liminality in relation to the established order,[28] it praises or mocks, badgers or satirizes, horrifies or cajoles. The trickster moves about in places where others, bound to the established order, are not allowed to go. Like dwarfs and jesters in court life, or the blind masseurs who pass unnoticed into the boudoirs of kings, the trickster knows all, sees all, and in the knowing can become the object of fear and ridicule. Symbolically, the trickster mediates between the community and the unknown, forcing people to confront their worst fears and fantasies even while providing relief and release from them.

Anthropologists such as Mary Douglas have tended to see the trickster as permanent outsider in relation to the established social order.[29] As a cultural broker between the outside world and the community, the trickster in its multiple roles from tension releaser to scapegoat makes it possible for the structures and institutions of society to be maintained. Indeed, as Victor Turner has argued, elaborate rituals in which those in established positions of authority reverse roles with social marginals are essential for preserving patterns of authority and institutional arrangements.[30] In that sense, much work on the trickster and other liminal figures presents a somewhat static picture of the social order, which stranger-outsiders help preserve rather than alter. Critics of such views, such as Barbara Babcock-Abrahams, however, see these betwixt and between figures as active mediators who are independent and both creative and destructive simultaneously, and who ultimately alter or stretch social and political boundaries and prevailing arrangements of authority.[31] This more recent work offers the basis for a view of the media in modern societies as trickster in a new guise. I argue that such a conceptualization captures the duality and seemingly contradictory nature of the media's various roles and thus clarifies the media's relation, symbolically speaking, to society and the state.

Trickster and Its Universe

Most social science research on political systems and their relation to the public continues to focus on the institutional dimensions of political systems—those institutions, formal and informal, that do the work of politics, the rules that govern them, the authorities who preside over them, and the policies that they make and carry out. Symbolic anthropology, as developed by Claude Lévi-Strauss, Turner, Douglas, Edmund Leach, and many others,[32] offers alternative visions in which the structural and symbolic are treated as distinct and are seen to be in a complex relationship with one another. Obviously, these authors do not all agree on the nature of that relationship, but their fundamental insights illuminate the symbolic dimensions of the world around us. Drawing on the work of Peter Berger and others, we can view structures as making up the domain of *nomos,* the existing order. In modern societies and political systems, the term would include state institutions, state policies, official statements, other social and political institutions (such as interest groups and legislatures), science and technology, weaponry, representational art forms, and so on. *Nomos,* however, can be seen as residing between two symbolic domains. On one side is cosmos, the domain of values and beliefs that give meaning to *nomos;* on the other is chaos, the unknown and feared. Only through continuing confrontation between the structural and the symbolic can structures be maintained, for it is through confrontation that the values and meanings that give life to structures and make it possible to live within them are reaffirmed and (as writers such as Babcock-Abrahams suggest) also transformed.[33]

In this conceptual universe, the trickster is to be found in the interstices of the social order, and from that position it mediates between *nomos* and cosmos on the one hand, and between *nomos* and chaos on the other. The trickster's domain lies in a zone of liminality or "periphery"[34] between the established order and the symbolic universe surrounding it. By mediating between the symbolic domain and the literal world of institutions or structures, the trickster constantly challenges the symbolic constructs upon which that world is based. The trickster is the ultimate nay-sayer to positive structural assertions, as Turner notes,[35] and therein lies its power. Yet at the same time, it is "in some sense, the source of them all," by creating, through linking the structural and symbolic domains, a "realm of pure possibility whence novel configurations of ideas and relations may arise."[36] These seemingly contradictory or dualistic elements of the trickster's role—in which it may create or destroy, challenge or legitimate—make the metaphor a compelling one for illuminating the media's role.

From a vantage point close to but outside the established order, the trickster simultaneously induces various effects. First, it *provides release* by bringing the world of fantasy to leaders and ordinary people alike.[37] It is prepared to mock and debunk what has been reified and institutionalized, and in doing so it makes the strains and tensions of current political arrangements endurable by providing release and escape. It is in this guise, among others, that the media as trickster serve the state. Also, because the trickster holds nothing permanently sacred, challengers of the established order (for example, protest or other organized movements) can fall prey to its mockery or skepticism; they, after all, are part of *nomos* as well.

In a second guise, the trickster *evaluates.* Everything that is part of the established order is fair game, and in confronting the world as it is (or seems) the trickster criticizes, analyzes, parodies, satirizes—all in ways that force the community to reexamine what has been accepted and reified. As a third effect, the trickster *horrifies.* It brings the community face to face with chaos, as discussed a moment ago: the unusual, the grotesque, the disgusting, the obscene, the bizarre, the pathetic; by this means the community is forced to confront the consequences of existing arrangements. Fourth, in so doing the trickster *induces reflection* on the nature of the established order on the part of the community, causing what Turner and others have referred to as "reflexivity" in people.[38] Finally, the trickster *bonds.* By forcing members of the community to reflect, it brings them together. In Turner's terms, it leads them to experience *communitas,* that fleeting sense of recognition within the group of an "essential and generic human bond" uniting them independent of all structures, without which there could be no society.[39]

Media as Trickster: The Concept Applied

Village idiots, jesters, diviners, and minstrels passed from the historical stage, like the agrarian societies of which they were a part but not a part. In their stead, the trickster in new forms has taken their place in industrial societies. As scattered communities became welded into mass societies, the media from their betwixt-and-between position in relation to social structure became the trickster most regularly before the public. From their insider-outsider vantage point, the media as trickster assemble a seamless stream of commentary, parody, analysis, evaluation, and satire about that world. Meanwhile, the media as the ultimate trickster organize and march other tricksters before us:

the gurus of the news shows or op-ed pieces, rap stars, stand-up comedians, the female impersonators of late-night Japanese television, the homeless, or terrorists as they emerge in news accounts.

In making the case for media as trickster, one crucial issue needs to be clarified. A basic element of the argument so far, derived from a symbolic-structuralist tradition, is that the trickster plays out its roles in society by virtue of its location "betwixt and between" the established order. Given the nature of media as big business today, how is it possible to even begin to think of the media as in any sense marginal? The starting point is to make the distinction, critical in the literature on the media, between media organizations and those at the front lines of gathering and creating news and commentary. Historically, at least in democratic societies, a degree of independence has always characterized journalists and other "creative types." And, even in today's large commercial media firms, it is possible to identify a number of means by which such practitioners—to varying degrees, depending on the organizational context—secure a measure of autonomy and space.

These features of media practitioners' place, both in relation to the social order and the organizational context in which they operate, emerge sharply in examining the media's development in Japan. According to most accounts, the earliest journalists were *rōnin*, or masterless samurai, who had lost their political power, their social status, and their pensions when the Tokugawa regime collapsed in 1868.[40] As one example, James Huffman's account of the life of ex-samurai Gen'ichirō Fukuchi, editor-in-chief of a major Japanese newspaper *(Tokyo Nichi Nichi)* in the 1870s and 1880s, indicates that even so distinguished a journalist saw himself as, and behaved as, an outsider for his entire career.[41] A government official in his earlier years, Fukuchi dropped out (a remarkable step in his day, given the high status of bureaucrats). His position as an outsider was further accentuated by two trips abroad that, according to Huffman, left him throughout his lifetime feeling the contrary pulls of East and West.[42] Ordinary journalists, as opposed to editors such as Fukuchi, were far more marginal in relation to the social status system. Kisaburō Kawabe, in a remarkable book written in 1921, describes the reporters of earlier days as an assortment of low-status men who, for the most part, were looked down upon by society.[43] Underpaid, they had to scramble for side jobs to make ends meet. While the leading papers were paying ¥500 a month to their editors, journalists were receiving only ¥30 a month with an allowance of ¥20 for car fare.[44] This was at a time, according to Kawabe, when employees of large business enterprises were getting "500 yen a month with bonuses of tens of thousands" of yen a year.[45] Ki Inukai, writing in 1917, described them as "rag-picker-wearing-frockcoat" men and noted that when they visited people, it was not uncommon for "things in the reception room (to be) found missing after they had left."[46]

Remnants of the early marginality or "free floating" position of journalists in relation to the established social hierarchy are suggested by their classification in the population census until the postwar era. From 1930 until 1950, the census routinely put reporters in the amorphous classification called *jiyūgyō*, "freelancers," which was clearly a residual category.[47] It contained an odd assortment of dancers and other entertainers, religious workers, and clerical workers, along with those holding the more prestigious jobs of teacher and medical worker. It was not until the 1950 census that reporters were promoted to the company of editors and grouped along with physicians, professors, and others (including artists and entertainers) in a new category called "professional and technical workers."[48]

With the explosion of mass media and the rise of modern media conglomerates, the marginality of media people, taken collectively, obviously ended in a social-structural sense in Japan as elsewhere as the twentieth century advanced. Yet that category contains vast diversity, from the highly paid entertainers-turned-talk-show-hosts of Japanese commercial television to poorly paid reporters for *Akahata*. The ranks of the antimainstream media have swelled in the free-press environment of postwar Japan. And despite the press club system and other features of the mainstream media that trigger critics' charges of media subservience, even well-paid professional journalists for top papers stand apart from media institutions in significant ways, even while they work within them. In a survey in 1974, 1,900 journalists (out of a total of 13,451) in Japan were asked what they saw as the three most important things in life; only 2 percent listed "social position" and only 6 percent listed "wealth."[49] When asked if they believed that the law should be respected at all times, only 17 percent replied in the affirmative, as compared to 43 percent of ordinary Japanese.[50] In a survey of journalists and bureaucrats reported in 1980, respondents were asked whether they thought that "the government may withhold information when its disclosure endangers national security." Of the bureaucrats, almost 70 percent agreed, while only 24 percent of the journalists concurred.[51] The professional norms reflected in these survey results are anchored in features of modern media organizations in Japan as elsewhere, especially in the print media. The work of Young C. Kim reveals numerous ways in which

the mass-circulation dailies with their ties to Japan's media conglomerates, create a margin of independence for those who report the
news: requiring rigorous competition for slots, including written
examinations; granting what amounts to tenured positions; delegating
responsibility to journalists for generating stories on their own; having organizational features that discourage uniformity of news product; and fostering norms that support adopting a critical stance.[52]

With all this said, numerous forces obviously constrain the autonomy and independence of media practitioners in today's information
societies. But the same may be said of other contemporary tricksters.
All have complex relations to structures in society. Novelists and
playwrights may be dependent on grants; scholars in public universities are government employees. Rap musicians, through their book-
ing agencies, are linked to the entertainment industry. In the same
way, editors, cartoonists, news anchors, and journalists, whether in
major commercial newspapers, television stations, *manga,* or scan-
dal-mongering magazines, ply their trade in business organizations
that are responsive to market forces. The economic arrangements in
which they find themselves inevitably constrain how and to what
extent modern tricksters can exercise a critical, debunking role. It is
worth remembering, however, that none of this is new. Historically,
tricksters were seldom totally independent of structures. Jesters performed at the monarch's pleasure and stayed within certain limits to
retain his largesse. Artists and composers often have been dependent
upon patrons. Tricksters have always exercised their critical role in
creative tension with structures that potentially bind them and limit
that role.

Casting the media today in a trickster role does not rest on evidence of media practitioners' independence alone. A more compelling argument arises from observing how the modern mass media
operate collectively in transmitting their messages. More than three
decades ago, Marshall McLuhan pointed out the particular structural characteristic of the media that, from the vantage point of this
analysis, appears above all to suit it to its role of trickster.[53] Historically, most tricksters, whether medieval minstrels or modern novelists, playwrights, and poets, have carried on their mediation between
nomos and the symbolic realm as single entities making their impact
on whatever audience was assembled before them. The novel, for
example, provides a single stream of meaning to whoever reads it.
The modern mass media, in stark contrast, present their messages as
a collage—or, as McLuhan refers to it, a "mosaic"—in which myriad
items are juxtaposed with no logical relation to one another.[54] Those

who reify are to be found alongside those who satirize or mock. The act of assemblage, both for newspapers and for television, is one that McLuhan compares to the work of a painter who, with palette and tubes of pigment, can produce any number of managed mosaic effects from the available subjects.

In the case of television, for example, one news item, with its own internal logic, presents one point of view, while another item—which could include commercials or talk-show content later in the same evening of viewing—may turn that same view into farce.

The same may be said of the mosaic presented by the press. Consider the following commonplace example in three items that all appeared on page 9 in the March 21, 1985, issue of *Asahi Shimbun:*

LDP and Business Exchange Demands and Opinions over Open Market Issue
   Business representatives paid an official visit to LDP [Liberal Democratic Party] headquarters on March 20 to make a request that the government lower tariffs on such items as wooden boards and boneless chicken, as ASEAN [Association of South East Asian Nations] countries have been strongly requesting.
   The government responded that it will deal with that issue according to its basic policy of free trade. The government added an explanation to the effect that if it reduces taxes on wooden boards, it would have to subsidize the domestic forestry industry.

Business Presents Open Request Calling for Employment of Foreign Teachers
   The Japan Chamber of Commerce approved an open request to be presented to the government. It includes, among other things, the request that foreign nationals be given equal employment opportunity in Japanese educational institutions; also, the request states its opposition to any laws that would provide for a reduction in working hours [for Japan's labor force].

Japan-Australian Industrial Cooperation Committee Set Up
   The Japan-Australian Industrial Cooperation Committee was set up on March 21, 1985. On the Japanese side, representatives of big business such as Toyota, Mitsui, and Kōgin are participating, along with governmental representatives, including the Ambassador to Australia.

Even these three routine pieces on one page of a single newspaper issue present subtly incompatible images of the nature of big business in Japan and of the character of the relationship between government and business. Business appears to be "liberal" when it is portrayed as requesting lower tariffs on behalf of the ASEAN countries or when it urges the employment of foreign nationals in Japanese schools. Yet on the same page, business representatives are depicted as "conservatives" who try to prevent workers from having shorter hours. The relationship between big business and the LDP appears to be adversarial over the issues of foreign teachers and tariffs on ASEAN products, but the two go hand in hand in establishing a Japanese-Australian Industrial Cooperation Committee. How each item alone portrays the character of big business or the business-government relationship is far less important than the presence of inconsistency. The juxtaposition of items in the mosaic presents the reader with multiple, mutually incompatible images. Far more striking examples could be found, in which newspapers and television in a single edition or day of programming offer up dazzling inconsistencies and conflicting images when items are juxtaposed.

This is true both for a given major commercial medium and for the mass media as a whole in relation to individual components. Not only is the individual newspaper a mosaic, but also the whole stream of media presents itself to the public as a large mosaic, a jumble of confusing, conflicting bits and segments of information and commentary. For the individual in mass societies, the mediator is ever present, and the collage is one to which the national community as a whole is exposed. Out of the common mosaic, members of the community are invited, on a do-it-yourself basis, to participate in the social construction of reality. No other trickster, past or present, operating as a single entity, has ever had the power to command such an audience and to engage it in such a vast communal task.

Consequences for the State

The tricksterlike quality of the media's role has been widely recognized. Daniel Hallin and Paolo Mancini, for example, see the media as a mirror of political life—reflecting its conventions and structures—and at the same time as an active constructor of meaning.[55] Peter Dahlgren similarly treats television news as a text whose structure and thematic content create a coherent symbolic world of events, people, and objects,[56] though his approach leads him to different conclusions from the ones set out in this chapter.

The implications of the trickster metaphor for evaluating the relationship between the media and the state in Japan and elsewhere deserve careful examination. The interpretations discussed so far of the media's role, and the implications of each for the media's relation to state and to society, are summarized in table 1.1.

A symbolic interpretation of the media's role sheds light on seemingly sharp incongruities found in other interpretations. It provides a way to take into account the unpredictability inherent in that role. It helps explain how Japanese television can support the authority of the state through its news programming (as Ellis Krauss demonstrates in the next chapter), and yet also, in the fateful summer of 1993, undercut powerholders (as Kristin Kyoko Altman shows later on in this volume). What the media elevate they soon may deflate, and indeed, individually and collectively, they are apt to do both simultaneously. Singly and cumulatively, the media are unreliable as allies.

The occasional bitterness of virtually all public officials in democracies—whether Spiro Agnew or Bill Clinton, Yasuhiro Nakasone or Morihiro Hosokawa—over wounds inflicted by the media attests to the media's fundamental tricksterlike unpredictability; what the media puff up they can puncture, as every spin-doctor knows too well. As noted earlier, media as trickster are by nature nay-sayers to positive structural assertions.[57] Powerholders are, in the same way, foreordained to be the object of debunking by virtue of their claims to being good and noble.[58] Marginals such as the trickster, who in a symbolic sense are located somewhere between purity and danger and who have close symbolic associations with dirt, can dismiss such claims a priori. The media as trickster will probe for soft spots, even while they elevate the object of their inquiry.

Evaluation, a task carried out by the media, has many consequences for powerholders and for accepted political arrangements. By simultaneously reporting and challenging claims of virtue made by public officials, the media as trickster may be seen as persistently shaking and subtly undermining authorities' basis for legitimacy and even as contributing to public cynicism. The reflexivity stirred in society as a result of the media's work leads the public into steady reexamination of those claims which, thanks to the media, can never be fully taken for granted. Furthermore, media as trickster offer the public new perceptions of reality. By blurring the boundaries of the existing order, the media are inherently revolutionary, in the broadest sense of the term. Thus, perspectives that cast the media as a passive spectator or as a predictably submissive servant of the state are certainly wide of the mark. The media are revolutionary without any conscious plan or strategy. Indeed, this fundamental characteristic of the media as trickster appears to be true to varying degrees, whatever the particular political or social system. Strategies of oblique criti-

Table 1.1 Competing Interpretations of the Media's Role

ROLE	WHOSE INTERESTS ARE SERVED	POWER OF MEDIA	RELATION OF MEDIA TO STATE	RELATION OF MEDIA TO SOCIETY	EFFECT OF MEDIA ON SOCIETY	EFFECT OF MEDIA ON STATE
Spectator	all	weak	dependent	neutral channel of information	none	none
Watchdog	society	strong	independent	resource	increases participation	spurs change
Servant	state	strong	dependent to limited autonomy	manipulator	increases quiescence	preserves status quo
Trickster	none	strong	independent	multiple/dynamic	builds *communitas*	transforms state over time

cism and resistance to state control by the commercial press and novelists alike in the heyday of prewar Japanese censorship illustrate the point (see the introduction to this volume). In a symbolic-structural sense, the same may be said about all tricksters, whatever their particular guise or sociopolitical context. Revolutionary claims for other tricksters and their functional equivalents, from surrealist artists to romantic poets and even children at play, have been made by a wide range of writers, from Herbert Marcuse to Friedrich Schiller, Johan Huizinga, and Georges Bataille.[59]

The media's evaluative role establishes some basis for adopting the position, as so many have done, that the media are first and foremost watchdogs on behalf of the public. But a view of the media as mainly watchdogs is fundamentally flawed. Even in their evaluative role as critics, the media are apt to be as skeptical of challenges to authority (protest movements, dark-horse candidates, claims of injustice by individuals and groups) as they are of authorities themselves.

Furthermore, other aspects of the media work against any claims that they are systematic critics. They are as likely to tweak as to condemn, and crucially in the mosaic form they have adopted, they do both simultaneously. The cumulative effect will be to disperse, dissipate, or fragment any effort on the part of the audience to agree on a systematic critique of the established order or to forge an alternative construction of reality that calls for profound political and social change. As noted earlier, new claimants for legitimacy and for recognition as standard-bearers of the noble and good suffer at the hands of the trickster in the same way as established authorities. They, too, are part of the established order in relation to the insider-outsider position occupied by the trickster. Opposition parties and protest movements face limits on what they can hope to gain from the media's scrutiny of their efforts to alter social arrangements. Thus writers like Gitlin have a strong basis for claiming that the mass media trivialized, marginalized, and disparaged the New Left in the United States in the 1960s and marginalized its members.[60] Similar charges abound among leaders of social protest movements in Japan, as David Groth chronicles in this volume.

Yet to observe this phenomenon is not to share the profound pessimism of many critics of the media who are advocates of political change and see the mass media defeating such ends. A view that the media serve the interests of the state leads one to overlook, or at least to underplay, the complex duality of the media's role, in which they serve state and society simultaneously but never in a predictable fashion. Though protest-movement activists sometimes denounce the

media, it is striking, as revealed in survey data, that both public officials and social-movement activists in Japan, the United States, and
Sweden have overall seen the media as a resource.[61] The dualism of
the media's role is well illustrated by such a finding.

The Future

Japan, the United States, and other advanced industrial societies
today are moving toward an uncertain future in the media age. Analyses of the role of the media in politics point in all directions regarding the implications of media growth and of new media technologies
for a future era of even greater penetration of society by the media.
Some accounts stress the positive effects of the media, which presumably can only increase. One obvious advantage will be an increase in
the range and sophistication of information available, which will
provide a sounder basis for policy making in government and a wider
knowledge of policies and their effects on society. Given the vast
expansion of bureaucratic tasks in an age of increasing governmental
complexity and scope, the revolution in information technologies
offers the hope of getting the work done, while the increasing media
sophistication and coverage make possible an otherwise hopeless
task: public scrutiny of the process.[62] Mass publics will gain greater
information about candidates for public office and about the performance of incumbents. The state will gain powerful new resources for
political socialization, while society will acquire new knowledge and
skills. If authors such as Phillips Cutright are correct in positing a
high correlation between levels of communication and political
development,[63] the new media technologies should benefit both the
state and society.

Much current research and theorizing is far more pessimistic,
however. According to some observers, the increased scope of
bureaucracy, and the expertise and specialized information it com-
mands, have made the job of monitoring policy too enormous for the
media to handle even today. In the United States writers such as Juergen Heise have claimed that the number of reporters would need to
be tripled (or quadrupled) to keep track of the manipulation of information by a single bureaucracy, the Pentagon—a claim that hardly
bodes well for the future.[64] Many other critics fear not too little, but
too much, media scrutiny: the effects of media saturation coverage in
trivializing events are undermining the credibility of public officials

and institutions. Saturation coverage in 1995 of the O. J. Simpson murder trial in America and of the activities of the Aum religious sect in Japan offers compelling examples. If the exercise of an evaluative role by the media, in the symbolic sense discussed in this chapter, undermines the state's claims for legitimacy and increases public cynicism today, then such effects presumably could only increase along with greater media saturation.

The interpretation that casts the greatest shadow over the future holds that the media, whatever else they do, strip away or deaden the reflexivity of their audience. According to this view, textual structure of the media message, the thematic content, and the contextual location all result in "nonreflexivity" on the part of the audience (specifically, television viewers), who see themselves not as participants in the construction of social reality, but as "merely acted upon by the social world."[65] The broader forces that purportedly promote this phenomenon—the dominance of experts (technical, scientific, and administrative), the "awesome display of technological capacity," the global reach of the medium of television "unhampered by factors of geography or time," and so on—will only increase in the future.[66] If these features of the electronic age do foster quiescence and passivity among mass publics in democracies, then the future is indeed grim.

This important issue requires further study. Three factors raise doubts about these authors' pessimism. The first concerns their data. Many scholars who study the media base their work primarily on content analysis, examining the content of media broadcasts or newspaper stories item by item or offering aggregate results of content analyses of entire broadcasting periods or newspapers over set periods of time. Television news, for example, is treated as a text whose structure and thematic content create a coherent symbolic world of events, people, and objects. The actual analysis, however, often rests on analyses of individual news items transcribed from broadcasts. In such a context, it is reasonable to conclude that viewers are demarcated as outsiders dependent on the teaching of television news and on officials and other experts; they are ultimately rendered subordinate and inefficacious, and are situated outside of history.[67] The validity of this method of analysis, useful as it is in many ways, seems open to question given the mosaic form that the media take. Traditional literary forms lend themselves to a "literatemental" approach, in which it is possible to examine texts and to explore them for continuity, uniformities, connectedness, and lineality.[68] However, the nature of media presentation, especially in the "tactile forms"[69] it takes in the electronic media, appears to defy or render obsolete that type of analysis. As noted above, the media mosaic is discontinuous, skewed, and nonlinear.

In a way that numerous scholars appear to ignore, readers are left to construct their own social world and point of view out of disjointed and incompatible items. The notion that mass quiescence or passivity results as media output increases appears to be undermined by the nature both of the media and of the audience's task.

The conclusions of those who see the media as undermining the basis for political participation in industrial democracies can also be questioned on empirical grounds. Despite media saturation, there appears to be little evidence that political participation in most countries (except, in some cases, by the measure of voter turnout) is on the decline, especially if we consider the more active forms of participation. In Japan, as a great body of empirical work on mass political behavior demonstrates, and as Flanagan notes in chapter 9, the media have had "a positive transforming role" in improving the quality of mass political participation since World War II. In short, there appears so far to be little justification for predicting declines in political participation in the electronic age. Certainly, far more research should be undertaken before such a conclusion is reached.

Finally, dire predictions about the mass quiescence induced by the media appear to ignore crucial aspects of the overall process by which the media relate to their audiences and of the functions they perform for them. In their role as trickster, the media create a sense of bondedness within the community, as members of society join together to create a collective social reality. Perhaps the high degree of media saturation in Japan—which by many measures exceeds the level in numerous other countries, including the United States—is a reflection of the importance of this bonding effect in a homogeneous society. Conversely, the value of bonding may be underplayed by Western political scientists and media specialists who place a higher value on the political efficacy of individuals and their active personal involvement in politics. The importance of the media in creating *communitas* in contemporary democracies may have been greatly underestimated. As rural and small-town communal life has given way to larger geographic entities and in turn to mass societies, the lack of means of connection among highly differentiated populations has become glaring. In the complex world of today and the future, the media are one of the few forces that make possible community and the construction of common realities in advanced industrial and postindustrial democracies.

Notes

I am grateful to Takako Kishima for her able research assistance in the preparation of this chapter, and to Ellis Krauss, David Groth, Emiko Ōnuki-Tierney, Patricia Steinhoff, Eleanor Westney, John Campbell, Murray Edelman, Richard Merelman, and others for their comments on earlier versions of this chapter.

1. See Timothy Crouse, *The Boys on the Bus* (New York: Ballantine, 1973), for an early and much cited statement of this view.
2. Ikuo Kabashima and Jeffrey Broadbent, "Referent Pluralism: Mass Media and Politics in Japan," *Journal of Japanese Studies* 12 (Summer 1986): 335–341.
3. Gladys Engel Lang and Kurt Lang, "Mass Communications and Public Opinion: Strategies for Research," in *Social Psychology, Sociological Perspectives,* ed. Morris Rosenberg and Ralph H. Turner (New York: Basic Books, 1981), pp. 653–682. For a more recent statement of this view, see William J. McGuire, "The Myth of Massive Media Impact: Savaging and Salvagings," in *Public Communication and Behavior,* ed. George Comstock, vol. 1 of 2 vols. (New York: Academic Press, 1986), 1: 175–257.
4. See Scott C. Flanagan, "Media Influences and Voting Behavior," in Flanagan, Shinsaku Kōhei, Ichirō Miyake, Bradley M. Richardson, and Jōji Watanuki, *The Japanese Voter* (New Haven: Yale University Press, 1991), pp. 298–301, for a discussion of the "minimal effects" hypothesis and of research efforts to establish independent media effects.
5. Shanto Iyengar, Mark D. Peters, and Donald R. Kinder, "Experimental Demonstrations of the 'Not-So-Minimal' Consequences of Television News Programs," *American Political Science Review* 76 (December 1982): 848–858.
6. Doris Graber, *Mass Media and American Politics,* 3rd ed. (Washington, D.C.: Congressional Quarterly Press, 1989).
7. See, for example, Eric Alterman, *Sound and Fury: Washington Punditocracy and the Collapse of American Politics* (New York: Harper Perennial, 1993); and Howard Kurtz, *Media Circus: The Trouble with America's Newspapers* (New York: Times Books, 1993).
8. Ralph Miliband, *The State in Capitalist Society* (London: Widenfeld and Nicolson, 1969).
9. Todd Gitlin, "News or Ideology and Contested Area: Toward a Theory of Hegemony, Crisis, and Opposition," *Socialist Review* 9 (November–December 1979): 11–54; Gitlin, *The Whole World Is Watching: Mass Media in the Making and Unmaking of the New Left* (Berkeley: University of California Press, 1980).
10. Murray Edelman, *Constructing the Political Spectacle* (Chicago: University of Chicago Press, 1988); and Edelman, *Political Language: Words That Succeed and Policies That Fail* (New York: Academic Press, 1979).

11. Peter Dreier, "Capitalists vs. the Media: An Analysis of an Ideological Mobilization among Business Leaders," *Media, Culture and Society* 4 (1982): 111–132.

12. See James D. Squires, *Read All About It! The Corporate Takeover of America's Newspapers* (New York: Times Books, 1993), for example. For an earlier version of the same type of argument, see Max M. Kampelman, "The Power of the Press: A Problem for Our Democracy," *Policy Review* 6 (Fall 1978): 7–39.

13. David L. Paletz and Robert M. Entman, *Media, Power, and Politics* (New York: Free Press, 1981). Also see Austin Ranney, *Channels of Power: The Impact of Television on American Politics* (New York: Basic Books, 1983).

14. Flanagan et al., *The Japanese Voter*, p. 302.

15. See chapter by Akuto in this volume.

16. Robert E. Ward, *Japan's Political System* (Englewood Cliffs, N.J.: Prentice-Hall, 1978), pp. 52–53.

17. I. M. Destler, Hideo Satō, Priscilla Clapp, and Haruhiro Fukui, *Managing an Alliance* (Washington, D.C.: Brookings Institution, 1976), p. 58. For the recent cases see Susan J. Pharr and Joseph L. Badaracco, "Coping with Crisis: Environmental Regulation," in *America versus Japan,* ed. Thomas McCraw (Boston: Harvard Business School Press, 1986); John Creighton Campbell, *How Policies Change* (Princeton, N.J.: Princeton University Press, 1992), pp. 140–141; on scandals see this volume, chapter 4.

18. Edwin O. Reischauer, *The Japanese* (Cambridge, Mass.: Belknap Press, 1978), p. 199.

19. Fukashi Horie, "Tōhyō kōdō ni miru 'min'i' " (The 'Will' of the People as Reflected in Their Voting Behavior) (1984), pp. 28–37.

20. Jun'ichi Kyōgoku, " 'Seken no jōshiki' to 'sekai no jōshiki' " ("The Popular Common Sense" and "the Worldly Common Sense"), *Bungei Shunjū,* January 1975, p. 118.

21. Nathaniel B. Thayer, "Competition and Conformity: An Inquiry into the Structure of Japanese Newspapers," in *Modern Japanese Organization and Decision-Making,* ed. Ezra Vogel (Berkeley: University of California Press, 1975), pp. 284–303.

22. Karel van Wolferen, *The Enigma of Japanese Power* (New York: Alfred A. Knopf, 1989), pp. 93–94. For a critical view by an American journalist, see Richard Halloran, "Japanese Newspapers, Their Approach to the News," *Asahi Evening News,* 6 December 1973.

23. See this volume, chapter 8.

24. Thayer, "Competition and Conformity."

25. Reischauer, *The Japanese.*

26. Symbolic anthropologists draw distinctions among different liminal figures, but tricksters have been central, and they offer a compelling way to think about the role of the media in contemporary societies. See Victor Turner, "Myth and Symbol," in *International Encyclopedia of the Social Sciences,* ed. David L. Sills, 19 vols. (New York: Macmillan and Free Press,

1968), 10:576–582. Takako Kishima, who as a research assistant worked with me in developing the theoretical framework for this chapter, has herself gone on to develop the notion of marginal beings and liminal states and to apply the concepts to Japanese politics (though not to the media). See Takako Kishima, *Political Life in Japan: Democracy in a Reversible World* (Princeton, N.J.: Princeton University Press, 1991), pp. 3–25. For a key work on the trickster, see Barbara Babcock-Abrahams, "A Tolerated Margin of Mess: The Trickster and His Tales Reconsidered," *Journal of the Folklore Institute* 11 (1975): 147–186.

27. Emiko Ōnuki-Tierney, *Illness and Culture in Contemporary Japan* (Cambridge: Cambridge University Press, 1984); Babcock-Abrahams, "A Tolerated Margin of Mess."

28. Victor Turner, "Betwixt and Between: The Liminal Period in Rites de Passage," in *The Forest of Symbols: Aspects of Ndembu Ritual* (Ithaca, N.Y.: Cornell University Press, 1967), pp. 93–111.

29. Mary Douglas, *Natural Symbols: Explorations in Cosmology* (London: Barrie and Rockligg, Cresset Press, 1970).

30. Victor Turner, *Ritual Process: Structure and Anti-Structure* (Chicago: Aldine Publishing, 1969).

31. Babcock-Abrahams, "A Tolerated Margin of Mess." Also see Kishima, *Political Life in Japan,* pp. 11–13, for a discussion of the transformative role of liminal figures.

32. Claude Lévi-Strauss, "The Structural Study of Myth," in *Structural Anthropology* (New York: Basic Books, 1963), pp. 206–231. Also see Turner, "Betwixt and Between"; Turner, "Myth and Symbol"; Turner, *Ritual Process;* and Turner, "Passage, Margins, and Poverty: Religious Symbols of Communities," in *Dramas, Fields, and Metaphors: Symbolic Action in Human Society* (Ithaca, N.Y.: Cornell University Press, 1974), pp. 231–271. Mary Douglas, *Purity and Danger: An Analysis of Concepts of Pollution and Taboo* (London: Routledge and Kegan Paul, 1966); Douglas, "The Social Control of Cognition: Some Factors in Joke Perception," *Man,* n.s. 3 (September 1968): 361–376; and Douglas, *Natural Symbols.* Edmund Leach, "Cronus and Chronos" and "Time and False Noses," in *Rethinking Anthropology* (London: Athlone Press, 1961), pp. 124–136; Leach, "Anthropological Aspects of Language: Animal Categories and Verbal Abuse," in *New Directions in the Study of Language,* ed. Eric H. Lenneberg (Cambridge: MIT Press, 1964), pp. 23–63; and Leach, *Culture and Communication: The Logic by Which Symbols Are Connected* (Cambridge: Cambridge University Press, 1976). Many others have also written on this subject.

33. Peter L. Berger, *The Social Reality of Religion* (London: Faber and Faber, 1969). See Kishima, *Political Life in Japan,* pp. 20–22, for an elaboration of this perspective.

34. Douglas, *Purity and Danger.*

35. Turner, "Betwixt and Between," p. 106.

36. Ibid.

37. Sigmund Freud, *Jokes and Their Relation to the Unconscious*, trans. and ed. James Strachey (London: Routledge and Kegan Paul, 1960).

38. Turner, "Betwixt and Between"; and Turner, *Ritual Process*.

39. Turner, *Ritual Process*, p. 97.

40. Ki Inukai, *Daigaku Hyōron*, August 1917, quoted in Kisaburō Kawabe, *The Press and Politics in Japan: A Study of the Relations between the Newspaper and the Political Development of Modern Japan*, (Chicago: University of Chicago Press, 1921), pp. 84–87.

41. James L. Huffman, *Politics of the Meiji Press: The Life of Fukuchi Gen'ichirō* (Honolulu: University of Hawai'i Press, 1980).

42. Ibid., p. 14.

43. Kawabe, *The Press and Politics in Japan*, p. 118.

44. Ibid., p. 117.

45. Ibid., p. 118.

46. Ki Inukai in *Daigaku Hyōron*, August 1917, cited in ibid., p. 118.

47. Sōrifu Tōkeikyoku, 1974: 318–361; other versions of the same were *jiyūgyōsha* (1940) and *jiyūshokugyō* (1947).

48. Ibid.

49. Nihon Shimbun Kyōkai (Japan Newspaper Publishers and Editors Association), "Survey of the Consciousness of Japanese Newsmen: Newsmen Believe Work Useful to Society and Proud of Profession," *The Japanese Press 1974* (Tokyo: Nihon Shimbun Kyōkai, 1974), p. 102.

50. Ibid.

51. Jung Bock Lee, "The Professional and Political Attitudes of Japanese Newsmen," *Asian Perspective* 4 (Spring–Summer 1980): 102.

52. Young C. Kim, *Japanese Journalists and Their World* (Charlottesville: University Press of Virginia, 1981). The recent and valuable work by Ofer Feldman, *Politics and the News Media in Japan* (Ann Arbor: University of Michigan Press, 1993) summarizes the findings of previous research on Japan's journalists and also provides a rich body of new data.

53. Herbert Marshall McLuhan, *Understanding Media: The Extensions of Man* (New York: McGraw-Hill, 1964).

54. Ibid., pp. 203–216.

55. Daniel C. Hallin and Paolo Mancini, "Speaking of the President: Political Structure and Representational Form in U.S. and Italian Television News," *Theory and Society* 13, no. 6 (November 1984): 829–850.

56. Peter Dahlgren, "TV News and the Suppression of Reflexivity," in *Mass Media and Social Change*, ed. Elihu Katz and Tama Szecsko (Beverly Hills, Calif.: Sage Publications, 1981), pp. 101–113.

57. Turner, "Betwixt and Between," p. 106.

58. McLuhan, *Understanding Media*, pp. 203–216.

59. Herbert Marcuse, *The Aesthetic Dimension: Toward a Critique of Marxist Aesthetics* (Boston: Beacon Press, 1978); Marcuse, "Nature and Revolution" and "Art and Revolution," in *Counterrevolution and Revolt* (Boston: Beacon Press, 1972), pp. 59–128; and Marcuse, *An Essay on Liberation* (Boston: Beacon Press, 1969). Friedrich Schiller, *On the Aesthetic Edu-*

cation of Man: In a Series of Letters, trans. Reginald Snell (London: Routledge and Kegan Paul, 1954); Johan Huizinga, *Homo Ludens: A Study of the Play-element in Culture,* trans. R. F. C. Hull (London: Routledge and Kegan Paul, 1949); Georges Bataille, "Sommes-nous là pour jouer? Où pour être sérieux?" *Critique* 7 (June 1951): 512–522 and 7 (August–September 1951): 734–748.

60. Gitlin, *The Whole World Is Watching,* pp. 58, 27–28.

61. Kabashima and Broadbent, "Referent Pluralism."

62. Juergen Arthur Heise, *Minimum Disclosure: How the Pentagon Manipulates the News* (New York: W. W. Norton, 1979).

63. Phillips Cutright, "National Political Development: Measurement and Analysis." *American Sociological Review* 28 (April 1963): 253–264.

64. Heise, *Minimum Disclosure.*

65. Dahlgren, "TV News and the Suppression of Reflexivity," p. 104.

66. Ibid. Also see Paletz and Entman, *Media, Power, and Politics;* Edelman, *Constructing the Political Spectacle;* Edelman, *Political Language;* and Gaye Tuchman, *Making News: A Study in the Construction of Reality* (New York: Free Press, 1978).

67. See the analysis offered by Dahlgren, "TV News and the Suppression of Reflexivity," p. 110.

68. McLuhan, *Understanding Media,* pp. 308–337.

69. Ibid.

PART II

Media Organizations and Behavior

2

Mass Media as Business Organizations: A U.S.–Japanese Comparison

D. ELEANOR WESTNEY

MASS media organizations rank among the major business firms in highly industrialized societies,[1] and the business side of the media is a continuing focus of research, regulatory scrutiny, and media attention. Changes in the strategies or performance of mass media firms, mergers and acquisitions, bankruptcies and start-ups, management difficulties and labor problems in media industries are reminders that media organizations are businesses, with business goals of returns on investment and vulnerabilities to changing business conditions. Such issues evoke long-standing anxieties about the potentially contradictory pulls between the two roles of mass media firms: as providers of the critically important public goods of information and values, and as businesses that buy and sell and are themselves bought and sold.

The business side of mass media firms has widely been viewed with suspicion. The figure of the press baron is a standard figure both of fiction and of media history, and illustrates one of the oldest fears about the business aspect of the media firm: that the pursuit of profits will foster sensationalism and a lowering of journalistic and artistic standards.[2] Another recurring fear is that the owners of media firms will suppress or distort information or values, out of a desire either to propitiate advertisers or to serve their own interests in other business ventures.[3]

The expansion of conglomerate ownership in the United States and Great Britain in the 1970s and 1980s generated a new anxiety: that the orientation to profits will drive managers to cut costs by reducing expenditures on information gathering or on the "quality" of their product.[4] Conglomerate ownership can also intensify a more general inclination on the part of media firms to increase profits by reducing competition, either by acquiring their competitors or by engaging in cutthroat competition to drive them out of business, thereby concentrating ownership in fewer hands. The international scope of a growing number of media conglomerates adds to the anxieties. Two aspects of media concentration have received extensive attention from regulators and media critics: cross-media ownership and the development of media monopolies within an industry, especially within regional media markets.[5] Both developments are seen as reducing the array of choice for media consumers, a reduction that is the more insidious because it is often invisible to them. Still another concern is that—at least in media industries where distribution is a significant element of cost structure, such as publishing, cinema, and cable television—media firms will make a considered judgment that certain segments of the market, such as isolated regions or low income groups, are simply not worth reaching in a business sense, thereby creating major inequalities in access to media within the society.[6]

These various anxieties can be grouped into three dimensions in which the business and public service aspects of the media may be in conflict: diversity within the media system as a whole, decision making within each firm about the information and values conveyed in the media "product," and audience access to the media through the distribution system. These dimensions in turn impinge directly on the ideals of the political role of the press in a liberal democratic society: pluralism, freedom of speech, and equality.

Given the importance of these ideals, owners and managers of media enterprises are not allowed to follow business self-interest without restrictions. Two other sets of stakeholders intervene to influence the behavior of media firms: the media professionals who generate and shape content and the authorities who regulate the operation of markets in media industries. Media professionals have focused their energies on limiting the business influences on the internal decision-making processes of the firm, largely by trying to establish strong norms of professional control over content-related decision making. Regulatory authorities have concentrated primarily on maintaining diversity in ownership by restricting the ownership and the buying and selling of media enterprises. As a result, the ownership and acquisition of firms are more highly regulated in the major mass media industries, particularly broadcasting, than in virtually any other industry. In addition, the state imposes varying legal restraints on journalistic freedom in the form of libel laws and laws governing the publication of information whose secrecy is deemed vital to the national interest.

Up to the present day, in most societies the third dimension of business influence, access to the media distribution system, has been seen as a legitimate preserve of business and left unrestricted by professional norms or regulation. The major exception is where distribution is assigned to public enterprises, as in public broadcasting. Increasingly, however, with the development of the new media, especially cable television, equality of access is becoming a much more salient regulatory issue, one that has yet to be satisfactorily resolved.

Efforts to control the business aspects of the mass media face a key paradox: the maintenance of the core values of journalistic freedom, diversity, and equal access requires media firms that are viable as businesses. Even public broadcasting systems are expected to perform in a financially "responsible" fashion. If the business side of media enterprises is overregulated, or if it is ineptly managed, media firms will either become bankrupt or require subsidies from the state or from private enterprise. Either choice betrays the original aims. Bankruptcies reduce the number of players in media industries and therefore reduce diversity and choice, but sustained subsidy threatens the autonomy of decision-making processes within the media firm.[7]

The tensions between the business aspects of media firms and their role as suppliers of public goods have been studied primarily from the viewpoint of the regulators (in a public policy framework) or from that of media professionals (in a sociological framework). A third well-established area of research is the economics of the mass media, a subfield much patronized by media firms themselves, which concentrates not on what media firms do but on the structure of media markets and the effect of changes in those markets on the potential resources available to the industry. But comparative research on the business behavior of mass media firms has received surprisingly little attention, despite its important implications for the political and social roles of the media in society.

Japan provides a fascinating case for the study of the business dimensions of the mass media. The fundamental regulatory structure of Japan's mass media system took shape during the Allied Occupation, and it was profoundly influenced by the long-standing Western concern with ownership as the key regulatory variable in ensuring the public service role of the mass media. The size of any single shareholding in media firms in Japan is limited by law, newspaper company shares can be held internally, and the creation of broadcasting networks is severely constrained by regulation. As a result, the sources of anxiety over the business dimensions of the mass media in North America and Western Europe are conspicuous by their absence. Japan has no newspaper chains, no large mass media conglomerates owned primarily by nonmedia corporations, a virtual absence of interlocking directorates tying the governance of media firms to leading industrial and financial corporations, a low level of investment in the media by nonmedia firms, and (as in so many industries) insignificant levels of foreign penetration. The national newspapers, whose shares are internally held and thereby protected from external acquisition, have avoided the differentiation into "quality" vs. sensationalistic "popular" newspapers that has been lamented in the British and North American press, and they have managed to keep newspaper circulations high and growing, in contrast to the decline of newspaper readership in most other advanced industrial societies.

The Japanese experience with the business aspects of the mass media, therefore, can be expected to differ from the North American experience, given that Japanese media regulation was consciously designed to avoid the major ownership problems experienced in the United States. Moreover, the business environment of Japan differs significantly from that of other advanced societies, particularly the much-studied United States. Exploration of the business side of Japanese media organizations can illuminate not only the nature of the mass media in Japan but also the variations across societies in the behavior of media firms.

Japanese Mass Media Firms: A Comparison with the United States

The twelve mass media firms that appeared among the top 500 firms for 1986 in Japan are presented in table 2.1.[8] They include three newspaper firms (two nationals and one of Japan's three "block," or regional, newspapers), three television broadcasting firms, five book and magazine publishers, and one cinema production and distribution company. Two major media organizations are not included. One is Nippon Hōsō Kyōkai (NHK), which has the largest revenues of any Japanese broadcasting organization, but which, as a public corporation, is not included in the data on which table 2.1 is based. The other is *Yomiuri Shimbun,* Japan's largest circulation national newspaper, which with a morning circulation of 9.75 million in the first quarter of 1990 is the world's largest circulation commercial newspaper. Until 1988 *Yomiuri* was produced by four legally separate companies, based in Tokyo, Osaka, Nagoya, and Kyūshū, which were linked by interlocking shareholding.[9]

Table 2.1   Mass Media Firms among Japan's 500 Largest
Corporations (1981 and 1986)

COMPANY	1981 RANKING (INCOME)[a]	1986 RANKING (INCOME)[a]	INDUSTRY[b]
Asahi Shimbunsha	114 (24,674)	440 (7,620)	N, M, B
Yomiuri Shimbunsha	213 (12,595)	[1,458][c]	N, M, B
Tokyo Hōsō	220 (12,554)	284 (10,913)	TV
Shūeisha	228 (12,187)	249 (12,840)	B, M
Nihon Terebi Hōsō	239 (11,482)	349 (9,123)	TV
Nihon Keizai Shimbun	241 (11,274)	213 (14,952)	N, M, B
Kōdansha	273 (9,848)	356 (8,983)	B, M
Shōgakkan	286 (9,495)	282 (10,987)	B, M
Gyōsei	289 (9,399)	409 (8,082)	B, M
Nihon Recruit Center	331 (8,201)	134 (23,713)	M, B
Zenkoku Asahi Hōsō	346 (7,838)	[1,512][c]	TV
Gakushū Kenkyūsha	373 (7,151)	[791][c]	B, M
Fuji Television	376 (7,113)	318 (10,103)	TV
Chūnichi Shimbunsha	414 (6,295)	420 (7,977)	N
Tōhō	—	482 (6,755)	C

Source: Tōyō Keizai annual ranking of Japan's companies, 1982 and 1987, ranked by taxable income as reported to the tax agency.

[a] Income unit is millions of yen.

[b] Industry code: N = newspaper publishing, M = magazine publishing, B = book publishing, TV = television broadcasting, C = cinema.

[c] In 1986 this company was no longer among the 500 largest.

The firms in table 2.1 exhibit a remarkably standardized pattern of involvement in the major media industries: the two national newspapers have the most diverse interests, crossing all three publishing industries; the three television firms are confined to broadcasting; and the five publishing companies are major players in both book and magazine publishing. That the newspaper companies are individual newspapers and not chains, and that the broadcasting firms are individual stations and not groups of stations, testifies to the effectiveness of Japan's provisions for protecting newspapers from external acquisition and of the ownership restrictions in Japan's broadcasting laws.

Table 2.2 provides similar data for the United States, although the data on which the ranking is based are the market values of shares

Table 2.2 Mass Media Firms among the 500 Largest U.S. Corporations (1986)

COMPANY	1986 RANKING	MARKET VALUE[a]	INDUSTRY[b]
General Electric	3	48,895	TV, R
Dun & Bradstreet	42	9,869	B, M
Westinghouse	45	9,260	TV, R, B
Gannett	60	8,017	N, TV
Walt Disney	63	7,930	C
Capital Cities/ABC	93	5,706	N, TV, R
Times Mirror	95	5,655	N, B, M, TV, R
Time	104	5,427	M, B, TV
Dow Jones	107	5,348	N, M, B
Gulf & Western	122	4,817	C, B, TV
Warner Communications	137	4,378	C, TV, B
New York Times	149	3,823	N, M, B, TV, R
CBS	151	3,818	TV, R
MCA	161	3,665	C, M, B
McGraw-Hill	163	3,556	M, B, TV
Tele-Communications	195	3,168	TV, M
Knight-Ridder	198	3,128	N, TV
Tribune	201	3,096	N, TV
Washington Post	258	2,411	N, M, B, TV
Viacom International	314	1,932	TV
Lin Broadcasting	316	1,912	TV, R, M
Affiliated Publications	349	1,672	N, M, R
Harcourt Brace Jovanovich	386	1,473	B, M
Taft Broadcasting	394	1,425	TV, C
Macmillan	438	1,291	B
Commerce Clearing House	494	1,134	M, B

Source: 1987 Business Week ranking of the top 1,000 U.S. companies, ranked by market value of shares. This table includes all firms listed under "Publishing, Radio and TV Broadcasting" and firms listed under other industry categories that have major holdings in two or more media industries.

[a] Market value unit = $ million.

[b] Industry code: N = newspaper publishing, M = magazine publishing, B = book publishing, TV = television broadcasting (including cable systems), R = radio, C = cinema.

outstanding rather than reported taxable income. The most immediate contrast with Japan is the larger number of firms with substantial media holdings that appear among the top 500 U.S. firms: 26, compared with 12 in Japan. And of these, 17 U.S. firms rank in the top 200, while only one of Japan's firms does so.

One reason is that the U.S. list contains several industrial firms whose primary base is outside the mass media, but which have major holdings in at least two media industries. The largest is General Electric (GE), whose acquisition of RCA added NBC to its already substantial radio and television holdings and made it the third-ranking corporation in the country. The others are Westinghouse, which long ago entered broadcasting from its base in appliances and receiving sets, and Gulf & Western, a huge conglomerate with more than a hundred subsidiaries in industries ranging from auto parts to lingerie.[10] Even if the data for Japan were consolidated, they would show no comparable involvement of non–media-based industrial firms in the Japanese media, although the new media (cable and satellite broadcasting in particular) have attracted the avid interest of firms in mature industries, such as steel and railways.

Finally, the range of media industries in which the U.S. firms are involved is considerably wider and less patterned than that of their Japanese counterparts. The "mass media conglomerates" of the United States, such as the Times Mirror Corporation, which has major holdings in all the media industries except the cinema, or Capital Cities, a broadcasting and newspaper firm that recently acquired ABC, have no obvious counterparts in Japan, where the top firms are apparently much more segmented by industry.

A comparison of tables 2.1 and 2.2 could give rise to three inferences. First, the mass media are big business in both countries, but they are bigger business in the United States. Second, there are closer connections between the mass media and the larger industrial system in the United States than in Japan. Third, the mass media industries themselves are more interconnected and more of a "system" in the United States than in Japan. However, a more detailed examination of each issue would find that while the first inference is valid, the second is only partly true, and the third is clearly wrong.

The Scale of the Mass Media

Japanese media firms remain comparatively small in scale, not only in comparison to other Japanese firms (as table 2.1 indicates) but also in comparison to U.S. media firms. Indeed, in general, the scale of both mass media firms and mass media industries is greater in the United States than in Japan. A key reason is the relatively modest scale of the Japanese advertising industry. The United States leads the world both in the absolute size of its expenditures on advertising and in the proportion of its GNP that goes to advertising. By the mid-1980s, total U.S. advertising expenditures were $424.07 per capita, or 2.43 percent of GNP. While Japan, which has the second largest economy in the noncommunist world, ranked second in the world in the absolute volume of advertising expenditures, it ranked seventh in per-capita expenditures ($150.81 per capita), and in terms of advertising as a percentage of GNP it ranked twenty-third (below Bolivia, Chile, and Jamaica), at 0.92 percent.[11] Advertising expenditures rose above 1 percent of GNP in Japan only in 1985. The so-called bubble years of economic expansion in 1989–1992 saw advertising reach a historic high of 1.3 percent of GNP, but with the collapse of the bubble in 1993 it fell to 1.16 percent.

The lower level of expenditure in advertising clearly affects the scale of the industries that rely on advertising for a significant portion of their revenues. In television advertising Japan ranked second after the United States in per-capita expenditures, yet the television industry in the United States earned $22.6 billion from advertising in 1986, while in Japan the amount was only $6.5 billion.[12] Even at the peak of the bubble (and aided by a strengthening of the yen by one-third of its mid-1980s value), television advertising expenditures reached only $13.3 billion dollars.

The smaller scale of Japanese media firms also reflects the effect of regulation in the newspaper and broadcasting industries, in contrast to the United States, where the multiple ownership of broadcasting outlets and of newspapers has contributed to the large scale of major U.S. media firms. Regulation has also tended to limit the expansion of broadcasting industries in Japan. The number of commercial AM radio stations was allowed to increase very slowly in the 1950s, while the licensing of FM stations was even more delayed through the 1960s and 1970s. Only with the revision of the Broadcasting Law in 1988 did the Ministry of Posts and Telecommunications officially embrace the principle of licensing four television stations in every region. Licenses were granted to cable television systems only toward the end of the 1980s. These constraints affected the distribution of advertising: in Japan by early 1990, only about 4 percent of total advertising expenditures were in radio, compared to 11 percent in the United States. Cable television has not yet begun to compete seriously with regular commercial broadcasting for advertising in Japan, as it has in the United States. In the early 1990s, only 0.2 percent of Japan's advertising expenditures found their way into the so-called new media (including videotext as well as cable television).

The Interpenetration of Media and Industrial Firms

As the comparison of tables 2.1 and 2.2 suggests, there are closer interconnections between the mass media and the larger industrial system in the United States than in Japan, at least in terms of controlling ownership of media outlets by industrial corporations such as GE, Westinghouse, and Gulf & Western. This is also true in terms of another pattern that has aroused considerable concern in the United States: interlocking directorates that put industrial leaders on the boards of directors of mass media firms and owners and chief executives of media firms on the boards of industrial firms. Ben Bagdikian, who has traced the major interlocks, states that representatives of "almost every major industry whose activities dominate the news of the 1980s—the leading defense contractors and oil companies—sit on controlling boards of the leading media of the country. There is hardly a major international bank or insurance or investment company that is not represented on boards of directors of the major media that control most of what Americans learn about the economy."[13] Such interlocks are extremely rare among Japanese mass media firms; like most Japanese firms, media companies have boards of directors composed almost exclusively of their own managers, past and present.

The indicators commonly used to measure interpenetration in the United States—interlocking directorates and cross-industry ownership of media companies—do not work very well in Japan. Japanese industry in the postwar period has generally exhibited a low level of cross-industry diversification that might lead industrial firms to buy into the mass media, and Japanese law provides protection for media firms against takeovers. Newspaper companies are particularly well protected: provisions in Japan's company law allow newspapers to hold their shares internally, even while they enjoy the legal protections of being limited-liability joint-stock companies, and 53 of the 101 daily newspaper companies in the Nihon Shimbun Kyōkai (Japanese Newspaper Publishers and Editors Association, equivalent to an industry association) have taken advantage of this. Twenty-eight have more than half of their shares held internally (eleven of these have all their shares held internally), and twenty-five have less than half held internally.[14] The intention of the law was to protect newspapers from acquisition by outside interests, but one consequence has been to exempt such firms from many of the normal public reporting obligations of incorporated enterprises. For example, according to one report, *Yomiuri Shimbun*, perhaps the most financially secretive of Japan's media firms, distributes a financial report at its annual shareholders' meeting but collects all copies at the end of the meeting to prevent the data from becoming public. One recent book on the newspaper industry has commented on the irony of the financial secretiveness of companies that in the course of their business insist on the public's right to information.[15]

Whatever the implications for internal governance, the ownership structures of Japanese media companies mean that the interpenetration indicators applicable for Japanese firms are not cross-industry ownership and interlocking directorates. Instead, the most applicable indicators are borrowing linkages with the leading banks, minority shareholdings, participation with other firms in government advisory councils *(shingikai),* and joint research and development projects with other firms.

On these indicators, Japanese mass media firms, particularly in newspaper publishing and broadcasting, are closely linked to the larger industrial system. The national newspaper firms are heavily tied to the major city banks: the low profit levels in the newspaper industry and the internal holding of shares that deprives the largest newspaper firms of recourse to the stock market for infusions of capital have made firms in this industry very dependent on bank loans for capital investment.[16] The transition to computerized cold-type systems in the 1970s and 1980s, at a time when the growth rates in the industry were slowing (and in some years even stagnating), has increased this dependence over the last decade and a half, a period when firms in other industries have been reducing their debt ratios and developing greater independence from the city banks. Broadcasting and other publishing firms have had greater latitude in raising capital through the stock market, but relatively few are listed on the Tokyo Stock Exchange, and even in these firms linkages with the banks are quite close.

Moreover, while industrial firms legally are prevented from holding controlling interests in either newspaper or broadcasting firms, they do hold shares in those that are publicly listed. Indeed, one of the unanticipated consequences of limiting any single shareholder to 10 percent of the total shares has been the involvement of industrial firms and banks in media ownership. All three of the block newspapers (regional, multiprefecture newspapers formed by the forced amalgamations of several prefectural newspapers during the Pacific War) and twenty-three of the ninety-five local newspapers listed in the *Nihon shimbun nenkan* in 1983 had industrial firms among their major shareholders. Most of these nonmedia corporate shareholders were local companies, but in some cases they were major corporations with a strong local presence. Blocks of shares in *Kōbe Shimbun*, for example, are held by Kawasaki Steel, Kawasaki Heavy Industries, and Takenaka Kōmuten (one of Japan's top five construction firms); shares in *Ehime Shimbun* of Shikoku are held by Sumitomo Metals and Sumitomo Chemicals. In addition, twenty of the local newspapers have banks among their institutional shareholders. In broadcasting, industrial firms were major shareholders for fifty-two of the ninety-five television broadcasting firms operating in 1983, and banks were major shareholders for forty-nine. This pattern of shareholding, however, does not involve representation on the media firm's board of directors (just as in the United States the appointment of leading industrialists to the boards of media firms does not necessarily involve shareholding).

Participation side by side with representatives of industrial firms in government advisory bodies is an indicator of interpenetration that has no real analogue in the United States. But in Japan, the leading mass media firms are very much involved in such bodies. At least one of the national newspaper firms is usually represented on various *shingikai,* not only those that directly or indirectly affect the media industries but also those that impinge on a wide range of public interest concerns (such as social welfare policy) and even industrial sectors. For example, the Ministry of Construction's Committee on Intelligent Buildings, which reported in 1986, included a department head *(buchō)* from *Nihon Keizai Shimbun.* Media representatives are there in a dual capacity, as spokespeople for public interests and as potential architects of public opinion who will probably provide some sympathetic coverage of the issues before the committees. Book and magazine publishers and private broadcasting firms are much less likely to participate in these groups (NHK is the usual representative of broadcasting industries).

On the fourth indicator of interpenetration, participation in joint research and development projects with industrial firms is precluded by the relatively small technology development capacity of most media firms. The major exception is NHK, whose sizable research laboratories have made it a key participant in government and indus-

try projects to develop new media technologies, such as the ill-fated
attempt to establish a global standard in high-definition television
(HDTV). In the development of computerized production and editing systems, however, the technical departments of both Asahi Shimbunsha and Nihon Keizai Shimbunsha worked closely with IBM for
several years, and indeed the importance of these two organizations
in shaping opinions and attitudes of both the general public and the
business elite was a key factor in persuading IBM-Japan's parent
company in the United States to continue the expensive and lengthy
development process.[17]

In projects related to the development of the new media, however, the national newspapers and major broadcasting firms are
working closely with Japan's leading industrial firms. The Japan
Satellite Broadcasting Company, for example, a joint-stock company incorporated in 1984 to develop delivery systems and programming for commercial satellite broadcasting, includes
representatives of the *Asahi, Yomiuri, Mainichi, Sankei,* and *Nihon
Keizai* newspapers on its board of directors, as well as representatives from three commercial broadcasting firms and such leading
industrial firms as NEC, Tōshiba, and Tokyo Electric Power. The
deputy chairman of Keidanren was the first chairman of the board.
All five national newspaper companies are among the shareholders,
along with fourteen broadcasting firms, six other newspaper firms,
seven major publishing firms, and more than a hundred leading
industrial and financial firms. Media firms are also in partnership
with industrial firms in the development of cable television and tele-
text systems.

It is ironic that by these various indicators of interpenetration,
the national newspaper firms are the most closely integrated with
the industrial system, although these are the firms that government
regulation of ownership has protected most assiduously. But as in
the United States, specifying the consequences of this interpenetration in concrete terms is far from easy. Critics such as Bagdikian
have gathered anecdotes of how pressures from nonmedia owners
have caused the suppression of certain stories or manuscripts in the
U.S. media, but as they themselves point out, the most important
effect of interpenetration is virtually impossible to measure: the type
of information that is not covered or is not covered critically. Large
business corporations rarely receive critical scrutiny from the media
in either country, until major crises emerge. How much of this is
due to the various modes of interpenetration of the media is difficult to assess.

The Interconnectedness of the Media System

The larger number of leading U.S. firms whose activities span the entire range of mass media industries suggests that the U.S. media system itself might be more interconnected. In fact, however, the Japanese media are more densely interlinked. The connections differ in kind as well as density and are the product of very different patterns of historical development and competition. The key nodes of interconnection are the national newspapers, which engage in activities that span the entire range of publishing and which have dense linkages with broadcasting.

The Japanese metropolitan newspapers from which today's nationals developed expanded their publishing activities very early in their history. Initially this was a response to the limit on the number of pages that could be printed each day, given the cumbersome and time-consuming nature of setting type for the complicated Japanese script. (The Japanese equivalent of the Linotype machine to streamline typesetting, introduced in the 1880s in the Western press, was not developed until 1920.) In the Meiji period, newspapers relied primarily on producing supplements inserted into the paper; in Taishō they expanded into the production of separate news magazines.[18] This was the beginning of the expansion of national newspaper firms into the magazine and book publishing that forms so important a part of their activities today. For example, in 1986 *Asahi* published five weeklies, five monthlies, two quarterlies, and eight annuals. In addition, it published more than 300 book titles, making it the twelfth-ranking Japanese publisher in terms of the number of new book titles. Both book and magazine publishing have obvious synergies with newspaper publishing, beyond the use of editorial and reporting staff. In 1990 both *Asahi* and *Nikkei* were among the top twenty-five book publishers, ranked by number of titles published; two others (*Mainichi* and *Nikkan Kōgyō Shimbun*) ranked in the top fifty. The newspaper provides a vehicle for effectively reaching the target audience with advertising for both books and magazines. In book publishing there is a further advantage: the national newspapers are disproportionately prone to publish reviews of books that they themselves publish.[19]

An even more important linkage across media industries in Japan is not apparent from table 2.1: the relationship between newspapers and broadcasting. When the Occupation authorities decided to break the broadcasting monopoly of NHK by allowing commercial broadcasting, the three major national newspaper firms (led by the presi-

dent of *Yomiuri*, Shōtarō Shoriki) joined forces with Japan's leading
advertising firm, Dentsū, to set up the first commercial broadcasting
station. They dealt with the potentially divisive problem of who
would direct the new enterprise by choosing as its first head the
former president of Ōji Paper (Japan's largest paper producer, which
had long-standing ties to all three newspapers), who was also an
officer of the Japan Chamber of Commerce. This foreshadowed the
close cooperation between the newspapers and industry in establishing Japanese commercial broadcasting. Each national newspaper
went on to invest in further broadcasting ventures, and as broadcasting licenses were granted outside the metropolitan areas, local newspapers took the lead in establishing broadcasting firms in their areas.

The legal ceiling on shareholding meant that newspapers could
not own broadcasting stations outright. Hence there was relatively
little anxiety among the regulatory authorities over the number of
stations in which an investor had this limited interest, and the
national newspapers went on to become the dominant shareholders
within the industry. By 1980, out of a total of 111 broadcasting companies, *Asahi* had holdings in 36, *Yomiuri* in 29, *Mainichi* in 13,
Sankei in 16, *Nikkei* in 7.[20] Thirty-four local newspapers were shareholders in their local television stations. These investments were by
no means passive. For example, newspaper companies supplied
many of the employees of the new enterprises. As late as 1975, 44.7
percent of the presidents of broadcasting companies had begun their
careers in newspapers, and for the companies established before
1967, the figure reached 66.1 percent.[21] But even more important
than the provision of investment capital and personnel was the role
of the newspapers in supplying news for both radio and television
broadcasting. The local newspapers supplied local news to the stations in which they held shares, and the national newspapers supplied news not only to the metropolitan stations in which they had
invested but also, through these stations, to Japan's emerging television networks.

Broadcasting networks emerged only very gradually in Japan.
Their development was hindered by regulations that prohibited any
contracts between a program provider and a broadcaster that
restricted the broadcaster's freedom to resort to other sources of programs.[22] However, given the need to spread the high costs of program production and the costs and complexities of effective
programming across several stations, networks of some fashion are
virtually inevitable in television broadcasting. Those that emerged in
Japan were centered on the five key stations in the nation's richest

market, Tokyo. The key stations supplied programs, especially news and prime-time programs, to stations in less affluent markets. Outside Tokyo and Osaka, there were fewer outlets, usually only two or three, so local stations could and did pick and choose their programming sources (cross-network), protected by the broadcasting law from having to develop an exclusive relationship with any one key station. Therefore affiliation came to be defined in terms of the key station that supplied national news programs. For support in producing these news programs, each of the major Tokyo stations relied heavily on the national newspaper that had invested in it. *Yomiuri* was the first national to develop a strong news network around its key Tokyo station, Nihon Terebi; *Mainichi* quickly responded by building a network around the Tokyo Broadcasting System (TBS); in 1957 *Sankei* cooperated with two existing broadcasting companies to develop the Fuji network; and in the late 1950s *Asahi* began to intensify its involvement with NET (renaming it Zenkoku Asahi Terebi in 1977). *Nihon Keizai Shimbun* was a relative latecomer, becoming involved in the operation of Terebi Tokyo in 1969 and building a relatively weak network around it over the next decade.

In consequence, the television companies themselves put relatively few resources into building an organization to gather and present news. In the early 1980s, when CBS had between 1,300 and 1,400 employees in CBS News,[23] the largest station in Tokyo, TBS, had 182 employees in its news department.[24] NHK was the only broadcasting organization to develop a full-fledged news organization, and its dominance of the field of news broadcasting in Japan owes much to the fact that commercial television news has long been controlled by the nation's top newspaper organizations, which were not eager to have commercial broadcast news develop into a competitor instead of an auxiliary.

The linkages across book and magazine publishing in Japan are evident from table 2.1. While only four of the twenty leading magazine publishers in the United States ("leading" meaning the companies that together accounted for over half of total magazine sales) were also among the nation's top book publishers,[25] in Japan the top publishing houses dominated both book and magazine sales. This linkage goes back to the Meiji period and was solidly established well before the Pacific War, when the industries were even more concentrated than they are today. Kōdansha, for example, accounted for 70–80 percent of the nation's magazine circulation in the early Shōwa period.[26] There are obvious synergies between magazine and book publishing. In Japan, the two industries use the same distribution channels (primarily wholesalers that distribute to small book-stores and newsstands) and identical distribution conditions: a fixed-price consignment system that began in 1908 for magazines and gradually developed to cover books as well.[27] The industries also share patterns of market segmentation, so that the editorial staffs develop expertise that can be applied in both magazines and books targeted at certain segments. These include textbooks for primary school and children's magazines, literary magazines and novels, and youth-market magazines and comics.[28]

The ownership connections between cinema and broadcasting observable in the United States (table 2.2), where firms own both broadcasting stations and cinema studios, are not found in Japan, although the major cinema companies are among the shareholders in several Japanese broadcasting stations. But one linkage between the two industries—the production of television programs by the major film companies—is the same. Like their U.S. counterparts, the Japanese film producers initially reacted with hostility to the new medium. In 1956 the five major studios forbade any appearances on television by movie stars under contract to them and refused to release any of their movies to television. As early as 1957, however, they were planning to produce programs under contract to the television stations, and when in 1961 a major film company (Shin Tōhō) went bankrupt and sold its film library to the television stations, the remaining producers began to release major films to television.[29]

Other Japanese cross-media linkages, however, have no U.S. analogue, especially those between the major newspapers and other media industries. For example, publishers are major advertisers in newspapers, providing more than 10 percent of total newspaper advertising revenues, second only to advertising from "service and entertainment." Newspapers still run serialized novels, which they often then publish in full. Newspapers carry television listings and—unlike in the United States where specialized publications such as *TV Guide* dominate the market—they remain the primary source of information on broadcasting programs (that section of the newspaper invariably has more regular readers than any other feature of the newspaper, including the front page). Nihon Shimbun Kyōkai includes broadcasting companies in its membership.

There is another set of linkages whose effects may be unmeasurable: those produced by the physical concentration of the media industries in Tokyo. The five national newspapers, the key stations of the five networks, all the major publishing companies, and 3,430 of the 4,258 publishing companies in Japan are all located in Tokyo, the political capital of the country. In contrast, of the twenty-six U.S. firms in table 2.2, fewer than half (eleven) are in New York, while the rest are scattered (three in California, two each in Illinois and Florida, and one each in Ohio, Pennsylvania, Connecticut, Massachusetts, Virginia, Ohio, Colorado, and the political capital, Washington, D.C.). The concentration in a single metropolitan center undoubtedly contributes to the development of shared communication networks and a common "media culture."

There are, then, clear differences between the United States and Japan in the scale of mass media firms and their linkages across the industrial system and within the mass media system. Some of these differences are the result of regulation, while some are the product of other factors, such as the structure of advertising. Are these differences accompanied by differences in the *behavior* of mass media firms in such areas as profits, competitive strategies, and diversification?

The Strategic Behavior of Media Firms

U.S. mass media firms have been roundly criticized for their orientation to profits, their strong predilection for monopoly (that is, for finding or creating a distinctive product or market that gives the firm a unique and profitable "niche"), and their short-term orientation (exhibited in such behavior as network unwillingness to give prime-time programs the chance to develop an audience over time and newspaper disinterest in "yesterday's story"). But media firms are not alone in exhibiting these traits. The rising chorus of criticism of U.S. management has focused on precisely these qualities as the achilles' heel of U.S. industry in international competition, particularly with regard to Japanese firms. While U.S. firms are profit oriented, according to these analyses, Japanese firms are growth oriented. While U.S. firms tend to pursue differentiation or "niche" strategies, Japanese firms tend to compete directly and aggressively, matching or slightly improving on the offerings of key competitors—but if the competition becomes mutually destructive or if the industry faces sudden external challenges, even the fiercest rivals will temporarily cooperate to deal with the threat. While U.S. firms tend to pursue short-term strategies, driven primarily by obligations to financial stakeholders, especially shareholders, Japanese firms pursue longer term strategies, driven primarily by obligations to their employees and sheltered by institutional shareholding from shareholders' demands for short-term profits.[30]

Do Japanese media firms, like their U.S. counterparts, exhibit the patterns of strategic behavior that are dominant in Japanese industry as a whole? The available data suggest strongly that they do, although the degree of conformity varies across the media industries. The model fits most closely in the newspaper industry. Profits there are extremely low by the standards of the United States, where, according to the *Economist,* "newspapers are among the most profitable businesses."[31] The average return on equity for the leading U.S. firms in publishing in 1986 was 19 percent. In Japan, in contrast, the financial performance of newspapers has long been below that of Japanese industry generally.[32] Nihon Shimbun Kyōkai's annual survey of newspaper performance for 1986 found an average operating profit of only 2.2 percent, although by 1988 it had risen to 4.7 percent, still well below U.S. levels.[33] The newspapers benefited from the expansion of advertising that accompanied the bubble economy of the late 1980s and early 1990s, and its collapse hit them particularly hard: profits fell in 1991 and fell further in 1992 and again in 1993. *Nikkei's* advertising revenue decreased by 30 percent from its bubble peak, and *Asahi's* by 15 percent. Circulations, however, continued to expand. In 1993 total newspaper circulation reached an all-time high of 52.4 million, an increase of 1 percent over the previous year at a time when the economy as a whole was actually contracting.[34]

The orientation of Japanese firms to growth ahead of profits has been exemplified by the national newspapers, whose growth strategy has focused on geographical extension of their markets and on aggressive distribution. Geographic extension began as early as the Meiji period, when the two leading Osaka dailies, *Asahi* and *Mainichi,* entered Tokyo, the nation's other major market, by purchasing and rehabilitating faltering Tokyo newspapers. One of the leading Tokyo dailies, *Jiji,* responded by setting up a sister paper in Osaka. During the Pacific War the government in effect created three additional major markets by consolidating local papers in each of the three largest markets outside Tokyo (Hokkaidō, northern Kyūshū, and the Chūbu region centered on Nagoya) into a "block" newspaper. All three—*Hokkaidō Shimbun, Nishi Nihon Shimbun* in Kyūshū, and *Chūnichi Shimbun* in Nagoya—have survived to the present. In the postwar period, however, as their markets were made even more attractive by rapid postwar urbanization, they faced increasingly stiff competition from the nationals. The three largest national newspapers have all established "headquarters" with the entire range of functions, from editorial to advertising, in Hokkaidō, Nagoya, and Kita-Kyūshū as well as in Tokyo and Osaka.

The introduction of facsimile transmission and computerized reproduction has expanded the options for geographic dispersion of printing plants, and the national newspapers have taken full advantage of them. Most of these printing plants either have been completely re-equipped or have come into operation since 1975, and they use the advanced "new media" technologies. Local newspaper firms have responded with investments of their own. Between 1987 and 1989, thirty-four new printing plants came into operation in the newspaper industry.[35] This represents an enormous investment in growth, and the availability of large loans from the major banks has been of critical importance in financing it. The bank loans in turn have probably reinforced the continued emphasis on growth by newspaper management; one of the explanations for the strong growth orientation of Japanese firms in the high-growth era was the high debt-to-equity ratio. In the 1980s, major industrial firms retired much of their debt, but the newspapers apparently remain locked into the earlier pattern.

The investment in production plant has been accompanied by continued reliance on aggressive distribution strategies. Virtually all of Japan's general-interest newspapers are sold through home delivery by exclusive distributors, whose door-to-door salesmanship often makes it less trouble for consumers to subscribe to a daily newspaper than to continue to fend off salesmen. In addition, distributors (with the tacit blessing of their newspaper) often provide lavish giveaways, including the distribution of free copies, cut-price subscriptions, and outright gifts, such as electric blankets or watches, in return for subscriptions. *Yomiuri,* which entered the postwar period with the weakest base outside Tokyo, has been the master of the aggressive sell and has often set the competitive pace in distribution.[36] Overly aggressive sales practices have provoked two responses from other newspapers: they have tried to match the distribution tactics, if only temporarily, and they have appealed to the industry's own association and to the Fair Trade Commission for restrictions on the "unfair" competition.

The Japanese newspaper industry exhibits a far higher degree of competition than that of the United States, where 98 percent of the cities with a daily newspaper are served by a single newspaper management, whose virtual monopoly of local print advertising gives it profits that have sometimes exceeded 20–30 percent of annual revenues.[37] In contrast, in most Japanese cities, even where there is a single local paper, it competes with the block newspaper in its region and with local editions of at least three of the national newspapers.[38]

The strong growth orientation of newspaper firms and the keen competition among them has kept newspaper circulations in Japan high and rising, despite continuing assertions over the last decade and a half that the limits of circulation have been reached. Between 1978 and 1990 the five national newspapers increased their total morning circulations to nearly 27 million from just over 23 million, an increase of more than 13 percent. Yet despite oft-voiced fears that the nationals' deep pockets will overwhelm the regional press in the intensified competition for readers, the nationals' share of total newspaper circulation remained virtually unchanged during the 1980s: 52.8 percent in 1990, compared to 52.6 percent in 1978. The growth strategies of the nationals have so far been countered effectively by the growth strategies of the block and regional dailies.

This growth is all the more remarkable in that the Japanese newspaper industry has shared with Japanese industry in general a concern that amounts to obsession with adjusting to the era of slow growth that followed the 1973 oil crisis, after decades of rapid expansion.[39] As one Japanese pundit put it, in terms much in vogue in Japanese business writing, television and radio broadcasting have entered a "winter age" in Japan (meaning an era of zero growth in revenues and markets), publishing has entered a "severe winter age," and the cinema is in an "ice age."[40]

The beginning of the low-growth era in the Japanese economy was the 1973 oil crisis. But the event that brought home to media managers the magnitude of the change in their own business environment was the 1976 bankruptcy of *Mainichi*, one of the "big three" of the Japanese newspaper world. Despite its circulation of more than 4 million, its already precarious financial condition was rapidly exacerbated by the slowdown in advertising and circulation revenues brought on by the economic recession of the mid-1970s. Relatively quickly, the banks stepped in to help reorganize the company and keep it operating, but neither the newspaper's image nor its circulation has regained its former luster. Because the shares of *Mainichi*, like those of the other major newspaper companies in Japan, were internally held, little information on the firm's financial performance had ever been publicly revealed. The revelations during bankruptcy proceedings of how much (and for how long) *Mainichi's* costs were exceeding its revenues called into question not only the competence of management but also the single-minded focus on expanding circulation that had for so long been the hallmark of Japan's newspaper industry.[41]

The newspapers' response to the low-growth era has involved

three major shifts: an increased attention to the management of advertising, the adoption of "lean management," and diversification, especially an eager embrace of the new media. The first, the publicly articulated concern for effectively managing advertising, runs counter to a long-standing ambivalence and even myopia in the Japanese national press concerning advertising. In the past the industry in general made strenuous efforts to hold advertising revenues to roughly half of total revenues: if advertising revenue began to outweigh circulation revenue significantly, firms generally supported an industrywide increase in the price of the newspaper. Within newspaper firms, the advertising department has long had low status and even lower influence. It would be virtually impossible to find a Japanese newspaper manager who would agree with the assertion of the publisher of the *Globe and Mail,* Canada's leading quality daily, that "by 1990, publishers of mass circulation daily newspapers will finally stop kidding themselves that they are in the newspaper business and admit that they are primarily in the business of carrying advertising messages."[42] Indeed, the dramatic rise of Recruit in the 1960s and 1970s, a company that built its enormously successful publishing empire largely on magazines that carried advertising, is seen as a symptom of the newspapers' lack of initiative in advertising because Recruit exploits advertising niches that are largely served by newspapers in the United States (particularly job listings and housing ads).[43] In 1987 the Tokyo editions of the nationals expanded their number of pages for the first time in seventeen years, from twenty-four pages in the morning edition to twenty-eight or thirty-two pages, and much of the increased space was taken up by advertising.

The second strategy to deal with low growth, "lean management" *(genryō keiei),* was widely embraced by Japanese industry in the wake of the first oil shock. It has meant combining increased investment in production technology that raises employee productivity with reductions in personnel (or at worst holding increases to a minimum). Between 1977 and 1987, sixty-one of the ninety-six newspapers of Nihon Shimbun Kyōkai (which account for virtually all of Japan's daily newspaper circulation) reduced the number of their employees. These reductions totaled 6,500 out of a total 1977 employment of 51,278—that is, 12.7 percent of the staff of these firms. While some of this decrease was attributable to reductions in printing staff, it is worth noting that because of the complexities of the Japanese language, the reduction attributable to the introduction of computerized typesetting is relatively small. Indeed, while sixty-one papers reduced staff overall, only fifty reduced the size of their printing force, and twenty-four newspapers actually increased it.

Both the greatest increases and the greatest decreases occurred, not surprisingly, at the national newspapers, which accounted for 44.5 percent of total employment of the Nihon Shimbun Kyōkai firms in 1977 and 45.1 percent in 1991. Four of the five nationals reduced their staffs in these years (table 2.3). The most dramatic reduction was at *Sankei,* but the change is more apparent than real: virtually all the newspaper's printing staff was transferred to a new printing subsidiary to serve the various publishing operations of the Fuji-Sankei group and to handle outside contract printing (a move that proved to be temporary). But even so, *Sankei* also undertook the greatest reduction in its editorial force. Only *Nikkei* expanded its work force during these years. These reductions in personnel have made it more difficult for the newspaper companies to face the next round of reductions (known this time as "restructuring") in the wake of the collapse of the bubble. Newspaper companies had fixed costs well in excess of Japanese manufacturing industry, due to large investments in new plant in the 1980s and to high personnel costs. When the bubble burst in 1992, newspaper companies once again

Table 2.3   Employment Changes at National Newspapers (1977–1987)

	YOMIURI[a]	ASAHI	MAINICHI	SANKEI	NIKKEI
Total employees					
1977	7,681	9,100	6,609	2,551	3,557
1987	7,428	8,335	5,009	951	4,049
% change	−2.8	−8.4	−24.2	−62.7	+14.1
Editorial					
1977	1,813	2,089	1,548	772	997
1987	1,909	1,917	1,118	450	1,164
% change	+5.3	−8.2	−27.8	−41.7	+16.8
Printing					
1977	2,357	3,086	2,315	1,017	988
1987	2,063	2,998	1,644	6	991
% change	−12.5	−2.9	−29.0	−99.4	+0.3

Source: Data from *Nihon shimbun nenkan* 1977 and 1987. Employment figures as of March of each year.

[a] These data understate the total *Yomiuri* employment; they do not include employees in the *Chūbu Yomiuri,* which in 1977 was not a member of the Nihon Shimbun Kyōkai.

targeted their personnel expenses, reducing bonuses, cutting back on hiring, and cutting top management pay.[44]

The changes in the national newspapers have occurred together with increasingly complex diversification strategies. The nationals had long been noted for their "competitive matching"; for example, each of the four general-interest dailies publishes a sports daily, and each publishes a weekly news magazine (sold separately on news-stands). But even before the low-growth era, each national newspaper had pursued some distinctive activities that shaped and reinforced its public image—and therefore enhanced its market position. *Asahi* sponsored cultural activities, while *Yomiuri* owned the Tokyo Giants baseball team (and its television station controlled the rights to broadcast Giants games, a factor credited with the rapid expansion of its network) and diversified into golf courses and other leisure-related activities. *Mainichi* eschewed professional sports in favor of sponsor-ing the national high school baseball championships. *Nikkei* has con-centrated on finding additional outlets for its business information, such as on-line data bases and overseas editions to follow the increas-ingly internationalized Japanese business firms. Recently all the nationals have added publishing outlets, launching new publications, such as *Kin'yū Shimbun (Nikkei), Katei Keizai Shimbun (Yomiuri),* and *AERA (Asahi).* Both the national and local newspapers print and distribute advertising supplements, free community papers, and so-called "free papers" filled with local advertising.

Indeed, the strategies of the nationals have begun to diverge even further. *Yomiuri,* now the circulation leader, is continuing to pursue a circulation-focused strategy and has announced its target of reaching 10 million. *Asahi* has proclaimed the goal of becoming an integrated information company, centered on its newspaper, by pursuing an aggressive expansion into the "new media" and "information busi-ness." Both *Mainichi* and *Sankei* are exploring (as yet unsuccessfully) alternative strategies to the circulation-oriented Big Press model. *Sankei Shimbun* has gone so far as to declare that it will follow a "niche" strategy of targeting families in which the husband is forty-three, the wife is thirty-seven, and they have one child.[45] The implica-tions of this strategy for newspaper content are unclear, as is *Sankei's* ability to implement it, given recent changes in top management.

On the other hand, *Nikkei,* having long occupied the profitable niche of business daily, is considering positioning itself as a general-interest daily. It has already expanded its international and national political coverage (see table 2.3). And as the general-interest press has moved to expand its business and economic coverage, *Nikkei* looks less and less like a "niche" newspaper. On the other hand, abandoning its position may have high costs. *Nikkei* has been able to avoid the huge investment in national distribution networks and printing plant because it has been able to piggyback onto the local dailies, which have been willing to distribute it through their own agents and to print it at their plants. If *Nikkei's* repositioning causes the locals to see it as a direct competitor, it would undoubtedly have to make enormous investments to maintain its current level of national distribution.[46]

The newspapers' involvement in the new media, accelerated by the prospect of an era of low growth in the traditional newspaper business, exhibits a long-term outlook associated with the prototypical Japanese firm. The nationals have each participated in various trials of the electronically delivered newspaper and have also used the computerization of their pages to set up on-line data bases. *Nikkei* has been most successful in finding markets for this service, mirroring the experience of the business press in the United States and the United Kingdom, which has the key competitive advantage of a well-defined audience with clearly identifiable needs for rapid and regular information. For all the nationals, however, the prospect of multiple distribution modes for the information they collect and process represents a diversification strategy of long standing, and the new electronic technologies are simply an enormously appealing extension of this tradition. Because of the lack of detail in the financial reporting of the national newspaper firms, it is not yet clear how much of a revenue stream these new media ventures are generating, but it is very unlikely that they will be abandoned because of low profits (as has happened with most U.S. counterparts). The belief that the newspaper of the future will have multiple distribution formats, both printed and electronic, seems now to be firmly entrenched in the Japanese industry.

The strategic behavior of commercial broadcasting firms has been far less typical of "Japanese management." They have enjoyed much higher profit levels than the newspaper industry, relatively high by Japanese industry criteria, although not up to U.S. standards. Companies that owned both television and AM radio stations in 1986 earned an operating profit of 6.9 percent, while those that had only television stations earned 7.5 percent, those with only AM radio stations earned 6.1 percent, and those with only FM radio stations earned an impressive 11.4 percent.[47] These higher profit levels have been accompanied by generally conservative strategies and a much less pronounced orientation to growth. The firms have been lukewarm about increasing the numbers of broadcasting licenses, even though the expansion of the number of stations in each market is crucial to the strengthening of the networks. The firms fiercely opposed the introduction of satellite broadcasting until it became clear that its development was unstoppable, at which point they began to demand access.[48] Many of the major initiatives in commercial broadcasting have come from outside the broadcasting firms themselves; for example, Dentsū's Radio and Television Department claims most of the credit for developing *News Station,* an innovative news program that was one of the first entries in the expansion of commercial news programs beyond their traditional time slots.[49] The initiative for strengthening the structure of the Asahi network in the mid-1970s came from the president of *Asahi Shimbun,* not from the management of Asahi Hōsō.[50]

The longstanding conservatism of commercial broadcasting management has been blamed only in part on regulatory restrictions; even within the industry, it has been attributed more to the restraining influence of the newspapers on the broadcasting firms. This influence was publicly denounced in the late 1970s by the chairman of Fuji Television, Nobutaka Kanai, who criticized the newspapers for retarding the development of the broadcasting companies associated with them and preventing television firms from becoming *kindai kigyō* (modern corporations).[51] Some support for this belief has been provided by the fact that the broadcasting firm most aggressive in entering new media business has been TBS, which has the weakest newspaper links, having been freed from its ties to *Mainichi* through that paper's financial troubles.

This casts an interesting light on the recent proclamations that commercial broadcasting has changed from an entertainment medium to an information medium.[52] Since 1992 commercial stations have engaged in what critics have dubbed the "news wars," with expanded time allocated to news programs and documentaries and growing investment by stations in developing and promoting their news shows. Clearly managers have seen this as justified by audience and advertiser response, but much of their eagerness may be propelled by a growing wish to assert the maturity of the management of commercial television with regard to the newspaper "parents," in the field that newspapers dominated for so long.

One area of diversification in which the associated newspapers are of little help is the rapidly growing industry of video "software" (recorded programs sold through retail outlets). Japanese broadcasting firms have identified "video soft" as a critically important arena of expansion; however, they are handicapped by their long tradition of contracting out most program production. Even more than their U.S. counterparts, the Japanese commercial stations have contracted out program creation and production to independent producers, as a way of holding down costs.

One of the more surprising participants in program creation and production is Dentsū, the advertising agency, which has a salience in the media system unmatched by any Western advertising firm. In 1984 Dentsū accounted for 20 percent of all newspaper advertising and 31 percent of all television advertising in Japan and employed 9 percent of all workers in the advertising industry. Dentsū has been actively involved in television programming for years, and in the low-growth era it has expanded its involvement. Dentsū participates in the development and production of series, such as the popular *Mito Kōmon,* as well as of information shows, especially "long specials" of over an hour's duration. One authority estimates that in recent years Dentsū has been directly involved in 80 percent of commercial television's long specials.[53]

Commercial broadcasting has been less threatened than the newspaper industry by the slower growth of the past two decades. Advertising expenditures in broadcasting have continued to increase, and the industry has not been afflicted by the enormous rises in costs that have faced publishing firms as the world price of paper has risen over the past decade. Of the 101 broadcasting firms operating in 1977, fewer than half (42 companies) had reduced their employment by 1987, while 57 had increased it (2 firms recorded no change). Employment in broadcasting firms had an aggregate increase of 11.5 percent over the decade, while in newspaper firms it fell by 8.7 percent. But the need for "lean management" varied somewhat across the broadcast industries (table 2.4). Companies engaged only in radio broadcasting faced increased competition for advertising from the growth of FM broadcasting and responded with deeper cuts in personnel. Firms that operated both radio and television stations tended to be the older companies, owning AM and VHF stations, characterized by more conservative management styles. But television broadcasting continued to be relatively healthy through the low-growth period before the bubble, and this was reflected in its expansion in employment. However, television broadcasting too suffered in the collapse of the bubble. Profits in 1993 at the five key stations fell dramatically (for example, by 71 percent for TV Asahi, by 64 percent for TBS, and by 30 percent for the most profitable station, Fuji). Unlike many newspapers, however, the television companies re-

**Table 2.4   Employment Changes in Broadcasting Firms
(1977–1987)**

	NUMBER OF EMPLOYEES		
	1977	1987	% CHANGE
Firms owning radio and television stations			
13 companies adding employment	4,972	5,400	+8.6
21 companies reducing employment	7,292	6,514	−10.7
Firms owning radio station only			
5 companies adding employment	547	604	+10.4
9 companies reducing employment	1,176	907	−22.9
Firms owning television station only			
39 companies adding employment	7,969	9,351	+17.3
12 companies reducing employment	2,843	2,733	−7.7

Source: Data from *Nihon shimbun nenkan* 1977 and 1987. Note: two firms
maintained their employment unchanged.

mained profitable and continued to hire new staff in anticipation of
future expansion.

The broadcasting organization that most closely fits the growth-
driven, competitive, long-term-oriented model of strategic behavior
of the Japanese firm is NHK. Although it is a public corporation, not
a private firm, it has been the most aggressively growth-oriented
organization in its industry. It has pushed for additional broadcasting
channels, was the prime mover in the application of satellite broadcasting, and has taken the lead in the development of HDTV. Its
articulation of a long-term strategy is supported by its technical
research capacity and by its extensive survey research organization,
which charts not only audience viewing habits but also a broader
range of lifestyle and socioeconomic trends on which to base its program and business planning. NHK has lobbied hard for the changes
in the Broadcasting Law to allow it to carry out its plans for diversi-
fying its fields of activity (a change that has been bitterly criticized by
the spokespersons for the commercial broadcasting industry).[54]
However, NHK is under strong and increasing pressures to "rationalize" its operations in the interests of economic efficiency—by
which is meant personnel reduction. Partly in response, NHK has
been setting up subsidiary companies to undertake many of its ventures into new business areas.

As an organization, NHK shares with the national newspapers
one critically important characteristic: a high level of vertical integra-

tion. Like the newspapers, NHK generates its own content; unlike
the commercial broadcasting firms, it does not contract out program
development and production. In consequence, NHK is in a much
stronger position than its commercial competitors in "video soft." It
is also, as a result, a very large organization, employing more than
16,000 people, more than ten times as many as the largest commercial broadcasting firm. Like other large Japanese firms (including the
national newspapers), NHK finds its strategies driven by the interests
of its employees in maintaining long-term-oriented growth strategies.
And like the newspapers, it is heavily involved in magazine and book
publishing, through a publishing subsidiary, Nihon Hōsō Shuppan
Kyōkai.

The business strategies of publishing firms exhibit greater varia-
tion and have attracted less systematic scrutiny than has been the
case for newspapers and broadcasting firms. But some generalizations can certainly be made. Publishing has been especially hard hit
in the low-growth era, and publishing firms have complained vocif-
erously about the necessity for cost reduction and the rationalization
of production. They have contracted out increasing amounts of
work, including the design of book covers.[55] The rapid adoption of
new technologies in Japan's printing industry has greatly speeded up
the physical production of books, which in Japan now carry the
month as well as the year of publication. One consequence has been
what some commentators have called the *zasshi-ka* (magazinification) of book publishing: the rapid production of competing books
on issues of current concern (what in the United States are often
called "instant books"). For example, in 1987, when Prime Minister
Yasuhiro Nakasone proposed a value-added tax, bookstores were
inundated within weeks with books from every major publisher on
the potential consequences of the tax. *Zasshi-ka* has undoubtedly
been influenced in part by the fact that the major book publishers
are also the major magazine publishers; the marketing and production expertise garnered in the magazine business has been applied in
the book trade.

Some of the recent major innovations in the book industry have
come not from the publishers but from firms in supporting industries. Book distribution in Japan now boasts an impressive electronic
infrastructure. Most retailers are now linked to the major distributors by on-line systems, and increasingly they are using catalogs on
compact disks rather than hard copy. Both these innovations were
initiated by the distributors and not the publishers. An innovation
that is potentially even more important is the establishment of book

delivery services by the national delivery firms. In 1986 Yamato Kyūbin set up a wholly owned subsidiary (Book Sābisu) in Okayama, its regional stronghold, in cooperation with a medium-scale book distributor. A customer could call the service and arrange by phone to purchase a book and have it delivered within two or three days. The service was so successful that it was extended nationally in 1987 and was joined by fourteen competing companies within a year.[56]

One further contrast in the business behavior of U.S. and Japanese media firms is the U.S. firms' preoccupation with "merger mania," to which the Japanese firms are largely immune. In 1986, for example, all three national broadcasting networks in the United States went though major ownership changes. Foreign firms have bought many U.S. publishing firms: the West German media conglomerate Bertelsmann has acquired Dell, Doubleday, and Bantam; Rupert Murdoch's Australia-based News Corporation owns Harper & Row as well as U.S. television stations and newspapers; the French firm Hachette recently purchased the U.S. magazine publisher Diamandis. The business press has hailed these developments as inaugurating an era of globalization in the mass media, one in which the same "products" are sold in an array of national markets by the same global firms, with earnings and management skills developed in one market being used to attain a competitive edge elsewhere.[57]

Given their shareholding structure—either internal shareholding or a set of stable institutional shareholders—Japanese media firms, like their industrial counterparts, have been largely immune to external acquisition, whether domestic or foreign. When foreign firms have made efforts to penetrate the Japanese market in publishing, they have tended to do so in partnership with Japanese firms. In 1988 more than thirty foreign magazines were published in Japanese editions, ranging in circulation from the 600,000 monthly copies of *Playboy* (published by Shūeisha) and *Penthouse* (published by Kōdansha) to the 28,000 copies of the Japanese version of *Scientific American* (published by Nikkei Saiensu). Virtually all were under license to Japanese publishing firms, which replaced or supplemented significant amounts of the content with Japanese materials, both in deference to the presumed interests of readers and to avoid paying additional royalties to foreign authors. The few joint ventures (such as TBS Britannica and Nikkei-McGraw-Hill) have tended to follow the traditional joint-venture pattern, whereby the foreign partner cedes control of the operations in exchange for the financial returns from the local market. In both cases, publications have been largely assimilated to the dominant Japanese model and have not had much influence in the industry in terms of either content or management strategies.

Part of this willingness of the foreign partner to cede control is resignation to competitive dynamics. Japanese firms have put up considerable resistance to efforts by foreign firms to penetrate their market more directly. For example, in the mid-1970s Readers Digest Corporation and West Germany's Bertelsmann each tried to take advantage of problems in book distribution by setting up book clubs in Japan. The clubs folded under stiff opposition from the Japanese book trade; at least one motive for this fierce competitive response has been suggested in a reference to the foreign-owned book clubs as "black ships," conjuring up an image of invasion.[58] However, with the rapid globalization of the Western publishing industry, large foreign firms are likely to look with increasing interest on the enormous Japanese market. Already satellite broadcasting is bringing Cable News Network directly onto Japanese television screens, and the increasingly competitive pursuit of "video soft" is increasing the flow of foreign materials into Japan. One of the few successful foreign entrants in publishing has been Harlequin Books, whose romance-novel recipe seems to have translated well into Japanese. Japanese firms are finding it more difficult to protect their turf. Yet they share with their industrial counterparts a finely honed capacity for competitive response—for matching the products of competitors, domestic or foreign.

Japanese media firms have responded relatively slowly to the opportunities that "globalization" presents to them beyond Japan. The national newspapers have been the leaders in this, as in so much else. *Asahi, Yomiuri,* and *Nikkei,* in keeping with their strategy of expansion, have all begun printing Japanese-language foreign editions to serve the growing Japanese expatriate community in the United States and Europe. However, *Nikkei* is virtually alone in aggressively pursuing an overseas market for its products. Its major "global" products—that is, products produced for and sold in major markets beyond Japan—are its English-language business weekly, the *Japan Economic Journal,* and its on-line data base service, NEEDS.[59]

In broadcasting, the first efforts to develop a global product have been made by NHK. One of the apparent motivations for NHK's advocacy of international standards for HDTV is its desire to turn technical leadership in the field into a position as a top international producer of HDTV programming. As yet, NHK's efforts in standards setting have been unsuccessful. Commercial broadcasting firms have been even less internationally oriented. Nevertheless, the growing demand for "software" (programming) in broadcasting is spurring some international ventures, although media firms have rarely taken the lead. For example, TBS was the first commercial broadcasting firm to venture significantly into foreign media business: in partnership with C. Itō and Suntory, it formed a venture called CST Communications Co. to finance Hollywood film production. Nippon TV and Fuji Television have each opened offices on the West Coast to buy and sell programming. For the most part, however, Japanese media organizations have fallen behind Japanese commercial and industrial firms in entering into media business overseas. It was C. Itō that took the initiative in CST Communications, and it is the other major trading companies that are becoming most active in film and television production in the United States.[60] The largest and most publicized overseas media acquisitions by a Japanese firm have been Sony's acquisition of CBS Records and Matsushita's purchase of MCA.

The Effects of Business Strategies: Diversity, Autonomy, Access

The principal justification for regulating ownership of media firms in the West has been the assumption that competition and diversity of ownership will produce diversity of content in the mass media. Japan boasts comparatively high levels of competition in broadcasting, where it has had five commercial networks and a two-channel public broadcasting network. It has much higher levels of competition in the newspaper industry than does any Western country. No single firm or person owns a controlling interest in more than one major media enterprise. Yet the single most common criticism leveled by Western and Japanese critics alike at the Japanese mass media, especially the press, is lack of diversity. Frank Gibney stated it dramatically: "No country, outside of the Communist world, can boast the terrifying homogeneity of opinion that the mandarins of the press put into Japan's newspapers."[61] A Japanese critic, Hideaki Kase, said of Japan's daily press that the member newspapers of Nihon Shimbun Kyōkai are as alike as identical twins.[62] Clyde Haberman, former *New York Times* staffer in Tokyo, said, "In the special brand of democracy that distinguishes postwar Japan, where the same party has governed for 33 years and may well govern for another 33, the range of opinions on any subject is extremely narrow."[63] This homogeneity is perhaps all the more striking when one considers that the leading media firms hire their staff not from journalism schools, which inculcate shared norms of professional journalism, but from general undergraduate programs, and that on-the-job training and "lifetime employment" provide a clear opportunity to develop a distinctive firm-level approach to the media "product."

There are many categories of explanation for this lack of diversity, but the impact of the business strategies of the top media firms is one that is frequently ignored by Western and Japanese commentators alike. The growth orientation of the newspapers in particular has meant that not alienating readers becomes more important than exciting them. Because so much of the competition among newspapers is externalized into the distribution system, the overriding concerns of the editorial side of the newspaper are to avoid offending readers and to provide a comprehensive product that gives its readers as much as its rivals offer. The power of the "Big Press" model was demonstrated in the aftermath of the *Mainichi* bankruptcy. There was much talk among *Mainichi* staff and within the media community of the reorganized *Mainichi* abandoning its old editorial strategy of matching the coverage and approach of the other nationals in favor of becoming a "quality" journal with a strongly defined editorial slant, on the model of the *New York Times* or the London *Times*. Yet the "new" *Mainichi* continued to follow the model of the old.

Because of the direct competition among national, block, and local dailies, the model set by the national newspapers, the most resource-rich competitors, holds across all three levels. The local paper emulates the format and content of the national, but adds a local slant to the news and offers greater local content than the local editions of the nationals. It too aspires to comprehensiveness because to be seen only as an adjunct to a national paper would be to shrink its market; a 1983 survey found that only 9.6 percent of newspaper buyers are multiple purchasers who buy both a national and a local or block newspaper.[64]

The ownership structure of the nationals may itself contribute to the lack of diversity. Although the strong influence of owners, such as that of Al Neuharth of Gannett on *USA Today* or of William Paley on CBS, has been criticized in the United States, the owners' personal beliefs about what kind of a media product they wanted had a decisive impact on creating a distinctive approach. In the Japanese nationals, where ownership is much more diffused, decisions are made collectively, and one of the barriers to the national press taking a strong stand on issues of the day is the difficulty of getting a consensus among the editorial staff on the appropriate approach.[65]

Given the dominance of newspapers in the information-gathering process of commercial television, the lack of diversity among them has widespread effects throughout the media system. The newspaper firms took over, to a large extent, the news component of the emergent medium of commercial broadcasting at the beginning of its development, and they are eager to do the same with the new media. The maxim of "one source, many outlets" captures the strategy of the nationals, and while this makes good business sense it does little for the diversity of the media system.

In broadcasting, one of the sources of diversity in the United States in recent years, the expansion of local television news programs, has been very slow to emerge in Japan. Although few U.S. media critics approve of the content of local news, it has been a force for diversity and change in the media system, effectively preempting the expansion of network news[66] and introducing new applications of video technology and modes of presentation. Only in 1986 did two Japanese local stations (Hiroshima Terebi and Nankai Hōsō) introduce hour-long, local evening news programs, which have been described as "aimed at opening an avenue to television-style programs that escape from the information styles of the newspaper model and the NHK model."[67] This comparatively slow development reflects the power of the newspaper and NHK models, the former reinforced by the ownership, personnel, and information linkages between local stations and local newspapers.

The lack of diversity in the major media should not obscure the very real diversity in other media, especially magazines and books. The major vehicle for the expression of opinion in the Japanese press is not the "op-ed" page of the daily newspaper but the pages of the weekly and monthly magazines, some of which enjoy very large circulations. In addition, many specialized and small-scale magazines are highly critical of political and business leaders and policies. In Japan the concern of the major media firms with maintaining a dignified and responsible public image works against their using material from the "little media," which are decidedly unprestigious sources. The "magazinification" of books has increased the role played by book publishing in public debates in Japan. Therefore, the expression of opinion and debate over public issues in Japan takes place in large part in media that most foreign media critics ignore and that do not feed into the standard international information networks of the wire services and international correspondents, for which newspapers provide the basic source material. Moreover, the competitive strate-

gies of the major publishers mean that one book on a subject is
quickly matched by half a dozen like it, reinforcing the perceptions of
sameness in the media.

The impact of business strategies on the content-related decision
processes of media firms is much harder to measure, and the topic
has not been much pursued by Japanese media scholars. The level of
such autonomy seems to have been fairly high in the past, but is currently diminishing and is likely to diminish further in the future. One
of the distinctive characteristics of newspapers (one that has long
been a point of pride in the press) is the relative insulation of the different activities of the value-added chain (reporting and editing,
advertising, marketing and distribution, production). Especially
important has been the separation of the reporting and editing function from the others, to shield the content of the newspaper from
undue influence from its role as a business. One of the trends in the
management of industrial firms in recent years has been increasingly
tight linkages across the value-added chain—between research
and development, manufacturing, and marketing. This principle of
"good management" has recently become accepted wisdom within
newspaper enterprises.[68] A recent survey of the Japanese newspaper
industry noted that newspaper firms were moving from an old-style,
high-growth-era strategy of selling the newspaper they produced
(tsukutta mono wo uru) to a strategy more appropriate to the low-
growth era, that of making a newspaper that could be sold *(ureru
shimbun wo tsukuru).*[69]

The pressures such an approach puts on journalists can be inferred
from the experience of U.S. reporters, but the topic has yet to be seriously investigated in the Japanese context. Perhaps one of the reasons for the lower level of concern about this issue in Japan,
compared to the United States, is that in America the change in orientation is likely to have been introduced from outside the firm, in
the context of a corporate takeover, usually by a media conglomerate, rather than initiated from within the firm.[70] U.S. journalists are
therefore more likely to resent the change.

One of the key decisions that affects media content, however, has
indirect rather than direct effects: the decision about how much of the
firm's financial resources to put into content-generation activities as
opposed to alternatives, such as investments in production technology, new business, or the disbursement of dividends to shareholders.
One of the features of "lean management" noted above is the reduction in personnel, and although newspapers have apparently made
efforts to hold cuts on the editorial side to a minimum, there have still

been cuts. Given the key role of newspapers in the Japanese media information system, reduction in their news-producing capacity affects the entire system. The difference has not been made up by the major wire services. Kyōdō Tsūshin had the same number of employees in 1987 as in 1977 (1,901) and Jiji Tsūshin added only 76 employees to its 1977 complement of 1,283. At the same time, virtually all the major media firms have been investing heavily in new media technology and new businesses, and very few of these investments have been in the content-generation side. Leaner resources constrain the decisions on content and also tend to reduce diversity because they produce a concentration on established "beats" and less slack for developing in-depth coverage and new sources of information.

Finally, in terms of consumer access to the media, the growth orientation of the newspaper firms in Japan has clearly made access to newspapers much more equitable in Japan than in virtually any other country, and the expansion of regional printing facilities by the nationals is increasing access. There is no evidence that newspaper firms have tried to shed readers of the "wrong" socioeconomic class, as has happened in Britain and the United States. They have virtually no incentive to do so, because advertising rates remain strongly correlated with circulation. Even in magazine advertising, the highest rates are charged by the weekly mass-circulation photo magazines, *Friday, Focus,* and *Emma,* which have the country's largest circulations.[71]

Access to magazines and books has been more skewed to metropolitan centers than in the United States, where publishing firms and distributors long ago developed ways of reaching the much more dispersed population through book clubs. The recent introduction of the book delivery service, however, has the potential for rapidly equalizing book distribution. This has been hindered by publishers' slowness in providing catalogs to individual customers, perhaps because the publishers were not the initiators of the service. Readers have had to rely primarily on publishers' advertisements, book reviews, and literary magazines for information about new books.

Access to broadcasting has been less equitable than access to newspapers, although more so than access to books and magazines. While NHK has had the responsibility for making its broadcasts accessible to the entire country, until the 1989 revision of the Broadcasting Law there was no commitment to equalize access to commercial broadcasting. The proximate cause of the slow expansion is the apparent unwillingness of the regulatory authorities to issue more licenses, but it is unclear how much of this reluctance can be ascribed to a bureaucratic perception that it is easier to control a small number of players and how much is due to pressures from existing firms to restrict the entry of competitors into regional advertising markets. There is also undoubtedly a tradition in Japan of trying to maintain the position of the public broadcasting network, whose public-service orientation is favorably contrasted with the more venial private broadcasters. But the ownership restrictions on broadcasting, which prevent existing firms from setting up wholly owned subsidiaries outside their own markets, have meant that firms in the industry have little motivation to press for expansion of the system. Perhaps the newspaper firms that are so influential in the broadcasting industry have also played a role in restraining the expansion of an industry that would compete for advertising expenditures, especially when their financial resources have been fully stretched over the last decade and a half in expanding their printing plants and coping with slower growth. The new Broadcasting Law, however, ensures broader access to commercial television broadcasting.

Diversity, autonomy, and access are features of the mass media system that are dynamic, not static. Both the regulatory regime of a society and the structure of media professions are critically important factors in shaping the changes, but increasingly, as the size of media corporations grows and what have in the past been domestic industries are increasingly subject to cross-national investment, the business organization of media firms and the business linkages among them are equally important.

Understanding more clearly the nature of and the changes in the diversity, autonomy, and accessibility of the mass media clearly requires an analysis of the business aspects of the media, not just at the level of the industry but also at the level of the firm—and at the level of the country. Both industry and country factors have important effects on the behavior of individual firms, although the former have received much more attention in the mass media literature than the latter. Country effects are created not just by the regulatory regime but also by the dominant patterns of business behavior in industry generally—patterns to which media managers look for models at times of crisis and change—and by potential negative models provided by other countries. Media firms in all the advanced industrial societies are facing roughly similar challenges from demographic changes in their markets, technological changes within their industries and in potentially competing industries, and changes in the cost structures of their markets. Yet firms are responding differently in different societies, and the direction and dynamics of that response will be the major determinant of the range, the quality, and the distribution of information in societies in coming decades.

Notes

1. *Business Week*, 18 July 1988, published a listing of the top one thousand companies in the world, ranked by market value of shares. Nineteen firms in publishing and broadcasting were listed: twelve from the United States, two each from Japan and Canada, and one each from the United Kingdom, Australia, and the Netherlands. The listing does not include companies that are not listed on stock exchanges or that are based in countries that substantially restrict foreign investment (such as Brazil, Mexico, South Korea, and Taiwan).

2. See, for example, G. Binney Dibblee, *The Newspaper* (New York: Henry Holt, 1913), p. 113: "It is impossible to deny that the recent commercialization of journalism is an irredeemable loss to this country."

3. This viewpoint has been particularly strongly stated by Ben H. Bagdikian, *The Media Monopoly* (Boston: Beacon Press, 1983).

4. See, for example, Canada's report from the Kent Commission on newspapers, published as *The Royal Commission on Newspapers* (Hull, Quebec: Minister of Supply and Services Canada, 1981), pp. 113–114: "The concentration of the press has had even more pernicious effects. The conformity it tends to impose, the constant search for even the smallest savings, and the recourse to tried and true news formulas has resulted in the development of a dreary uniformity in the handling of news." The report contains detailed stories of the cost-cutting steps taken by the major Canadian chains. See also Andrew Krieg, *Spiked: How Chain Management Corrupted America's Oldest Newspaper* (Old Saybrook, Conn.: Peregrine Press, 1987).

5. See Benjamin M. Compaigne, ed., *Who Owns the Media? Concentration of Ownership in the Mass Communications Industry* (New York: Harmony Books, 1979).

6. See James Curran, "Advertising and the Press," in *The British Press: A Manifesto* (London: Macmillan, 1978), pp. 229–267.

7. The case of Britain's *Observer* provides perhaps the most famous example. In 1976 the increasingly unprofitable paper was purchased by Atlantic Richfield, which continued to subsidize it until 1981. Media critics pointed out that a firm under pressure from public opinion because of the energy crisis and eager to win contracts in the North Sea oil fields would likely find the purchase of a failing prestige newspaper attractive for reasons beyond the business opportunity. In 1981 the paper was purchased by the conglomerate Lonrho, which was apparently willing to subsidize it in exchange for its presumed influence on public opinion. See Jeremy Tunstall, *The Media in Britain* (London: Constable, 1983), pp. 80, 180–181; and Peter J. S. Dunnett, *The World Newspaper Industry* (London: Croom Helm, 1988), p. 138.

8. Getting detailed information on the business operations of mass media companies is difficult in most countries, given the persistence of privately held firms, particularly in the print industries. It is especially difficult in Japan, where so many newspaper companies hold their shares internally and are exempt from standard financial reporting requirements. The main source

of financial performance data in Japan is therefore the tax office, whose data on the reported taxable income of corporations form the basis for the annual publication of the Japanese equivalent of the "*Fortune* 500." Like all tax-based figures, these do not provide total operating income but only income after allowable deductions, such as those for new production capacity. And the Japanese data have a further problem: they are unconsolidated, which means that the income of subsidiaries, even those that are wholly owned, is not included.

9. A company called Yomiuri Kōgyō, a wholly owned subsidiary of the Tokyo-based *Yomiuri Shimbun,* owned the Kyūshū and the Chūbu companies. It also owned the Tokyo Giants, and the revenues from that immensely profitable baseball team helped underwrite Yomiuri's aggressive expansion into those two regions. In effect, the various companies were branches of the parent, but because they were all legally separate companies, and because the tax data are unconsolidated, each reported separately. This organizational structure allowed one Yomiuri company to violate fair trade agreements in the pursuit of circulation without bringing down sanctions on the other companies. By 1990 the companies had been consolidated, with a structure similar to that of *Asahi* and *Mainichi.*

10. Bagdikian lists Gulf & Western's extensive industrial interests in *The Media Monopoly,* pp. 30–31. Gulf & Western owns Paramount Pictures, Desilu Productions, Simon & Schuster, and Pocket Books, as well as Fruit of the Loom, Dutch Masters cigars, Simmons Mattresses, the New York Knicks, and 8 percent of the arable land in the Dominican Republic, among other holdings. As Bagdikian points out (p. 31), "There is hardly a major issue in the news that does not affect Gulf & Western."

11. The advertising data are taken from *World Advertising Expenditures: A Survey of World Advertising Expenditures in 1986* (Mamaroneck, N.Y.: Starch Inra Hooper, Inc., 1986).

12. CBS, the U.S. network that in 1986 was the least diversified of the firms owning major television broadcasting properties, earned $4.75 billion in 1986; Tokyo Broadcasting System earned ¥1.38 billion, which at the 1986 exchange rate (¥150 = $1.00) was equal to $9.2 million.

13. Bagdikian, *The Media Monopoly,* pp. 25–26.

14. *Asahi,* with just over 8,000 employees, has 3,919 internal shareholders; *Nikkei,* with 4,500 employees, has 3,279 internal shareholders. Internal shareholders cannot dispose of their shares publicly, so they "sell" them to the equivalent of an internal trust when they leave the company. They can collect dividends, but one source found that only 4.6 percent of profits in the newspaper industry were distributed to shareholders, compared to 10.6 percent in Japanese industry as a whole, suggesting that internal shareholders' identity as employees takes precedence over their identity as shareholders. Puresu Netowaku 94, ed., *Shimbun no ura mo omote mo wakaru hon* (Tokyo: Kabushiki Kaisha Kanki Shuppan, 1994), p. 164.

15. Ibid., p. 163.

16. Ichirō Tōgō, "Shimbun keiei no genjō" (The Current State of Newspaper Management), *Shimbun Kenkyū* (Newspaper Studies) 284 (1975): 74.

17. Takao Sugiyama, *Media no kōbō* (The Rise and Fall of the Media) (Tokyo: Bungei Shunjū, 1986), pp. 21–22.

18. For a more detailed analysis of the technology and organization of the Meiji newspapers, see D. Eleanor Westney, *Imitation and Innovation: The Transfer of Western Organizational Forms to Meiji Japan* (Cambridge: Harvard University Press, 1987).

19. Masami Kataoka, "Shimbun shohyōran no rikigaku" (The Dynamics of Newspaper Book Review Columns), *Sōgō Jānarizumu Kenkyū* (Journalism Studies) 71 (Winter 1975): 65–75.

20. Takayuki Ochiai, *Nihon no terebi kigyō: buraunkan no oku no ningen dorama* (The Japanese Television Industry: The Human Drama behind the Picture Tube) (Tokyo: Kitsugyō no Nihonsha, 1980), p. 324.

21. Ibid., pp. 204–205.

22. This distrust of the U.S.-style exclusive networks was not uniquely Japanese; Australia's Broadcasting Control Board recommended in the late 1950s that new broadcasting licenses be granted only on condition that the recipients undertook not to join networks. George Munster, *Rupert Murdoch: A Paper Prince* (Australia: Penguin, 1985), p. 47.

23. Peter McCabe, *Bad News at Black Rock: The Sell-out of CBS News* (New York: Arbor House, 1987), p. 29.

24. This number was significantly larger than at the other Tokyo stations, because by the early 1980s TBS' affiliated national newspaper, *Mainichi,* was the weakest of the nationals and had cut back on its own staff, giving TBS somewhat greater responsibility for its own news presence.

25. Bagdikian found that in 1981 twenty corporations controlled just over half of magazine sales within the United States; of those, Time, McGraw-Hill, Times Mirror, and CBS were also among the eleven firms that accounted for more than half of the country's book sales. In 1986 CBS sold both its magazine- and book-publishing operations. Bagdikian, *The Media Monopoly,* pp. 10–15.

26. See Fumio Yamamoto, *Nihon no masu komyunikēshon shi* (The History of Mass Communication in Japan) (Tokyo, 1970), pp. 166–171.

27. Etsuo Ishizaka, *Shuppan sangyō* (The Publishing Industry) (Tokyo, 1987), p. 127.

28. Youth-market magazines and comics are a rapidly growing sector of the industry in Japan, accounting for 4.8 percent of total publication sales in 1976 and 10.7 percent by 1985. Ibid., p. 136.

29. Ochiai, *Nihon no terebi kigyō,* pp. 266–268.

30. See, for example, James Abegglen and George Stalk, Jr., *Kaisha: The Japanese Corporation* (New York: Basic Books, 1985); and Masahiko Aoki, *Information, Incentives, and Bargaining in the Japanese Economy* (New York: Cambridge University Press, 1988).

31. "American Newspapers—The Only Rag in Town," *Economist,* 9 August 1986, pp. 57–58.

32. Tōgō, "Shimbun keiei no genjō," pp. 73–76.

33. Based on a survey of forty-one of the association's members, from Nihon Shimbun Kyōkai, *Nihon shimbun nenkan 1987* (The Japanese Press

1987) (Tokyo: Nihon Shimbun Kyōkai, 1987); and Nihon Shimbun Kyōkai, *Nihon shimbun nenkan 1990* (The Japanese Press 1990) (Tokyo: Nihon Shimbun Kyōkai, 1990).

34. Data from *Shimbun no ura mo omote mo wakaru hon,* p. 187.

35. Yoshio Sorita, "Shimbunkai ni ima nani ga okite iru no ka" (What Is Happening in the Newspaper World Now?), *Tsukuru* (Create) 18, no. 6 (June 1988): 32–40.

36. See Saburō Ina, "Chūbu Yomiuri Shimbun mondai to konmei suru shimbunkai" (Confusion in the Newspaper World from the *Chūbu Yomiuri Shimbun* Problem), *Sōgō Jānarizumu Kenkyū* 73 (Summer 1975): 6–12.

37. Bagdikian, *The Media Monopoly,* p. 76.

38. The national newspapers produce a large number of local editions to compete with the local newspapers (a practice that, like geographic dispersion, began in the Meiji period). These have one or two pages of local news contained within the standard national edition. In 1986, according to the *Nihon shimbun nenkan, Asahi* was producing 129 local editions; *Mainichi,* 109; *Sankei,* 23; and *Nikkei,* 22.

39. Kenkyū shūdan komyunikēshon 1990, *Masu komi no asu wo tou: henbō suru masu media* (Inquiry on the Future of Mass Communication: Mass Media in Transformation) (Tokyo: Daigetsu Shoten, 1985), pp. 3–5.

40. Isao Shimano, *Hikaku Nihon no kaisha: hōsō* (Comparison: Japanese Broadcasting Companies) (Tokyo: Jitsumu Kyōiku Shuppan, 1987), pp. 2–3.

41. Atsushi Kuse, "The Big Press in Japan: Images and Realities," unpublished paper, 1985; Nihon Jānarisuto Kaigi (Journalist Conference of Japan), *Mainichi Shimbun kenkyū: hirakareta shimbun wo mezashite* (Research on Mainichi Shimbun: Moving toward a More Open Newspaper), Mainichi Shimbun Studies (Tokyo: Yūbunsha, 1977).

42. Quoted in Bagdikian, *The Media Monopoly,* p. 197.

43. The publishing side of Recruit has apparently been unaffected by the Recruit scandal of the late 1980s concerning the company president's lavish donations of stock in new companies. See the assessment in Nihon Keizai Shimbun, ed., *Kaisha jitsuryoku rankingu '90* (Company Rankings 1990) (Tokyo: Nihon Shimbunsha, 1989). Perhaps one explanation for the zeal with which the Japanese media pursued the Recruit scandal was that the target was an aggressive new competitor in media businesses.

44. *Shimbun no ura mo omote mo wakaru hon,* p. 42. *Nikkei,* for example, cut the salaries of the members of its board of directors by 15–25 percent.

45. Yoshio Saitō, "Toppu kyūshi de dō naru Sankei daikaikaku" (What Will Happen to Sankei's Major Reorganization with the Sudden Death of Its Head?), *Tsukuru* 18, no. 6 (June 1988): 77.

46. Tarō Koitabashi, "Nikkei Shimbun, senmonshi kara sōgōshi e no henshin" (*Nikkei Shimbun,* the Transformation from a Specialist to a Generalist Paper), *Tsukuru* 18, no. 6 (June 1988): 71–72.

47. Shimano, *Hikaku Nihon no kaisha: hōsō,* p. 150.

48. Japan's first satellite was launched in February 1983; in October

1982 the annual conference of commercial broadcasters reversed its position of opposition to satellite broadcasting and demanded a role in its application. Nobuo Shiga, *Nyū media bijinesu* (New Media Business) (Tokyo: Kioi Shobō, 1983), pp. 8–12.

49. "Nyūsu no ikioi wa tomaranai" (The Power of the News Does Not Stop), *Hōsō Hihyō* (Broadcasting Review) 227 (1 June 1988): 22–30.

50. Ochiai, *Nihon no terebi kigyō*, pp. 325–326.

51. Cited in ibid., p. 205.

52. See, for example, the editorial in *Hōsō Hihyō* 227 (1 June 1988): 7.

53. Shimano, *Hikaku Nihon no kaisha: hōsō*, p. 99.

54. Yukio Ōmori, "Mondai haramu hōsō hō kaisei" (Broadcasting Law Revisions Full of Problems), *Shimbun Kenkyū* 442 (May 1988): 28–32.

55. Ishizaka, *Shuppan sangyō*, p. 140.

56. By May 1988, Book Sābisu was receiving 400–500 requests a day, with an average of 3 volumes per request. There is a flat ¥300 delivery charge anywhere in Japan. "Takuhaibin sanyū de gekihen suru hon no ryūtsū" (With Home Delivery, a Sudden Change in Book Distribution), *Sentaku* (Choice) 14, no. 5 (May 1988): 116–117.

57. See, for example, "The Advent of the World Book," *Economist,* 26 December 1987, pp. 109–114; and "Magazines for the Global Village," *Business Week,* 9 May 1988, p. 91.

58. Ibid., p. 117.

59. According to one commentator, *Nikkei* is alone in regarding its foreign operations as potentially rewarding in business terms; *Asahi* is content to have them exist, because they are necessary to maintain its image of a top-quality newspaper. Koitabashi, "Nikkei Shimbun," p. 73.

60. See "On Location in Hollywood: The Japanese," *Business Week,* 21 March 1988, p. 160.

61. Frank Gibney, *Japan: The Fragile Superpower* (New York: W. W. Norton, 1975), p. 246.

62. Tsuneari Fukuda, ed., *Shimbun no subete* (Everything about Newspapers) (Tokyo: Takagi Shobō, 1975), p. 78. A 1972 list of faults of the Japanese press, drawn up by a group of Japanese media critics, included the following statement: "Unlike most foreign newspapers, which each have their own particular character, Japanese papers are much the same in outlook." Quoted by William Horsley, "The Press as Loyal Opposition in Japan," in *Newspapers and Democracy,* ed. Anthony Smith (Cambridge: MIT Press, 1980), p. 222.

63. Clyde Haberman, "The Presumed Uniqueness of Japan," *New York Times Magazine,* 28 August 1988, p. 39.

64. Nihon Shimbun Kyōkai, *Nihon shimbun nenkan 1985* (The Japanese Press 1985), (Tokyo: Nihon Shimbun Kyōkai, 1985), p. 37.

65. This was asserted in two separate conversations, one with a reporter from a national newspaper and one with an academic, both of whom asked not to be cited publicly.

66. When CBS proposed in 1981 to expand its evening news to a full

hour, its affiliates "didn't just reject the expanded news plan; they assaulted it." Peter J. Boyer, *Who Killed CBS? The Undoing of America's Number One News Network* (New York: Random House, 1988), p. 97.

67. NHK, *NHK nenkan '87,* (Tokyo: Nihon Hōsō Shuppan Kyōkai, 1987), p. 416.

68. See, for example, Jon G. Udell, *The Economics of the American Newspaper* (New York: Hastings House, 1978), pp. 49–50.

69. Sorita, "Shimbunkai ni ima nani ga okite iru no ka," p. 32.

70. See, for example, Krieg, *Spiked.*

71. Data from *Dentsū Japan Marketing Advertising Yearbook 1988* (Tokyo: Dentsū, Inc., 1988).

3

Portraying the State: NHK Television News and Politics

ELLIS S. KRAUSS

IN most industrialized democracies in the 1990s, television has become a main, if not *the* main, source of information about government and politics for the average citizen, and thus it has become the major creator of images of what the state is like, how it operates, and how it relates to society. This chapter analyzes how Japan's major television channel, NHK (Nihon Hōsō Kyōkai, the Japan Broadcasting Corporation), has portrayed the state in its main television news program, the 7 P.M. news. It explores why NHK depicted the state as it did and the possible effects on politics of such a portrayal.

Why television's treatment of the state matters is an important question. Some media analysts have argued that the portrayal of government and politicians in television news has contributed substantially to Americans' alienated and cynical views of the political process. Is there evidence of this in Japan? Do technology and the reportorial and production requirements of television news have similar consequences everywhere? Or does television news portray the state differently in Japan as compared to the United States, with different implications for politics? These are some of the questions this chapter will explore.

The field research reported in this paper was conducted between 1983 and 1985.[1] During and after these two years, the process and organization of the NHK 7 P.M. news changed in several ways. Although for convenience the present tense may be used, the chapter describes a news organization and process in effect for much of the post–World War II period until the mid-1980s, but not necessarily as it is today.[2]

Television News and NHK

Television news may well be the prime source of information for the average Japanese. Considering the much vaunted reading habits of Japanese, who consume more newspapers per capita than almost any people in the Western world, this statement may come as a surprise. Yet public opinion surveys confirm that Japanese depend on television news for information as much as or more than they depend on the newspaper. Television is preferred over newspapers by twice as many people for knowing what occurs in the world.[3]

For much of the postwar period, NHK was the primary source of television news in Japan. Like the British Broadcasting Corporation (BBC) in England, NHK is a public service broadcasting *(kōkyō hōsō)* organization, not a national broadcasting *(kokuei hōsō)* agency. It receives its revenue from receivers' fees rather than from central government allocation. The government has no direct control over its day-to-day administration. In this sense, NHK is an independent broadcast agency. However, governmental purview is not completely lacking and is exercised through various financial and bureaucratic mechanisms. For example, the NHK board of governors is appointed by the prime minister, and its overall yearly budget and any receiver fee increases must be approved by the minister of posts and the Diet. NHK may be characterized as autonomous from, but somewhat accountable to, government. Equally true for NHK would be Tom Burns' characterization of the BBC as a "quasi-autonomous, non-governmental organization."[4]

NHK for some time has competed with a full range of private, commercial *(minpō)* stations and "networks." From the 1960s to the 1980s, however, NHK dominated the competition. In the late 1980s it employed approximately 16,000 people, making it the second-largest broadcast agency in the world after the BBC, and it commanded a budget of more than ¥480 billion (more than $3.5 billion per year at 1992 exchange rates). More than 30 million households in Japan have contracts with NHK to pay receivers' fees, 93 percent of them for color television sets.[5]

Especially in television news, NHK has no peer in Japan or the world in sheer amount of coverage: in the early 1980s it broadcast more than two and a half times as much news on a weekly basis as the commercial stations. Around one-third of its entire programming (about forty hours) falls into this category, more than double that of the private networks' offerings to the public.[6] Indeed, NHK broadcasts, in both number of programs and total minutes per day, more television news than any other major news organization in the West or in democratic Asia and Oceania.[7]

Quantity of news broadcast was only part of NHK's domination of its competition in television news. On an average weekday, between one-third and three-quarters of viewers with their televisions on were watching its major morning, noon, and evening (7 P.M.) news broadcasts,[8] rather than the competing commercial networks. Asked in surveys to compare their trust in NHK television news with commercial stations' news, an overwhelming majority of the public trusted NHK as much as or more than the private stations.[9] Indeed, NHK occupied a special place in Japan. According to surveys, it was the most trusted institution in Japanese society, outstripping government bodies, the police and the courts, business and labor, and other media in this regard.[10] If Japan is an information-oriented society, television is the primary means of dissemination of information, and NHK news in the mid-1980s was the primary source of television information.

When my research began in 1983, NHK was broadcasting fifteen news programs per day. There were four major national news programs, numerous five-minute news updates during the day, and also local news programs. Although the 7 P.M. evening news program, then and now, does not have the largest audience share of NHK's news programs (that honor belongs to the morning news show), it still obtains about one-third of the nationwide viewing audience at that time slot[11] and is considered the prime news of the day for broadcast journalists, just as network evening news programs are in the United States.

Style and Content: A Typical Evening News Program

An American in 1983 tuning in to the 7 P.M. news for the first time would be impressed, first and foremost, with the seeming homogeneity of television news around the world. At first glance, the format of the program appears to be strikingly similar to U.S. commercial network news. There are "anchors," one male and one female. Behind them, backboards display the "headline" of the story segment and sometimes graphics. At the beginning of each broadcast, the anchors mention the day's "headline" stories. Correspondents sometimes do "standup" live remote reports.

Unlike U.S. network news, the NHK news program has no commercials, but it divides the presentation of the news into sections, just as commercial breaks do. The first part of the program consists of "hard news," followed by a part called *naigai wadai,* or "domestic and foreign topics," providing more superficial and topical entertainment and curiosity news. Then follow features and other less important news stories. Sports and weather close the program.

As she watches the 7 P.M. news over a longer period, however, our hypothetical American viewer begins to discern differences in style and content from American news. For example, the anchors do fewer short "reads" from the wire services than in American news; indeed, the anchors seem to do little more than read the headlines, and from a script, not a teleprompter; they then provide occasional straightforward voice-over for some stories.

The anchors present a different appearance and style, too. They are generally conservatively dressed, with the unsmiling male anchor looking particularly stolid in his round-rimmed glasses, having the look and demeanor of a serious businessman. The female anchor smiles more often, but would pass unnoticed among younger middle-aged mothers at a PTA meeting in Japan. No avuncular and craggy, or hirsute and boyish good looks distinguish the man; no "professional woman" or starlet image characterizes the woman. Neither infuses the program with much personality, and neither uses any trademark sign-off—no "that's the way it is" or "courage." Rather, they both bow deeply to the audience before the female anchor gives a tentative bow in the male anchor's direction, one that he seems to acknowledge as an afterthought as the program goes off the air. This is the only on-screen interaction between the two in the entire program.

Looking beyond the anchors, our viewer would notice that the backboard emphasizes written sentences rather than flashy visuals. Indeed, to a viewer used to American television, the visual segments would seem somewhat stodgy, with many shots of "talking heads," usually several people sitting around a table. Her attention would not be grabbed by stories and visuals with high drama, violence, or individual conflict or tragedy. Neither would the world outside Japan intrude into the living room as often as it seems to back home in America. For someone eating dinner while watching the news, there are fewer disturbing images of war, death, and pestilence. As for the correspondents appearing on camera at the scene of events, the viewer usually will not recognize their faces, for different ones covered stories the night before. These correspondents present not the glamorous aura of their sometimes trench-coated and wind-whipped

American counterparts, but more the appearance of overworked clerks. They often are seen in the summer with ties askew and shirtsleeves rolled up.

An American, used to a different style of news, is likely to conclude eventually that NHK's 7 P.M. news, with its absence of flashy format, of action and dramatic visuals from at home and around the world, or of anchor, correspondent, and subject "personality," is boring, "cold," parochial, and staid. But such judgments are not the only ones possible. Just as many Britons appreciated the BBC's similar "reading" of the news, Japanese overall obviously have found NHK's style highly satisfactory. In their eyes, NHK's format in 1983 was a solid, straightforward presentation of the news as it should be presented, providing information rather than entertainment and inspiring trust rather than stirring doubts that accuracy, relevance, and significance had been sacrificed in a visual appeal to emotions.

A Day in the Life . . .

To illustrate the kind of news content the average Japanese saw on a daily basis, I will briefly describe one typical evening's broadcast, that of July 21, 1983.[12]

The broadcast begins with the anchor behind a desk announcing the two top stories of the day (almost invariably the first two news items to follow), whose headlines appear behind on a backboard. Tonight, as usual, the first two headline stories involve government and politics. The first story's headline is "Debate Concerning Tax-Cutting Bill: No Agreement to Adjust Proposal Time—Government–Opposition Parties' Diet Strategy Committees." The story concerns the conflict between the Liberal Democratic Party (LDP) and the opposition parties over a tax-cut bill the LDP has promised to introduce. The LDP wants to postpone implementing its pledge; the opposition parties (as well as some LDP members) want the bill introduced sooner. To try to resolve the conflict, the chairmen of all parties' Diet Strategy Committees, the party organs responsible for handling party strategy in the Diet and sometimes for negotiating with the other parties, held a meeting. The visuals for the item are a videotape showing the chairmen sitting around a circular table in the Diet Building talking to each other, obviously just before or after their actual meeting. We do not hear any of their voices, however, for the only sound is the narrator's voice-over discussing the story. As he talks about the inter- and intra-party conflicts over this issue, the camera pans from face to face, and we see the chairmen chatting rather amicably, some smiling at each other or at the camera.

The second (and other "top" story of the day) has the headline "Western Japan Railroad Raises Fares 14.9 Percent from Next Month." This story might not appear from the headline to be a "political" story, as it concerns a private railway. Like most society or economic stories, however, it does have a governmental or political, usually bureaucratic, component. In this case, the story is that the Transportation Advisory Council attached to the Ministry of Transportation approved the railway's request for a fare increase, its first in two years, and that the minister of transportation is expected to approve the increase. At the end of the segment there is a brief discussion of the probable effect of this increase on other railway fares.

The visuals for this story again concern various meetings. The Transportation Advisory Council meeting of that day is shown (again without actual sound), and its members are shown with serious countenances looking through a document. Then the scene switches to the chairman of the council entering the transportation minister's office and bowing to him as he presents the minister with the council's report. A close-up shot shows the cover of the report. Finally, there is a still photo of a railway train.

The third item is a foreign story, and typically, one that concerns the United States, conflict, and the military. The U.S. House of Representatives, in a close vote, approved the construction of the MX missile, and over a video (no sound) of the House debating the bill and of file film footage of U.S. missile launches and of Soviet missiles in a May Day parade, the foreign correspondent in Washington, D.C., discusses the implications of the vote for President Reagan, the latter's relations with Congress, and budget expenditures.

The fourth item is the one story involving violence that will appear on the news that night. It deals with the continuing police investigation of a murder. A member of a private university's board of trustees *(riji)* had been stabbed to death at the university by a staff member. The content concerned the police taking testimony from the head of the office staff and searching his home for evidence that might implicate the administrative faction at the university that had had acrimonious relations with the murdered trustee's group. The video first shows the staff chief's home that is being searched and its surroundings. Then there is a replay of the scene at the campus on the day of the murder. One sees a series of confusing, but obviously dramatic, shots of reporters and cameramen running toward a building on campus, and then an ambulance leaving from the front of the building. Finally, the alleged murderer is shown being led out of the building in handcuffs by the police.

The next two stories involve strictly domestic "social" news, the only two items of the night that do not involve politics or government. The first is about a former thalidomide baby, deformed at birth, who has given birth to her first, normal, child. The hospital where the birth occurred is shown, and an NHK local reporter interviews the director of the hospital about the birth. File footage then depicts the mother going to her wedding, seemingly a conventional bride in veil and gown although it is apparent that she has no arms. The final scene shows her in the same bridal outfit at a press conference after the wedding. In the other story, a convicted murderer by the name of Menda, released from prison by a court retrial of his case after spending thirty-four years on death row, visits Tokyo to express his thanks to a Japanese lawyers' organization for their efforts on his behalf. He is first shown on the airplane to Tokyo, then visiting the head of the lawyers' group, and finally posing with him for the press.

The seventh story of the night involves a government decision concerning an environmental court case and a protest against it. A pollution-disease case had been decided in the plaintiffs' favor by a court. The defendants, the national and prefectural governments, have decided to appeal the case to a higher court, and the victims are protesting that decision. Visually, the item first has the head of the Environment Agency and the governor of Kumamoto prefecture meeting in the former's office after the court decision. Then we see the pollution victim/protesters in front of the Environment Agency gate behind a police barricade, shouting. Finally, the leader of the protesters is seen talking at a press conference before a final view once again of the protesters sitting at the gate.

The next-to-last story of the night again concerns a bureaucratic arm of government, this time the Economic Planning Agency. The agency is distributing a report about loan sharks who (legally) charge outrageous interest rates and whose "victims" have become a major social problem in Japan. The report warns against using the loan sharks and suggests that the public think twice about the interest rates they are asked to pay. The visuals are all graphics, cartoon graphics of a "salaryman" and a loan shark, followed by a written list of measures against loan sharks and another list of the contents of the report. Finally, there is another cartoon showing a figure labeled "Economic Planning Agency" pulling a salaryman away from an angry loan shark.

The ninth and final item on the news that night is about the visit to Japan of former U.S. president Jimmy Carter. It appears with the headline "Former President Carter Indicates 'Search for Policy to Break the Deadlock in the Middle East.'" That day Carter had met with Prime Minister Yasuhiro Nakasone and stated that he wanted to use his Emory University Peace Center to look for ways to break the Middle East stalemate, and that there would be a meeting next month there with various sides attending. The visuals show Carter entering a room where he meets and shakes hands with the prime minister. Then the two are seen sitting together and talking (again, no sound but announcer voice-over), toasting each other, and finally sitting at a meeting table. Lastly, there is a scene of Carter being greeted by former prime minister Takeo Fukuda.

The program just described is a typical 7 P.M. news broadcast, different from the norm in only a few respects. It contains only nine items, instead of the average twelve or thirteen, and lacks the usual "Internal and External Themes" segment of the program in which various human interest and unusual short items from Japan and abroad are presented. Further, it actually has more items involving conflict than one usually finds: party conflict in the story on the Diet, a murder case, and a protest.

What were some of the major distinctive features of this program? Political and governmental news items dominated and were given priority in the top stories of the day, particularly items involving bureaucratic agencies, advisory councils connected to bureaucratic agencies, and policy innovations or changes. There was little "pure" social or economic news that did not involve the state in some way. Conflict, violence, and weapons of violence were rarely portrayed visually, and when they were, the events took place abroad, or involved crimes for which the perpetrator(s) were being or had been arrested or punished. Visuals of staged events such as meetings or interviews, or still visuals, predominated; stories about conflict or disagreement were often shown with visuals that did not illustrate conflict, but rather showed the opposite: people meeting, often with no visible indication of hostility, to try to resolve conflict.

Portraying the State

News Items

This chapter focuses on how the state is portrayed, but there is no agreement among social scientists on how to define "the state." Some take a broad view, seeing it as encompassing "all public officials—elected and appointed, at high and low levels, at the center and the peripheries—who are involved in the making of public policy."[13] Others use the concept more narrowly to refer primarily to the executive and the national bureaucracy, the "core" elements of the state.[14] In the following discussion, I will delineate how the state was portrayed, in both senses of the term.

I will present data from a content analysis of the NHK 7 P.M. weekday news programs for a three-week period in July 1983, a total of fifteen programs.[15] The number of news items in each program varied, but generally there were about twelve or thirteen (excluding sports and weather), taking up a bit over twenty-three minutes of the total twenty-five-minute program. Each of the 193 separate news items on the 15 programs during this period was categorized and/or described as to content, length, order in the program, visuals used, and so on.

Two major news items occurred during the three-week period. The most important was the release of the convict Menda after he had spent thirty-four years in prison for murder. The second was extensive flood damage along the seacoast in northern Japan. Apart from these two stories, the period was a quiet one, especially politically. There were no plenary sessions of the Diet. The Japan Socialist Party (JSP) was involved in the preliminary stages of finding a new chairman, but no nationwide elections were held or about to be held. The content analysis thus encompasses a rather "slow to average" period for political news.

The first, basic question we may ask about the portrayal of the state on NHK television news is how much attention and time are devoted to the news about politics and government in general, that is, to the state in its broader conception. A preliminary indication of the relative importance of news about the state is shown in table 3.1, which gives the percentages of total items and total time for stories related to politics/government, society, economics, and foreign affairs/defense. Stories could be classified in up to, but no more than, two categories.[16]

Table 3.1   Percentage of Total Items and Total Time Related
            to Type of News (NHK)

	POLITICS/ GOVERNMENT	SOCIETY	ECONOMIC	FOREIGN/ DEFENSE
Items (N = 193)	52	56	10	26
Time (N = 20,967 secs)	61	61	11	19

Note: Percentages total more than 100 percent because each item could be
categorized into two (but no more than two) categories.

Remarkably, more than half the items, and three-fifths of the time, involved stories that had some relation to politics and government. The same was true for items about society. Stories involving foreign countries or national defense were a distant third, and least frequent were items related to economics (including business, labor, and general economic trends and events). Further, the difference between item frequency and time indicates that although slightly fewer stories involve government and politics than society, they are on average of longer duration (indeed, the average time per story involving some political aspect was slightly over two minutes, but slightly under two minutes for items involving society).

To appreciate the remarkable emphasis on the state in the evening news in Japan, it is also necessary to look more closely at the stories in the other categories. In the case of the "society" stories, for example, more than half of their number (and 60 percent of their time) also had some connection to politics and government. Only a little less than half the items during these three weeks were "purely" about society without involvement of governmental or political elements.

In the case of "economic" stories, the role of government and politics is even greater: nearly two-thirds of the stories concerned with economics (71 percent of the total time) also involved political or governmental aspects. Only a bit over one-third (35 percent) of all the stories and time devoted to economic issues on the evening news were purely about economic matters with no reference to the state. Similarly, about one-quarter of the items (about one-third of the total time) devoted to foreign countries or defense matters also had connections to Japanese government and politics.

If stories related to the state, broadly conceived, occupy such a large percentage of the stories and the time in NHK evening news, what specific aspects of the state and politics are portrayed? Using the broad conception of the state does not tell us whether the focus is the "core" state of national executive and bureaucracy, or local officials, or legislators. Nor does it tell us whether the state's symbolic and policy-making aspects are the target of coverage, or whether the focus is on opposition to them. It would also be useful to know whether the coverage given specific actors and institutions in Japan is similar to or different from that in other countries.

Unfortunately, there are no content-analysis data in other countries exactly comparable to my data about Japan. Most content analysis of television news has been done in the United States or Britain, and many of these studies have been more narrowly focused, using different time periods, coding, or analysis methods.[17] We can find some comparable data, however, in two studies conducted on television news in the United States.

The first is a one-month portion of data from a year-long study in 1976 conducted by Doris Graber,[18] which I recategorized to approximate roughly the NHK data.[19] If we take the percentages that different types of news occupy of the total number, NHK and ABC news look quite similar. Both paid most attention to politics and government—the state in its broadest conception (45 percent of mentions on ABC, 45 percent of classifications on NHK)—followed by economics, society, and other stories as a combined category (39 percent on ABC, 39 percent on NHK). Least attention was paid to foreign affairs (16 percent on NBC and about the same on NHK), although for NHK the category also included defense-related stories, and it is unclear whether or not it did for ABC).

Thus far, the great attention paid to the state on NHK news and the time devoted to different types of news do not appear to be unique. When we look at what kinds of items were covered concerning government and politics, however, we begin to discover some significant differences. These are shown in table 3.2.[20] There is a fair degree of similarity in the percentages for some of the categories—for example, in the degree of attention to local government and the courts. There is less similarity, but no overwhelming difference, on such items as elections, policy innovations and changes, and party and national legislative politics. The breakdown on legislature/parties in Japan, incidentally, reveals that NHK covers the government and opposition parties relatively evenhandedly.[21]

The two differ enormously, however, on the exceptionally large percentage of stories related to the bureaucracy and its advisory councils in Japan (together occupying 36 percent in the Japanese sample versus only 2 percent for mentions of bureaucracy in the American sample), and in the predominant attention given to the president and his cabinet in the United States (41 percent of the total

Table 3.2   Content of News about Government and Politics
(Japan and United States)

JAPAN (1983) NHK[a]		U.S. (1976) ABC[b]	
TOPIC	PERCENTAGE	TOPIC	PERCENTAGE
Prime minister	7	President	25
Cabinet	4	Cabinet	16
Political parties/factions	11	Congress	8
Diet	3		
Bureaucracy	26	Bureaucracy	2
Advisory councils	10		
New policy or policy changes	13	Domestic policy & other politics	20
Elections	5	Elections	2
Local government	3	State and city government	5
Courts	9	Judiciary	10
Police	8	Police	3
		Miscellaneous	9
Total	100		100
	n = 148		n = 485

[a] NHK data are percentage of domestic news stories only that contained some aspect related to political topics. Some stories contained one, some two, and some three of the topics. The total *n* is the total number of categorizations in this sample. The content analysis includes three weeks of 7 P.M. news programs, July 1983.

[b] ABC data are percentage of mentions of domestic political topics, as recalculated from data supplied by Doris A. Graber, based on one month of national evening news programs, 1–31 December 1976. For the results of her year-long content analysis of all three news networks and major newspapers, see Graber, *Mass Media and American Politics* (Washington, D.C.: Congressional Quarterly Press, 1980), table 3-2, pp. 99–100. The total *n* is the total number of mentions in this sample, with up to three possible.

political mentions versus only 11 percent in Japan). NHK news seems bureaucracy-centered, with more than one-third of the Japanese items related to it, while American news seems executive-centered. The news gives the most attention to the "core" of the state in both cases, and even with a narrow definition of the concept, the state is central to news coverage; but the core is different for the two countries.

The results of this content analysis are confirmed by another study done in Japan for a four-week period during 1981. Yoshiaki Kobayashi found that NHK covered stories of domestic politics and government, particularly bureaucratic agencies, more than the commercial stations, and it gave less coverage to stories of society and individual citizens. NHK also tended to focus more on the government as a whole rather than on the individual in stories about the prime minister.[22]

The great emphasis on the bureaucracy in the Japanese sample seems to be a unique and integral aspect of NHK coverage of politics. This emphasis on the administrative organs of the state is striking in itself, and especially so in comparative perspective. The major role played by the state, particularly the core bureaucratic state, in NHK evening news is further demonstrated by analyzing the order of stories presented. In our sample, there were thirty-five "headline" stories in the three-week period (usually two or three per program). These are the stories emphasized by the announcer at the start of the program with a brief "headline" of their content displayed on a drop—the equivalent of "page one" stories in a newspaper. Four out of every five of them involved politics and government. Of the politically related headlines, 36 percent concerned the bureaucracy, the largest proportion of all the political categories, and 18 percent involved bureaucratic advisory councils.

Although stories involving the cabinet were only a small proportion of the total stories broadcast (see table 3.2), about one-quarter of all the political headline stories were related to the cabinet, indicating that this aspect of government is given a high priority, if not a great proportion of the items or time on the news. News involving political parties and factions took up a smaller proportion of the headlines than their frequency or time among all news items, indicating a lower priority given to this type of political news. The percentage of headlines for all the other categories was similar to their proportion of all political news items.

There is other evidence that the Japanese news differs from American news, especially in its great attention to certain kinds of activities related to the state. These data are found in table 3.3. Herbert Gans analyzed a month of CBS evening news broadcasts in 1967, not according to political or governmental institutions, but according to type of activity dealt with in the news.[23] The NHK data were classified according to the same types of activities for domestic news only. There are only slight differences in most of the categories: The American news, for example, pays somewhat more attention to crimes, scandals, and investigations, to disasters and accidents, and to births, weddings, and deaths than NHK news; NHK news gives slightly more attention to government personnel changes. Further, some differences appear in two categories related to conflict: American news gives greater attention to conflict within the government, conflicts against the government (protests and strikes), and conflict within society. Japanese news pays more attention to the unusual and the bizarre (15 percent in Japan and 2 percent in the United States).

By far the greatest difference is in the category of "government decisions, proposals, and ceremonies." Nearly two out of every five stories on NHK news relate to these basic core state activities, more than three times the attention paid to them by U.S. news.

Government decisions and rituals occupy a prominent place in NHK news. The particular aspect of the state that occupies the greatest amount of attention and priority in Japan is the bureaucracy and its advisory councils. These findings differ greatly from data on American network news. Clearly, the portrayal of politics and government, particularly the administrative state, is one of the most important and seemingly distinctive aspects of the content of NHK television news compared to American network news.

Table 3.3   Comparison of NHK 7 P.M. News and U.S. News on Activities in Domestic News (Percentages)

	JAPAN (N = 143)	UNITED STATES[a] (N = 392)
Government conflicts and disagreements	12	17
Government decisions, proposals, and ceremonies	39	12
Government personnel changes (including elections)	9	6
Protests and strikes	6	10
Crimes, scandals, and investigations	23	28
Disasters and accidents	9	14
Change and tradition	9	8
Births, weddings, and deaths	0.7	4
Unusual activities	15	2
Other	6	0

[a] U.S. data are for one month of CBS news in 1967. See Herbert J. Gans, *Deciding What's News* (New York: Vintage Books, 1980), table 4, p. 16. Although he does not report it, Gans' data appear to have been categorized into mutually exclusive categories, whereas the Japan data were categorized allowing for the possibility of one item falling into more than one category, and thus add up to more than 100%.

Visuals

Television is a visual medium, and much of its power rests with its ability to communicate events pictorially. The visual images telecast in each story during the three-week period under analysis were described in outline, and from this description the visuals were categorized in four general groups. These categories, each containing several specific visual types, are:[24]

Nonmoving visuals: still photos of people, graphics, cartoons, and so on, and still photos or videos of building exteriors.

Moving visuals of staged action: journalists reporting, people entering or leaving a building, people posing for cameras, speeches before audiences, and various other kinds of meetings, press conferences, and interviews.

Moving visuals of limited action: ordinary scenes or activities from daily life, unusual or bizarre activities or scenes.

Moving visuals of drama, conflict, or violence: arrests or scenes involving courts or crime evidence, armed forces or weapons not in combat, dramatic but nonviolent scenes, nonviolent conflict or confrontation (protest, debate, altercations, and so forth), and actual violence, brutality, or combat or their consequences.

Each item was given up to three classifications based on these subtypes.

All but 7 of the 193 news items had some kind of visual, and most stories included some use of videotape or film. In this sense, NHK evening news is quite visual and does not have as many of the "tell" stories found each evening in U.S. network news, in which the anchor will merely read a short news item without an accompanying videotape (although she may have a graphic or still picture behind her).

Nearly one out of every five NHK stories involved a nonmoving visual, the least exciting form of visual portrayal. Another 22 percent involved moving visuals but of limited action. By far the most common type of visual classification (45 percent) was the staged event. The least frequent type was the moving visual of drama, conflict, or violence; only 16 percent were in this category. The most frequent of this latter type were visuals having to do with arrests, courts, or crime evidence; nearly two out of every five of this type visually portrayed police, crime evidence, or courts. All the other subtypes made up only 2–3 percent each of the total number of visual classifications, with the least common being nonviolent dramatic scenes or scenes of violence or its consequences. Indeed, another content analysis found that NHK emphasized visuals less, and talk more, than Japan's commercial stations.[25]

Even the small proportion of conflict visuals in our data exaggerates their importance in television's portrayal of the state in Japan. Three of the eight visuals directly showing any sort of violence, conflict, brutality, or their consequences took place abroad or in fiction. One involved a file film of rioting in Northern Ireland, another the damage resulting from a race riot in Sri Lanka, and the third, battle scenes from the American movie *Star Wars*. Similarly, three of the ten nonviolent conflict visuals took place abroad, showing peaceful demonstrations in Britain against the death penalty, the U.S. House of Representatives debating the MX missile, and American baseball manager Billy Martin shouting at an umpire.

The forces or weapons in noncombat roles are foreign military troops and their hardware: five of the nine armed forces visuals were of foreign troops and weapons (four of them the U.S. military). Scenes that we labeled "dramatic" (but not involving conflict) were homegrown. Five of the eight did not encompass manmade drama, however, but were videos of the damage caused by the forces of nature (such as flood rains or tsunami).

If NHK news is "visual," in that pictorial images other than the face of the newscaster accompany almost all news, it is not visually dramatic. It tends toward the staid, the staged, or the nonconflictual. When violence, conflict, drama, and the military appear, much of the material comes from outside Japan.

Drama enters into visuals related to politics or government news items as little as or even less than it does in the sample as a whole. Items related to the state in its broadest sense contained a higher proportion of staged visuals (53 percent of the classifications for political stories), a slightly higher proportion of nonmoving visuals (20.5 percent), an equal proportion of dramatic or conflictual visuals (16.5 percent), and a lower proportion of common or unusual activities or scenes (only 7 percent). Conflict or violence is portrayed no more frequently in political news than in other news on NHK, which is to say not very frequently, and visual images of staged events or nonmoving pictorials illustrate political news more frequently than other kinds of news.

The most common type of visual used in stories about government and politics depicts meetings of various kinds. Over one-quarter of all the political classifications involved videos of meetings in progress or participants sitting around a table, visits of a person or delegation to meet another person, and speeches being made at formal meetings. Another quarter of all political stories either depicted people merely entering or leaving a building or directly involved the press in some way, as in posing for cameras, press conferences, interviews, or journalist comments.

On the other hand, by far the most frequent single subcategory of conflictual visual involving politics or government was related to crime or the courts. Usually, however, what is depicted is not crime per se, or its consequences, or even court battles, but rather a criminal suspect being arrested or a defendant being led into or out of court under heavily armed guard. Twelve of the twenty-one classifications in this category included these kinds of scenes. Only four stories in the three weeks' worth of news actually showed scenes of a crime or evidence of crimes, and in only two of these was there also no visual portrayal of police arresting the suspects.[26] During the entire three-week period, only two stories showed actual violence or its direct consequences. One of these used file footage of a violent student demonstration with police several years previously in a story about the chief defendant in the case receiving a life sentence. The other showed blood on the street in a story about gang warfare in a Japanese city. In other words, news about crime and courts on NHK news most usually shows the suspect or defendant in the custody of the state, and it rarely portrays criminal behavior or courts.

Finally, the data seem to indicate a disparity between the content of political news items and their visual portrayal. According to this analysis of the activities in the news, 12 percent of the domestic news items concerned governmental conflicts and disagreements; 6 percent, protests or strikes; and 23 percent, crimes, scandals, or investigations. One might expect such content to show up in equivalent percentages in the visual classifications of nonviolent conflict and crime and courts. Yet while these themes were found in 41 percent of the news-item content classifications, they were found in only 9 percent of the visual classifications. The translation of conflictual political items to the screen thus loses the drama inherent in the events.

Comparing visual patterns at NHK to U.S. news is difficult, as most content analyses of American news focus on the story contents rather than the visuals used to illustrate them. However, all analyses of American network news have emphasized that one of the chief criteria for selecting national news in the United States is the value placed upon drama, conflict, and violence, especially when pictorial images of these are available for showing. Gans found that stories about citizen versus government combined with intragovernmental conflict were the activities portrayed most frequently in the news, and Graber argues that one of the most important elements of American media "newsworthiness" is *"violence, conflict, disaster, or scandal."*[27]

Producers of American network news assume "that the home audience is more likely to be engrossed by visual action than a filmed discussion of issues, or 'talking heads,' and so they place high value on action film," with "visually identifiable opponents clashing violently."[28] One unpublished study shows that television is much more likely than local newspapers to cover noncriminal violence.[29] Yet we have found little evidence for these same values in the visual images on NHK evening news in 1983.

There is one exception to this visual dissimilarity: foreign news. On NHK, stories and images involving conflict and violence are more prevalent in foreign news items than in domestic ones. U.S. network news tends to the same characteristic.[30]

Explaining the Patterns

News and Reality

How does one explain the patterns found in Japanese television news?[31] One tempting explanation is that television news is essentially a mirror of reality, merely transmitting to us, with relatively little distortion, the events and conditions in a particular country. Thus if Japanese television offers more news about the administrative state and provides fewer images of conflict and violence than American news, it is simply because the state bureaucracy is more powerful in Japan and because there is less crime, violence, and conflict in that society.

There is some truth to this. After all, television news does not completely invent what happens. According to many analyses of Japanese politics, bureaucracy is more important and influential in Japan than in the United States, and statistics show that the crime rate is much lower. But attributing the differences in television news solely to the different contexts in which they operate can explain only part of the results. No news organization—even one with the great resources and large staff of NHK—can cover everything that happens in a society, and none can perfectly reflect an objective reality.

Choices have to be made as to which twelve or thirteen stories will be featured on a given night's newscast; what priority, order, and time they will be given; and how they will be portrayed visually. These choices mean that we are no longer dealing with reality itself, but with how a news organization has chosen to portray it. As Austin Ranney has cogently observed, television news is not so much an "electronic mirror" as it is a "flashlight in the attic," illuminating whatever it briefly shines its beam on and leaving the rest in the dark.[32]

Furthermore, although some of these findings seem to reflect common beliefs about Japan (held by foreign observers and the Japanese themselves), some findings do not seem to fit well and others are questionable. For example, although Japan does have a lower crime rate and is widely believed to be a less conflictual society than the United States, it is also believed to be a society in which courts play only a minor role in resolving disputes. And yet, as we have seen, crimes, scandals, and investigations represent a surprisingly high percentage of the stories on NHK news, nearly as much as on American news. The courts are featured in the news as much in our NHK analysis as in Graber's on ABC evening news, and the police more so.[33]

Further, although the bureaucracy may be more powerful in Japan than in the United States, the extent of that power has been widely debated among political scientists and print journalists. Some have presented evidence that the power of LDP politicians and big business relative to the bureaucracy has been greater than previously thought and that it is increasing.[34] Indeed, the incumbent prime minister at the time of this content analysis, Yasuhiro Nakasone, has been one of the most active and influential of Japan's postwar leaders, and one whose political style attempts to circumvent reliance on the bureaucracy.[35] Yet we find little reflection of these other possible "realities" in the data.

If news organizations must select and present only part of a society's daily story, and if television news seems to reflect reality in some ways, but not in others, then one cannot use "reality" as an explanation of all one finds on the news. There is no question that events "out there" do define the daily pool of stories that might be presented, but within that very broad limit, "reflections of reality" cannot completely explain our findings.

Nor can the simple assertion of journalists' political bias explain the results. In the case of NHK, for example, findings that the administrative state and nonconflictual images predominate do not square with the frequent assertions by politicians that individual journalists are generally government critics and supporters of the opposition parties. This explanation does not accord either with the nature of broadcasting organizations or with the research that has been conducted on them. The journalistic process is a collective, organizational one run by professionals in which one individual's partisan views do not have much influence. Indeed, most studies have indicated that existing biases in the presentation of news seem to be the result not of individual political bias but rather of "structural bias," the constraints and exigencies of the organization that produces the news.[36]

A recent trend in scholarly study of the media in the United States and other countries thus has been to conduct studies of the organizational process of television broadcasting. These go beyond the naive assumption that the "media is only the messenger" transmitting an objective reality. The titles of some of these works are indicative of more sophisticated assumptions: it is not *News from Nowhere* that appears on our television screens nightly, but a question of *Deciding What's News,* of *Putting 'Reality' Together,* and sometimes even of *Creating Reality.*[37] Michael Reich finds that in Japan what is defined as newsworthy in newspapers is the result of a complex bargaining process between the news company and its sources.[38]

These works have in common the assumption that what is defined, selected, and presented as "news" has much to do with the organization that gathers and transmits it. In other words, they are concerned with "the effect of the processes of a news organization on the news product,"[39] which produces a "structural bias" in the news. Obviously, what happens in the world defines the universe of potential news stories; within that rather wide sample, however, *which* stories are selected as "news," what priority they are given, and how they are presented are very much functions of the information-gathering and decision-making process of the news organization. Among the many organizational factors that may influence that process are the relationship of journalists to their sources, perceptions of the audience and its values and preferences, economic factors, the political and legal environment, the structure of the decision process, the organization's professional "ideology," shared organizational and professional norms of what constitutes the news, and the role of the journalist.

Organizational factors and the "gatekeeper" norms of journalists seem particularly relevant to explaining the pattern of news about the state in Japan, because NHK's news organization has been constituted very differently from American network news. The NHK television news organization until 1984 was structured much like a Japanese newspaper. This "newspaper model" of organization encompassed a specialized assignment structure for reporters, a desk-centered process of story selection, and print journalists' norms guiding the production process. The structure of NHK news organization as it combined with the exigencies of television as a medium may go a long way toward explaining the news patterns found in this analysis.

News-gathering Organizations: The Reporters' Clubs

Unlike newspaper reporters who are assigned to specific "beats," most American television correspondents (with the typical exception of those assigned to cover the president, Supreme Court, or State Department) are generalists covering all the news in a geographical region and therefore lacking the expertise and background to cover particular topics in depth. Conversely, of course, they are also freer from the institutionalized relations with sources that develop when reporters continually cover specialized beats.

By contrast, Japanese reporters are assigned to highly specialized beats and are in institutionalized relationships with their sources revolving around "reporters' clubs" *(kisha kurabu)*. Journalists for the major newspapers and television news organizations in Tokyo, including NHK, are assigned a specialized beat to cover in the major governmental, political, and societal organizations.[40] At the institution they cover, reporters use the club as something of a "home base" and press room. Begun as a social club, the reporters' clubs have come to be intimately involved in the news-gathering process, and today most of the major presses' news-gathering activities are organized around them.[41]

The Japanese reporters' clubs have received a great deal of critical attention from Japan specialists and others.[42] Their most important aspect from the standpoint of this analysis, however, is that they induce and encourage dependence of reporters on their sources and a tendency to report the news as their sources see it. "Beat" journalists who cover the same organization or person over time become specialists on what they cover and also tend to see the world as their sources do. They often can become prisoners of official handouts and leaked information provided by their sources. Attached on a long-term basis to an organization, journalists know that if they alienate their sources they cannot do their job, and this dependence sometimes makes these journalists more transmitters of official information than independent and objective observers.[43]

Like that of the major newspapers, NHK's news-gathering operation is highly dependent on the specialized reporters assigned to important clubs or "beats." The most important clubs are found in the agencies of the government: each of the major ministries, the prime minister's office, the two houses of the Diet, the LDP, the opposition parties, the police and courts all have reporters' clubs. Thus the news-gathering process of NHK, closely tied to these institutions of reporters' clubs, makes the news highly dependent on official and political sources.[44]

Further, because the reporters' clubs extend to each of the major government agencies, news gathering in bureaucratic agencies tends to be heavily represented. For example, the total number of NHK political reporters assigned to bureaucratic agencies is approximately equal to the number assigned to the clubs at the parties and the Diet. When one adds the prime minister's office, which has the single largest political reporters' club, nearly three out of every five NHK political reporters are assigned to the executive agencies of government rather than to the "political" beats of parties and parliament.[45]

The club system's effect on news gathering is magnified in the case of television news. Because of the need for visual materials to accompany the news, advance warning of where and when stories are likely to break is crucial. This is why "staged events," such as press conferences and interviews, play such a large role in the presentation of television news and why predictability is such an important criterion in the selection of stories for U.S. network evening news.[46]

In American network news, the program's executives learn of coming events primarily from the wire services (AP and UPI). More than two-thirds of the stories on network news have as their source the wire services; only a small percentage originate from correspondents or other in-house sources.[47] Choosing stories from the wide pool of possibilities provided by the wire services allows for the inclusion of many different types of items for potential viewing.

At NHK almost all domestic news originates with its own reporters, most of whom, as we have seen, are stationed in reporters' clubs. Such reporters function as the "advance warning" system for informing the news organization about coming events, tipping off the newsroom up to a month in advance. Because of the need for advance information to dispatch camera crews, "predictable" news originated by club reporters becomes a major source of stories. And since the reporters are dependent on officials and politicians as sources, the pool of stories filmed tends to overemphasize governmental news.

Thus the allocation of reporters to the numerous reporters' clubs attached to governmental organizations, and not merely the reportorial process that occurs in those clubs, shapes coverage to a great degree. The club system and the demands of television ensure that news about the state in general and the core bureaucracy in particular will play a major role in NHK television news, greater than in Japanese newspapers or American television news.[48]

The News Selection Process: Organizational and "News Value" Norms

Perhaps the four most important "gatekeepers" in U.S. television news are the program's executive producer and associate producer, who have final responsibility for news inclusion, priority, and presentation; the anchor(s) who often participate in these decisions and also frequently edit the final copy of their script; and the assignment editor, who is responsible for selecting in advance which stories to assign crews to film.

At NHK the gatekeepers and process are quite different. There is no nonjournalist executive producer responsible for the entire production, but rather several journalists who rotate the job of coordinating and producing the evening news program. Instead of an assignment editor, there are several specialized sections that supervise the gathering and editing of news. There is no influential anchor, but rather two nonjournalist announcers whose sole job is to read the news clearly and who take no part in editing decisions.

Because the NHK news organization resembles a Japanese newspaper, the various "desks" or sections *(bu)*—the social desk *(shakaibu)*, the political desk *(seijibu)*, the economic desk *(keizaibu)*, and the foreign desk *(gaishinbu)*—play a major role in the selection and editing of national news. All reporters belong to a desk and those in the field are directly responsible to it. The desk is composed of experienced reporters who function as the editors and assignment editors for the news. Reporter and desk are in frequent communication about potential stories and about which ones to pursue in more detail.

Desks assign priorities to the stories they expect to come in on a given day and suggest them to yet another desk—the "control" desk *(seiribu)*—which has responsibility for actually producing each segment. It is the duty head of the control desk, an experienced reporter referred to here as the "main producer," who decides what will be included in that evening's program. The main producer functions essentially as the executive producer, and new duty heads are rotated each week from among several "main desk" personnel.

Such specialized assignment and coverage procedures might be expected to result in a fair balance of governmental and political news with economic, social, and foreign news, especially since the political desk is only the second largest (after the social desk). This is not the case, however, because even the social and economic desks have many of their reporters assigned to governmental and political organizations.

Of the approximately eighty social-desk reporters in the field (excluding those working in the newsroom or those assigned to cover sports), half are assigned to some government agency, including the courts, the major ministries, the police, the Tokyo prefectural government, and even the Diet. The other half are "troubleshooters" *(yūgun)* who go where they are needed, developing a particular story on their own, or who are assigned to particular areas. The same is true for the much smaller economics desk, half of whose thirty-odd reporters are assigned to government agencies to cover economic stories. The remainder either are assigned to a functional topic (such as "energy," "trade," or "stocks") or to the major business association (Keidanren), or act as troubleshooters. Many of these reporters may also wind up gathering information at government agencies, depending on the story they are covering.

Incidentally, having so many reporters assigned to specific government agencies is the result of organizational practice and is not necessarily the preference of reporters. Although reporters may express their wishes concerning assignments, the ultimate decision as to where they go is made by the organization, ostensibly in accord with the reporter's suitability for the post and with what is thought best for the development of the reporter's career training. Actually, many journalists prefer being a freelance *yūgun* because it offers them some freedom to develop their own stories and gives them a freedom from fixed schedules that those assigned to reporters' clubs do not have.[49] Thus, organizational tradition and norms determine the distribution and assignment of reporters; the preferences of reporters have not created the organizational tradition and norms.

The important role of these specialized desks, therefore, does not decrease the likelihood of government-related or political stories being covered and suggested for inclusion. Rather, it increases the odds. Even though the main producer responsible for putting the program together will attempt to include at least one item from each desk each day, many of the items suggested by desks other than the political desk will involve government and politics anyway.

What are the most important norms governing the assignment, coverage, and suggestion of stories by the desks, and the inclusion, priority, and time decisions of the main producer? Reporters have difficulty articulating norms for what they consider "newsworthy." They place great store on experience and on development of an instinct for what is important. There is no set "formula" for determining news value. The main producer agonizes, both individually and sometimes with colleagues, each night over priority and time decisions. Nevertheless, I was told by some experienced newsroom personnel in 1983 that if they had to articulate criteria of newsworthiness at NHK, they would say that a story has to (1) be national in scope; (2) have an impact on people's daily life; and (3) be of concern to taxpayers. This generalization seems confirmed by the results of our previous analysis and description of one evening's broadcast. Such norms are also common in American evening news,[50] but when combined with the particular reporters' club/desk system for fostering and selecting news items, and the traditional Japanese print journalism norms of giving priority to political and governmental affairs, the norms result in a pool of potential stories loaded with items about the state in general, and about its bureaucratic elements in particular.

Newsroom Authority, Gatekeeper Norms, and Visuals

Traditional norms of Japanese print journalists not only influence the main producer's decisions as to the choice of headline stories and news order, they also permeate the entire news editing and production process at NHK. A basic division in a news organization is the one "between journalists (notably reporters) who judge a story from the perspective of sources and those, such as top producers and editors, who look at it from the viewpoint of the audience."[51] Although neither "side" can focus completely on either sources or audience, but must take both into account, these do represent different approaches to story and programming decisions. A main-desk reporter at NHK rephrased this dichotomy in simpler terms by saying there were two kinds of news, news "they want to have" (audience perspective) and news "we want them to have" (journalist-source perspective). This also closely overlaps the distinction often made between "soft news" and "hard news."

In American network news, executive producers and assignment editors—some of whom may have backgrounds in the entertainment divisions of the networks rather than in journalism—play a major role. This is probably a major factor accounting for the proclivity of American news for drama, action, and violence in visuals. As one former vice president of ABC indicated, American television news is transmitting what it thinks the viewers want to see and hear rather than what they ought to know.[52]

At NHK, however, journalists and their norms are much more dominant in the process from development to broadcast decisions. Journalists on the various desks make the crucial decisions with club journalists about the pool of stories, and career journalists are the key actors in producing each segment and the program as a whole. Each individual news story on the program described earlier was produced *separately* by *different* control desk "producers"—many of whom were career reporters —responsible for coordinating the script and the visuals and packaging them into a final story item. Even the "main producer" of the night's program was a reporter.

The "main producer" of the program, therefore, has responsibility primarily for coordinating the various segments and deciding on the allocation of order and time of news items in the broadcast. Some programming and audience considerations enter into these calculations, but because the broadcast has a fixed format (hard priority news, human-interest items, then softer news), the packaging, pacing, and audience considerations are minimal compared to U.S. network news. Thus, news based on journalistic criteria, or source-perspective news, predominates over audience-perspective news at NHK. Because of the news-gathering system in place, sources are likely to be official, governmental, or bureaucratic sources. News "we want them to have" takes precedence over news "they want," and although the "we" refers to journalists, invariably it also must involve journalists' official sources.

In American network news, professional story writers are responsible for writing scripts. Sometimes stories are filmed first by the camera crew, then the story is rewritten by the scriptwriters. For other items the correspondent writing the story and a producer edit the visuals together in the field before sending the segment package back to the studio.[53] At NHK, however, the writing of a script is always the responsibility of the reporter covering the story, who then transmits it to the newsroom to be edited by another reporter at the main desk. The camera crew merely films the visuals while accompanying the reporter, and then the visuals are edited back in the newsroom to conform to the reporter's draft. As a result, while in American network news a determining aspect of visual production is the visuals themselves and the story line, molded respectively by nonreporter producers and scriptwriters, the determining aspect of NHK visuals is the reporters' stories written by the journalists themselves.

Herein lies a major explanation for the nature of political visuals on NHK evening news. The norms guiding the process of filming and visual editing are those of the professional journalist, and the focus of production is the story written by that journalist. Visuals, in other words, rarely have priority on their own merits; rather, they are designed to illustrate the reporter's story and to be an adjunct to it. With the news-gathering and editing process of journalists resulting in frequent news about bureaucratic and policy-making decisions and processes, this type of news dominates story selection. The function of visuals is relegated to merely illustrating such stories and the script of the covering reporter, so that "talking heads" in meetings tend to be a common sight on the evening news.

There is also a problem with the visual presentation of political news that emphasizes bureaucracy and policy making. Even when such news concerns conflict among rivals or adversaries, how does one portray this visually? Aside from debates in the Diet and in Diet committees, what does one show to illustrate a story on disagreements within the state? Clearly, little can be shown except the relevant personnel in still photos or in a group before or after their actual meeting.

In a culture such as Japan's, in which basic interpersonal courtesy and formal and correct public behavior are of paramount value, such footage would rarely display overt conflict or hostility. One of the visual editors at NHK complained that this was one of the chief problems of editing political visuals: a reporter's script describes conflict or disagreement among actors in the political process, but the only videotape available to illustrate the story shows politicians, advisory committee members, or bureaucrats sitting amiably around a table chatting and posing for the cameras. Behind this complaint may lie other reasons for the benign visual images of conflict stories, including implicit norms against portraying powerful political actors negatively, and widely accepted routines for illustrating certain types of stories.[54] All these factors contribute to the disparity in the results presented earlier: visuals are even less likely to portray conflict than are the contents of the stories themselves.

Audience Concerns and the Political Environment

Organizational ideology, partially shaped by the political environment in which the broadcasting agency operates, can also influence the selection of the news. NHK news prides itself on presenting "news one can trust." This core principle of NHK policy and image derives in part from the political environment in which NHK operates. As a public service broadcasting agency collecting fees from the public, but whose budget is passed by the Diet, NHK depends for its existence and operating resources on the goodwill of both the public and political authority.

Commercial television news stations feel indirect pressure to be responsible and sensitive to the public because of their dependence on commercial sponsors, which are in turn dependent on the public to sell their products. Public service broadcasting agencies such as NHK and the BBC experience this pressure even more directly; they cannot afford to alienate the public and must actively cater to it to reinforce a positive image. Only by public support can a station rationalize its existence before the public's representatives who have some control over its finances. NHK is particularly sensitive to this need because, as mentioned earlier, its receiver fees (like the BBC) as well as its yearly budget must be approved by the Diet.[55] The image NHK has cultivated to gain the support it needs is that of providing the most accurate and responsible news possible. Philip Elliot has hypothesized a relationship between the extent of political control over media organizations and the degree to which they emphasize a style of "factual news";[56] such a relationship appears to be well borne out in Japan.

Audience factors reinforce both the national trust and norms of the evening news. The 7 P.M. news audience tends to be older, rural, female, and less educated. This is because in an urbanized, commuter, and work-oriented society, males who are younger, educated, urban, and middle-class usually do not return home until later in the evening. Also in some rural areas NHK is the only, or one of a few, television channels. There is therefore a consciousness at NHK that its news audience wants news that is simple, direct, and reliable rather than flashy and sophisticated.

News from and about official government easily fits these criteria. It is national and reliable, and can be presented with directness and authority. As an added functional consequence, the straightforward, "factual," and responsible presentation of hard-news items originating in government agencies is unlikely to engender controversy that might undermine the public image and political credibility of the broadcasting agency.

"Structural Bias" and NHK Television News

As a result of the overall news production process of NHK, the gatekeeper norms of journalists, the environment in which NHK operates, and television's characteristics as a medium, a pattern of portrayal of government and politics emerges.[57] This does not appear to be the result of any explicit NHK policy toward covering government or of its news personnel's political biases. Many NHK reporters themselves might be surprised or even appalled to discover these systematic results of their organization and work. Certainly, many of the news personnel at NHK hold an image of themselves similar to the self-image of American journalists—independent professionals free of political bias.

On the other hand, some American observers and many conservative politicians have characterized Japanese journalists as left-wing, "mandarin" critics of government.[58] If this view has any validity for television, one would expect to find patterns of television news that emphasize the conflicts of government, opposition parties and protest movements, and the failure of policy. But this is not the case. Instead, *the structure and process of the media organization, partially conditioned by its institutionalized relationship to the state and its audience,* mold the news product. The particular nature of these factors at NHK results in a different type of product than that of American news. Television's technology and some of its news format may be universal, but the ways in which technology and format combine with the structure and process of news gathering, editing, and production create distinctive types of news.

In April 1984 NHK television news revised its format and organization for the 7 P.M. news. It attempted to move away from the "newspaper model" and adopt instead some of the elements standard in American news and in its more innovative news programs (for example, *News Center 9 P.M.*). The 7 P.M. news now benefits from increased organizational integration and task coordination of reporters and producers; younger, better-dressed, and more appealing announcers; greater use of interesting visuals; and so forth. NHK has constructed a state-of-the-art news center that in some respects has brought the news process into the television age. The rise of competition from commercial stations has also taken its toll on NHK's dominance of news. The news styles and organization analyzed here have faded and are already becoming just a part of journalistic history. The fundamental structure of the news process, however—reporters' clubs, the central role of journalists, and the legal environment—remains essentially unchanged in the 1990s.

Television News and the Portrayal of the State in Japan: "Video-Legitimation"?

The origin of the NHK news product in the early 1980s may have been only indirectly political, and the product may already have changed; nonetheless it may have had significant political consequences by helping to determine how Japanese citizens perceived their state for much of the postwar era. Japanese citizens viewing the NHK evening news received the following images of what their state is or does:

The salient state. The state is omnipresent in NHK television news, portrayed as not only the most frequent and important definer of events in Japan, but also as involved in almost all aspects of social and economic life as well. Society and the economy are rarely portrayed as having a "life of their own."

The administrative state. Most state activities presented involve the bureaucracy or bureaucracy-related organs, such as advisory councils. The "input" actors—politics, parties, interest group pressures, and protest movements—are given far less attention than these "output" actors. Even the prime minister is shown more frequently in his role as representative of the nation in relations with other countries or in ceremonial roles than as a politician or policy maker. The "core" bureaucratic state predominates. This is in marked contrast to the portrayal of politics on American television news, where the conflicts of president, Congress, and the political parties are given much more attention than the bureaucracy.[59]

The state as ritualized rule maker. The bureaucracy is not shown actually *implementing* policy. Emphasized instead are the public rituals involved in the process of making goals and rules for society. The announcement of final decisions is sometimes speculated upon but rarely shown.

The impersonal state. Politicians and government officials are rarely depicted as private individuals or in spontaneous situations. Rather, they are almost invariably portrayed in the performance of their official roles and are usually seen engaging in a ritual activity (ceremonies, posing for cameras, and so forth). Individual politicians, officials, or advisory council members are rarely the focus of a story or accompanying visuals. Party politicians and Diet members will sometimes be shown with their actual voices broadcast in debates, speeches, or interviews, but bureaucrats and advisory council members generally are shown without a soundtrack. This serves to reinforce the image of impersonality and anonymity of these state actors.

The state as paternal, active guardian. The state, particularly the bureaucratic state, is portrayed as guardian of the public's interests, taking care of the problems that arise in society. Bureaucracy and advisory councils are constantly portrayed considering new policy, changing old policy, or quickly pursuing the culprits of scandal or criminal activity. The visual images of criminals almost inevitably in, or being taken into, custody is one example. The news item on loan sharks using cartoons is also graphically symbolic of this state portrayal: a government agency is shown "saving" the average citizen from himself or herself and from unscrupulous others. If, as Murray Edelman argues, one of the functions of politics is to offer symbolic "reassurance" rituals,[60] television news in Japan underlines the bureaucratic state performing this function.

Stories sometimes appear critical of a part of the state, and correspondents may very occasionally make negative comments. Almost inevitably, though, such comments will be made or legitimized by another part of the state. Thus, during the three weeks under analysis, the two most critical stories concerned an overly optimistic projection on economic recovery made by the Economic Planning Agency and a reporter's emotional criticism of an apparent error made in the case of the convict Menda. In the former case, however, the Ministry of International Trade and Industry voiced the criticism of the agency, and in the second case, the reporter made his critique only after the court itself had decided that a miscarriage of justice had occurred.

The state as conflict manager. The state portrayed in NHK television news is not necessarily a "harmonious" one. A fair amount of attention is paid to conflicts within and between parties and government agencies. The visual image, however, is one in which conflicts are managed or resolved. Also, actors are shown relating to each other in a nonconflictual manner, so that conflicts appear to be manageable or less serious than the words imply.

What is fascinating about these images of the state is how much they contrast with the images portrayed on American network news. Analysts have found that U.S. network news tends to ignore bureaucracy; concentrate on "input" institutions, individual leaders, and personalities; emphasize conflict, chaos, and violence; portray itself as the "watchdog" of government; and be interpretive, negative, and anti-institutional in its portrayal of politics and political actors.[61] Although American network news may reinforce basic support for the political system through the affirmation of democracy and the capitalist system and its attention to rituals or patriotism, it may also produce alienation from the actors and institutions of that system.[62]

Indeed, some have gone so far as to argue that American television news is responsible for "video-malaise," apathy, cynicism, and instability at the regime level in American politics.[63]

Further research may well ask whether NHK, the chief source of television news in Japan, has by contrast performed the function of *video-legitimation* of the Japanese state. Such legitimation may have operated to reinforce support for the system and the regime by emphasizing positive, active, and effective images of the actors and institutions of Japanese politics, particularly the "core" bureaucratic state. Before one can come to such a conclusion, however, further research must be done on the effects of the image portrayed in television news on individual attitudes in Japan.

Some indirect evidence indicates that there may be a link between the amount of coverage given to particular political actors and viewers' positive attitudes towards those actors.[64] Yet many factors may intervene to inhibit or modify the meaning of such news products for the individual. These include citizens' comparison of the media message to their own experience and the competing influence of other factors in the context in which political learning takes place.[65]

The question of how such NHK television news images interact with those of other media in forming the image of the state for Japanese citizens is particularly crucial in Japan, where newspapers are often seen as having a negative tone and critical attitude toward government.[66] A recent survey conducted in Machida City outside Tokyo by Hiroshi Akuto and associates (see chapter 10) indicated that of those who followed political news on television always or sometimes, 81 percent did so by watching NHK, and four out of five of these persons also always or sometimes read political articles in the newspapers.

We should remember, too, that the 7 P.M. news is not the only television news and information show broadcast by NHK. The news programs may not elicit much controversy because of their basically factual style of presentation, but some NHK documentaries have become the target of government criticism and have been controversial. This may indicate that a more critical and interpretive view of government is being presented through documentaries. The viewing audience that tunes in the commercial stations' news programs also gets somewhat different messages; some of these news programs have become more freewheeling and interpretive in style. Finally, "entertainment" and other nonnews television programs on both NHK and the commercial stations also may provide messages with important implications for political legitimacy.[67] Thus major questions about the image of the state projected by NHK are whether it had a superseding or merely countervailing function with regard to the printed press and other types of news, information, and entertainment programs, and whether it had a formative or merely reinforcing role in the overall political socialization process.

This analysis of NHK's major evening news broadcast also raises difficult questions about the role of a public broadcasting agency in a democratic society. The emphasis in the 7 P.M. news on "hard," factual, and authoritative news conforms to many people's idea of what "unbiased," "objective" news reporting should be. Yet, as we have seen, the result is a different form of bias, one that may well reinforce political authority. Less state-centered information with more critical, interpretive news about government might contribute to the undermining of political authority even while broadening the scope and intensity of political debate in Japan. Is there any way out of this dilemma? Is a public broadcasting agency, so dependent on the goodwill of both audience and political authority for its operation, capable of producing more critical and less authority-reinforcing news? Should it try to do so?

These questions lead to others. Does the diversity of programs within a public broadcasting agency like NHK and within the mixed public-commercial broadcasting system in Japan provide enough information for most citizens to mitigate the implicit bias of any particular program or network? If there is genuine diversity, does it result in a stratification of information, creating and reinforcing each audience's own biases and stereotypes, leading to a segmented polity? Or does it result in a confusing welter of information and images with less predictable results? In a democracy, should all news outlets strive for "objectivity," or should competing and variously biased transmitters provide that information? All modern democracies confront these dilemmas and questions. Perhaps Japan, with its extensive mass media, intensive dependence on information, and news-dominant public broadcasting agency in a mixed public-commercial television system, faces them more urgently than most.

Notes

1. The first field research took place during the summer of 1983 when I was a Fulbright Senior Research Fellow in Tokyo, the second during the spring of 1985 under a grant from the Joint Committee on Japanese Studies of the American Council of Learned Societies and the Social Science

Research Council. The Northeast Asia Council of the Association for Asian Studies and the Bureau for Faculty Research, Western Washington University, provided small grants that aided the content analysis. Grants for research assistance from the Japan Council (Japan Iron and Steel Federation funds) and a research leave from the University of Pittsburgh facilitated some parts of the research and the revision of this article. I am grateful to the Japan Council and to Peter Koehler, dean of Pittsburgh's faculty of Arts and Sciences, for their financial support. Takeshi Ishida and the Institute of Social Science of Tokyo University (1983) and Yasunori Sone and Keiō University (1985) were helpful and hospitable hosts for the field research.

None of the field research, which included direct observation of the news process at NHK's Shibuya complex, would have been possible without the help of Koji Sakakura, a former managing director; Tetsu Tsukawa of the Broadcast Culture Institute; Yoshimi Obata, assistant head of the news division; and Kenji Aoki, head of the Editing Center in 1985. Among the many journalists, producers, and newscasters I spoke with, Yasuyoshi Yamamura, Kazurō Katō, and Akira Naitō were particularly helpful in teaching me about the details of the news and editing process at the newscenter. Many of those who aided the research may not agree with the analysis and interpretations in this paper, but I hope they know that I am grateful to them for their help.

I also very much appreciate Doris Graber and Hiroshi Akuto allowing me to use some of their data. The comments and suggestions of Michael Reich and David Paletz, and of fellow participants in the "media and politics" project, especially Susan Pharr, John Campbell, and Eleanor Westney, were extremely helpful.

The research presented here is part of my ongoing book project, "NHK and the State in Postwar Japan: The Politics of Broadcasting and the Broadcasting of Politics."

2. One of the few articles in English to deal with NHK in its political context, and one that also touches on some of the present stimuli to change at NHK, is Michael Tracey, "Japan: Broadcasting in a New Democracy," in *The Politics of Broadcasting,* ed. Raymond Kuhn (New York: St. Martin's Press, 1985).

3. Terebi Hōdō Kenkyūkai (Research Council on Television Coverage), ed., *Terebi nyūsu no kenkyū* (A Study of Television News) (Tokyo: Nippon Hōsō Shuppan Kyōkai, 1980), p. 12. Similar information given me at the NHK Broadcast Research Institute in Tokyo in 1983 also indicates that television news is the most trusted source of news; only in information depth do Japanese prefer their newspapers over television, and even here the trends over the last twenty years indicate an increase in those preferring television and a decrease in those preferring newspaper news.

4. Tom Burns, *The BBC: Public Institution and Private World* (London: Macmillan, 1977), p. 192.

5. Nippon Hōsō Kyōkai (Japan Broadcasting Corporation), ed., *NHK nenkan '91* (Radio and Television Yearbook '91) (Tokyo: NHK, 1991), pp. 63–64 (NHK budget and finances).

6. NHK Sōgo Hōsō Kenkyūjo (NHK Broadcast Research Institute), "Hōsō jijō chōsabu, dēta de miru Nihon no masu komi no idō to genjō" (The Flow and Current State of Mass Communication in Japan as Seen through Data: A Study by the Broadcasting Affairs Research Division) (Tokyo: NHK, March 1983).

7. Terebi Hōdō Kenkyūkai, ed., *Terebi nyūsu no kenkyū* (A Study of Television News) (Tokyo: NHK Publishers, 1980), p. 11.

8. For example, see the ratings for Wednesdays in NHK Hōsō Yoron Chōsajo, *Terebi-rajio bangumi shichōritsu chōsa* (Survey of Viewer and Listener Ratings of Television and Radio Programs) (Tokyo: NHK Hōsō Yoron Chōsajo, November 1982), pp. 31–32.

9. NHK Hōsō Yoron Chōsajo, "Zenkoku hōsō ikō chōsa" (Tokyo: NHK Broadcast Research Institute, 1975). This interview survey had a nationwide sample of adults over twenty years old.

10. NHK Hōsō Yoron Chōsajo, "Nihonjin no terebi-kan—chōsa" (Survey of How Japanese View Television) (Tokyo: NHK Hōsō Yoron Chōsajo, 1978). The survey was conducted on a nationwide sample of adults on 3 December 1977 using the interview method. Similar surveys in the United States showed that in 1966 and 1972 the percentage of the public expressing a "great deal" of confidence was the lowest for television news (with "the press" next lowest) among all major institutions except organized labor. See Gabriel A. Almond and Sidney Verba, eds., *The Civic Culture Revisited: An Analytic Study* (Boston: Little, Brown, 1980), p. 190, based on a 1973 report by a subcommittee of the U.S. Senate Committee on Government Operations.

11. NHK Hōsō Yoron Chōsajo, *Terebi-rajio bangumi shichōritsu chōsa: zenkoku sūbetsu kekka hyō* (Survey of Viewer and Listener Ratings of Television and Radio: A Numerical Chart of National Results) (Tokyo: NHK Hōsō Yoron Chōsajo, November 1982), pp. 13–14, 27–28.

12. Naturally, there is really no such thing as a completely "typical" news day. This day was chosen because its news contained examples of most of the content and visual patterns discussed below; it was not very deviant statistically from the percentage findings on political news for the total sample of stories for which I conducted content analysis; and it was a "normal" news day without any extraordinary event overshadowing most others.

13. Eric A. Nordlinger, *On the Autonomy of the Democratic State* (Cambridge: Harvard University Press, 1981), p. 10.

14. Ibid., p. 9.

15. An initial content analysis was performed on about half the programs by two Japanese students. I reviewed their initial work and categorized the remaining ones.

16. The "politics/government" category was broadly defined to include aspects of stories related to national or local governmental officials, politicians, processes, or decisions, opposition or protest related to these, courts and police, or elections—i.e., those involving governmental authority. The "society" category included aspects of stories that involved the activities,

interaction, problems, or concerns of individuals or groups not normally engaged in political or governmental activities. Thus, a story about a crime in which a suspect committed a murder but was caught by the police and was to be tried would have been classified as both "societal" (criminal activity) and "political" (if courts and police were also involved). A protest against environmental pollution similarly would have been coded in both categories: "societal" because the problem had an impact on normally nonpolitical actors, "political" because they were involved in challenging governmental authority. Natural disasters, social and recreational activities, and crime or environmental stories in which the police or government were not mentioned, for example, would have been classified only as "societal."

17. As a public service broadcasting agency, NHK could most appropriately be compared to the BBC in England. Unfortunately, content analyses of BBC broadcasts have primarily been on specific themes. For example, see the Glasgow University Media Group's series of publications—beginning with *Bad News* (London: Routledge and Kegan Paul, 1976) and including G. Cumberbatch et al., *Television News and the Miners' Strike* (London: Broadcasting Research Unit, 1986)—that deal primarily with industrial relations and use very different coding categories. Although I hope in the future to unearth more data to compare the BBC's treatment of political and governmental news, this article focuses on comparisons with U.S. network news most familiar to Americans.

18. Doris A. Graber, *Mass Media and American Politics* (Washington, D.C.: Congressional Quarterly Press, 1980), table 3-2, pp. 66–67; this same table also appears in the second edition (1984), pp. 82–83. I am grateful to Graber for providing me with the raw data for reanalysis.

19. NHK data are a percentage of domestic news stories only, which contained some aspect related to the political topics given below. Some stories contained one, some two, and some three of the topics. The N is the total number of categorizations in this sample. The ABC data are a percentage of mentions of domestic political topics, recalculated by me from raw data supplied by Doris A. Graber based on a month's national evening news programs, 1–31 December 1976. The N is the total number of mentions in this sample, with up to three possible. Graber classified her data according to the "number of mentions" of a topic, rather than by item per se. This is not exactly the same as our method of classifying an item, but because we allowed for multiple classification of an item, it is close.

20. Here we calculated our NHK data in terms of percentages of the total number of classifications of stories related to politics and government and recalculated Graber's data on number of "mentions" of a category similarly. The NHK data are for a three-week period in July 1983, weeknights only; the ABC data are for the month of December 1976.

21. Twenty-five percent of the stories involving political parties concerned the LDP only, 37.5 percent the opposition parties only (just the JSP in this sample), 31 percent both government and opposition parties, and 6 percent smaller parties in the upper house. The fact that this period included

various activities related to the selection of a new JSP chairman undoubtedly accounts for both the slightly greater coverage given to the opposition parties and particularly to the JSP here. Yoshiaki Kobayashi ("Terebi nyūsu no hōdō ni kansuru naiyō bunseki" [Content Analysis of Television News Coverage], *Keiō Daigaku Hōgaku Kenkyū* [Keiō University Law Journal] 55, no. 9:35–36) conducted a content analysis of Japanese television news and found that NHK gave more equal treatment to the LDP and opposition parties than did the commercial networks, and that it was the only network to cover all the political parties. Kobayashi's sample, it should be noted, included *all* news programs on each station, including NHK, and was not confined to the main evening news programs.

22. Ibid., pp. 32–42.

23. Herbert J. Gans, *Deciding What's News: A Study of CBS Evening News, NBC Nightly News, Newsweek and Time* (New York: Vintage Books, 1980), table 4, p. 16. One difference, however, was that Gans' data categories appear to be mutually exclusive, while in the NHK analysis, it was possible for the same item to appear in more than one category (although most actually fit into one or at most two).

24. *Nonmoving visuals* show people and events statically, without human action. *Moving visuals of staged action* portray people and events in action, but in contrived situations purposely arranged in advance. This type of television visual has sometimes been called "pseudo events," "media events," or even "medialities," because they might not have occurred, or might not have occurred in the same way, had the cameras and reporters not been present. See, for example, Austin Ranney, *Channels of Power: The Impact of Television on American Politics* (New York: Basic Books, 1983), pp. 22–23; Timothy Crouse, *The Boys on the Bus* (New York: Ballantine Books, 1972), pp. 149–150. *Moving visuals of limited action* are those in which people act in common or uncommon situations not covered by the preceding category and which do not involve great drama, conflict, or violence. *Moving visuals of drama, conflict, or violence* show confrontation and tension with and without actual violence.

25. Kobayashi, "Terebi nyūsu no hōdō ni kansuru naiyō bunseki," pp. 37, 40–41.

26. Additionally, two other visuals concerned civil suits over malapportionment of electoral districts. Four visuals showed the reaction to the announcement and release of Menda, the convicted murderer exonerated by the courts after thirty-four years in prison—an uncommon, indeed unprecedented, event.

27. Gans, *Deciding What's News*, p. 17; Graber, *Mass Media and American Politics*, p. 63 (emphasis in original).

28. Edward Jay Epstein, *News from Nowhere: Television and the News* (New York: Vintage Books, 1973), pp. 172–173.

29. Cited in Michael J. Robinson, "Public Affairs Television and the Growth of Political Malaise: The Case of the 'Selling of the Pentagon,'" *American Political Science Review* 70 (June 1976): 428.

30. Gans, *Deciding What's News*, p. 35.

31. The following discussion is based on the "four models of newsmaking" discussed in Epstein, *News from Nowhere*, pp. 13–43; and in Graber, *Mass Media and American Politics*, pp. 70–71.

32. Ranney, *Channels of Power*, p. 19.

33. This finding, incidentally, was probably not an artifact of the particular time period in which we conducted our content analysis, during which the Menda case received great attention. Kobayashi's 1981 study of all NHK programs also found that criminals were the third most frequent type of actor to appear in the news, following ordinary citizens and government agencies; they appeared in almost one out of ten news items in his study. See Kobayashi, "Terebi nyūsu no hōdō ni kansuru naiyō bunseki," table 3, p. 35.

34. Discussion of this trend among scholars of Japanese politics may be found in Michio Muramatsu, *Sengo Nihon no kanryōsei* (Postwar Japan's Bureaucracy) (Tokyo: Toyo Keizai Shimposha, 1981); Michio Muramatsu and Ellis S. Krauss, "Bureaucrats and Politicians in Policymaking: The Case of Japan," *American Political Science Review* 78 (March 1984): 126–148; Takashi Inoguchi, "Politicians, Bureaucrats and Interest Groups in the Legislative Process," paper presented at the Workshop on One-Party Dominance, Cornell University, Ithaca, N.Y., 7–9 April 1984; Seizaburō Satō and Tetsuhisa Matsuzaki, "Jimintō chōchōki seiken no kaibō" (The Anatomy of Ultra-long-term LDP Rule), *Chūō kōron*, (November 1984): 66–100; Chalmers Johnson, "Tanaka Kakuei, Structural Corruption, and the Advent of Machine Politics in Japan," *Journal of Japanese Studies* 12, no. 1 (Winter 1986): 23–28. Even the printed press in Japan has come explicitly to acknowledge this scholarly trend. See "Theories of the LDP's Ascendancy over the Bureaucracy Become Stronger," *Asahi Shimbun*, 14 September 1985 (evening).

35. Michio Muramatsu, "In Search of National Identity: The Politics and Policy of the Nakasone Administration," in *The Trade Crisis: How Will Japan Respond?*, ed. Kenneth B. Pyle (Seattle: Society for Japanese Studies, 1987), pp. 193–228.

36. Ranney, *Channels of Power*, pp. 37–42.

37. The latter two works, not previously referred to in this chapter, are Philip Schlesinger, *Putting Reality Together: BBC News* (Beverly Hills, Calif.: Sage Publications, 1979); and David L. Altheide, *Creating Reality: How TV News Distorts Events* (Beverly Hills, Calif.: Sage Publications, 1976).

38. Michael Reich, "Crisis and Routine: Pollution Reporting by the Japanese Press," in *Institutions for Change in Japanese Society*, ed. George DeVos (Berkeley, Calif.: Institute for East Asian Studies, 1984), pp. 148–165.

39. Epstein, *News from Nowhere*, pp. xvii–xviii.

40. Although reporters' clubs exist throughout Japan and not just in Tokyo, NHK reporters in local bureaus are often more generalists covering all types of news in their locales. So many of the "hard news" stories on the

national evening news being considered here originate in Tokyo, however, that the generalizations made here about the impact of reporters' clubs still generally hold.

41. Young C. Kim, *Japanese Journalists and Their World* (Charlottesville: University Press of Virginia, 1981), pp. 45–47. The closest equivalent to reporters' clubs in the American press is the White House press room for the White House press corps. See the description of White House reporters in Michael Baruch Grossman and Martha Joynt Kumar, *Portraying the President: The White House and the News Media* (Baltimore: Johns Hopkins University Press, 1981), pp. 36–38; and in Crouse, *The Boys on the Bus,* pp. 203–212.

42. Among the complaints about reporters' clubs is that the constant interaction among reporters of different papers is one of the prime causes of the conformity of the Japanese press and the lack of differentiation in the news of the major dailies. See Nathaniel B. Thayer, "Competition and Conformity: An Inquiry into the Structure of Japanese Newspapers," in *Modern Japanese Organization and Decision-Making,* ed. Ezra F. Vogel (Berkeley, Calif.: University of California Press, 1975), pp. 296–303. In this sense, reporters' clubs are an extreme and institutionalized form of "pack journalism" common wherever the same journalists cover the same events together over a period of time. See Crouse, *The Boys on the Bus,* pp. 7–8 and passim.

43. Some have even said that newspapers and reporters in Japan have been "poisoned" by the reporters' club system because it makes them dependent on official sources, turns them into outlets for official handouts, and ultimately results in boring news. See Jirō Koitabashi and Kenjin Onose, "NHK vs. minpō: shiretsu na hōdō sensō no jittai" (NHK vs. the Private Broadcasting Companies: The True Story of the Intense Battle over News Coverage), *Tsukuru* (Create), June 1986, p. 85. For a case study of Japanese print reporters' relationship to their sources, see Reich, "Crisis and Routine"; for an American example involving Henry Kissinger's masterful use of this weakness in the "beat" press, see Roger Morris, "Henry Kissinger and the Media: A Separate Peace," *Columbia Journalism Review* (May–June 1974): 155–167. On the general problem of reporters' relations to sources and specialized beats in the United States, also see David L. Paletz and Robert M. Entman, *Media–Power–Politics* (New York: Free Press, 1981), pp. 20–21, 55–56, 201–202.

44. See Thayer, "Competition and Conformity," pp. 299–300; and Kim, *Japanese Journalists,* pp. 47–48.

45. An NHK internal document, "Political Desk Club Distribution," dated 8 August 1983, lists nine political reporters assigned to the prime minister's office, eight to the LDP, three to the opposition parties, and one each to each chamber of the Diet. Thirteen reporters are assigned to nine major ministries and agencies. For a similar lineup of political reporters at a Japanese newspaper, see Thayer, "Competition and Conformity," p. 293.

46. Epstein, *News from Nowhere,* p. 31, estimates that for 90 percent of all stories used on the evening news, producers had at least one day's

advance warning, and that only 2 percent of the filmed stories were totally spontaneous or unpredictable events. On the importance of staged events and predictability, see pp. 133–134, 146–147. See also Gans, *Deciding What's News,* pp. 87–88.

47. Epstein, pp. 141–144, 37.

48. The different allocations of space and time in newspapers and television also ensure a greater proportion of political news at NHK than in the printed press in Japan. Japanese newspapers have a set format for presentation of news: after the major "newsworthy" stories on page one, there is a fixed format with particular kinds of news appearing on particular pages, and all articles are complete on the page on which they begin. Therefore, all types of news will have a relatively fixed share of space in a Japanese newspaper and will be placed in a predictable location for the reader. See Thayer, "Competition and Conformity," pp. 287–288. In television news, however, stories related to politics and government can appear in NHK news in any proportion, subject only to vague criteria of "newsworthiness" and the desire for some "balance" in the program.

49. See Kiyoshi Kuroda, *Shimbun kisha no genba* (On the Scene with Newspaper Reporters) (Tokyo: Kōdansha Gendai Shinsho, 1985), pp. 70, 76–77. Kuroda is discussing newspaper reporters here, but I assume the same applies at NHK, which has the same personnel practices and organization as a newspaper.

50. See, for example, Gans, *Deciding What's News,* p. 20.

51. Ibid., p. 89.

52. Quoted in Hiroshi Matsuda, "Ima, terebi jānarizumu no kōzō wo tou" (An Inquiry into the Current Structure of Television Journalism), *Hōsō Bunka* (Broadcasting Culture), August 1983, p. 57.

53. Av Westin, *Newswatch: How TV Decides the News* (New York: Simon and Schuster, 1982), pp. 83–88. Although Westin, an executive producer at ABC News, stresses the importance of words, he also says (p. 89), "If a picture can do the work, let it. Narration should add to what the picture already tells us."

54. I am grateful to Michael Reich for pointing out these other possible explanations for the patterns found.

55. The British government, through the postmaster general and by means of the provisions of the BBC license, retains some latent power to interfere in actual programming. See Walter B. Emery, *National and International Systems of Broadcasting* (East Lansing: Michigan State University Press, 1969), pp. 98–100. Although such powers are rarely exercised, incidents under the Thatcher government illustrate the extent of the British government's direct powers in this regard.

56. Philip Elliot, "Production and the Political Content of Broadcasting," in *Politics and the Media: Film and Television for the Political Scientist and Historian,* ed. M. J. Clark (Oxford: Pergamon Press, 1979), pp. 20–21.

57. Key questions, of course, include which of these various factors—news-gathering mechanisms, editing and selection organization and norms,

or audience and political environment—is most important and what is the relative weight of each in contributing to the image of the state presented. The organization and norms of editing and selection have changed substantially at NHK since the research presented here was conducted, and another news program, *News Center 9 P.M.*, operates more like American network news. I hope to answer these questions in the future by a comparison of the more recent news process and *News Center 9 P.M.* to pre-1984 7 P.M. news.

58. Frank Gibney, *Japan: The Fragile Super Power* (Rutland, Vt.: Charles E. Tuttle, 1975), chap. 11.

59. Ranney, *Channels of Power*, p. 153.

60. Murray Edelman, *The Symbolic Uses of Politics* (Urbana: University of Illinois Press, 1964), pp. 41–43.

61. See, for example, Robinson, "Public Affairs Television and the Growth of Political Malaise," especially pp. 427–432; Ranney, *Channels of Power*, chap. 3.

62. This seemed to be the general interpretation emerging from the discussion in a panel of media experts at a roundtable, "Do the Media Support or Subvert the Political Status Quo?" at the annual meeting of the American Political Science Association, Washington, D.C., 28–31 August 1986. See also Ranney, *Channels of Power*, pp. 34–43, for a summary of rightist and leftist critiques of American television news and his conclusion that there may be truth to both critiques but the source of deviation from "objectivity" is more usually "structural" rather than political bias.

63. See, for example, Robinson, "Public Affairs Television and the Growth of Political Malaise," especially pp. 427–432; Ranney, *Channels of Power*, pp. 58–87.

64. Kobayashi, "Terebi no nyūsu no hōdō ni kansuru naiyō bunseki," pp. 35–36, found that when amount of coverage (particularly in terms of time) given to specific political parties was matched with a Tokyo survey of viewing habits and party preferences, there was a perfect match between station coverage and station viewers' party preference. In other words, for example, there were more LDP supporters among viewers who got their political news from the stations that covered the LDP more than the opposition parties. As he points out, it is impossible to know whether this was the result of the coverage or of selection of the channel by a particular party's supporters.

65. For a concise discussion of the methodological problems in media research and the difficulties of assuming impact from product, see Doris A. Graber, "Media Images and Status Quo Enforcement—Summing Up the Evidence," paper prepared for the roundtable, "Do the Media Support or Subvert the Political Status Quo?" at the annual meeting of the American Political Science Association, Washington, D.C., 28–31 August 1986.

66. See the chapters by Akuto and by Takeshita and Takeuchi in this volume on the amount of bias in newspaper coverage of elections and candidates.

67. See for example, Paletz and Entman, *Media–Power–Politics*, chap. 10.

PART III

The Role of the Media in Politics and Policy

4

Japan's Press and the Politics of Scandal

MAGGIE FARLEY

OF the many functions filled by the press in a modern democracy like Japan, none is more essential than that of "watchdog," ferreting out and exposing the wrongdoing and incompetence of those in authority. Governments everywhere seek to transmit only what makes them appear wise, efficient, and good, and to hide whatever will arouse anger, shame, or ridicule and thus decrease support for the regime and its incumbents. Indeed, government officials often seem to lose the distinction between what is merely embarrassing to an individual or party and what may endanger national interest or security—that is, between the controversial and the politically dangerous. The press draws those distinctions and can bring down governments.

Although other institutions—opposition parties, parliamentary question-and-answer sessions, or legislative committees—may function in the watchdog role, their work has little meaning unless it is also reported and disseminated in the media. Further, there may be conflicts of interest in or pressure brought to bear on those other bodies capable of investigation because they are all related to the state in one way or another; in democratic polities, only the media are autonomous from the state. And the media have the motivation to play such a watchdog role because of both journalistic norms and commercial self-interest. A scoop, bluntly put, sells papers; a scandal lures viewers.

This chapter assesses how well or poorly the Japanese press performs this important democratic function. Japan provides an especially important context for exploring the watchdog role of the press. First, because the Liberal Democratic Party (LDP) held power for almost four decades, Japan's opposition parties had less leverage in checking governmental power than do opposition parties elsewhere, which have the prospect of "turning the rascals out." It was left to the press to be the major institution capable of limiting elite power through exposure and the reaction of public opinion.

Second, the especially close relationship of Japanese business and other major interest groups with the LDP and an electoral system that has required astounding amounts of money to maintain representatives in power have led to frequent scandals and charges of corruption involving politicians, especially those of the LDP. Among these affairs are several that eventually helped to set the stage for the LDP's split and loss of power in 1993. What role has the press played in raising and pursuing these allegations?

Third, Japan's history and culture would seem to pose an obstacle to the press in its role as watchdog. Government restrictions on the press were in place almost from the beginning of Japan's modern era following the Meiji Restoration of 1868, long predating the even more draconian restrictions employed by the military in the late 1930s and early 1940s. Japanese culture traditionally also has deemphasized conflict and controversy. Whether the press has been more influenced by this historical background or by the Allied Occupation's attempt to bring democratic pluralism, responsible criticism, and independent and unbiased reporting to the Japanese media's relationship to government is an important question.

Finally, Japan's media organizations have some unique features. For example, the "reporters' clubs" through which most news is gathered do not exist in the same way and to the same extent in other democratic nations. How do these influence the ability of the press to perform its watchdog role?

The answer to the question of whether the Japanese press—in the context of a dominant-party regime with close and sometimes scandalous relations with major interest groups, of a historical tradition of press restriction, and of unique journalistic institutions—is able to perform the watchdog function well is by no means clear even today. The press commits itself formally to norms of independence, impartiality, and truthfulness, and even "to ensure the democratization of Japan."[1] Major press leaders perceive themselves to have a special responsibility in this dominant-party system to check the government. Yukio Matsuyama, the former editorial chairman of *Asahi*, has stated that "with the Liberal Democratic Party as the *de facto* ruling party, there is collusion between the legislative, judicial, and executive branches. If there is no confrontation between the three big powers, then it falls upon the fourth estate to provide opposition to government."[2] Indeed, some American observers have criticized the

Japanese press for taking this role too far, even to the point of biased opposition to government, as in the crisis surrounding the 1960 United States–Japan Mutual Security Treaty.[3] Certainly, in its frequent "campaigns"—drives for social reform—the national press has lived up to the image of social and political critic, placing on the public agenda such issues as bullying *(ijime)* in the schools, the environment, organized crime violence, and administrative reform (see chapter 6).

Yet other foreign observers, such as two journalists formerly stationed in Tokyo, Richard Halloran and Karel van Wolferen, argue that the Japanese press is a mere tool of the government. Halloran writes that the press there "has not developed a tradition of independence but has been subject to domination by the authorities or to their indirect influence."[4] Van Wolferen insists that the newspapers' criticism of government is superficial and empty adversarialism.[5]

Responsible watchdog of a dominant party government? Biased and extreme opponent of legitimate authority? Or coopted and conformist tool of the state? This chapter looks at the evidence on how the Japanese press has and has not played its watchdog role with regard to government by analyzing how the structure of Japanese journalism has affected press coverage of public figures, especially the pursuit of corruption and wrongdoing in some of the major scandals of the postwar period.

Government-Press Relations: The Reporters' Clubs

To understand how the press has covered major scandals, it is crucial to distinguish between the establishment press and the "outsider" press. The most important component of the establishment press is the major national newspapers whose news coverage of governmental and societal organizations is institutionalized through reporters' *(kisha)* clubs, which are attached to nearly every government office, ministry, and major corporation.

The clubs are open only to accredited members, and some are furnished with beds, telephones, and computers. Reporters from major newspapers and television stations are assigned to a certain club, where they are guaranteed up-to-the-minute briefings and close access to officials. Until recently, the foreign press was banned from all clubs (their access remains somewhat limited), and Japanese magazine reporters and freelance journalists are still largely excluded.

A reporter from *Asahi Shimbun* insists that nonmembers do not

miss much groundbreaking information but that they do miss close access to important sources. "No scoop ever came from a press club. It's all just official business and press releases," says Masaru Honda of the paper's political section. The real information, he says, comes from the relationships cultivated at the club and the resulting off-the-record disclosures from politicians over lunch or dinner.[6]

The closest equivalent to the *kisha* club in the United States, according to Japanese journalists who have worked in America, is probably the White House press corps. A bureau chief of *Asahi Shimbun's* Washington office, Akio Nomura, has said that inside the corps, reporters' work and their relationships with sources and government officials are essentially the same as those within the Japanese *kisha* clubs. The main difference is that only the White House and the State Department have institutionalized press followings, while in Japan *kisha* clubs are attached to every agency and major corporation. Further, the U.S. press corps is open to any accredited journalist, including foreign correspondents, and the questioners at press conferences are randomly selected by the speaker, not organized and rehearsed before the conference by a club "overseer," as they often are in the *kisha* club system. Most significantly, U.S. reporters are given time and encouragement to conduct independent, investigative reporting beyond the official story.[7]

There are both advantages and disadvantages to Japan's *kisha* club system. At the clubs, reporters are constantly fed official government announcements, press conferences, and regular background briefings. That relieves them from having to chase down information about the government's daily activities, and it guarantees each paper equal treatment. But the regulated dissemination of information, though efficient and convenient, amounts to a monopoly of the news. By so coopting the journalists and their time, the system effectively prevents or discourages independent investigation to counterbalance official announcements that invariably cast the government in a favorable light.

Well-timed press conferences can also stifle stories. If a company fears a reporter has wind of a story it does not want published, it will call a press conference and announce the story to all the reporters—off the record. If a reporter then prints the story, even if the information was obtained independently beforehand, the reporter appears to be in violation of the rules and will be censured accordingly.[8]

The *kisha* club system also contributes to the homogenization of news, since the reporters get their information from the same source and often decide together how to report the story. There is a saying in the *kisha* clubs that "no scoop is everybody's happiness." If one reporter's story includes information that was embargoed by the source or that other reporters agreed to leave out, that reporter may lose membership in the club or be ostracized.[9] Sonoko Watanabe, a young reporter for *Nihon Keizai Shimbun,* says: "The club is bad because everybody writes the same thing strictly from the information released. . . . If I have a scoop I can't write it, because the club won't let me. Individuality can get you punished."[10] With the papers working together to make sure no one is left out or behind, front pages of the major papers consistently feature the same stories and sometimes even the same headlines.

Kisha club reporters supplement their daily diet of official news with off-the-record comments from the politicians and officials they cover. After working the same beat for months on end, the supposed adversaries often establish relationships, trading toasts and information after hours. Many reporters stake out officials' houses late at night, hoping to be invited in for a nightcap and some candid discussion. A select few have "refrigerator privileges," meaning they are trusted to wander into the kitchen and help themselves to a beer.[11] If the official is not at home, the reporters leave their namecards on the door and hope for a courtesy call the next day. Some may return the next morning for *asagake* (literally, "morning attack"), and the most favored few sometimes join the official they are covering for a ride to work and a private chat in his chauffeured car.[12]

Although these off-hour visits may seem a surprising invasion of privacy by American standards, journalists and those they cover consider it all in a day's work. "You have to work on building a relationship," says Honda of the *Asahi Shimbun.* Former vice minister of finance Makoto Utsumi shakes his head at the memory of avid reporters hovering on his doorstep at all hours when he was assistant to the chief cabinet secretary in the early 1980s, but he explains that he put up with it: "It was part of my job to ensure friendly treatment by the media for my boss."[13] And by the unspoken rules of the game, journalists are careful to protect their close access by concealing the source of controversial information or not reporting it at all. "In Japan," says one newspaper reporter, "you'll get no information from a news source who doesn't trust you. This trust refers to refusing to write stories which could be troublesome to the source."[14]

Every journalist must find a balance between the need to maintain credible sources and the desire to reveal potentially newsworthy information. The *kisha* club, however, as Ellis Krauss argues in chapter 3, encourages dependence on sources and skews this balance in their favor. Unity is prized, entrepreneurial reporting is not. The close relationships cultivated in and out of the club, therefore, may make the reporters more informed but leave the public less so. The press clubs ultimately become arenas of information "of, for, and by the insiders."[15] The more the reporters become coopted by the system, the less they want to threaten their privilege and access with hard-hitting stories.

Other Structural Constraints: Norms and Self-interest

Even outside the reporters' clubs, journalists' norms and commercial and other pressures place additional constraints on aggressive coverage and investigative journalism. Japanese newspapers consider themselves the upholders of public morality and eschew certain topics out of "dignity"—a position that limits the kind of news they will print. *Asahi's* former editorial chairman, Yukio Matsuyama, says, "There's scarcely any news we avoid," and he explains the reasoning behind the absence of certain subjects in the paper. In the early 1990s organized crime *(yakuza)* received coverage when ties between leading LDP politicians, such as former prime minister Noboru Takeshita, and underworld figures came to light in a major scandal. But before that time, according to Matsuyama, newspapers considered *yakuza* to be unworthy of notice. As for issues of discrimination, especially against *burakumin,* Japan's cultural underclass, "nobody likes to read those stories."[16]

Notions of "decency" dictate the treatment of the emperor and his family, limiting reporting on public figures to "above the waist,"[17] a norm the British royal family would undoubtedly like to see followed in their national press. In 1988 it was agreed not to disclose to the public that Emperor Hirohito was dying of cancer, despite detailed reporting of his food intake, transfusion record, and bowel functions. That he had cancer was revealed only after his death in early 1989. In February 1992 the press called a voluntary three-month halt to coverage of the crown prince's search for a bride, "out of respect for the privacy of the women and families under consideration."[18] The head of the social affairs division at Nippon Television explained, "We are not prohibited from collecting information. We just cannot broadcast it until a decision on the princess is made. We are doing this to create a good environment for choice."[19] Also in February the main newspapers and networks agreed to hold stories about the impending Sagawa Kyūbin bribery scandal, which linked organized crime to politicians and businesses, until the prosecutor's office began issuing arrest warrants.[20] The serious papers leave most stories concerning sex, gossip, and organized crime to the popular magazines and sports papers until they gain some sort of wider relevance.

The Japanese press is further limited by commercial considerations. As journalism has turned into big business, reporters are supposed to "make newspapers that sell" as opposed to "sell newspapers they make."[21] Advertising constitutes one major source of financial support for newspapers, and it also imposes constraints. Reporters understand that they are to go soft on big advertisers, and when they forget, pressure from advertising agencies on behalf of their clients will quickly remind them.[22] Dentsū, the world's largest advertising agency, has a chokehold on the market and the media; at some prime-time hours, all national television advertising is arranged by Dentsū exclusively. Though specific instances of Dentsū manipulating news coverage of its clients are often rumored, they are difficult to prove. But the possibility worries even the government. A Fair Trade Commission report on commercial influence warned that "[Dentsū's] influence over the media and . . . trend towards oligopoly could accelerate."[23]

The media also are affected by the close reciprocal relationship between the business sector and Japan's ruling party. The country's most popular news show is anchored by Hiroshi Kume, a reporter known for his candid—and often critical—on-air remarks about the government. Several years ago, Toyota Motor Corporation dropped its sponsorship of Kume's program when LDP officials expressed concern that one of Japan's leading manufacturers supported such a show.[24] In 1989 the minister of post and telecommunications pressured Fuji Television not to run a documentary that showed a former vice minister of international trade and industry confessing that Japan had indeed promised the United States 20 percent of the semiconductor market in a confidential sideletter, instead of merely promising "efforts to achieve" that amount, as they later claimed. To a lesser extent, newspapers as business enterprises are affected by similar political and commercial pressures.

The effort to attract the widest possible audience keeps the news moderate and essentially nonpartisan. Commercial concerns seem to underlie the common newspaper practice of not endorsing political candidates, unlike newspapers in other countries. According to Matsuyama of *Asahi*, the paper fears that if it comes out in favor of one candidate it would lose readers who support the other candidates, a loss that could amount to hundreds of thousands of subscriptions.[25]

These organizational constraints and their effects on reporting do not go unnoticed by the public. The annual Media Credibility Survey of Nihon Shimbun Kyōkai (Japan Newspaper Publishers and Editors Association) showed that in 1989, after it became clear that members of the media had knowledge of Recruit's dealings and Prime Minister Sōsuke Uno's relation with a geisha long before those scandals surfaced (see below), evaluation of press credibility temporarily dipped to 54 percent from 89 percent two years before.[26] Ratings were also hurt in 1989 by the *Asahi* "coral incident," in which a news photographer, illustrating a story about a vandalized coral reef, recarved the vandal's fading initials so they would show up better in the photograph. The 1989 *Asahi Shimbun* readers' poll revealed many complaints about biased stories, sensationalism, and lack of accuracy in reporting. Readers stated that other news sources, such as television and magazines, highlighted newspapers' biases or inaccuracies, and 64 percent thought that newspaper coverage was swayed by outside forces.[27] The media audience believed that they were not getting all the information they should and were frustrated that the journalists were not protecting "the people's right to know."[28]

The Outsiders

As a result of the complex and highly controlled structure of the media in mainstream Japan, a peripheral wellspring of journalism exists. It is effectively an outside press corps that, while not completely free of the constraints that limit the insider journalists, is less affected by them. Thus it is responsible for most of the investigative reporting in Japan—and much of the scandal coverage. These outsiders—namely, the magazine reporters, freelance writers, and foreign journalists excluded from the press clubs, and the small newspapers and rural bureaus detached from them—have greater distance, perspective, and freedom from personal relationships with sources. In many cases, they are the only ones able to scrutinize aggressively and critically the government and big business. It thus falls to this outer ring to break most scandals.

Given the symbiotic relationship between *kisha* club members and their sources, it often takes an outsider to bring about the disclosure of accumulated inside information. Journalists excluded from the *kisha* clubs can and must create their own information pipeline and are less reliant on the ruling LDP. They are therefore quicker to question politicians' actions or inaction. Weeklies and monthlies have the luxury of time to step back and analyze trends, and foreign journalists are known for their constant questioning of (what seem to them) curious patterns of behavior and for attempts to reconcile the gap between *honne* and *tatemae* (the real story versus the official version) that domestic reporters often let pass. The outside press also attracts tipoffs from other outsiders with an axe to grind—opposition party members, disgruntled civil servants, businesspeople passed up for promotion, even other frustrated journalists.

The *Economist's* former Tokyo bureau chief, Nick Valery, relates how a reporter from a major Japanese paper handed him a story about 100,000 NTT (National Telephone and Telegraph) shares that were "lost" at the Ministry of Finance when NTT went public. The reporter discovered the results of the ministry's internal investigation, which concluded that 20,000 shares had gone to the president of Recruit, thus linking the previously untainted finance ministry to the Recruit scandal, and another block of shares had gone home with a certain minister when he retired. But the same reporter was told that the story could not be published and, disenchanted, he pointed the *Economist* in the right direction.[29]

On the less noble side, magazines are also willing to publish what the newspapers will not: personal items, speculation, and rumor. Weeklies are known to buy information from insiders and to reward underpaid writers from major newspapers handsomely for freelancing under an alias. Nor are they shy about basing an entire story on a single, unnamed source. Although some magazines are more credible than others, and though their motivations tend to be more commercial than moral, these outsiders hit the target often enough to retain the public's attention. They serve the important function of unearthing information that would otherwise remain buried and placing it in the public domain. Critic Joyce Milton lauds the nonmainstream press for offering an alternative to the official view: "Indeed it might be argued that the history of the free press is the history of sensationalism."[30]

Some of the closest readers of the weeklies are members of the public prosecutor's office, who use the magazines as tip sheets; once they begin an investigation, the issue is legitimized for the mainstream press.[31] One of the most famous criminal cases ever uncovered by the outside media was the Miura Incident. The wife of a Japanese businessman was killed, allegedly by a mugger, while they were on vacation in California. Mr. Miura was transformed from a figure of national sympathy to one of morbid fascination when the weekly magazine *Shūkan Bunshun* revealed through an independent investigation that Miura had arranged his wife's murder for the insurance money.

Some "outside press" is attached to the inside press: namely, newspapers' branch bureaus and affiliated weekly and monthly magazines. Newspapers commonly route items they believe are important but below newspapers' standards of decency to their magazines and use their weeklies to test public reaction to a story. These publications gain in prestige and credibility because of their association with the newspaper group, making them "inside outsiders."

When former prime minister Uno's disaffected geisha mistress came to *Mainichi Shimbun* to tell her story, the editors directed her to their affiliated magazine, *Sunday Mainichi*. Only after the *Washington Post* picked up the account and an opposition party member brandished a copy of the *Post* in the Diet, accusing Uno of showing disrespect to women and making Japan look foolish in the eyes of the world, did the major papers publish the story. Even then, people were less surprised by the fact that the prime minister had a mistress—most politicians do—than by how cheap Uno was (her $2,000 a month "pin money" was less than one-third the standard rate) and by his inability to keep her quiet.[32] The scandal ultimately forced Uno's resignation and raised awareness of women's issues.

The relationship between tabloids and the "quality" newspapers in the United States in some ways mirrors the situation in Japan, as illustrated by the Gennifer Flowers scandal during the U.S. presidential campaign in 1992. When Flowers, candidate Bill Clinton's alleged former mistress, told the supermarket tabloid the *Star* that she had had a twelve-year affair with the Arkansas governor, the *New York Times* and other highbrow papers initially ignored the story, even after the governor and his wife had made a much watched appearance on national television to confront the issue. Only after deciding that the accusations were threatening Clinton's candidacy and had gained relevance as "a character issue" did the standard-bearing *New York Times* give the story much coverage.

But there are also significant differences between the American and Japanese approaches. While the American press draws the line between what a politician does as a public official and as a private citizen and excludes the private unless it bears on public performance, the Japanese mainstream press tends to concentrate on the façade a politician offers for public consumption, rather than the reality behind it. For example, during testimony about the Sagawa Kyūbin scandal, Ichirō Ozawa (then LDP secretary general) described a meeting between LDP power broker Shin Kanemaru, former prime minister Noboru Takeshita, and the president of Sagawa Kyūbin, where they discussed payoffs. Ozawa claimed he was not involved in the discussions and did not hear what was said because he was busy pouring drinks and emptying ashtrays. Ozawa resigned along with Kanemaru and Takeshita, but the secretary-general-cum-busboy was handled gently enough in the media to be able to rise again as a leader of a new "reform" party of former LDP members and to claim Kanemaru's position as the power behind the new coalition government's prime minister in 1993.

This dichotomy can best be understood by using the previously mentioned Japanese cultural construct of *honne* and *tatemae,* or "real intentions" versus "stated principles." Japanese cultural norms dictate that one should acknowledge only the surface, even if what is going on underneath is well understood. Such norms obviously represent a problem for the mainstream press, for they mean that taking notice of shady dealings is somehow unseemly. A senior writer for *Nihon Keizai Shimbun,* Kazutami Yamazaki, blames this practice for muting the responsibility of the press: "At first glance, the Japanese media seem to be a watchdog, but their anti-government stance is superficial, another reflection of our *honne-tatemae* culture."[33] This self-restraint puts the responsibility for breaking scandal on the shoulders of the outside press.

How Scandals Break

Political scientist Theodore Lowi has said that "scandal is corruption revealed,"[34] implying that the absence of scandal does not necessarily mean an absence of corruption. Corruption can be defined as "behavior that deviates from the formal duties of a public role for private, monetary or status gain; or violates rules against the exercise of influence for private purposes."[35] For corruption to become scandal requires public awareness: scandal depends on the public reaction to deviation from norms or violation of rules. If nobody cares, there is no scandal, and thus it is the media that turn the existence of corruption into scandal.

In most countries, society is divided by a dual normative structure: the symbolic or normative dimension, where the idealized vision a society has of itself is embodied in its rules and laws, and the operative dimension, where the ideals lose out to the improvised rules of personal gain and political expediency.[36] In Japan this duality is clearly seen in electoral politics. Japan has the most restrictive

campaign regulations of any democracy to ensure fairness and prevent corruption and undue influence on the voter (see chapter 10).
The press' and the public's expectations of propriety in this area also
are high.

Yet at the operative level, there is a general acceptance that politics
is very expensive, due to an electoral system where intraparty competition for seats forces each candidate to maintain a costly political
machine. Constituents expect not only large-scale pork-barrel provisions for their districts in exchange for their votes, but also attendance and monetary gifts at celebrations. "You don't understand
how expensive it is," lamented top LDP politician Michio Watanabe
to a group of foreign correspondents. "Everyday before I go to work
I put a white tie in my right pocket [for weddings], a black tie in my
left pocket [for funerals], and a stack of ten-thousand-yen notes in
my inside pocket [for gifts]."[37]

A 1989 study by an LDP research committee showed that the
average cost of maintaining a district for a junior Diet member was
¥110 million (around $850,000) a year.[38] The *Economist* figures that
"the most junior politicians need to raise $1 million in a non-election
year; by one estimate, faction leaders need ten times that. Multiply
everything by three if there is an election to fight."[39] And that is only
what is disclosed. Politicians have devised alternate routes for "donations" and what they do to earn them is not publicly discussed. The
electorate shares in the benefits, through gifts and favors doled out
by politicians, and this makes people complicit in and perhaps more
tolerant of larger abuses: they know where the money comes from.
Thus, corruption is defined in part by how much the public knows
about the extralegal dealings and its level of acceptance of them. The
media have much to do with both.

If it were not for the outside journalists, Japan would have considerably fewer scandals—and, some might argue, more corruption.
Several of the most significant scandals of the past few decades have
been unearthed, not by those in the best position to expose them—
the reporters in the press clubs—but by the outside press. Once the
scandal is broken, an avalanche of information descends as the
retaining walls crumble and the big-time insider journalists are freed
to release their hoard of information and begin a real investigation.
"Every scandal is pursued by the [major] media," said *Asahi's*
Nomura when he was Washington bureau chief, "but not many are
initiated by them."[40]

Journalist John Roberts aptly captures the cathartic effect: "When
a big scandal breaks the public is suddenly immersed in a torrent of

revelations that gush forth from the newspapers, magazines, and broadcasting stations day after day, week after week, until the scandal itself seems to be the whole political process, unique and unrelated to anything else in the past. For that reason, scandal after scandal erupts and subsides, yet no political lessons are learned and no real reform is achieved."[41] Lowi identifies the two stages of scandal—the break and the flood—as the substantive and procedural stages. The first stage begins with the exposure of the breach of a legal or societal norm—the substantive scandal. But while it is still in the realm of accusation and not yet fully proven, the scandal usually enters a second stage in which further illicit actions occur. Usually aimed at cover-up, these include lies, destruction of evidence, suppression of information, and coercion of witnesses—and sometimes go well beyond the effort to keep the corruption concealed. This is known as procedural scandal, and the series of revelations and developments it engenders keeps the scandal alive much longer than if the initial accusations had simply been acknowledged in the first place.[42]

Indeed, the procedural scandal can subsume the substantive scandal. In the Watergate affair in the United States, the initial breach was a burglary and the calculated violation of campaign laws—trivial offenses in comparison with the ensuing procedural scandal that caused Richard Nixon to resign and disgraced his administration.[43] The same pattern can be seen in Japan's Lockheed and Recruit scandals, which began with revelations of bribery and ended by bringing down an entire tier of political leaders.

In Japan it is usually the outsider press that breaks the substantive scandal; after that, however, the insider press takes over and covers the procedural part in painstaking detail as it monitors daily—even hourly—developments. Often the press focuses so intently on the main part of the scandal and the ensuing revelations that it misses the big picture—the underlying causes. This, of course, is hardly a uniquely Japanese problem. In the case of Watergate, for example, the U.S. press focused mainly on whether Nixon was personally corrupt; it largely ignored the bigger issue of the potential for official misuse of the huge U.S. intelligence system and campaign financing, and gave little attention to the problem of how to guarantee that similar abuses would not happen again.[44] In the same way, the Japanese coverage of the 1976 Lockheed scandal substituted the simple slogan "money politics" for an investigation into the actual nature of Japanese political power.[45]

Although never planned, an occasional scandal serves several purposes: it serves as a check on excessive power; it purges bad elements

(at least temporarily); it shakes up a power structure otherwise
locked in an ossified balance, allowing opportunity for change; and it
reminds the players of the rules of the game. Moreover, scandals are
essential for the media to make their self-proclaimed role of watchdog more than merely nominal. During a scandal, the unspoken rules
that normally govern the reciprocal power relationships between
journalists and their official sources apply less strictly, allowing
reporters to betray confidences, release information, and provide
background and details that usually never reach print.

Cases of Scandal

The clearest evidence of the importance of outsiders in shattering the
normal reticence of the inside press emerges from a brief review of
several scandals of the postwar period. The description focuses not
on the substantive issues at stake in the scandals, but on the roles
played by the establishment and outsider press and how the scandals
were revealed and covered.

Kakuei Tanaka and the Lockheed Scandal: Money Politics Revealed

Former prime minister Kakuei Tanaka has come to symbolize the
collusion between government and business known in Japan as
"money politics." Business wants politicians to pass legislation and
push for policies favorable to industry's interests. Politicians, in turn,
need the financial contributions of business to maintain their political machines and fund their costly reelection campaigns. This reciprocal relationship was built in a high-growth economy, where
stability and economic development were agreed to be top priorities.

Scandals resulting from this sort of symbiotic relationship are
nothing new. France, Germany, and the United States have all experienced similar scandals in recent years.[46] In Japan almost every postwar prime minister has been tainted by suspicion of corruption,[47] but
Tanaka has come to symbolize the phenomenon at its extreme.

Tanaka, the LDP kingpin who served as prime minister from 1972
until he was forced to step down in 1974, was legendary for his ability to work the system, knowing that "money is the mother's milk of
politics and that whoever controlled the largest amounts of it in the
political system controlled the system."[48] Tanaka, who did not come
from a monied family, once having gained an LDP seat, was said to
have used his political position to build up a strategic treasure chest.

Much of the funds came from real estate dealings guided by inside information garnered in the Diet, such as the purchase of land in the path of the then newly developed transnational bullet train. He also reaped profits through construction firms he owned in Niigata (his home prefecture), which engaged in pork-barrel public works projects he brought there. Success bred success: as his money made him more powerful, Tanaka pulled in larger political donations because he could get things done. While serving as minister of posts, Tanaka also took a particular interest in controlling the media, once bragging that he had the press in his pocket.

In 1974 a team of investigative journalists ran two long exposés of Tanaka's questionable maneuverings in the monthly magazine *Bungei Shunjū.* The leader of the investigation, Takashi Tachibana, was actually a freelance writer at the time, though he had previously worked for the magazine. He thus had even greater distance from the power center, and less to lose, than most outsider journalists.[49] Parallels can be drawn to the investigative reporting by Bob Woodward and Carl Bernstein—two *Washington Post* metropolitan reporters at the time, not part of Washington's press elite—who exposed the Watergate affair.[50] Tachibana's articles were carefully researched and detailed Tanaka's questionable financial dealings, including how he had constructed several "paper" companies to obscure his personal income and "gray" transactions.[51]

The general press ignored the articles at first; it was old news to them, and Tanaka had not explicitly broken any laws. But at a press conference with Tanaka at the Foreign Correspondent's Club in Tokyo, *Los Angeles Times* reporter Sam Jameson led the foreign journalists in intense questioning about the articles' revelations, thus launching the story internationally. Only then did Japan's insider journalists, led by *Asahi Shimbun,* jump onto the story, bringing it back into the country and onto the front pages of the major newspapers. A predictable storm of criticism and press attention followed, ultimately forcing Tanaka out of office. Tanaka resigned the prime ministership just four months after Nixon stepped down from the U.S. presidency.[52]

That, however, was just a squall compared to the hurricane of Lockheed in 1976. After his resignation (from the premiership, but not from his Diet seat), Tanaka began working on a comeback, retaining his trademark favor granting and deal making as well as the leadership of the most powerful and largest faction in the Diet. Then, through the investigations of U.S. senator Frank Church's subcommittee, it emerged that Tanaka had accepted almost $2 million in bribes from the American aircraft company Lockheed to help smooth the way for sales of its Tristar airplanes in Japan. Tanaka was indicted on charges of bribery and of violation of the foreign exchange and foreign trade control laws, and was ultimately found guilty.[53]

Again, the source of the revelation was on the outside—this time, the U.S. Securities and Exchange Commission. And again, the story boomeranged into Japan, where the press launched a vehement anti-Tanaka, anti–money politics campaign. The attacks reached a fever pitch in 1983 after Tanaka was found guilty of bribery but glibly appealed the decision and refused to resign. Van Wolferen describes his portrayal in the media as that of "a villain whose conduct was unbecoming in a Japanese and who therefore deserved to be ejected from society."[54] But by making Tanaka into a villain, the "watchdogs of democracy" avoided examining the flaws of the system that the former prime minister had exploited to become so powerful, and failed to apply concerted pressure to stimulate reform. Without fundamental changes, the same type of scandal was bound to happen again.

The Recruit Scandal: Stocks for Favors

In the spring of 1988 a big story fell through for the cub reporters of *Asahi Shimbun's* Yokohama bureau: the police had decided not to arrest the deputy mayor for taking a bribe from Recruit Cosmos Company—the property subsidiary of information services firm Recruit Company Limited—because the three-year statute of limitations for bribery had passed.[55] Usually, the reporters would have moved on, but Hiroshi Yamamoto, the bureau chief, had a hunch and decided to pursue it. Three months later, after several secret late-night meetings with sources and many hours of investigative drudgery to confirm tips and leaks, the team ran the first story of thousands to come about Recruit's attempt to trade stocks for political favors. The article did not even make the front page.[56]

It did, however, attract tips that even bigger fish had received Recruit shares. Several weeks later the front page of *Asahi Shimbun* declared that aides to Prime Minister Takeshita, LDP Secretary General Shintarō Abe, and Finance Minister Kiichi Miyazawa, among others, had received stock. *Asahi Journal,* the newspaper's affiliate weekly magazine, picked up the story and wrote an article titled "Recruit's Dirty Dealings Taint Political, Mass Media World" (Sei-masu komi kai wo osen suru rikurūto shōhō), which sparked the resignations of Hiromasa Ezoe, chairman of Recruit Company, and of Kō Morita, president of *Nihon Keizai Shimbun,* who also had taken stock.[57] *Yomiuri Shimbun* vice president Iwao Murayama also stepped down after later revelations that he had acquired shares as well.

Only after the newspapers conducted an internal poll to confirm that none of their employees were implicated did the papers fully pick up on the story.[58] But from that point on, Recruit subsumed all other news. By the time the dust settled, thirty-one politicians, aides, and business leaders had resigned, thirteen had been indicted, and Prime Minister Takeshita's secretary had committed suicide.

In light of the amount of attention the Recruit scandal received and the impact it had on the political system, it is hard to believe that the scandal almost did not break at all. Yokohama bureau chief Yamamoto's description of the difficulties he and his reporters faced while gathering information for the study underlines the unspoken division between the inside and outside reporters. Even though they were working for *Asahi Shimbun,* the young journalists were consistently denied interviews with politicians. They were reluctant to ask their press club colleagues for help, not for fear the Tokyo reporters would steal the story, but because they were afraid they would warn their government sources about what was coming.[59] But once the story had broken, it was taken out of the Yokohama bureau's hands and given to the Tokyo bureau and the press club reporters. The final irony: the Nihon Shimbun Kyōkai award for investigative reporting went to *Mainichi Shimbun*—not to the *Asahi* team in Yokohama.

The Compensation-for-Loss Scandals: Bureaucracy and Leaks

Just as the Recruit scandal was fading into the past and tainted politicians were resuming positions of power, another saga of wrongdoing emerged. It was revealed that the "Big Four" securities firms—Nomura, Daiwa, Nikkō, and Yamaichi—had been manipulating stocks and compensating major clients for their losses. In defiance of a specific Finance Ministry order to stop the practice of guaranteeing returns to clients, the Big Four had not only indemnified certain major accounts against losses but also illegally raised certain stock prices to generate the necessary funds. Almost as surprising as the actual scandal, and highly revealing about the relationship of the press with Japan's bureaucracy, was the way the story surfaced. This time the revelation was not due to investigative reporting or to any action of the press at all. Instead, the information was leaked to *Yomiuri Shimbun* by middle-ranking Ministry of

Finance officials. Apparently, the ministry's National Tax Administration Agency was exasperated, not by the firms' financial maneuverings, but by their arrogance in demanding that they be allowed to write off the compensation payments against the tax they owed. One ministry official likened it to "a car thief claiming that his jimmy is one of the tools of his trade and its cost should be deductible."[60] Nomura's attempt to use its political connections to intimidate the agency into allowing its claim was the last straw. In June 1991 someone placed a call to *Yomiuri.*

The papers became the forum for a bitter and ever widening scandal. Yoshihisa Tabuchi, then chairman of Nomura, struck back, claiming at a press conference that the Ministry of Finance had known all along about the indemnification practices and condoned them. Outraged at the implication, the Finance Ministry released more details, which prompted an outpouring of damaging information and led to the exposure of several more unrelated financial scandals.

Why did the official call *Yomiuri?* "Because it was their turn" is the answer of one Finance Ministry source, revealing the orchestration behind the information network.[61] In 1989, when the ministry was having trouble controlling Daiwa-Yamaichi, the leak went to *Mainichi,* as the round-robin continued. The official's comment shows that there is at least one element of fairness in the press-government relationship. It also clearly demonstrates why the press, in order to keep the "leak line" open, would soft-pedal coverage or accede to "administrative guidance" not to report a story.

Although the Tax Agency itself triggered the scandal with its leak to the mainstream press, there is another story behind the story and another scandal behind the scandal, both of which reveal the outside media's role. Twenty days after the Tax Agency leaked to *Yomiuri,* the weekly magazine *Shūkan Themis* went to press with an article alleging wrongdoing in the Ministry of Finance: it claimed not only that the ministry condoned the security industry's practices but also that certain ministry officials made considerable profits from inside information about preflotation stocks provided by the securities houses.[62] The day before the magazine went on sale, *Themis'* distributors were asked to return their copies, and the magazine announced that it was suspending publication due to pressure from the Tax Agency. The agency denied that it had pressured *Themis* but said the article was "libelous" and "had no root in fact."[63] Tabuchi of Nomura later repeated the charge that ministry officials were well aware all along of the company practices that came under scrutiny thanks to the Finance Ministry's leak. *Shūkan Themis* is out of business and claims it was a victim of "media oppression."

Sagawa Kyūbin —The Fall of the "Don"

The slowly breaking saga of the Sagawa Kyūbin scandal is the perfect illustration of the interplay of forces involved in scandals. It had all the elements of a great story: a fast growing delivery company with *yakuza* ties allegedly was making gargantuan donations to politicians in exchange for favors. Yet, even though the scandal was rumored to dwarf the Recruit scandal that brought down the government in 1989, the mainstream media at first soft-pedaled coverage.

The scandal broke in July 1991 in the weekly magazine *Shūkan Shinchō,* with an article detailing the power struggle between the chairman of Sagawa Kyūbin, Kiyoshi Sagawa, and its Tokyo president, Hiroyasu Watanabe. When the president conspired with Sagawa's son to take over the company, Chairman Sagawa exposed Watanabe's involvement with organized crime figures and accused him of bribing ministry officials for trucking and land permits and of making illegal "donations" to more than 100 politicians. Watanabe retaliated by revealing details about Sagawa's ties with another mob group. The article led to an investigation by the Tokyo district public prosecutor's office, which resulted in the arrest of Watanabe and three other directors about seven months later, on February 15, 1992.

The arrests marked only the beginning of the scandal, as investigators went on to explore the links between Sagawa Kyūbin, organized crime, and the donations of up to ¥80 billion ($600 million) to selected politicians. Contributions to a single politician of more than ¥1.5 million a year are illegal, and those over ¥1 million must be registered in the donor's name. The arrests also mark the beginning of scandal coverage by the major media. Despite rumors and leaks, and the fact that a list of politicians who had received money had circulated among journalists for several months, there was a "gentleman's agreement" among the major media not to report anything until it could be confirmed by the prosecutor's office.[64]

The investigation of the most important matters—which politicians received money and whether it could be proved that the money had influenced their legislative decisions—was left to the prosecutor's office; the major media remained content merely to publicize the office's findings. Leaks from the investigators revealed that five senior politicians—including chief lieutenants of the Takeshita faction, the largest in the LDP—had allegedly received ¥5 billion each

($38 million), and that there was a possible connection between the money and the liberalization of a parcel-delivery law in 1990 that significantly benefited Sagawa Kyūbin.[65]

There were several indications that legal authorities themselves were in no hurry to press the case because of their fear of damaging Prime Minister Kiichi Miyazawa's fragile support base in the party, in which the Takeshita faction played the critical role. It also appears that the inquiries were timed to take place after the July 1989 upper house elections, "out of a bureaucratic sense of fairness."[66] The press likewise did little to further the investigation of the blossoming scandal.

Following the election Shin Kanemaru—a senior leader of the Takeshita faction, "don" of several "tribes" *(zoku)* of politicians that broker policy for major interest groups, and probably the most powerful politician in Japan until his fall in 1992—publicly admitted that he had accepted $4 million in illegal contributions from Sagawa Kyūbin. The public prosecutor, however, initially let him off with a negotiated "punishment" of a fine of less than $2,000. Only at that point did the mainstream press, which had widely covered Kanemaru's admissions, finally erupt in criticism of this bald discriminatory leniency toward a powerful politician, forcing Kanemaru's resignation from the Diet.[67]

When the "Watchdog" Doesn't Bark

The Sagawa Kyūbin case shows what it takes for a scandal to become a scandal: an apparent violation of accepted rules, exposure, legitimization of the issue, pressure to drive the investigation, and a high level of public interest. The last of these usually is mobilized only belatedly by the mainstream media. When there is little pressure, either from opposition parties or from a press that is being reactive instead of proactive, authorities can prolong, delay, and even attempt to circumvent justice.

This dimension of media behavior in the Sagawa Kyūbin scandal shows the potential for cases of corruption to escape becoming scandals. Whether the stuff of scandal is pursued has to do with the way news about corruption breaks and the nature of the players involved. Along with the outbreak of the financial scandals, news also briefly surfaced about illegal dealings of Japan's trust banks. In much the same way that the securities companies had been indemnifying big customers against losses, the trust banks were found to have been protecting their big clients against losses by shifting assets from smaller clients. In effect, they were taking money from smaller pension funds or investors to pay bigger pension funds or investors. In contrast to the compensation payments, which were made in flagrant defiance of a Finance Ministry directive but were illegal only if specifically promised to clients, the trust banks' actions were clearly against the law.

Finance-industry observers were waiting for the scandal to blow sky high and destroy the already severely weakened trust banks; the news, however, merely died. Henny Sender, formerly a journalist for *Institutional Investor* who now writes for the *Far Eastern Economic Review* and has close connections to financial officials, speculates that "the situation was so critical, so bad, that it would have brought down the trust banks if it had been exposed. [The Finance Ministry] asked the media to sit on it"—something she says happens quite frequently. Valery of the *Economist* adds that the Bank of Japan also called media heads and told them not to write about it. "If it were to have been exposed, it would have been a disaster—much bigger than the [U.S.] savings and loan crisis. People would have really lost their savings. The Bank of Japan said the media would be responsible if people lose their money."[68]

Sender cites another unreported scandal at a small *shinkin*, or cooperative bank, in northern Japan. If the bank's troubles had become known, the news could have sparked a minor financial panic or bank runs. "They had all sorts of emergency measures ready, but the papers never ran it. The Bank of Japan did not explicitly ask the papers to *not* print it, but let it be known that 'we would prefer this story not appear—it would create instability in the banking system.' And the papers didn't." A Bank of Japan official later confirmed both stories—off the record.[69]

There are also known practices parallel to those behind the Lockheed and Recruit episodes that have never become scandals. It was known in the 1970s, for example, that other airplane manufacturers—Boeing, McDonnell-Douglas, and Grumman—were doing the same sort of behind-the-scenes "fixing" as Lockheed.[70] Three years after Tanaka's arrest, it was revealed that McDonnell-Douglas had paid ¥500 million to the director general of the Self-Defense Agency—the same amount Tanaka had received from Lockheed.[71] In the same vein, Recruit Company certainly was not the first to make large political donations with the expectation of favorable government treatment in exchange. Recruit chairman Ezoe was merely plugging into the well-oiled machine of money politics.

Much of the behavior in all these cases was in the "gray" area, not clearly illegal. The question, then, is why the Lockheed, Recruit, and loss-compensation cases all became scandals, while numerous others did not.

Ingredients for Scandal

The answer has much to do with how outsiders, as opposed to insiders, are treated. In Japan the demarcation between inside and outside, *uchi* and *soto*, is rigidly observed.[72] Part of the reason why the Lockheed and Recruit scandals blew up is that they were revealed by media outsiders, as suggested above. The additional fact that foreigners uncovered the Lockheed bribery case made it nearly impossible to ignore in Japan.

But another element has to do with the outsider-insider distinction in yet another way. It arises out of the never-ending struggle for power among the elite in Japan and the personalities of the players involved. Almost all corruption is caused by the desire to obtain or hold onto power without going through the sanctioned channels (to the extent that such channels exist). Scandals arise in Japan mainly when outsiders try to buy their way in or insiders try to lock outsiders out. Lockheed was an outsider, and so was Recruit chairman Ezoe. And even though Prime Minister Tanaka was the consummate insider in many ways, his stubborn flouting of the rules—which dictated that he be discreet about how he got his money, bend to the will of other senior leaders, and quietly bow out after bringing disgrace on his party and country—made him an outsider in fundamental ways.[73] Covering his downfall was thus much easier for the insider press—once the outsider press had begun the process.

Ezoe was a fast-rising newcomer who had figured out the system, much like Tanaka. Indeed, so unerring was his judgment of whom to target for stock deals that leaders who were *not* favored were reportedly jealous and resentful. Further, new information magazines published by Recruit were beating out the mainstream media's rival publications and rapidly drawing advertisers away from newspapers and traditional magazines. It may not be entirely coincidental that the scapegoat for money politics was also a media rival. In any case, once again, the outsider media found a vulnerable target, though a powerful and well-connected one.

In the financial scandals the insider-outsider factor entered in a more subtle way. In the initial compensation-for-loss scandal, the Tax

Administration Agency was the underdog. Relatively weak compared to other bureaus connected to the Ministry of Finance, it seemingly felt impotent against the big securities firms' defiance and clout with politicians, so it turned to the press for additional power. The media then did the rest.

The targeting of Nomura Securities illuminates another element in all three scandals: hubris or its opposite (that excessive arrogance must be punished and excessive power checked). Sender says, "During the scandals, no one said, 'What Nomura did was so terrible—they manipulated Tokyo stock.' Instead, they said 'Good. Nomura is so arrogant—all those *kachō* [managers] saying it was their genius in picking stocks [that lay behind Nomura's big profits] and not the market or the way they manipulated it. They deserve to be punished.' "[74] Tanaka and Ezoe similarly were perceived as becoming too powerful.

The final, and perhaps most important, element in whether or not a potential scandal becomes an actual one is whether or not those in power want a scandal. The financial scandals demonstrated the power of the Ministry of Finance and Bank of Japan to reveal or conceal scandals. The Tokyo district public prosecutor's office held a similar power. The prosecutor's office defied political pressure to stifle the Recruit scandal by steadily "dripfeeding" news to the press. They would announce carefully staged raids and arrests to the media to keep the investigation on the front pages and on the evening news. It became a self-propelling cycle: the public prosecutor discreetly prodding the press, the press giving the revelations high exposure and mobilizing popular interest, public interest adding impetus to the investigation. In the Sagawa Kyūbin case, the Tokyo prosecutor's office, which prides itself on its autonomy, faced a stiffer challenge because of the stakes involved and had to negotiate a token punishment for Kanemaru. It was only the belatedly fierce pressure from the press and the public that wound up truly "punishing" the perpetrator.

Does Scandal Lead to Reform?

If the media are truly watchdogs, then it is reasonable to ask whether or not their coverage of corrupt behavior leads to genuine reform. Because scandals over money politics and related issues surface so frequently, the media's role in spurring reform is in doubt. There is a crucial step between condemning the transgressors and providing a basis for reforming the system. The possibility of voters translating their disapproval into action depends on their perception of the issue. There are three basic conditions for this to happen. The first is the clarity of the issue: whether voters see the accused party as guilty or not, and the system as broken and requiring repair. The second is whether voters consider the issue relevant to their interest and serious enough to require reform. The third is whether they relate the issue to a particular party, and their votes to a particular outcome (for example, "the LDP is corrupt and should be punished and without voter support will lose power").[75] Although the media cannot ensure reform, they are most effective in marshaling public opinion and helping readers link issues and action, such as connecting their concern about corruption, on the one hand, with voting against the LDP, on the other.[76]

But if scandal becomes a regular feature of life, voters may become inured to corruption rather than inspired to correct it, as they come to doubt that their vote will make a difference.[77] If the media themselves are fatalistic about prospects for reform, or even the need for it, then there is little basis for readers to be more optimistic. A former editor of *Sunday Mainichi*, Shuntarō Torigoe, who reported the story about Prime Minister Uno and his geisha, says, "There are those in the media who are set in their old way of thinking: that it doesn't matter if politicians have money or women problems, as long as they are strong leaders." Voters, then, may well mirror such feelings. If the politicians are all "corrupt," it matters only which of them is better at working the system to win pork-barrel projects for the home prefecture.

The July 1989 upper house elections were a good test case of voter attitudes. The ruling LDP was not only tainted by the Recruit scandal but also faced voter disenchantment as a result of an unpopular consumption tax, the much protested liberalization of beef and oranges, as well as of Uno's geisha incident—issues that dominated the media. Political analysts predicted that 1989 could be the year in which the LDP would lose its unbroken thirty-four-year reign.

The LDP did take a beating; it came out of the election with the lowest number of seats in the upper house it had ever had. But it had weathered an election in spite of four negative issues, and when the more important lower house election rolled around the following February, the LDP was able to hold its majority. Several years later, almost all the LDP politicians who had resigned because of Recruit were back in positions of equal or greater power (with Prime Minister Miyazawa as a paramount example). Indeed, several resigned yet again as a consequence of their involvement in the next round of scandals. Not until 1993, after the Sagawa scandal had fully erupted, did there seem to be a real correlation between the media's exposure of wrongdoing and popular action leading to political change. The difference this time, after four decades of boom-bust scandal cycles, was that the media had clarified the issue, personalized it, and suggested a solution. The combination of politicians' excesses and economic recession made people hunger for change.

Once the Sagawa scandal had broken, the press followed up with a steady stream of exposés about *yakuza* involvement in politics and the influence of right-wing nationalist groups—topics the media had previously backed away from.[78] Although many voters were aware of politicians' involvement in unsavory activities to gain and maintain power, many were shocked by the revelations of how deep and how far the connections reached.

Television also played a major role in hastening political change by targeting and personalizing the issue of political reform. TV Asahi's chairman, Sadayoshi Tsubaki, let it be known that the station had a mission: to bring down the LDP. The station created debate shows and explanatory newscasts that engaged viewers and inspired imitations at other news stations.

Kristin Altman has written in detail about how television eliminated the *kisha* club buffer between politicians and the public by questioning Diet members on the air "live" (see chapter 5). Politicians suddenly became vital characters in a political drama; broadcasts repeatedly juxtaposed images of white-haired LDP politicians committing gaffes and making unfulfilled promises, with images of the youthful leader of the opposition coalition, Morihiro Hosokawa, descendant of a samurai and the new leader of reform.

Symbols of corruption—Kanemaru's stash of gold bars and his cash-filled shopping cart—became rallying points for public protest, and demand for change among a normally cynical and disaffected electorate became palpable. The NTV news announcer, Yoshiko Sakurai, captured and fueled the popular sentiment when she began one evening's newscast with an announcement: "There is a new force in Japanese politics tonight. It is called people power and it will change the country."[79] In June 1993 the LDP government fell in a no-confidence vote after nearly four decades in power.

Despite what newly elected Prime Minister Hosokawa called "a new wind sweeping Japan" that year, the change in leadership turned out to be a short-lived internal power play masquerading as grassroots reform. Hosokawa ultimately resigned after revelations that he too had received questionable loans from Sagawa. "The voters did not throw the rascals out," said Tokyo-based reporter Quentin Hardy, "the rascals just changed their stripes."[80]

In the euphoric period after the LDP fell, both the press and political structures seemed to be undergoing a revolution: newspapers were running more investigative pieces, Sunday television talk shows raised the level of debate, and some weeklies dared to broach the ultimate taboo: criticizing the empress.

Most important, the dissolution of the LDP's hold on power broke up some of the entrenched *kisha* club relationships. A senior political reporter at *Asahi Shimbun* described the difficulty in trying to cover the new opposition parties, as coalitions evolved and disintegrated. No longer could reporters rely on their favorite highly placed official to give them reliable information off the record. Unlike in the days of LDP-orchestrated politics, nobody could tell what would happen next.[81]

Despite the changes, the pendulum soon began to swing the other way. Politics began to revert to business as usual, and slowly a chill fell over the press. Tsubaki of TV Asahi apologized to the Diet for his "inappropriate comments" during the 1993 campaign, reporters began to rebuild *kisha* club relationships, and magazines backed off from discussing the royal family after severe criticism from the Imperial Household Agency and an oblique rebuke from the empress herself. "It was two steps forward, one step back," says Honda of *Asahi Shimbun*. "The people of Japan were severely disappointed."[82]

Will the events of 1993 result in structural reforms that change the face of "money politics" in Japan? Cutting those traditional channels of political and financial support is like, as the Japanese phrase aptly puts it, "eating one's own legs." Analyses of the behavior of Japan's ruling party in other areas indicated that it may institute reforms only when it is convinced that change will not jeopardize its maintenance of power. This may be even more true of the new rulers, as they struggle to retain their delicate hold on control—and thus dampen the chances of real follow-through on promises of revolutionary structural reform.[83]

Indeed, van Wolferen holds that scandal actually helps perpetuate and refine underground dealings, not stem them. Scandals "help curb excess, and in doing so they help preserve the informal extra-legal political and economic system."[84] That the Sagawa Kyūbin scandal was just a replay of the 1989 Recruit scandal on a larger scale supports such a theory. Yoshiki Hidaka, managing director of NHK, has said that the only real change after the Recruit scandal was that

Recruit stopped its political donations—which was not necessarily a positive outcome, as it led directly to politicians' dependence on one of the few remaining sources, Sagawa. Hidaka insists that money will always find a way in because pragmatism is replacing the society's earlier moral structure.[85]

Conclusions

Uncovering scandal is a chief aim of a watchdog press. But in Japan, ironically, the journalists who are best positioned to ferret out truth—the reporters in the cozy press clubs that cover major institutions—have seldom been responsible for exposing the major scandals of the last two decades. Rather, those stories were broken by a press corps outside the center of power. All the scandals surfaced from sources outside the mainstream media: the foreign press, outsiders' investigative reporting, or leaks given to passive insider journalists. The insiders and outsiders of the media world have an almost choreographed interplay with the insiders and outsiders of the political, bureaucratic, and business worlds. The outside press acts to pull information out of the inner sanctum. Once the news has been leaked, the inside press works to maintain the outflow and to condemn the transgressors. In all the major scandals over the past two decades, extensive press coverage of wayward behavior has forced officials to step down but has not, at least so far, resulted in real reforms. The pattern revealed by this analysis of scandal confirms Ellis Krauss' observation that the establishment press in Japan ultimately may be a better "guard dog" than watchdog: pursuing the criminal once his existence is revealed, but doing little to initially point attention to the wrongdoer.[86]

This pattern is a telling indicator of the nature of power and relationships in Japan, and of the dual role of the press in Japanese society. Press coverage of scandal reveals that both Japan's prewar tradition of press control and the postwar role of the press as democratic critic are operating and that both those who tout the press as a guardian of the public interest and those who criticize it as a tool of authority are correct. The reporters' clubs and the inner and outer networks of journalist-government relations create a particularly severe duality between investigative journalism of the kind that leads to revelations and coverage journalism that merely reports wrongdoing once it has been revealed. That the latter predominates, at least for the mainstream media, suggests a more limited form of watchdog role overall for the Japanese media. This combination of inside and outside media can serve the Japanese public fairly well, but not always, and only when the watchdog outsider is alert and the guard-dog insider is prepared to cooperate.

Notes

1. These commitments appear in the Canons of Journalism issued by the Nihon Shimbun Kyōkai (Japan Newspaper Publishers and Editors Association) and its publications. See Jung Bok Lee, *The Political Character of the Japanese Press* (Seoul: Seoul National University Press, 1985), p. 2; and Nihon Shimbun Kyōkai, *The Japanese Press 1991* (Tokyo: Nihon Shimbun Kyōkai, 1991), p. 4.

2. Yukio Matsuyama, "The Miyazawa Administration and His Leadership," paper presented to the Harvard University Program on U.S.–Japan Relations, Cambridge, Mass., 5 November 1991.

3. See, for example, George R. Packard III, *Protest in Tokyo* (Princeton, N.J.: Princeton University Press, 1966), especially pp. 278–284.

4. Richard Halloran, *Japan: Images and Realities* (Tokyo: Charles E. Tuttle, 1969), p. 160.

5. Karel van Wolferen, *The Enigma of Japanese Power* (New York: Alfred A. Knopf, 1989), p. 93. See also British scholar William Nester's critique that concludes that the media cannot truly be considered a "fourth estate": "Japan's Mainstream Press: Freedom to Conform?" *Pacific Affairs* 62(1) (Spring, 1989): 39.

6. Masaru Honda, personal interview, 17 November 1991.

7. Akio Nomura, bureau chief, *Asahi Shimbun,* personal interview, Washington, D.C., 27 April 1992.

8. Nick Valery, personal interview, 29 April 1992, and personal experience working in Japan's press corps, 1988–1990.

9. Van Wolferen, *The Enigma of Japanese Power,* p. 95.

10. David Brock, "Gentlemanly Press Gets Gloves Dirty," *No. 1 Shimbun,* March 1990, p. 3.

11. Young C. Kim, *Japanese Journalists and Their World* (Charlottesville: University Press of Virginia, 1981), p. 175.

12. Yukio Matsuyama, personal interview, 7 December 1992.

13. Makoto Utsumi, personal interview, 8 December 1991.

14. Michio Uchida, "Japan's Newspaper 'Disease,'" *Tokyo Business Today,* March 1992, p. 20.

15. David Broder, warning of the hazards of symbiosis, in Lewis W. Wolfson, "Through the Revolving Door: Blurring the Line between the Press and Government," R-4 (Cambridge: Joan Shorenstein Barone Center for Press, Politics, and Public Policy, Harvard University, June 1991).

16. Yukio Matsuyama, personal interview, 23 September 1991.

17. Ibid.

18. *Nihon Keizai Shimbun,* 13 February 1992.

19. Steven R. Weisman, "Is the Prince Courting? Not a Peep from the Press," *New York Times,* 14 February 1992, p. 4.

20. "Special Delivery," *Economist,* 1 February 1992, p. 38.

21. Yoshio Sorita, "Shimbunkai ni ima nani ga okite iru no ka" (What Is Happening in the Newspaper World Now?), *Tsukuru* (Create) 186 (June 1988): 32–40. See also this volume, chapter 2.

22. Philip Meyer, *Ethical Journalism* (New York: Longman, 1987), p. 39.

23. Karl Schoenberger, "Ad Giant in Japan Sells Clout," *Los Angeles Times,* 14 June 1990, p1.

24. Kay Itoi, "Tokyo TV: Heeere's [*sic*] Hiroshi!" *International Herald Tribune,* 28 February 1990, p. 9.

25. Matsuyama interview, 23 September 1991.

26. Nihon Shimbun Kyōkai Research Institute, *Henka suru media kankyō to shimbun dokusha—zenkoku shinraido, dai ikkai sōgōchōsa, 1989* (Comprehensive Nationwide Newspaper Credibility Survey, 1989) (Tokyo: Nihon Shimbun Kyōkai, 1989). The 1989 poll was of 4,000 randomly selected respondents.

27. *Asahi Shimbun,* readers' poll, 14 October 1987.

28. After the drop in ratings, the major national newspapers established an ombudsman system to handle readers' complaints and instituted in-house review boards, with a resulting rise in perception of credibility to 73 percent by 1991. See Nihon Shimbun Kyōkai, *NSK Bulletin,* December 1991, pp. 3–4.

29. The story that resulted is "The Monsters Stalking Politicians' Dreams," *Economist,* 29 April 1989. Valery covered the Recruit link but could only allude to the suspect minister.

30. Joyce Milton, *The Yellow Kids* (New York: Harper and Row, 1989), p. 14.

31. Confirmed in interview with Shigeru Yotoriyama, Organized Crime Unit, Japan Police Force, 27 April 1992.

32. Matsuyama interview, 7 December 1991; and other reports.

33. Kazutami Yamazaki, "Press Freedom Japan-Style: Bow and Scrape," *Nikkei Weekly,* 3 April 1992.

34. Andrei S. Markovits and Mark Silverstein, eds., *The Politics of Scandal* (New York: Holmes and Meier, 1988), p. vii.

35. This definition is based on that of Joseph S. Nye as given in his "Corruption and Political Development: A Cost Benefit Analysis," in *Political Corruption,* ed. Arnold J. Heidenheimer et al. (New Brunswick, N.J.: Transaction Press, 1990), p. 966.

36. Jeanne Becquart-Leclercq, "Paradoxes of Political Corruption: A French View," in *Political Corruption,* ed. Heidenheimer et al., pp. 191–210.

37. Michio Watanabe, speech at Tokyo Foreign Correspondents' Club, 24 September 1991.

38. *Yomiuri Shimbun,* Report of the Utopia Political Research Committee, 4 March 1989.

162   *Maggie Farley*

39. *Economist,* 18 March 1989.
40. Nomura interview.
41. Van Wolferen, *The Enigma of Japanese Power,* p. 95.
42. Markovits and Silverstein, *The Politics of Scandal,* p. viii.
43. Ibid.
44. Lance Bennett, *The Politics of Illusion* (New York: Longman, 1988), p. 55.
45. Karel van Wolferen, "Agreeing on Reality: Political Reporting by the Japanese Press," *Speaking of Japan* 5, no. 44 (August 1984): 20–23.
46. Examples of scandals involving symbiotic relationships include the Carrefour scandal in France in March 1986 and the Flick scandal in Germany in 1982.
47. Van Wolferen, *The Enigma of Japanese Power,* p. 136.
48. Chalmers Johnson, "Tanaka Kakuei, Structural Corruption, and the Advent of Machine Politics in Japan," *Journal of Japanese Studies* 12, no. 1 (1986): 8.
49. Markovits and Silverstein, *The Politics of Scandal,* p. 222.
50. Robert C. Christopher, *The Japanese Mind* (London: Pan Books, 1984), p. 202.
51. Markovits and Silverstein, *The Politics of Scandal,* p. 223.
52. Johnson, "Tanaka Kakuei," p. 12.
53. Van Wolferen, *The Enigma of Japanese Power,* p. 129.
54. Ibid., p. 128.
55. Fred Hiatt, "Uncovering a Scandal," *Washington Post,* 20 February 1989, p. A36.
56. Ibid.
57. *Asahi Jānaru* Henshūbu, ed., *Rikurūto gēto no kakushin* (The core of Recruit-gate) (Tokyo: Suzusawa Shoten, 1989).
58. From conversations with reporters in Tokyo, 1988. Confirmed by Masaru Honda, *Asahi Shimbun,* personal interview, 18 August 1993.
59. Hiatt, "Uncovering a Scandal," p. A36.
60. Kevin Rafferty, "Old Boys in Hot Water," *CEO/International Strategies* (September/October 1991): 42.
61. The official does not wish to be named.
62. "Samitto chokuzen, naze shōken sukyandaru wa riiku sareta shinkyū kokuzei chō chōkan ga antō no hate ni" (Why the Stock Scandal Was Leaked on the Eve of the Summit—The Secret Strife between the Incoming and Outgoing Tax Agency Directors in the Final Stage), *Shūkan Themis,* 17 July 1991 (the banned issue).
63. "*Shūkan Themis:* 'Meiyo kison' to kaishū, kyūkan" (With Charge of Libel, the Roundup and Suspension of Publication of *Shūkan Themis*), *Mainichi Shimbun,* 10 July 1991.
64. "Special Delivery," *Economist,* 1 February 1992, p38.
65. "Pass the Parcel," *Economist,* 22 February 1992, pp. 28–29.
66. Interviews with Yoshiki Hidaka, NHK, 15 April 1992; Shin Yoshida, *Asahi Shimbun,* Washington, D.C. bureau, 27 April 1992.

67. David E. Sanger, "Japan's Top Politician Quits Posts over Mob Scandal," *New York Times,* 15 October 1992.

68. Nick Valery, personal interview, 29 April 1992.

69. Personal interview, 1992.

70. Johnson, "Tanaka Kakuei," p. 12.

71. Van Wolferen, *The Enigma of Japanese Power,* p. 137.

72. Chie Nakane, among others, in ibid.

73. Van Wolferen, *The Enigma of Japanese Power,* p. 137.

74. Henny Sender, personal interview, 26 April 1992.

75. Ikuo Kabashima, professor of political science, Tsukuba University, personal interview, 8 April 1992.

76. See this volume, chapter 9.

77. Ikuo Kabashima and Jeffrey Broadbent, "Referent Pluralism: Mass Media and Politics in Japan," *Journal of Japanese Studies* 2 (Summer 1986): 358.

78. T. R. Reid, "Japan's Feisty New Press," *Nieman Reports,* Fall 1993, p. 14.

79. Ibid., p. 15.

80. Quentin Hardy, telephone interview, Tokyo, 9 August 1993.

81. Masaru Honda, personal interview, 18 March 1994.

82. Ibid.

83. Kent Calder's theory of crisis and compensation—which holds that the LDP stays in power by compensating, then coopting, the creators of crisis—reaffirms this conclusion. See also Elpidio R. Sta. Romana, "The Politics of Liberalization of the Japanese Agricultural Market," research paper 12 (Singapore: Department of Japanese Studies, National University of Singapore, 1991). He shows that the LDP began its moves toward agricultural liberalization only after carefully calculating that it could "dump" the farmers and still survive. The same strategy was used before agreeing to electoral reapportionment.

84. Michael Shari, "How Foreign Analysts in Tokyo See It," *Nikkei Weekly,* 3 August 1991.

85. Yoshiki Hidaka, personal interview, 15 April 1992.

86. See Ellis S. Krauss, "Japan," in *Media Technologies and Democracy,* ed. Anthony Mughan, Richard Gunther, and Paul Beck (forthcoming).

5

Television and Political Turmoil: Japan's Summer of 1993

KRISTIN KYOKO ALTMAN

O N October 25, 1993, millions of Japanese gathered around their television sets to witness an unprecedented political show-down. The conflict—which took place within the stately chambers of the national parliament building and was broadcast on live televi-sion—pitted the Liberal Democratic Party (LDP), the conservative party that had dominated Japanese politics for nearly four decades, against the Japanese press. The occasion for this confrontation: the appearance of former TV Asahi news executive Sadayoshi Tsubaki before the Japanese Diet. Tsubaki, the first journalist ever sum-moned to testify before the Diet, stood accused of slanting his net-work's coverage of the LDP in the July 18 election that led to the party's downfall.

The role of television news coverage had been hotly debated in the months since the LDP's defeat. "The LDP Lost to TV," wailed a head-line in one respected magazine, which argued that without television many of the young reformers who formed the new government could not have been elected.[1] "Television Fascism," declared another.[2] Indeed, some pundits christened the new government "the Kume-Tahara Coalition Government," a nickname that suggested the Hosokawa Coalition had been created by Hiroshi Kume and Sōichirō Tahara, two of the nation's most influential television anchors.[3]

On September 21, two months after the July elections, scholars and top executives from Japan's largest news organizations gathered to ponder those issues at a closed-door meeting of the Japan Com-mercial Broadcasting Association (Nihon Minkan Hōsō Renmei). In the course of their discussion, Tsubaki—then the head of TV Asahi's news department—offered a remarkably blunt defense of his net-work's aggressive coverage of the ruling party during the July elec-tion. Tsubaki complained bitterly that for the preceding several years, TV Asahi had been unfairly bullied by the LDP and officials at the Ministry of Posts and Telecommunications to water down its coverage of the party's leaders. To put an end to such strong-arming, Tsubaki said, he and TV Asahi colleagues had decided that the network "must crush the LDP" in the July elections. "There's no question we resolved that in this election, we must use our news coverage to absolutely obliterate the LDP's thirty-eight-year rule," he declared, according to a transcript of the meeting.[4]

The meeting was intended to be private, but three weeks later Tsubaki's comments were splashed across the front page of *Sankei Shimbun,* the most conservative of Japan's five major dailies. The headline read: "Instructions to Create a Non-LDP Government."[5] Immediately, the Ministry of Posts and Telecommunications began an investigation into TV Asahi's coverage of the elections. The LDP politicians, the victims of the network's alleged bias, roared on the floor of the Diet that the network must be punished. They then issued a subpoena for a hearing, in which Tsubaki was to be questioned under oath about his comments.

Critics seized on the comments as proof that Japan's big television stations had abandoned all pretense of objectivity and fairness, and instead had launched a vendetta against the ruling party. Others saw Tsubaki's combative statements as evidence that Japan's television stations, after decades of craven subservience to the nation's political establishment, had finally come of age; they decried the subpoena as a violation of press freedom. Underlying the controversy was a deeper, more complex debate about the role of the press, the limits of free expression, and the nature of democracy in Japan's fast changing post–Cold War political structure.

Traditional Press-Politics Relations in Japan

In the world of Japanese political journalism, television historically has played a minor role compared to the print media.[6] Political news tended to avoid challenging the LDP, reflecting in large part the decades of trust and cooperation nurtured by Japan's cozy *kisha* (reporters') club system.

The Kisha Club

The *kisha* clubs largely control political reporting in Japan, as described in chapters 3 and 4. The system began, however, as a way to help news organizations pool their resources to maximize their ability to cover the government. The system has succeeded in giving *kisha* club reporters tremendous access to the government and political parties at the expense of the regional and foreign press, whose reporters are not members of the club. Only the major news organizations that belong to Nihon Shimbun Kyōkai (Japan Newspaper Publishers and Editors Association) are granted membership. While insiders are constantly provided with updated, detailed information by their sources, outsiders struggle to obtain any type of information. For this reason, foreign correspondents have often referred to the *kisha* clubs as "news cartels."[7]

The three main political *kisha* clubs have been the Hirakawa Club, the Shakaitō Club, and the Nagata Club. The Hirakawa Club, named after its location in Hirakawa-cho at the LDP headquarters, reports on the LDP. The Shakaitō Club, also called Yatō Club (opposition club), traditionally covered the opposition parties out of the headquarters of the Japan Socialist Party (JSP), the largest opposition party. The Nagata Club, located at the prime minister's office in Nagata-chō, is responsible for covering that office. Reporters in each of these clubs are provided a room with equipment and staff by the organizations they cover. So, for example, the LDP has provided phones, desks, and long couches—used as beds by some reporters—to the journalists in the Hirakawa Club. Because the LDP also distributes updated news material throughout the day, reporters spend the majority of their time at their clubs. In this way, the *kisha* club system fosters an interdependent relationship between reporters and their sources.

Reporters in the same *kisha* club also become close with one another. In the small overcrowded room, desks of reporters from competing news organizations are situated side by side, leaving no room for privacy. Over the years reporters have tended to cooperate with one another, discussing what the news is and building a consensus over what to report for the day. The relationship is so collegial that, according to one reporter at the Shakaitō Club, when someone oversleeps or is absent during important briefings, colleagues from rival news organizations will cover for the absent one, later providing the news material needed to file a report. Such a cooperative system among *kisha* club members tends to produce uniform political news. All five national newspapers usually have the same political headlines on any given day.

Each of the major news organizations belonging to the *kisha* clubs typically assigns one or more reporters to follow full time the leaders of the organization they cover. These reporters, usually younger journalists just beginning their careers, are known as *ban-kisha* (the word *ban* is derived from the Japanese character "look out"). For example, within the Hirakawa Club, there always have been *ban-kisha* for the LDP's top three leaders as well as the leaders of each of the LDP factions. These reporters are expected to keep watch over their politician's house in the mornings and the evenings. If the reporters are lucky, they will get a ride to work with their politician. This is called *hako-nori* (literally, "riding the box"). Furthermore, if the reporters are deemed trustworthy by their politician, they will be invited into the home at night when the politician returns from work. The reporters' ratings go up as they progress from the entrance of their politician's house to the living room and finally to the refrigerator door in the kitchen. After proving their loyalty to their politician through sleepless nights and days of following the politician's every footstep, the young reporters are able to obtain some information. Early in their careers, reporters are trained in this way to develop and value a close relationship with political leaders.

The veteran Japanese political reporter is one who has mastered the art of *kondan* (friendly chat)—that is, the behind-the-scenes talks that take place among politicians and reporters. Hidden from the public, politicians and reporters exchange information, advice, and sometimes even favors. Press conferences have been a sham in which reporters and politicians trade vague questions and evasive answers for the sake of appearances. Fearful of offending the politician in public, but also knowing that the real issues will be discussed in the *kondan*, the reporter asks only polite questions at a press conference. A former editor of *Shūkan Mainichi* recalled, "Occasionally, a young reporter would ask some question at a press conference, and the veteran reporters in the back of the room would chuckle to themselves over the naivete of the new reporter. The best reporters were the ones who kept silent during the press conferences and would ask questions at the exclusive *kondan*." The press conferences, he explains, were regarded as only *tatemae* (superficial), while the *honne* (the real story) was revealed in the *kondan* to which only a few reporters had access.[8]

Kondan usually take place under an implicit agreement that the source will not be identified; often they are *ofureko* (off the record). Most of the information reporters gather from a *kondan* does not get into print. One political reporter for *Asahi* explained, "I cannot write it because I would lose the trust of the politician and that would be the end of my career."[9]

The president of the Foreign Press Club in Japan, Lewis Simons, who has covered Japan for nearly a decade, observes, "Japanese political reporters are by far much more knowledgeable about their subject than their counterparts in the United States or any other country, but it's shocking how little of what they know actually gets in the paper. As a result, journalism suffers."[10]

Japanese political reporters frequently have been criticized by foreign reporters for "not taking on the system." But in Japan, traditionally, a political reporter's idea of reporting has been to talk exclusively about policy. Questions about whether a politician received illegal contributions are considered dirty and beneath a political reporter's responsibility. Social reporters, not political reporters, are responsible for dealing with such matters. However, social reporters have often been constrained because if they offend a politician, their political colleague—and thus the entire paper—is punished by having all political access cut off.[11] Consequently, political reporting tends to parrot the government line. Tetsuya Chikushi, a former print journalist who now works as an anchor at TBS, one of Japan's five private networks, says, "Most of the time the Japanese press has acted as the mouthpiece for those in power. Newspapers were created with the belief that important news comes from those in power."[12]

Typifying the view held by most political reporters, a former senior editor at *Asahi Shimbun,* one of Japan's major newspapers, defended the traditional system: "A trusting relationship with a politician is essential because we need to know what the politician's *honne* is—what he is really thinking—in order to understand and get the whole picture of politics. . . . Politics is a special field where misinformation can bring down a government. We must be accurate."[13] This kind of cautious thinking by journalists, taking political responsibility as a duty, helps perpetuate status-quo reporting.

Political Reporting in Television

Conventional television news has operated under the same rules of *kisha* club reporting in the print-dominated world of press and politics. As discussed in chapter 3, from the advent of television news in the 1950s until the mid-1980s, NHK, Japan's public broadcasting system, was the primary source of television news in Japan. But the legal and political framework of NHK subjected it to political pressures. Structured very much like Japanese newspapers, NHK stations its reporters in the *kisha* clubs and adheres to the same rules of reporting as the print media. Tied to these old-boy networks, NHK's news-gathering process is highly dependent on official and political sources. In addition, because NHK is Japan's public broadcasting organization, its board of directors is appointed by the prime minister, and its annual budget and receiver fees are submitted to the Ministry of Posts and Telecommunications and the Diet for approval. Former president of NHK, Keiji Shima, recalls how he faced constant pressure from the LDP: "Because broadcasting is a licensed operation, a television station is in a weak position. In particular, NHK had to submit its annual budget to the Diet. The LDP used their *yūsei zoku giin*—members of the so-called policy tribes associated with the Ministry of Posts and Telecommunications—to pressure us. Among the former prime ministers, there were those who would summon me and point out the inconvenient parts from a printed transcript of our news."[14] Some staff members who worked at NHK referred to the evening news as the "LDP hour."[15]

The style of NHK news—its use of complex literary vocabulary in detailed accounts of ongoing political issues—has also been strikingly similar to the print media. Much of the news was focused in an impersonal fashion on the various bureaucracies and institutions. Politicians and government officials were rarely depicted as private individuals. For most Japanese, NHK's style of news presentation—with conservatively dressed, unsmiling anchors who more or less read the news—was equated with reliability and trust.

The private networks have followed NHK's lead for much of the postwar period. Political journalism in Japan has thus tended to be a uniform governmental account of politics, the result of a structural system that upheld a close relationship between journalists and the government. Only insiders and those who studied the system understood the full meaning implied in the complex political stories. For most Japanese people, politics was a gray haze. Faceless politicians mumbled noncommittal bromides about issues that were never really explained. Political stories were complex and dry, using a language very different from daily Japanese. Finally, much of the information, buried forever in off-the-record *kondan,* never reached the people, leaving most of the nation in the dark.

The Emergence of a New Media and the 1993 Elections

News Station

A television program called *News Station,* a live prime-time program that began airing in the fall of 1985 on TV Asahi, revolutionized conventional reporting in Japan. *News Station* first transformed news by translating the complex news vocabulary to a level the public could understand; then it began questioning and criticizing government actions.

The program, which became a controversy overnight, employed Hiroshi Kume, a former pop-music show host, as its anchor to lead the hour and a half of nightly news. Kume set out with one goal: to make the news understandable to everyone. Using charts and maps of the world and speaking in everyday language, Kume tried to make the news as visual and simple as possible. He believed every Japanese—from junior high school students to the elderly—was entitled to a full explanation of the nation's news. Lacking a background in journalism, Kume ignored conventional rules and taboos.

Critics complained that Kume's simplicity was dangerous, and politicians publicly urged viewers to boycott program advertisers. Former minister of health Tokuo Yamashita openly called on viewers to stop buying products advertised on *News Station,* and former LDP secretary general Seiroku Kajiyama pressured sponsors to withdraw their commercials.[16] Backed by strong public support, the program survived these political pressures. An average of 20 million viewers a night for the last eight years has kept *News Station* on the air. A public poll conducted in the beginning of July 1993 in Tokyo shortly before the historic election showed that 60.2 percent of Japanese watched *News Station* for political news, while 38.3 percent watched the NHK news.[17]

In August 1992 Shin Kanemaru, Japan's most powerful political boss, admitted taking $4 million in illegal campaign contributions from a mob-affiliated trucking company, Sagawa Kyūbin. Kanemaru was let off with a fine of $1,700 and was preparing to reenter office. The media barely moved and the public was hardly shaken until *News Station* began featuring the Kanemaru scandal nightly. T. R. Reid, the Tokyo bureau chief of the *Washington Post,* wrote:

> Japan's most popular and powerful newscaster, Hiroshi Kume of TV Asahi's national evening news show, used to tell his viewers "this stuff is complicated, but it's important that you understand it." A laid-back fellow with no pretensions, Kume used stuffed dolls and play money to demonstrate how illegal payoffs moved from business to politicians, and how the politicians and the bureaucracy paid back their benefactors with government contracts and other goodies. At first, I laughed at this; it seemed so childish to see a national news anchor playing with dolls. In fact, though, Kume-san helped me—and, presumably, millions of voters—to understand just how corrupt the old system was.[18]

Kume did not hide his outrage at the politicians involved in the scandals, even going so far as to comment on air that these people should resign. "Kume . . . reported each scandal to hit the LDP with sarcastic commentary and disbelieving stares. The public loved it," wrote Reid.[19] The *Wall Street Journal* stated that "it was Japan's often-ignored public opinion, whipped up by the likes of Kume, that made it untenable for Kanemaru to stay in office."[20]

News Station kept its focus on political reform throughout the year, airing for the first time relatively unknown politicians calling for reform. One of these was Morihiro Hosokawa, who became prime minister after having been dismissed by senior politicians of the LDP as a minor figure at the time. Unlike the older, powerful politicians who shunned television and relied on off-the-record chats with print reporters behind closed doors, the young, reform-minded politicians were part of an image-conscious generation that had grown up with television. Many of these young politicians saw television as their natural medium and eagerly sought its exposure. More important in 1993, television allowed them to break from the iron control of party seniors and appeal directly to the public.

Talk Shows and the Fall of Kiichi Miyazawa

Another program that challenged traditional reporting was Sōichirō Tahara's Sunday-morning live political talk show, *Sunday Project,* on TV Asahi. The combative style of the program's moderator was unprecedented. This program became a forum for open political debate among young reform-minded politicians challenging the LDP. "Previous political talk shows . . . by NHK had been *tatemae* [superficial] debates where participants who had been chosen for their powerful names performed a script on which there already was a consensus. . . . [The new style of talk show] allowed people to see politicians' real faces and made people think, 'There are such interesting people in politics,'" said Yasuhiro Tase, a senior editor at *Nihon Keizai Shimbun,* one of Japan's major newspapers.[21] A politician's statement made on *Sunday Project* often became the headline news in the papers the next morning, and soon political reporters began coming to the studio for news. Then other networks started creating similar programs.

It was not long before the older politicians began to realize the impact that this new style of raw political talk was having on the public. So much so that then prime minister Kiichi Miyazawa felt compelled to accept the invitation of an "anything goes" interview with Tahara. This was the first time a Japanese prime minister had agreed to a television interview without any preset restrictions on the type of questions to be asked. But if Miyazawa's intention was to reestablish his credibility with voters, the program had just the opposite effect. The interview triggered the downfall of his government. In the interview, which first aired on May 31, 1993, Tahara pinned the prime minister to a pledge that he would achieve political reform during the June Diet session. Prime Minister Miyazawa's failure to deliver on this promise allowed his opponents to attack him as a liar, leading to the no-confidence vote against him on June 18 and, ultimately, to the Diet's dissolution.

Minutes before the interview, Miyazawa declared that he would not answer any questions about political reform, Tahara recalled after their encounter. But Tahara was adamant. "Political reform is the issue voters want to hear about. . . . If you avoid the question, voters will think you are no good," he said. Miyazawa apparently concluded that he had no choice but to go along. As the interview proceeded, he promised repeatedly to address political reform before the Diet session ended. With remarkable lack of deference, Tahara pushed the prime minister to make his position explicit. "Are you going to carry out political reform or not?" he demanded.

"Yes, I will," Miyazawa said. "I promise I will."

"Will you do it during this Diet session?"

"I will do it," Miyazawa said again. "It is my responsibility."[22]

In the end Miyazawa, weakened by repeated scandals within his own party, was unable to deliver on his promise. Networks broadcast the exchange with Tahara over and over again as proof of the prime minister's inability to lead the government. Detractors used the Tahara interview to brand Miyazawa the "lying prime minister." In short order, his political enemies forced a vote of no-confidence against Miyazawa, and the Diet was dissolved.

During the election campaign that followed, the leaders of the three dominant reform parties—Morihiro Hosokawa, Tsutomu Hata, and Masayoshi Takemura—appeared daily on television. These reformers had strong character images: Hosokawa, a direct descendent of a great Japanese warlord, was "the samurai king." Hata, known for his clean political record, was "the devoted reformist." Takemura, who had round, soft features, reminded people of a chubby, gentle, popular cartoon character named "Moomin Papa."[23] Compared to the colorful images that these new leaders projected on television, the senior LDP members were ineffective on the screen. They had had little experience communicating directly with voters. The LDP style of campaigning—branded as the "politics of Santa Claus" by media pundits—was one in which politicians often delivered "presents" like bridges and roads to the people. While the young politicians appealed for political reform, the traditional power barons were caught on live television stammering without a clear message.

Tahara once suggested to Prime Minister Miyazawa, "Stop the goofy meaningless smile and speak out clearly" when on television. But Miyazawa responded saying, "I don't like such performance gimmicks. It has nothing to do with politics."[24] This attitude was typical of most senior politicians, who had little respect for television and chose to rely for the most part on the print media.

A Shift from the Old to the New

Like their political leaders, voters traditionally relied on the print media for their political information. But as programs like *News Station* and the *Sunday Project* began to change the style of news—and an increasing number of programs on other networks followed their lead—people began to turn to television.

A poll taken at the end of the July 1993 election campaign (between July 15 and 17, one day before the elections) asked voters which medium had helped them make their final decision. The result showed a huge turnaround from several years before. Thirty-four percent responded that special political programs on television had made the difference, while 26 percent said the newspapers had helped them.[25] That television would surpass the print media was unthinkable several years earlier. Tase of *Nihon Keizai Shimbun* explains, "As television programs like *News Station* and *Sunday Project* introduced a different perspective of politics, everyone reading the papers began questioning the gap between political reality and the articles. Newspapers came to be perceived as *tatemae,* advocating only the official view."[26]

Television was able to confront politicians more directly because it had a smaller stake in the old political system. Newspapers have a long history in the *kisha* club system, where there are unspoken rules, such as the one that says reporters should not ask a politician about his love affairs or his tax evasions. But the commercial television networks developed later and were less bound by such rules. "We are ignorant. We don't have the experience and don't know the limitations of the rules," says Tahara. "That's why we can ask."[27]

Nihon Keizai Shimbun called the July campaign "the Television

Election." On election day the networks made a spectacle of the race: Fuji TV tracked voting results with three-dimensional graphics updated every few seconds. NTV tallied electoral results alongside the strike count during its broadcast of the Yomiuri baseball game. TBS dispatched a record number of 700 camera crews across the nation. At TV Asahi, Kume and Tahara led a live debate with party leaders and representatives. NHK conducted polls at 1,400 places across the nation with 140,000 voters and computerized the results. Never before had voters seen anything like this on television. The ratings showed that the political programs on June 18 were immensely popular.[28]

Without television, many of the newly elected politicians would not have been successful. The fact that the three new parties—Nihon Shintō, Shinseitō, and Shintō Sakigake—were able to round up 103 seats, surpassing the JSP to become a new political force, was due in important ways to television. No election in Japan had ever felt the impact of television as did the elections of July 1993.

The Beginning of Television Politics

The end of LDP rule has brought new challenges to the conventional press structure. The fundamental pillars that have upheld traditional Japanese press-politics relations—the *kisha* club, the *ban-kisha* and the *kondan*—tottered in the aftermath.

One week after the election Ichirō Ozawa, a central figure in the new Hosokawa governing coalition, abolished *kondan*. Ozawa told *ban-kisha* from the many newspapers and networks who followed him day and night not to bother hanging around his house anymore; he would not be giving background briefings. Instead, he would hold open press conferences in which journalists outside the *kisha* club, such as reporters from the regional press and foreign correspondents, were welcome to participate.

"Japanese politics has always had a *honne* and *tatemae* which made the process ambiguous and murky," Ozawa said. "We have been elected to carry out political reform, to make the process more transparent and open. *Kondan* are a thing of the past."[29]

Ozawa's decision deprived *kisha* club reporters of one of their most important political sources at a crucial time. Though *ban-kisha* assigned to Ozawa continued to follow him, they were no longer able to gather information in the traditional way. This increased the turmoil in the *kisha* clubs already resulting from the political change.

The Yatō Club, the opposition party club that had mainly covered the JSP for the past thirty-eight years, struggled most. Suddenly reporters faced the task of covering seven different parties, which included many new faces. Confronted with the lack of a system for assignment responsibilities and a shortage of facilities—not enough phones, faxes, or even chairs to allow them to do the job—the *kisha* clubs had to scramble to adapt.

Adjusting to Image Politics

As the conventional press struggled to redefine itself, old-guard politicians began shifting their attention to television, the new medium in politics. LDP leaders, recognizing that their disdain for television had contributed to their defeat, groped for a new strategy. "Television attracted voters by its colorful presentation of politics," said Yoshirō Mori, secretary general of the LDP on the TBS nightly news program *News 23*. "Our old style was considered *dasai*—drab. We must adopt a policy that uses television more."[30] In an astonishing move, the LDP invited Tahara to preside over its party convention in September. A program featuring a cross-talk session between senior members of the LDP and media pundits from popular television talk shows was televised on TV Asahi. Not all LDP members could swallow such a strategy, and there were complaints that the party had gone too far.

The new prime minister, Hosokawa, himself a former print journalist who knew the media well, was one step ahead of all other prime ministers in his knack of handling the media. Putting an end to the old-style press conference, Hosokawa opened his press conferences to non-*kisha* club reporters and transformed the meetings into lively sessions where he gave straightforward answers. "From the regional reporters to celebrity reporters on tabloid shows, everyone came to Hosokawa's press conferences. The room reverberated with questions," said Kazu Ogawa, a reporter for *Mainichi Shimbun*, one of Japan's five major newspapers.[31] Hosokawa's bold style of standing during press conferences and calling on reporters by pointing to them directly with a pen was unprecedented. It attracted much admiration as well as criticism. The critics dismissed the prime minister's new style as a shallow performance, an imitation of U.S. president Bill Clinton. In the fall Prime Minister Hosokawa attempted to use the teleprompter for the first time when announcing the opening of Japan's rice market nationwide on television. Impressed by Clinton's use of the teleprompter to speak directly to the people, Hosokawa decided to give it a shot. The experiment was not entirely success-ful—the teleprompters were set up much too close to the prime min-ister—but it marked one of the first attempts by a prime minister to convince the Japanese public of a particular policy through televised communication. The prime minister's image consciousness extended to changing the chairs in the cabinet meeting room because he thought the old seats looked "imperialistic" and projected the wrong image to voters. Critics shrieked that the new prime minister was turning Nagata-chō into "a stage for television."[32]

But Hosokawa's popularity prompted other politicians to follow his example. When a television camera crew entered the headquar-ters of Shinseitō for a scheduled interview with Ichirō Ozawa, the stocky power broker motioned the camera crew to stop filming. He then proceeded to shave with a high-tech electric razor while the camera crew politely waited. Upon finishing, he signaled permission to resume.[33] The *Wall Street Journal* wrote, "What's Out: Drab. What's In: Fashion," and noted that Hata, the leader of Shinseitō, had taken to wearing "an unusual jacket with half-sleeves, not exactly haute couture but weird nonetheless for a Japanese politi-cian." And in the Diet, the *Wall Street Journal* noted, Hata "some-times wears a blue shirt, a departure from LDP regulation white."[34]

The public relished this image makeover by Japanese politicians. Politics remained all the rage on television, and ratings soared even higher. Jacob Schlesinger, the *Wall Street Journal*'s Tokyo correspon-dent, observed that "one night recently, regulars at a public bath here rushed out of the water, clutching their little towels to themselves, to catch the political news on TV. Unheard of." Schlesinger also noted that *Spa!*, a magazine for young people, devoted six pages to "How to Tell Who's Really a Reformer." One thing to watch out for, the article claimed: "oily skin caused by living high on the hog. Oily-faced people do bad things."[35] Never before had image entered into the Japanese assessment of politicians.

On the one hand, television was making the political process clearer and closer to the people. On the other, it was making political leaders increasingly concerned with image and performance. As a result, Japan's "exclusive" system of *kisha* clubs and cozy relations between press and politicians was starting to look more like the American system. The triangular relationship between television, politics, and elections that characterizes American politics was begin-ning to emerge in Japan.

Parallels with American Television Politics

The Japanese revolution in press-politics relations in the summer of 1993 in many ways echoes the shift of power that occurred during the 1992 U.S. presidential campaign. Just as the balance of power established between American political leaders and journalists in the post-Watergate years was challenged by the emergence of television talk shows, the changes in Japan in 1993 reflected a shift of power from the conventional press to popular television programs such as *News Station* and *Sunday Project,* characterized by live political talk and interviews.

In 1992 Bill Clinton, battered by a series of accusations—sexual misconduct, drug use, and draft dodging—that would have destroyed most other politicians, survived partly because of his skillful use of live television programs and talk shows. Marvin Kalb, director of the Barone Center on the Press, Politics and Public Policy at the John F. Kennedy School of Harvard, explains: "He survived because he adopted a new approach. . . . The new approach was rather than deal with the traditional press, the Washington press corps, he decided to go around them. . . . He did this by going on programs like the Larry King show, by going on Arsenio and playing sax, by trying to convey a non-traditional political approach to the presidential campaign—and he succeeded."[36]

These talk shows represented a sharp departure from traditional press coverage. Previously candidates, if they had appeared on a talk show at all, had stuck with hard-news programs such as *Nightline* or *Meet the Press,* in which they faced tough questions from veteran political journalists who knew Washington. By contrast, in 1992 candidates Ross Perot, George Bush, and Bill Clinton regularly appeared on television talk shows: *Larry King Live, Today Show, 60 Minutes, Phil Donahue,* and *Arsenio Hall.* Indeed, for many television viewers, the most memorable moment in the 1992 campaign was Bill Clinton's saxophone performance on the *Arsenio Hall* show. Clinton later joked that such programs had "liberated" him from the traditional press.

Mark Gearan, director of communications in the Clinton White House, explains the Clinton media strategy: "Americans today learn from a variety of news sources. . . . It used to be the networks and newspapers. Now with specialty news programs, cable TV, wires . . . we've seen an explosion of new news organizations. We try to observe that. We try to think how people get information they want."[37]

Hosokawa and his fellow reformers clearly took a cue from the Clinton approach. When they were able to view politics without the filter of the *kisha* clubs, Japanese voters found that some politicians actually had interesting personalities. The new media kindled the interest of alienated voters who previously had cared little about politics. Yōhei Kōno, Miyazawa's successor as LDP leader, said recently, "For a long time it was said that our people were not interested in politics. I believe these television programs helped stir up political interest in the people."[38] Both in Japan and in the United States, 1992–1993 were watershed years in the relationship between the media and politics. The nontraditional media, which included television talk shows and interview programs, loosened the establishment media's grip on the portrayal of political leaders and the government. In both countries, power to influence public opinion shifted from the traditional network news in America and *kisha* club reporters in Japan toward nontraditional professional interviewers, such as Larry King and Sōichirō Tahara.

Backlash: The Japanese State Strikes Back

To some observers in the summer of 1993, the relationship between the press and politicians in Japan appeared to be converging with the U.S. model. "In general, Japan's mass media performed very much like the American press would have in a similar period of political uproar," concluded Reid of the *Washington Post*. "The shortfall in print coverage was largely filled by aggressive and innovative TV reporting. . . . Far from advocating the status quo or protecting the System, the Japanese press corps seemed, to this reader at least, to be hell-bent for change."[39]

Conservatives in Japan, however, saw this transformation as a plot. Masashi Nishizawa of *Nihon Keizai Shimbun* argued that media coverage of the elections was tilted too far in favor of the new parties. "Television stations in particular bordered on covering the new parties to an unreasonable extent," he wrote. "The coverage of Shinseitō was the most excessive." Noting that Shinseitō leader Hata made about thirty-five television appearances during the time when Shinseitō was being established, Nishizawa charged that "members of Shinseitō—who voted against Miyazawa—appeared on television practically every day."[40]

Some media critics, for example, were disturbed by what they deemed excessive use of one image that was unflattering to the LDP.

The controversial scene depicted Seiroku Kajiyama, then secretary general of the LDP, whispering to Koko Satō, chairman of the LDP Policy Coordination Committee and a key figure in the Lockheed bribery scandal. Aired repeatedly, this footage served as a vivid reminder of the conservative party's shadowy past.

In an article in *Bungei Shunjū,* Satō objected to the use of the image, which "made us seem like the evil men in the samurai movies." He protested, "This raises the question of whether television has been manipulating images to sway public opinion."[41] Such resentment over the way television covered politics gradually produced a backlash that exploded in the fall of 1993, after Tsubaki of TV Asahi boasted about television's new powers at a meeting of the National Broadcast Association. Tsubaki had said that he and his colleagues had been determined "to defeat the LDP in this election."[42]

As noted earlier, Tsubaki was summoned before a Diet committee on political reform for his comments. The hearing took place five days before TV Asahi was to have its license renewed by the Ministry of Posts and Telecommunications for five more years. Bowing deeply, Tsubaki apologized for "my unnecessary, indiscreet, and inappropriate remark." But when charged by the committee members with "unfair" and "distorted" reporting, he defended the TV Asahi reports, saying that its coverage of the election on July 18 adhered to the principles of fairness and neutrality. "It is true I held a personal view, but I never instructed my staff to carry it out." Asked his current occupation, he replied, "Currently unemployed." He had been forced to resign from TV Asahi. The hearing continued for several hours, with LDP members repeatedly criticizing Tsubaki and the former news executive repeatedly apologizing. During this time, the question of whether the LDP had used political pressure on the network was never raised.[43]

Because the session focused on Tsubaki's statements without examining TV Asahi's programming material, the session became more a forum for LDP members to vent their frustration than a critical examination of television coverage of the election. The *New York Times* wrote of the LDP's subpoena, "now the losers are out for revenge, trying to put the genie back in the television tube."[44] Reid of the *Washington Post* wrote, "TV Asahi's reporting was not any different from the other networks. The LDP was angry with the media in general and needed a scapegoat. Tsubaki's statement provided them that opportunity."[45]

The Diet proceedings triggered a protest from several key members of Nihon Minkan Hōsō Renmei. They argued that the Diet proceedings threatened the freedom of the press and resigned from the association hoping to bring public attention to the issue. In another show of protest, the nation's most famous television newscasters issued a joint statement denouncing the government effort to bring the media under control.[46]

The Tsubaki subpoena divided the Japanese press. The traditionally conservative press supported the subpoena and demanded more than an apology. The liberal press protested that the subpoena violated freedom of press and criticized Tsubaki and TV Asahi for complying with the government. Speaking shortly after Tsubaki's subpoena, a senior TV Asahi executive said, "We had to bow down in order to survive. We're facing enormous pressure and harassment right now from the Ministry of Posts and Telecommunication."[47]

Toshio Hara in *Shūkan Kinyōbi*, a magazine recently started by a group of journalists concerned with the future of Japanese journalism, wrote, "I've always feared that at the moment of government intervention, our media would split into the conservative *Sankei, Yomiuri,* against the liberal *Asahi, Mainichi.* As a result of Tsubaki's statement, my fears have come true."[48]

An editorial in *Newsweek International* criticized the split: "When there is government pressure, the press needs to stand up to it together."[49] Similarly at a journalists' meeting in Tokyo, Reid of the *Washington Post* spoke about how the *New York Times* had backed the *Washington Post* when President Nixon had tried to take away one of its affiliate stations during the Watergate uproar. Those sorts of observations by American journalists in Japan prompted a bleak assessment from one senior TV Asahi executive: "This is not America," he said. "Here in Japan, journalism is still years behind. We're back to where we were before. Nothing has changed."[50]

Political Fairness

The Tsubaki subpoena raised several crucial questions for the future of political reporting in Japan. In theory, Article 21 of the Japanese Constitution guarantees absolute freedom of speech. Newspapers and magazines are free to publish anything they wish. However, television and radio are regulated by the Broadcasting Law, which stipulates that because of their highly public nature, television stations should maintain political "fairness." Compliance with this law is a condition for obtaining a broadcasting license from the government. Government charges that TV Asahi had violated the Broadcasting Law served as the basis of Tsubaki's subpoena.

Keiichi Katsura, a professor at Tokyo University, has argued that the actions the government took—"demanding public disclosure of the private records from the Japan Commercial Broadcasting Association, issuing a subpoena, and threatening non-renewal of TV Asahi's broadcasting license"—violated Article 21. The Tsubaki subpoena, he claims, sets a dangerous precedent.[51] Two fundamental questions were debated after the subpoena: Should the government be responsible for licensing and enforcing broadcasting laws? Should political fairness be regulated at all?

In the United States the Federal Communications Commission (FCC), a neutral third party, regulates broadcasting. Until 1987 the FCC had what was called the Fairness Doctrine, similar to Japan's Broadcasting Law. The original rationale for this regulation was that only a limited number of broadcasters could use the air at one time. But modern technology has made this premise obsolete. With the spread of cable television, the Fairness Doctrine was abolished on the grounds that it stifled freedom of expression and thought.

Those who argue that Japan should follow the example of the United States say that political fairness cannot be regulated because any criticism of the government may be seen by the Ministry of Posts and Telecommunications as unfair or irresponsible. Only the people can determine whether what they see or read is fair. If they believe it to be unfair, they can switch to another channel or buy another paper. Those who argue that political fairness should be regulated say that if Japan abolishes the Broadcasting Law, more government intervention in television could result. Takashi Tachibana, an independent investigative reporter, says, "We know from Mr. Tsubaki's statements that TV Asahi had received a lot of pressure from the government in the past. Had there not been a Broadcasting Law, TV Asahi might have given in to their demands more easily." What needs to be done first of all, argues Tachibana, is to create an independent organization that regulates Japanese broadcasting.[52]

The Future

While the Tsubaki subpoena reminded private Japanese networks that they are still legally under the control of the Ministry of Posts and Telecommunications, in reality technology has freed them to a large degree from the government's watchful eye. Live television is difficult to regulate; once the images are on air, they cannot be called back. No previous screening or checking is possible. Many of the television programs that influenced Japan's political transformations—including *News Station* and *Sunday Project*—are live programs. TBS anchor Chikushi says, "Producers are in constant fear of protests from sponsors, but they can't do anything about it. Once we're on air live, we control everything."[53] No one can stop or change the programming of live television.

Television unleashed its power for the first time in the summer of 1993, tipping the political scale to topple a government that had monopolized power for nearly four decades. Its inexperience allowed it to break taboos, challenging the establishment and exposing the rotten roots of one-party rule. Its technology enabled young reformers to unlock the exclusive political world controlled by traditional journalists and political barons and to sell their ideas directly to the people. The transition of power was at first denied by the establishment that saw its power erode but was soon reluctantly accepted when it was clear that an irreversible change had occurred. What does this revolutionary change signify for the people of Japan?

If the American experience is any guide, the change will be a profound one. In the 1960s television news became an integral part of U.S. politics and changed the process from top to bottom. Television news helped build and destroy the careers of political leaders. After defeating Nixon in 1960, President John F. Kennedy commented, "It was television more than anything else . . . that turned the tide."[54] Now more than ever, politicians are obsessed with sound bites and image making. Indeed, campaigns are run through the newsrooms, and as a result agenda setting is often at the discretion of journalists. "Every political leader is judged in part by how well he or she can speak to people through the medium of the age," says pundit-cum-presidential counselor David Gergen. "Today that medium is television."[55] As Gergen's own prominence attests, keenly honed media skills have become a crucial weapon in the Washington power game.

As Japan struggles to redesign its power game, critics warn of the dangers of "television politics." Traditional intermediaries, such as political parties and print journalists, they contend, have helped maintain political stability in Japan. These critics fear the emergence of an ill-informed public led by television, an immature commercial medium driven by ratings and popular personalities.

These concerns merit debate, but they underestimate the democratizing effect of Japan's television revolution. In the summer of 1993 Japanese politics emerged from the smoke-filled back rooms of elite politicians and journalists, where it had been confined for decades, and reached out to ordinary, everyday people, who got a firsthand view of the problems and issues their nation faces. Political debate, which had been almost nonexistent in Japan, suddenly became popularized through television as politics entered voters' living rooms. The television revolution accelerated Japan's long march toward increased democracy. As Japan's political leaders struggle to create order out of the present political turmoil, the media will also struggle to define their new role. The question is whether politicians as well as journalists can put to best use the new democratizing power of television.

Notes

This chapter appeared in a somewhat different form as an Occasional Paper of the Program on U.S.–Japan Relations, Harvard University, 1994.

1. *Chūō Kōron,* October 1993, p. 31.
2. "TV fashizumu no jidai" (The Age of TV Fascism), *Bungei Shunjū,* December 1993, p. 144.
3. Ibid., p. 154. Yasuhiro Tase, political reporter of the *Nihon Keizai Shimbun,* first coined the term.
4. *Sankei Shimbun,* 23 October 1993.
5. *Sankei Shimbun,* 13 October 1993, p. 1.
6. Aiji Tanaka, "Media and Politics," *Asahi Shimbun,* 1 November 1993.
7. Leslie Helm, "All on Board," *Daily Yomiuri,* 1 May 1993, p. 8.
8. Shuntarō Torigoe, personal interview, 3 February 1994.
9. TV Asahi political reporter, personal interview, 10 August 1993. Interviewee was promised anonymity to promote frank and open discussion.
10. Lewis Simons, personal interview, 6 August 1993.
11. Kazu Ogawa, "Seijihōdō no genjō to mondaiten" (The Reality and Problems of Political Reporting), *Hō to Minshushugi* (Law and Democracy), November 1993, p. 9.
12. Tetsuya Chikushi, "Honmono no janarizumu wo mezashite" (Striving for Real Journalism), *Hō to Minshushugi,* November 1993, p. 34.
13. Toshio Wada, personal interview, 11 August 1993.
14. Keiji Shima, "Jimintō ni hōsō no chūritsu ga ieru no ka" (Does the LDP Have the Right to Talk about Neutral Broadcasting?), *Shūkan Asahi,* 5 November 1993, p. 32.
15. *New York Times,* 7 November 1993, p. 16.
16. Makoto Sataka, *Ekonomisuto,* 30 November 1993, p. 68.
17. Shunji Mikami, *The Role of Mass Media in the 1993 National Election in Japan* (Tokyo: Tōyō Daigaku Shakaibu, 1994), p. 49.
18. T. R. Reid, "Japan's Feisty New Press," *Nieman Reports,* Fall 1993, p. 15.
19. Ibid.

20. Jacob M. Schlesinger and Masayoshi Kanabayashi, "Japanese TV News Anchor's Antics Stirred Sentiment against Kanemaru," *Wall Street Journal,* 16 October 1992, p. A11.

21. "Terebi seiji no kōzai" (The Merits and Demerits of Television Politics), *Chūō Kōron,* November 1993, p. 33.

22. Sōichirō Tahara, "TV ga kimeru seiji" (Politics Dictated by TV), *Bungei Shunjū,* September 1993, p. 166.

23. Ibid., p. 164.

24. Tetsuya Chikushi, "Sutajio ni wa mamono ga hisonde iru" (There's a Beast in the Studio), *Chūō Kōron,* October 1993, p. 50.

25. Mikami, *The Role of Mass Media in the 1993 National Election in Japan,* p. 56.

26. "TV fashizumu no jidai," p. 156.

27. Chikushi, "Sutajio ni wa mamono ga hisonde iru," p. 54.

28. "Bijuaru senkyo, terebikyoku mo daigekisen" (The Visual Election), *Nihon Keizai Shimbun,* 18 July 1993, p. 18.

29. Ichirō Ozawa, personal interview, 11 August 1993.

30. *Ekonomisuto,* 5 October 1993, p. 53.

31. Ogawa, "Seijihōdō no genjō to mondaiten," p. 9.

32. Kaoru Moroi, "Kyodaikenryoku terebi no mujikaku wo tōu" (Questioning the Unconsciousness of Television Power), *Chūō Kōron,* November 1993, pp. 38–45.

33. Ozawa interview.

34. Jacob M. Schlesinger, "In Japan, the Torch Has Been Passed to a New In-group," *Wall Street Journal,* 10 August 1993.

35. Ibid.

36. Marvin Kalb, personal interview, 25 January 1994.

37. Mark Gearan, personal interview, 24 January 1994.

38. "Terebi seiji no kōzai," p. 32.

39. Reid, "Japan's Feisty New Press," p. 15.

40. Masashi Nishizawa, "Election Coverage Raises Bias Question," *Yomiuri Shimbun,* 21 July 1993, p. 3.

41. Koko Satō, "Tenkano akuyaku ōini kataru" (The Villain Speaks Out), *Bungei Shunjū,* December 1993, p. 158.

42. *Sankei Shimbun,* 23 October 1993.

43. T. R. Reid, "Tokyo Legislators Probe Press Bias," *Washington Post,* 26 October 1993.

44. David E. Sanger, "Japan's Old Guard Flails at the Talking Heads," *New York Times,* 7 November 1993, p. 16.

45. T. R. Reid, "The Constitution Is above the Law," *Shūkan Kinyōbi,* 12 November 1993, p. 34.

46. *Asahi Shimbun,* 26 October 1993, p. 1.

47. Senior executive at TV Asahi, personal interview, December 1993.

48. Toshio Hara, "Tsubaki hatsugen tekihatsu no shisō to masukomi no shisei" (The Thinking behind Accusations of Tsubaki's Statement and the Media's Response), *Shūkan Kinyōbi,* 12 November 1993, p. 31.

49. Bill Powell and Hideko Takayama, "Kikai naru ka Nihon no masukomi" (The Odd Japanese Media), *Newsweek International*, 27 October 1993.

50. Senior executive at TV Asahi, interview.

51. Keiichi Katsura, "Kōsei to jiyū wo ikani ryōritsu saseru ka" (How to Balance Freedom and Fairness), *Ekonomisuto*, 30 November 1993, p. 66.

52. Takashi Tachibana, "Media to seiji" (Media and Politics), *Asahi Shimbun*, 25 November 1993, p. 19.

53. Chikushi, "Sutajio ni wa mamono ga hisonde iru," p. 55.

54. Theodore H. White, *The Making of the President* (New York: Atheneum, 1961), p. 294.

55. David Gergen, personal interview, 24 January 1994.

6

Media and Policy Change in Japan

JOHN CREIGHTON CAMPBELL

IN the United States the mass media are often called the "fourth branch of government," on a par with the executive, legislative, and judicial branches. The Japanese mass media have similarly been called the "fourth authority" *(daiyon no kenryoku),* ranked along with the familiar power triumvirate of *sei-kan-zai,* or the ruling Liberal Democratic Party (LDP), the bureaucracy, and big business.[1] Their pervasive influence is well attested by leaders of various social groups who were asked in 1980 which groups had the most influence over daily life. The mass media *(masu komi)* were ranked number one, markedly higher than the bureaucracy, political parties, and big business, and they were given this top ranking by all the groups except journalists themselves.[2]

Why should the media be so powerful? A fundamental proposition of democracy is that the ultimate source of legitimacy is the opinion of the public. That government will be responsive to the public is fundamentally guaranteed by elections, of course, but elections occur infrequently and their messages about what people want and do not want are often ambiguous. On a day-to-day basis, the mass media operate as the most important link that conveys the preferences of society to the state.

My own experience over twenty years in conducting interviews about many public policy matters confirms the importance of this linkage. Time and time again a bureaucrat or politician would mention some desire or antipathy among the general public, and when asked how he or she knew, would nearly always answer, "The newspapers."[3] Everyone around the Japanese government seems to read three papers a day and to take from them his or her own notions of what problems facing the nation deserve attention and what might be done about them.

187

It would seem the media could virtually dictate the policy agenda to the government—or that an individual or group wanting to get something done or seeking some change in public policy would have no better strategy than to enlist the media as an ally. But here we find a contradiction. The political science literature contains many studies of media and politics, and many detailed case studies of particular governmental decisions. However, the former rarely discuss actual decision-making processes, and the latter usually mention the media only in passing, or in any case do not see them as an important direct cause of policy change.

On the one hand, political scientists who study the media tend to focus on what stories appear or on their effect on readers. "Agenda setting" is often mentioned, but it usually refers to what the general public thinks is important without much explicit attention to how such ideas impinge on government, except with regard to social movements.[4] On the other hand, with some distinguished exceptions, most studies of the decision-making process have focused on the direct causes of change and on what might be called the "enactment" stage, in which specific proposals are considered and fought over. Less attention has been paid to the more diffuse agenda-setting process by which social problems come to be seen as worthy of attention.[5]

Because it is at the agenda-setting stage that the media may be most important, studies employing conventional methodologies or conceptual frameworks may well have substantially underestimated the role of the media in policy change. A broad survey would produce fragmentary and perhaps quite misleading results. For this reason, I will not try to generalize across policy areas, but instead will concentrate on a single policy area: policy toward the elderly in the postwar era, which is a subject I have studied in some detail.[6] Along with environmental policy, this is probably the policy area in Japan in which the media have been most important as a cause of change. It therefore provides several good illustrations. Before undertaking this account, however, we need some theoretical perspective on how the media fit into the process of policy change.

Energy, the Media, and Policy Change

A useful metaphor for understanding policy change is to see governance as a billiard ball in motion, moving in a straight line in the sense that simple momentum will keep producing the same old policy day after day, year after year, unless some new force is applied.

Understanding policy change requires us to grasp how this force or energy is generated, as well as its "direction," or the goals being pursued. Such purposeful actions are not the only cause of policy change—for example, changes in the environment and simple accidents often affect policy—but we are here mainly interested in how individuals, groups, or institutions consciously try to change policy. Call them "sponsors" of issues or of policy proposals. Possible sponsors include political leaders, parties, groups of rank-and-file politicians, interest groups, social movements, governmental agencies, individual bureaucrats, academic experts, foreign countries, newspapers—any actor, inside or outside the governmental system, that seeks to start a new program, end an old one, or markedly alter the goals, methods, or size of some existing activity.

The sponsor's task is to mobilize enough force behind a policy idea to overcome inertia plus any opposition. Small matters or those on which there is not much disagreement require little energy; big or controversial issues require more. Occasionally a sponsor will have enough power to change policy on his or her own (for example, a chief executive with regard to some foreign policy matter), but most often support from other actors will be needed, and strategies must be devised to attain it. The key lies in deciding whom to try to attract. The sponsor will favor those who, first, have a great deal of power (or the potential for it) and, second, can be relied upon to support the sponsor's ideas.

Analyses of policy-making processes in the United States, Japan, and elsewhere often center on tracing how supporters, such as politicians or interest groups, are brought into a campaign to enact or oppose a new law or some other policy change. The process is sometimes called "coalition building," a term that evokes a legislature making decisions by majority vote. Most processes of policy change are more complicated and ambiguous, but they can nonetheless be seen as the mobilization of energy by attracting supporters.[7]

How do the media fit into this general picture? If our concern is policy change, we must look beyond the nagging of newspaper editors deploring corruption, secrecy, or insufficient attention to the public interest, or urging that the government behave more virtuously. Long-term espousal of some policy position, such as opposing high defense spending or favoring a more liberal policy toward China, also rarely shows up as a major factor in understanding why a concrete change in policy happened. The long-term climate of press opinion may help account for why some proposals never get aired at all, but it does not explain the processes of policy change.

On occasion, a newspaper or television station may itself take the role of a positive "policy-change sponsor." The media as a whole played a leading role in putting political ethics on the agenda and driving politicians from power during the scandals of the late 1980s and early 1990s (see chapter 5), but more narrowly focused examples can be found as well. The best is Hideo Ōtake's account of the 1969 automotive-safety recall issue, in which the newspaper *Asahi Shimbun* was the main protagonist.[8] As Michael Reich has noted, *Asahi* also came close to becoming a central protagonist in several pollution-related issues.[9] Media-led opposition to some initiative by the government can be even more significant; witness the press campaign against the Ōhira cabinet's indirect tax proposal, which is well described by Hiroshi Andō.[10] Indeed, as Yoshikazu Iwabuchi points out, the mass media can sell a negative image, such as Japan being "victimized" in U.S.–Japanese trade disputes, even without explicitly expressing any opinions.[11]

More such examples could be cited, but overall media organizations rarely push for policy change on their own,[12] and even in opposition to some proposal they are generally reflecting the views of other important social groups rather than initiating resistance. Their more important role is actually as an ally of some other sponsor of policy change, pro or con. For our purposes, it is useful to see the media less as an "actor" than as part of a strategy by other sponsors seeking to advance or oppose a proposal for policy change.

The media's strategic role is important, quite simply, because no supporter has more potential power than "the people." A proposal with "the people" behind it carries both democratic legitimacy and the practical promise of electoral benefits or costs. At the same time, it is difficult to get "the people" to sympathize, more difficult to get them to do anything positive, and hardest of all to keep them interested and active for more than a fleeting moment. This is why the media are potentially so powerful in a country like Japan, which Ikuo Kabashima and Jeffrey Broadbent have called a "referent pluralist" system.[13] That is, given the highly centralized nature of the newspapers and television networks plus the high levels of literacy and media consumption in society—plus the propensity noted above for Japanese decision makers to take press attention as a surrogate for public opinion—it would seem that no supporter of policy change would be a more attractive ally in Japan.

Often such positive uses of the media involve no more than providing them with routine advisory committee reports, giving briefings to friendly reporters, and staging "media events" aimed at gaining favorable coverage. Sometimes much more is involved. Japanese political scientist Jun'ichi Kyōgoku calls attention to how officials and politicians use the media to generate the sense of crisis necessary to shift the policy "mood" toward a new "common knowledge" that favors their objectives.[14] Richard Boyd provides a fine example: The phrases "structurally depressed sector" and "structural recession" were not much heard before June and July 1977, when officials began to use them; journalists picked them up as the new thing, and the phrases gained wide currency.[15] Recognition of this new conception of post–oil-shock economic problems was a necessary precondition for the Ministry of International Trade and Industry (MITI) to push its "Special Measures for the Stabilization of Specific Depressed Industries Law."

But from a policy sponsor's point of view, the potential power of the mass media as a supporter is offset by substantial costs and risks. The media are fickle, with short attention spans. A media campaign that does not succeed quickly will fail quickly. Moreover, it cannot be tried again soon—nothing looks more stale than last year's popular slogan. And the media are not just unreliable, they can be positively dangerous. Susan Pharr identifies the mass media with the anthropologists' idea of the "trickster," the jesters and fools of traditional society; tricksters may parody and criticize the status quo, but they are just as likely—if not even more so—to mock and undermine serious attempts to change the status quo as well (see chapter 1). Journalists may be concerned about truth, virtue, and the well-being of the nation or of themselves, but they are likely to be even more interested in making trouble.[16]

From the viewpoint of policy actors, then, the media threaten to bring a random, unpredictable, even irrational factor into what might otherwise be an orderly process of decision making. Understanding and controlling the decision-making process—who will be participating, when things will happen, what ideas will be prominent—is often the key to successful policy sponsorship. Sponsors find it hard to predict and harder to influence whether reporters will show up and when, and what aspects of an issue the media will emphasize. Partly, of course, this unpredictability stems from the public itself; it is not always easy to foresee how ordinary citizens will react to some idea, and the media will always be ready to follow a trend in public opinion. But to the bureaucrat, politician, or interest-group representative, it is the reporter who combines so much power with so much unpredictability, and thereby inspires so much fear.

For these reasons, although not much happens in modern politics without considerable attention paid to the media, many media strategies are essentially negative rather than positive. Attempts to channel or manipulate press attention are ubiquitous in the policy process, but many are defensive rather than offensive, aimed more at controlling damage than at maximizing support. In particular, Japanese politicians, government agencies, and other organizations typically maintain close relations with a closed group of reporters (formal or informal "press clubs") with whom they trade access, information, and other favors for predictability and some protection against what will be published and how.[17] These stable structures are of course designed to protect the status quo, but sponsors of policy change as well may be much more concerned with limiting than promoting media attention to their proposals, out of fear that the media might hurt them more than help them.

Despite the risks, however, positive media strategies are by no means uncommon. What conditions determine whether they are likely to be used? I will suggest three sets of conditions. The first set has to do with the motives of the sponsor. Positive media strategies are likely when reaching the mass public is an important goal, not just one possible means toward achieving policy change. For example, a politician who has some new proposal may be interested in enhancing his reputation with voters as much as, or more than, he is concerned with actually getting some program enacted. Or a sponsor may seek to bring about a change in the behavior of the public as well as of the government, such as more consideration for the handicapped or not drinking before driving. The media provide almost the only means for success in such cases.

The second set of conditions is whether or not the sponsor has good alternative strategies available. If sponsors cannot themselves catch the attention of the relevant decision makers, or if they cannot find reliable supporters with enough power to push through desired change, they are almost forced to turn to the media. Examples might include groups linked to opposition parties, which would be automatically disliked and excluded from influence by bureaucrats and politicians in power, or environmental protest groups.[18]

In Japan as elsewhere, however, relatively few policy changes are the direct result of such bottom-up, antagonistic social movements, and groups that are too radical will not likely get much cooperation from the establishment media in any case.[19] More common are examples of sponsors that are not really outsiders and may even be quite comfortably situated. These have enough power to counter threats to their position (which probably don't amount to much anyway), but when they want to change policy, or to get the government to do something or to stop doing something, they lack the power or the supporters to overcome opposition or even the simple inertia of existing policy. In the 1980s, the "administrative reform" period in Japan, Keidanren, Japan's leading business organization, needed the press to push its "fiscal reconstruction without a tax hike" slogan. Even a governmental ministry can find itself in this situation: a Labor Ministry official once told me that his agency relied heavily on "mood building" *(mūdo zukuri)* tactics to get new programs approved and to expand its budget precisely because it lacked strong support from interest groups and politicians. That meant coming up with clever ideas and backing them with plausible arguments and studies, as well as using direct public relations techniques. Such methods were not seen as working very well, but were considered to be the best available means.[20]

The third set of conditions concerns characteristics of the issue itself, as they affect a calculation of the costs and benefits of media strategies. A proposal will be attractive to the media, and thus make media strategies more beneficial and perhaps less dangerous to a sponsor, if it is easily understandable (not highly technical), human and concrete (not abstract), in line with conventional social values (does not make people uncomfortable), and benefits the public as a whole (not "special interests").

In summary, sponsors of policy change view using the media as a "second-best strategy," inferior to more reliable methods of mobilizing power, such as interest-group ties or political deals. When other resources are lacking, however, media strategies may be the best available, particularly when the issues involved are attractive to journalists. Often most important are defensive media strategies, aimed at preventing opponents from using the press to attack a proposal or, more generally, at insulating the decision-making process from the unpredictable and disruptive effects that media attention often brings. All these points are well illustrated by examining how policy toward the elderly developed in Japan.

The Media and the Elderly

Old-age policy is a good area for studying policy changes because there have been so many of them. In the period immediately following World War II there was almost no concern for the elderly as a special class, while today the "aging society" *(kōreika shakai)* is touted everywhere. Japan is hardly a welfare state on the Swedish model, but today its programs for older people (including pension, health care, employment, and others) compare favorably at least with those of the United States and Great Britain. All these programs are expensive: social security spending has risen to more than 15 percent of national income from about 5 percent of a much smaller total in the 1950s, and on the basis of existing legislation it is expected to exceed 25 percent by 2010.[21] While social security also covers spending on the poor, the handicapped, and so forth, most of this growth has been in programs for the elderly. How did this happen?

The development occurred in three stages, in response to a series of problems addressed by the Japanese government. The first could be called the "aging problem" *(rōgo mondai)*, the need to provide for the future retirement of current workers, associated with the development of pension programs in the 1950s and 1960s. Second was the "old-people problem" *(rōjin mondai)*, the plight of those already old, which began in the 1960s and peaked in a rapid expansion of many programs for the aged in the early 1970s. After the economic slowdown caused by the oil shock, attention turned to the "aging-society problem" *(kōreika shakai mondai)*, the burden on the society and the economy caused by the need to care for the growing numbers of the elderly. This problem led to attempts to cut back or at least rationalize programs for the elderly, proposed from 1975 and enacted in the administrative reform era of the early 1980s. Incidentally, more recently Japan has again moved to a more expansive posture, trying to deal with all three old-age-related policy problems at once. These varied experiences offer ample materials to examine the role of the media in policy change.

We would expect that role to be extensive, given the three sets of conditions outlined above. Consider the case of the "old-people problem" in the early 1970s. First, characteristics of the issue itself: the elderly are an exceptionally attractive group for the media. Unlike the handicapped, they are not "different" from the rest; everyone will one day be old. Both traditional and modern values—Confucianism and welfarism—dictate special regard for the elderly. The rationales that those who built Japan should not be suffering and that Japan is far behind the West in welfare policy are clear and persuasive. Finally, old people are photogenic—*kawaii obāchan* (adorable grandmas) are a mainstay of magazines and television.

Second, those seeking more programs for the elderly have often lacked direct strategies. The elderly do not appear to vote as a bloc, and they are difficult to organize politically, especially in Japan. The Federation of Old People's Clubs has an enormous membership and has sometimes been mentioned as an important interest group, but in fact its political pressure has been aimed mainly at protecting its own small government subsidy. Service-provider groups such as the National Social Welfare Council are well organized but small and not very powerful outside their limited domain. The relative lack of interest-group support has meant that rank-and-file politicians have not seen old-age issues as closely connected with either votes or campaign contributions for themselves. While the LDP's social welfare *zoku* (Diet members' policy group) is powerful, it has generally been more interested in medical care (particularly protection of the interests of physicians) than in old-age issues. Even the opposition socialist parties—not the best route to influence in any case—have been less reliable supporters than one would expect, given their key role in European welfare states, because for historical reasons they have concentrated more on foreign policy and civil rights than on social policy. Labor unions have been somewhat more consistent supporters, but their efforts have often been undercut by narrow concerns for their members' interests. And notwithstanding some foreign criticism of the economic advantage Japan gained by low social expenditure (welfare dumping), *gaiatsu* (external pressure) was not an important factor.

This list is oversimplified; at specific junctures many actors have been influential in old-age policy making. But it suggests that compared with many other areas in which there has been considerable policy change—agriculture, small business, industrial policy, financial liberalization—the area of old-people policy is relatively lacking in the more direct methods of mobilizing power.

Third, although old-people policy is not a good area for direct appeals to particular constituencies, it has potential for appealing to voters in general. A prime minister or a political party wants to be seen as doing something for such a deserving group (compared with, say, doctors). Also, old-age specialists are naturally eager to heighten regard for the elderly among ordinary people. Because the mass media are the only way to communicate with the general public, one can expect to find attempts to gain media coverage for reasons beyond simply trying to bring about policy change.

For all these reasons, positive media strategies should play a particularly important role in policy changes that involve expansion of programs for the aged, with negative strategies becoming critical when cutbacks or consolidations are on the agenda. We will find ample support for both propositions. Further, the first wave of change in policy toward the elderly illustrates two additional propositions: participants will prefer safer strategies when they are available, and reliance on the media can be very dangerous.

The Aging Problem and the Expansion of Pensions

During the 1950s and 1960s several pension programs were set up or substantially reorganized and enlarged to deal with the problem of how current workers would be supported after retirement. These important policy changes fall into four patterns with regard to their relationship to the media.[22]

First, the Employee Pension established in 1954 was actually a reconstruction of a prewar system made unworkable by postwar inflation. The initiative was taken by the Ministry of Health and Welfare, which negotiated a series of compromises with the employers' association (Nikkeiren), the labor unions, and the Ministry of Finance. This policy change received relatively little publicity, apparently because none of the participants saw enough advantage to its own interests to warrant mobilizing mass political energies, even though the program would affect nearly half the population of Japan. The participants may have feared pressure from those not covered (especially farmers) or "irrational" interventions by political parties. In any case, despite the size and importance of this program, virtually all decision making was confined within narrow boundaries; the outcome was a quiet deal among the actors most directly concerned.

Second, several campaigns by powerful interest groups resulted in special pension programs for their members or advantageous treatment within larger programs. These included the initiation of Mutual Assistance Associations by private school teachers (1953) and agricultural cooperative employees (1958); a "farmers' pension" program aimed at encouraging retirement as well as better benefits (1969), sponsored mainly by the Chamber of Agriculture pressure group; tax breaks for private pensions (1951, 1962) and then provision for "contracting out" of the Employee Pension into new Employee Pension Funds (Kōsei Nenkin Kikin) (1965), all pushed by Nikkeiren representing big business employers. All these proposals encountered substantial opposition, but their proponents did not rely on media strategies for two reasons. They knew that appeals to the media might backfire, since "special interests" were being advanced, and they knew that this second-best strategy was not really needed because the group could get what it wanted by mobilizing its supporters among politicians or bureaucratic agencies.

The third case was the National Pension, created in 1959 to cover nonemployees. The main sponsor was Prime Minister Nobusuke Kishi, who saw it as a way for the newly created LDP to strengthen its appeal to farmers and more generally to respond to the threat from the Japan Socialist Party (JSP) with people-oriented programs. ("Pensions for everyone" [*kai nenkin*] was a major slogan in the 1958 election campaign.) These motivations required publicity.

Once the newspapers have been attracted to an idea, however, they need something to write about. When neither LDP policy organs nor the Ministry of Health and Welfare (MHW) could come up with convincing, concrete plans very quickly, media attention was drawn to squabbling among bureaucrats, experts, interest groups, and politicians. The result of this intense but confusing coverage was Japan's first grass-roots social movement among potential beneficiaries of an old-age program, which ironically was a movement *against* the National Pension (mainly among farmers, who protested having to make contributions). The National Pension was enacted anyway, but it was very poorly designed; problems with its inadequate financial provisions, separation from the Employee Pension, and the unworkable system of voluntary enrollment by housewives plagued Japanese decision makers for the next thirty years and were only partially solved by the 1985 pension reform.

A key factor in the National Pension case was timing. The issue came up when tensions were rising over the United States–Japan Security Treaty, the "reverse course" against Occupation-era democratization reforms, and Prime Minister Kishi's high-handed leadership. Perhaps it was inevitable that all these political energies could not be excluded from the pension decision-making process; in particular, both the JSP and Kishi's factional rival Ichirō Kōno were delighted to use the National Pension and anything else at hand to attack the administration. But the case was also a failure of policy sponsorship. Creating a new pension system is a formidable undertaking in technical and political terms. Unless the decision-making process is carefully managed, pressures may build up and disrupt reasonable policy development—both the process of thinking up ideas and that of arranging the compromises necessary to secure agreement.[23] In particular, the media, once given their head, can be very disruptive.

Finally, the fourth pattern demonstrates that this lesson was not lost on MHW's Pension Bureau, which ten years later turned its attention to improving benefits in both the Employee and National Pensions. Campaigns for the "¥10,000 pension" and "¥20,000 pension" were carried out during the regular 1966 and 1969 budget processes. These campaigns were quite narrowly focused, orchestrated by the Pension Bureau, and based mainly on support from local government officials and a large but quite passive group of LDP Diet members. There was little opposition to these rather moderate proposals, so that limited pressure was enough without the risk of politicizing pension issues by bringing in the mass media.

Pension policy changes up to the early 1970s thus illustrate the point that even with a relatively popular issue, sponsors will often not turn to media strategies. The National Pension case illustrated why concerns over turning to the media are justified.

The Old-People Problem and the "Boom"

After 1960 the media were not a significant factor in any sort of old-age policy until the early 1970s, when they played a crucial role in an extraordinarily rapid and large-scale policy expansion. Between 1969 and 1976, the percentage of national income devoted to social security jumped from 5.6 to 10.5 percent. Much of this growth was due to two big policy changes: a major increase in pension benefits (for example, from ¥20,000 to ¥50,000 per month in the Employee Pension) and a new program of "free" medical care for the elderly. These policy changes were discussed and decided from the summer of 1971 to the end of 1972 and then took effect in 1973, which became known as *fukushi gannen*, or the "first year of the welfare era."[24]

The story goes back to the early 1960s. In and around the passage of the Welfare Law for the Aged in 1963, several very small service programs for the elderly had been initiated by the Social Affairs Bureau of MHW, and the Welfare of the Aged Division was established. The process was mainly confined to social welfare specialists. Some lower-level opposition and LDP politicians were involved, but not the leaders, and there was little mass media coverage. The law, in effect, created a new organizational and policy niche, leading to the development of an "old-age welfare policy community" comprising MHW bureaucrats, several service-provider interest groups under the umbrella of the National Federation of Social Welfare Councils, a growing number of academic social gerontologists, and a few sympathetic rank-and-file Diet members. Year by year existing programs were expanded and some new ones added. The specialists devoted much of their energy to discovering new ideas about the problems of the elderly and possible solutions, mostly by studying overseas programs.

This process had begun with a relatively narrow conception of the old-people problem, one appropriate to the range of potential solutions within the purview of the Social Affairs Bureau. Over time, as its officials and their growing number of allies thought about the issue, they came to see new aspects of the problem that required solutions in the policy areas of pensions, health care, employment, housing, and education. When they approached the agencies in charge of these policy areas, however, they were ignored. All the old-age specialists had were ideas; they lacked the resources even to catch the attention of those in other specialized areas, let alone push them into starting programs with their own money, or to fight for additional funds for these purposes. The amount of money needed to meet the apparent problems of the elderly was so large that a major commitment by political leaders would be necessary.

The main challenge was to take the old-people problem beyond the narrow confines of the old-age policy community and onto a broader policy agenda. If the beneficiaries of the intended policy change had been farmers, veterans, retail shopowners, or local governments—groups that were already politically sophisticated and well organized—the obvious next step would have been to mobilize electoral pressure on LDP Diet members and let them carry the case to the party leadership, the prime minister, and the Ministry of Finance. As noted above, however, the case of the elderly was not well suited for such direct techniques. Therefore, a media-based "mood building" strategy was adopted.

Members of the policy community worked hard on publicity. The entry on old-age welfare in MHW's 1966 White Paper was fourteen pages long, more than twice the length of the previous year's entry. Several bureaucrats wrote magazine articles, notably the "specialist" official of the Welfare of the Aged Division, Mikio Mori.[25] Mori also played a more indirect role: in the late 1960s he spoke at length with the famous social-problem novelist Sawako Ariyoshi, after she had encountered the old-age problem in newspaper stories and called MHW for more information. The resulting book about a family trying to deal with a senile old man, *Man in Ecstasy,* became the number-one bestseller in Japan in 1972 and is remembered by many as the reason they first thought about old people.[26] Full of facts on problems and programs, it reads in spots like a bureaucatic white paper.

But such indirect media strategies were not enough, and in 1968–1970, MHW officials, the National Federation staff, and several academic experts cooperated closely in a variety of tactics aimed directly at attracting the attention of newspapers and television. These included the following:

A major Economic Planning Agency report on the old-people problem expressing (as the former MHW official who headed the project put it in an interview) the overwhelming need to "raise consciousness" *(kanshin wo takameru)* (September 1968).

A massive nationwide survey of the bedridden aged, a highly dramatized targeting of the group within the elderly most likely to attract broad public sympathy (reported December 1968).

A Central Social Welfare Council project calling for a national consensus and comprehensive government planning to aid the elderly (1969–1970).

The National Conference for a Rich Old Age, a replication of the successful American media event called the White House Conference on Aging, in which participants from all over Japan discussed for three days an agenda drawn up by MHW (1970).

A special cover-story report in the annual MHW White Paper (1970).

The lead in the latter three efforts was taken by Hideo Ibe, an entrepreneurial MHW official who had become chief of the Social Affairs Bureau in 1969. When asked in a 1976 interview about the origins of the National Conference for a Rich Old Age, Ibe said that up until then policy for the elderly had been limited to low-income people, the bedridden, and so forth. "I saw the need to think about all old people, or all society. . . . There was little interest in old people even in the Welfare Ministry, no 'problem consciousness.'" Ibe's motivation was to raise the status (and budget) of the Social Affairs Bureau by attaching it to an issue with potentially great popular appeal. His strategy paid off. By stimulating reporters to notice the old-people problem and then providing them with ideas about solutions, these efforts helped touch off a real "boom" in media coverage and public opinion.

The process of building this "boom" was subtle and can be seen in the different patterns among three indicators of attention. First, the number of articles on gerontology or old-age policy problems in specialized magazines and newsletters began to grow in 1967, and growth continued at a rapid and steady pace. Second, coverage in the regular mass-market newspapers peaked sharply in 1970–1971. Third, as revealed by a periodic opinion poll, the percentage of the public who selected "completion of social security" *(shakai hoshō jūjitsu)* as their top priority among several policy choices jumped from 9 percent to 20 percent from 1969 to 1970—the biggest one-year shift ever in this survey. This figure rose further to 25 percent in 1972 (actually during 1971, since all these surveys were taken in January). A jump in just two years from one-tenth to one-quarter of Japanese voters picking social security as their number-one policy desire is quite impressive.[27]

The relationships among these three indices are more complex than one-way cause and effect. In particular, the surge in public opinion was no doubt a cause as well as an effect of mass media coverage—the newspapers stepped up their coverage when their stories were well received. Similarly, media coverage and public opinion were not the sole causes of policy change. But it is highly suggestive that the period of top-level discussion and decision making (summer 1971–December 1972) was preceded by so substantial an increase in media and public attention to the elderly.[28] That was precisely what Ibe and others interested in old-age welfare policy had set out to achieve.

Not readily apparent at the time, however, was an inherent weakness in basing a strategy for policy change on mass media and the general public. Policy specialists are solution-oriented, but the mass media and general public tend to be attracted to problems. The community of those interested in old-age welfare policy had developed an agenda of desired solutions and took pains to include these in all its public relations efforts. However, none of these received much attention from newspapers or television. Instead, the mass media put the emphasis on the neglected virtues of respect for the aged, on how much today's prosperous Japan owed to the efforts of those now retiring, on the desperate plight of many elderly as evidenced by high suicide rates, and on the social policy "gap" with other advanced countries. These concerns were immediately translated into demands for government policy, but the demands were not attached to the solutions the promoters had in mind.

The best example is health care. In the 1960s the specialized policy community had carefully nurtured a proposal to meet the health care needs of the elderly with a differentiated system of specific services to treat geriatric diseases and chronic conditions, with a heavy emphasis on preventive medicine and health maintenance. Several programs reflecting this public health approach, such as free physical examinations by government doctors and a subsidy for cataract operations, had already been initiated. But this issue area was soon captured by outsiders, notably Tokyo governor Ryōkichi Minobe, who largely on his own initiative started a program that simply reimbursed doctors for all charges to nearly all patients aged seventy or above.

The Tokyo plan, addressing as it did the simple problem of costs, was much more appealing than MHW's argument that the health needs of the elderly would not be met by simply pumping more money into a medical system that was oriented toward curing acute illness and contained financial incentives for hospitalization and heavy drug prescription. The concept of "free" medical care received extensive media coverage and diffused rapidly among other local governments, resulting in intense pressure on the central government. The LDP responded in 1972 with a nationwide program that was actually enacted over the objections of MHW. Its heavy costs severely inhibited the development of programs in rehabilitation and other chronic medical treatment, long-term institutional care, and in-home services—the jurisdiction of the Social Affairs Bureau—that were strongly favored by old-age specialists but lacked much public appeal.

Incidentally, another effect of intensive media coverage can be observed during the "old-people boom." In 1971–1976, more than fifty small programs for the elderly were initiated by the Japanese government, most of them by agencies that previously had shown little interest in the problems of older people—for example, the Agriculture, Labor, Posts and Telecommunications, and Home Affairs ministries and the National Land Agency. In nearly all these cases, it was by reading the newspapers that officials came to think that the old-people problem deserved attention and that proposing a new program in that area would probably meet with success. Despite the near absence of pressure from interest groups or politicians, these small peripheral programs increased at a much higher rate than did social service programs in this period.[29]

One is tempted to conclude that the old-age policy community won the war but lost the battle. It is ironic that a mood-building strategy that succeeded brilliantly in bringing a problem to the national agenda should then have failed to lead to solutions that brought much direct benefit to its sponsors. The media truly can be "tricksters."

The Aging-Society Problem

Handling the media is likely to be trickier still for policy sponsors seeking to cut back rather than expand popular programs. After the 1973 oil shock and the shift from rapid to moderate economic growth, the Finance Ministry, the Economic Planning Agency, and others concerned with the nation's fiscal health began pointing with alarm at the implications of the welfare expansion of the early 1970s. The key slogan was the "aging-society problem" *(kōreika shakai mondai),* which focused not on the plight of the elderly but rather on the burdens being placed on the economy and society by the ever growing old-age population. Along with calls to "reexamine welfare" *(fukushi minaoshi)* or to develop a "Japanese-style welfare society" *(Nihongata fukushishakai)* that would rely on traditional supports and avoid the "English disease" of overdependence on government, this phrase appeared frequently in newspaper, magazine, and television reports through the second half of the 1970s and soon became the conventional wisdom.[30] Clearly, this was a very effective media strategy.

However, the first serious attempt at policy change ended in humiliating failure. In 1979 MHW was pushed by the Ministry of Finance into suddenly proposing that the age for receiving the Employee Pension be raised gradually from sixty to sixty-five, which was supposed to cut outlays by some 20 percent by the year 2000. Media strategies were not carefully considered, and this particular reform effort turned out to be extremely vulnerable. The idea of waiting five more years was distasteful to many workers, and further the proposal played directly against two "gaps" that labor unions and the opposition parties had already publicized intensively in opposing conservative attacks on social welfare. One gap was between the mandatory retirement age of fifty-five in most companies and the age for eligibility for pensions; the other (called *kanmin kakusa*) was between the generous treatment given retiring government officials and the lower benefits at a later age available to private employees. Although the government was implementing partial remedies for both these gaps, its efforts lacked the media appeal of such easy-to-understand "fairness" issues.

The result was that the age-hike proposal met with so hostile a reaction from LDP as well as opposition politicians that it had to be withdrawn from the Diet six weeks after formal cabinet approval—a disaster for the bureaucrats in charge.

After this débâcle the perception throughout the government was that tinkering with entitlement programs is dangerous and that large reductions may be impossible. Nonetheless, just five years later, a major reform of the pension system was achieved, which reorganized the entire pension system and restrained projected future benefits substantially. The most remarkable aspect of this process was that it proceeded at MHW's "pace." There was little serious opposition, and discussion in both the mass media and the Diet focused almost exclusively on the problems and solutions formulated within the ministry.

Why were the experiences of 1980 and 1985 so different? One reason is that to avoid media exploitation of the "gaps," MHW was clever enough in 1985 not to include the pensionable age hike in its reform, although a future hike was called for in the legislation (this was postponed again in 1990, for similar reasons).[31] Nonetheless, it does seem strange that the media were quite so cooperative. For example, two points were barely mentioned, even though a great many people were affected by them: first, projected benefits for many future recipients were being reduced by one-third, compared with what they would have received if the system had not been reformed; second, longer periods of contributions would be required for eligibility. Also, single employees, and especially all self-employed people, appeared quite disadvantaged compared with married employees; one would think this should have become a "fairness" issue ready-made for editorial writers.[32]

Some credit for the bureaucrats' success in minimizing press opposition belongs to positive media strategies pursued by Pension Bureau chief Shinichirō Yamaguchi. He talked frequently with reporters and had his bureau prepare a barrage of brochures on the pension "crisis," with lots of simple charts and cartoons. The master stroke was a brand-new public relations device: a detailed opinion survey called "Survey of Intellectuals concerning 'Pensions in the 21st Century,'" administered by mail to 1,000 leaders in late 1982. This tactic had been opposed by many of Yamaguchi's colleagues, who preferred more traditional negative media strategies. Said one:

> What do you do if the answers to the survey are different from the ministry's ideas? It's rash and stupid. That's why there was so much opposition. That is, when you want to carry out a reform that is tough on the public, you have to make it so the problems are difficult to see, make it as confused and vague as possible, then cut a deal with the opposition parties behind the scenes, and slip it through fast. That's only common sense. Deliberately revealing everything in your hand—

all the problems, everything the public will hate—is the dumbest of the dumb. It will make the possible impossible—that's what they all thought.[33]

In the event, the survey was not that dangerous. Although the questions were detailed, their wording, the selections of answers provided, and the accompanying forty-seven-page explanation of pension problems were designed so that embarrassing results were unlikely. The results by and large endorsed the Pension Bureau's views about reform, and the survey was well covered in the press, publicizing not only the seriousness of the pension "crisis" but also the bureaucrats' specific proposal and its rationale.

Another key factor was that Yamaguchi worked hard at prenegotiations *(nemawashi)* with nearly everyone concerned with pensions. This meant, first, that many of those with enough expertise to effectively criticize the proposal were already on board and, second, that potential opponents (especially the labor unions) were induced to press for specific concessions rather than mounting a press campaign against the entire plan. Without a real sponsor leading the opposition, journalists were on their own. They found it difficult to cope with bureaucratic expertise on so technical an issue—especially when MHW worked hard to portray it as densely technical.[34]

Perhaps the fundamental factor, however, was the eventual success of the decade-long media campaign to convince the Japanese public of the importance of the "aging-society problem" of having to support so many elderly people in the future. It was helpful that this slogan had become an important theme of the Administrative Reform campaign of the early 1980s, constantly reiterated as a justification for cutting "wasteful" public spending. This success put potential opponents of pension reform and other welfare consolidations on the defensive, since they were obliged to say how they themselves would deal with the aging-society problem. Only the MHW bureaucrats had a solution that seemed plausible to the media and the public.

In the usual dialectical irony of media strategies, however, the very success of the campaign to justify welfare cutbacks by talking about the burdens of the elderly soon undercut itself. The Ministry of Finance was the victim. It had long sought a new value-added or consumption tax, but by the mid-1980s it found that arguments about stable revenue sources or the fairness of indirect taxes had little appeal for the media or public. The ministry therefore picked up on the "aging-society problem" as the main justification for the new tax: the government had to get ready for all the old people. Opposition parties and newspaper editorial writers understandably responded that this appeal was quite abstract, with no indication of how the money would actually be spent. Facing a general election in which the consumption tax would be the number-one issue, the LDP came up with a new "Gold Plan" or "Ten-Year Strategy for Old-Age Health and Welfare" (Kōreisha Hoken Fukushi Suishin Jūkanen Senryaku) to attach to its tax-reform proposal. In television debates LDP spokespersons heralded this plan, which called for a major expansion of home helpers, nursing home beds, and so forth, as a justification for the tax, and the party pushed substantial increases in the MHW 1990 budget for such programs.[35] The "aging-society problem" slogan had actually led to an expansion of programs and the inevitable increase in burdens.

Conclusions

It used to be said in the Reagan White House that there is no such thing as a free lunch, especially if you are dining with the press. This survey of forty years of important changes in policy toward the elderly demonstrates that while media strategies have often been important to policy-change sponsors (or opponents), they can also be a double-edged sword. That the 1959 National Pension was so poorly designed is due in part to its becoming a media circus. That is why those who have enough resources will try to get what they want without the media, as was true in many of the pension-policy changes of the 1950s and 1960s. The key lesson here—one well learned by Pension Bureau director Yamaguchi in the 1980s—is that a sponsor of policy change has to think carefully about both negative and positive, or defensive and offensive, media strategies.

Such considerations about media strategies are important in nearly all policy areas, although the mix of strategies chosen will vary depending on circumstances. These show up with unusual clarity in the old-age area precisely because, for the reasons noted above, it is an unusually "people oriented" case. A comparison with environmental problems will make the point, since this is the area most often seen as a policy response to public pressure.

In the environmental case, one can see the various citizens' movements *(shimin undō)* as the sponsor for policy change, which then signed up the media as an ally. Michael Reich has described the close relationship between *Asahi Shimbun's* special antipollution "team" and movement activists in the early 1970s.[36] It is important to note that representing "the people" in this sense does not require much support from the general public to be effective—overall public opinion appeared relatively indifferent to pollution.[37] Direct political pressure in several important local areas (especially as exemplified by antipollution politicians winning local elections) plus support from the press adds up to "the voice of the people" in the eyes of decision makers. Incidentally, direct pressure from local governments, including the problem they presented for the central government by enacting more stringent regulations than theoretically allowed by law, was another very important cause of the burst of pollution legislation in 1970.[38]

The old-people case was different. There was little in the way of a large-scale social movement, and to the extent that the media were enlisted by a sponsor of policy change, that sponsor was a government agency (the Social Affairs Bureau) and its surrounding old-age policy community. For a government agency and its allies to use public relations as a weapon in a dispute with another agency is quite common, and the effort includes such devices as articles based on White Papers, advisory commission reports, and even a "national conference."[39] The key difference in the old-people-policy boom was the public response. The readiness of ordinary Japanese to see the elderly as a problem not only for themselves personally but also for the nation and the government was reflected in the poll results cited above and in letters to the editor and other indicators of readers' or viewers' intense interest in a story. No doubt that intense interest explains the speedy growth of media coverage. I would argue that this "boom" in media attention and public opinion was itself the primary cause of the major policy changes of "free" medical care and the enormous pension benefit increase, with pressure from local governments or other interest groups a secondary factor.

This interpretation differs, at least in emphasis, from the argument by American political scientist Gerald Curtis and others that the expansion of "quality of life" programs, such as environmental and social welfare policy, in the early 1970s was a deliberate strategy on the part of the LDP to attract a new, urban constituency.[40] Although I would not deny that LDP support for such expansion was crucial and that leaders such as prime minister and LDP kingpin Kakuei Tanaka may well have been worrying about attracting young and urban voters, I would put less weight on tactical maneuvers from above and greater weight on the surge of real pressure from below, as represented by media coverage. Indeed, a ruling political party would have to be inept not to respond to the "boom" of press coverage of both pollution and the "old-people problem" in the early 1970s.

In both these cases, the media ably represented "the people," though in somewhat different senses. But it should not be concluded that the media are any more dependable representatives of the "public interest" than they are dependable allies of specific sponsors of policy change. In the twin pension-reform cases of 1979 and 1985, media opposition was immediate and substantial against the age-hike proposal of 1979. Yet the same mass media allowed MHW to push through several strong reforms in 1985 with relatively little dissent. The differences had little to do with how many people were concerned or how seriously they were affected. Rather, the key factors were whether issues were simple or complicated, whether the bureaucrats in charge paid careful attention to media strategies, and whether a "sponsor" appeared on the opposition side.

The lesson, again, is that the media are tricksters, supporting one moment but mocking the next, essentially unreliable. When the media are drawn to an issue, they bring unpredictability and danger. In a sense, this makes them the natural ally of change rather than of the status quo. As many sponsors of policy change have discovered, however, what sorts of policy changes will be favored by media involvement cannot always be controlled. The media are a powerful but undependable ally.

Notes

A revised version of this chapter was published in Japanese: "Media to sei-saku tenkan: Nihon no kōreisha taisaku" (Media and Policy Change: Policy toward the Elderly in Japan), *Leviathan* 7 (Fall 1990): 49–74.

1. Hiroshi Andō, *Sekinin to genkai: Akaji zaisei no kiseki* (Responsibility and Limits: The Mystery of Deficit Finance), vol. 2 (Tokyo: Kinyū Zaisei Jijō Kenkyūkai, 1987), p. 250. *Sei* stands for *seitō* (the ruling party); *kan*, for *kanryō* (bureaucracy); *zai*, for *zaikai* (big business).

2. The Japanese version of the question was: "Kaki no shogurūpu ga wareware no seikatsu ni dono teido eikyōryoku o motte iru." See Ikuo Kabashima and Jeffrey Broadbent, "Referent Pluralism: Mass Media and Politics in Japan," *Journal of Japanese Studies* 12, no. 2 (Summer 1986): 329–361.

3. Public opinion polls are frequent and include many questions pertaining to public policy. Yet few people mention them in conversation, and even when prompted by specific questions, most cannot cite survey results. Incidentally, television was not often mentioned in a general sense, but sometimes a recent program (generally an NHK "special") would be noted as a focus of public attention.

4. A classic account is that of Robert W. Cobb and Charles D. Elder, *Participation in American Politics: The Dynamics of Agenda-Building* (Baltimore: Johns Hopkins University Press, 1972). For a more recent American account of methodological and substantive issues, see Shanto Iyengar and Donald R. Kinder, *News That Matters: Television and American Opinion* (Chicago: University of Chicago Press, 1988).

5. An exception is John W. Kingdon, *Agendas, Alternatives, and Public Policies* (Boston: Little, Brown, 1984). In the Japan field, note that an excellent recent book of essays on the policy process, aimed in part at demonstrating how much influence unorganized groups have attained over public policy, does not have an entry for "media" in its index, and the subject is not taken up systematicallly in the text: Gary D. Allinson and Yasunori Sone, *Political Dynamics in Contemporary Japan* (Ithaca: Cornell University Press, 1993).

6. This research is reported in John Creighton Campbell, *How Policies Change: The Japanese Government and the Aging Society* (Princeton, N.J.: Princeton University Press, 1992.)

7. An extreme example would be the use of *gaiatsu* (external pressure) by the Foreign Ministry or the Ministry of International Trade and Industry, to enlist U.S. support to carry out some policy change facing political and bureaucratic opposition.

8. Hideo Ōtake, *Gendai Nihon no seiji kenryoku keizai kenryoku* (Political Power and Economic Power in Contemporary Japan) (Tokyo: San'ichi Shobō, 1979), pp. 25–68.

9. See Michael Reich, "Troubles, Issues, and Politics in Japan: The Case of Kanemi Yushō" and "Crisis and Routine: Pollution Reporting by the Japanese Press," in *Institutions for Change in Japanese Society,* ed. George DeVos (Berkeley: Institute of East Asian Studies, University of California, 1984), pp. 114–165; and Susan J. Pharr and Joseph L. Badaracco, Jr., "Coping with Crisis: Environmental Regulation," in *America versus Japan,* ed. Thomas K. McCraw (Boston: Harvard Business School Press, 1986), pp. 229–259.

10. Andō, *Sekinin,* pp. 253–259.

11. Yoshikazu Iwabuchi, "Nichibei masatsu mondai ni okeru masu media no yakuwari" (The Role of the Mass Media in U.S.–Japanese Trade Frictions) *Leviathan* 12 (Spring 1993): 161–172.

12. Compare Kingdon's observation for the United States that the "media report on what is going on in government, by and large, rather than having an independent effect *on* governmental agendas" (*Agendas,* p. 62 [emphasis in original]).

13. Kabashima and Broadbent, "Referent Pluralism."

14. See Jun'ichi Kyōgoku, *Nihon no seiji* (Japanese Politics) (Tokyo: Tokyo Daigaku Shuppankai, 1983); and Kyōgoku, *The Political Dynamics of Japan* (Tokyo: Tokyo University Press, 1987).

15. Richard Boyd, "The Political Mechanisms of Consensus in the Industrial Policy Process: The Shipbuilding Industry in the Face of Crisis, 1973–1978," *Japan Forum* 1, no. 1 (April 1989): 1–17, at p. 6.

16. The media have often trivialized the messages of feminist groups and other protest movements, even though journalists no doubt shared many of their values. The media have attacked even environmental groups (with which they are generally sympathetic) for opportunism or "egoism." For an example, see David Groth's analysis of the movement to oppose Shinkansen noise pollution (this volume, chapter 7).

17. A good overall account is Young C. Kim, *Japanese Journalists and Their World* (Charlottesville: University of Virginia Press, 1981).

18. Kingdon (*Agendas,* p. 64) quotes an American "outsider" with limited access to decision makers as saying, "If there is a strong organized interest in keeping the status quo, you have to overcome it somehow. Your only hope is to go public." He is contrasted with an "insider" who says, "Mass media coverage is not critical. It is one of your vehicles. . . . We have alternatives of leverage on the system, and we don't have to use the media very much."

19. Direct pressure is a more feasible strategy for groups such as the student radicals of the late 1960s and the *burakumin* (whose media strategies are mainly defensive). Of course, such groups will use or create more narrowly focused media resources.

20. The official sadly remarked that "campaigns for public support and campaigns for Finance Ministry support do not have much connection." See John Creighton Campbell, *Contemporary Japanese Budget Politics* (Berkeley: University of California Press, 1976), p. 36.

21. This relatively conservative forecast is by the International Monetary Fund, and includes education. See International Monetary Fund, *Aging and Social Expenditure in the Major Industrial Countries, 1980–2025* (Washington, D.C.: International Monetary Fund, 1986).

22. For a detailed discussion of old-age policy and decision, see Campbell, *How Policies Change,* chap. 3; and Paul M. Lewis, "Family, Economy and Polity: A Case Study of Japan's Pension Policy," diss., University of California, Berkeley, 1982.

23. A point well demonstrated by the tortuous process of making decisions about U.S. Social Security in the 1980s: see Paul Light, *Artful Work: The Politics of Social Security Reform* (New York: Random House, 1985); for a magisterial study of effective policy sponsorship, see Martha Derthick, *Policymaking for Social Security* (Washington, D.C.: Brookings Institution, 1979).

24. See Campbell, *How Policies Change,* chap. 5.

25. Mori's work fills 27 pages of a 117-page standard bibliography of social gerontology covering 1960–1973: Tokyoto Rōjin Sōgō Kenkyūjo, ed., *Rōnen kenkyū bunken mokuroku: shakai kagaku hen* (Bibliography of Gerontology Research: Social Sciences) (Tokyo: Tokyoto Rōjin Sōgō Kenkyūjo, 1975).

26. This story was told in a publicity brochure included with the book, and was confirmed by Mori in an interview in 1977. *Kōkotsu no hito* (Tokyo: Shinchōsha, 1972) was translated as *The Twilight Years* (Tokyo: Kōdansha, 1984) and also made into a powerful and very popular movie.

27. For details see Campbell, *How Policies Change,* pp. 140–142. Sources for these three indicators are Rōjin Sōgō Kenkyūjo; *Rōnen Kenkyū;* the bi-weekly newsletter *Kōsei Fukushi* (Welfare); the "morgue" at NHK News; the Newspaper Clipping Section (Shimbun Kirinuki Shitsu) of the National Diet Library; and the "Kokumin seikatsu ni kansuru yoron chōsa" (Opinion Survey on National Life), conducted by the prime minister's office from 1963, as reported in the annual editions of *Yoron chōsa nenkan* (Yearbook of Opinion Surveys).

28. Such cases are relatively rare. For the United States, Jack Walker showed that even for such a high-visibility policy area as health and safety regulation, media coverage generally follows rather than precedes government action: Jack Walker, "Setting the Agenda in the U.S. Senate: A Theory of Problem Selection," *British Journal of Political Science* 7 (1977): 423–445.

29. In 1976–1977 I interviewed the officials at the section chief *(kachō)* or assistant section chief *(kachō hosa)* level in charge of nearly all the programs for the elderly in the national government. A similar pattern explains many of the new programs for old people at the local level initiated in this period.

30. For example, Ezra Vogel reported a consensus throughout the Japanese establishment that welfare spending should be curtailed: Ezra Vogel, *Japan as Number One* (Cambridge: Harvard University Press, 1979).

31. That is, the measure was simply too vulnerable to opposition attacks using the media. In 1994, however, the government and opposition coalitions got together to raise the pensionable age to sixty-five over a thirteen-year period beginning in 1991. Clearly, passage of this bill was much easier because the JSP, the group most likely to go to the press, was then in the government. See *Asahi Shimbun,* 3 November 1994, p. 1.

32. The 1985 reform should be seen more as a consolidation of gains than as a step backward in the development of the welfare state, but unquestionably there was much to object to. See Campbell, *How Policies Change,* chap. 10; for the most complete account of the politics of this policy change, see Junko Katō, "Nihon no seisaku kettei katei" (Policy-making Process in Japan), M.A. thesis, Tokyo University, 1986.

33. Unnamed Welfare Ministry official, quoted by Sōichirō Tahara, *Nihon daikaizō: shin-Nihon no kanryō* (Japan's Great Reconstruction: The New Japanese Bureaucrats) (Tokyo: Bungei Shunjū, 1986), p. 310.

34. All these tactics were long used as well by the U.S. Social Security Administration; see Derthick, *Policymaking.*

35. For example, the weekly NHK debate, 14 January 1990; for the budget, *Asahi Shimbun,* 29 December 1989. Long-time welfare supporter and then finance minister Ryūtarō Hashimoto took the lead in this initiative. The "Gold Plan" was effective public policy and public relations; in the mid-1990s a "New Gold Plan" was offered to boost the targets for long-term-care provisions still further.

36. Reich, "Crisis."

37. In the annual survey of what people want from the government, cited above, environmental policy was never chosen as the top priority by more than 6 percent of the public (1972); it was only 2 percent in the survey taken just before the period of rapid legislative change in 1970.

38. See Steven R. Reed, *Japanese Prefectures and Policy Making* (Pittsburgh: Pittsburgh University Press, 1987).

39. As noted above, this strategy is often found in budgetary politics, particularly for agencies without much direct political strength, such as the Labor Ministry or, in later years, the Environmental Protection Agency. Reich describes EPA's cultivation of reporters in the late 1970s in his "Troubles" and "Crisis."

40. Gerald L. Curtis, *The Japanese Way of Politics* (New York: Columbia University Press, 1988).

7

Media and Political Protest:
The Bullet Train Movements

DAVID EARL GROTH

LEADERS of protest movements face difficult dilemmas in dealing with the mass media, which can be both an invaluable resource and a devastating enemy. As Todd Gitlin has noted, "people find themselves relying on the media for concepts, for images of their heroes, for guiding information, for emotional charges, for recognition of public values, for symbols in general, even for language."[1] A sixty-second spot on the evening news gives movement leaders access to a vast audience, larger than they could reach in a lifetime of giving speeches at community rallies, and enables them to send messages directly to powerholders.[2]

But being in the media spotlight involves serious risks. The mass media can distort messages and trivialize goals, perhaps at best providing superficial coverage of a movement's most flamboyant leaders. In his analysis of the media's coverage of the new left and the anti–Vietnam War movement in the United States during the 1960s, Gitlin concluded that by "processing" social opposition, the media tended "to control the image and to diffuse it at the same time, to absorb what could be absorbed into the dominant structure of definitions and images and to push the rest to the margins of social life."[3]

How and to what extent can protest movements use the media as a political resource? What media strategies do protest movements adopt? What impact have the media had on protest movements? In this chapter, I seek answers to these questions by examining a particular type of protest movement in Japan: citizens' groups that have opposed the construction of the Shinkansen (bullet train) or the pollution (noise and vibration) caused by its operation. During 1980–1982 I conducted field research on such movements in Nagoya, Tokyo's Kita Ward, and three cities (Toda, Urawa, and Yono) in southern Saitama Prefecture. The protest in each area involved coalitions of citizens' movements that received support at various times from local governments; neighborhood associations; opposition political parties, notably the Japan Communist Party (JCP) and the Japan Socialist Party (JSP); and labor unions. The citizens' movement in each area brought a lawsuit concerning the Shinkansen, and litigation became a major stategy.[4]

The Shinkansen Citizens' Movements and the Context of Japanese Politics

The postwar Japanese state has given top priority to economic growth. Because the Japanese government has implemented specific policies, such as the "income-doubling plan" of 1960, to achieve high growth rates, some scholars have emphasized the state's role in promoting economic development. Chalmers Johnson, for example, has described Japan as a "developmental state," in which the central bureaucracy identifies the industrial sectors that should be developed and chooses the best means to achieve national economic goals.[5]

The creation of the Shinkansen by a public corporation, Japanese National Railroads (JNR), symbolized the state's commitment to development. Although JNR was "privatized" in April 1987, it was a public corporation while the Shinkansen system was being built. It thus came under the control of the Ministry of Transportation and had its budget approved by the Japanese Diet.[6] *Shinkansen* means "new basic line" in Japanese, suggesting the perceived national importance of the project. Former prime minister Kakuei Tanaka described its expansion throughout Japan as one of "six general principles of urban policy" for building a new Japan.[7]

The Shinkansen developed in several stages. The Tōkaidō Shinkansen linking Japan's two largest cities, Tokyo and Osaka, began operation in 1964, and the project was extended to Kyūshū in southern Japan in 1975. The Tōhoku and Jōetsu lines to northern Japan were built to link Tokyo with Iwate and Niigata Prefectures, which contained the electoral districts of several powerful politicians, including Tanaka. JNR opened these lines in 1982 from Ōmiya, about twenty kilometers north of Tokyo, rather than from the capital because citizens' movements had prevented the completion of the projects. They were finally extended to Tokyo in 1985.

State emphasis on economic growth above other goals has given rise to significant political protest at the grass-roots level since the mid-1960s. Some groups have challenged state priorities by demanding greater attention to social welfare and related issues; others have protested the pollution that has resulted from Japan's rapid economic growth and the construction of projects such as the Shinkansen. Indeed, according to one observer, citizens' movements opposing various types of pollution represent "the largest and most significant social movement in Japan's recent history."[8] A directory of Japanese citizens' movements, published in 1980, listed more than a thousand environmental citizens' movements active in Japan during 1979–1980.[9] An earlier directory had identified 6,427 grass-roots political organizations in Japan, including environmental, consumer, and pacifist movements, as well as organizations promoting goals such as educational reform, protection of cultural assets, and civil rights for the disabled.[10]

None of these movements has encountered more formidable problems than were faced by the groups protesting the Shinkansen. Much citizen protest has centered on the consequences of private industrial projects that directly benefit relatively few people; examples include the Minamata mercury-poisoning case and the Yokkaichi asthma case. The Shinkansen, in contrast, is public and directly benefits millions of people. By 1980 it was transporting about 340,000 passengers per day. Even leaders of the Shinkansen citizens' movement in Nagoya used the Shinkansen for trips to meet government officials in Tokyo.

At the same time, the Shinkansen has adversely affected hundreds of thousands of people. Some 50,000 households were evicted for the construction of the Tōkaidō Shinkansen;[11] according to one estimate, about 130,000 households suffer from Shinkansen-related pollution along its corridors between Tokyo and Kyūshū alone.[12] Between the late 1960s and early 1980s, about one hundred citizens' movements dealing with the Shinkansen sprang up throughout Japan.

A diverse group of people joined the movements I studied. Members ranged in age from the late twenties to the mid-eighties. Members and supporters of the ruling Liberal Democratic Party (LDP), JSP, JCP, and several "new left" movements all participated. Both men and women held leadership positions. Several of the leaders had doctorates or medical degrees from leading universities, while others had not even completed prewar Japan's six years of compulsory education.

The Shinkansen citizens' movements have dealt with two basic problems: noise and vibration pollution caused by the trains and compensation for residents evicted because of the project. In cities such as Nagoya and Yokohama, the Shinkansen runs through heavily populated residential areas only a few meters from homes. With trains roaring by about every ten minutes from early morning to late at night, some residents living near the lines complain that they cannot sleep while the Shinkansen is in operation and that the noise interferes with conversations. The vibrations are equivalent to minor earthquakes, causing walls and tiles to crack.[13] In a densely populated, industrial country like Japan, very little land is available for sale. Residents evicted because of the Shinkansen have thus faced extreme difficulty in finding alternative sites of land. Some have been forced out of their homes, off their little pieces of land, and into apartments. These people have protested that compensation for their land and property was grossly inadequate. Owners of large tracts have been no less vocal, complaining about the high taxes they must pay on the money they receive.[14]

Because of the immense importance of the Shinkansen to Japan, the citizens' movements did not oppose the Shinkansen per se. Rather they sought comprehensive solutions to the problems caused by the project. During 1980–1982 only the radical fringe of the movements in Tokyo and Saitama could be described as "anti-Shinkansen."

The Media as a Political Resource

John McCarthy and Mayer Zald have argued that several forces must be considered in the study of social movements: the resources that the movement mobilizes; its linkages to other groups and organizations; the dependence of the movement upon third parties for success; and the tactics used by the state to defeat, coopt, or incorporate the movement.[15] The "resource mobilization" model of McCarthy and Zald thus stresses both the resources within a society that can be mobilized to support a movement and the constraints that a society or its government imposes on the movement.

The mass media are one of several major resources that the citizens' movements used in trying to resolve problems caused by the Shinkansen project. Other strategies of the citizens' movements included the following:

Working with local governments and neighborhood associations to oppose the national government's Shinkansen policies
Soliciting support from opposition politicians, particularly those from the JCP and JSP

Negotiating with representatives from JNR, the Ministry of Transportation, and the Environment Agency (EA)[16]
Filing lawsuits against JNR or the Ministry of Transportation
Establishing formal (in Kita Ward) or informal (in Nagoya) alliances
   with labor unions and relying on labor unions to organize rallies
   and to provide participants for demonstrations and other activities
Mobilizing members and supporters for confrontations, such as sit-
   ins, pickets, vigils (used in Kita Ward and Saitama but not in
   Nagoya), and mass rallies (used in all areas)

To explore the media's role as ally—or alternately, as a constraint on
the movements' success—it is first necessary to provide a sense of the
nature and evolution of the movements themselves.

The Shinkansen movement in Nagoya involved residents who
lived within about sixty meters of the Shinkansen line. In an attempt
to eliminate the pollution, movement leaders initially tried to negotiate with officials from JNR, the Ministry of Transportation, and EA.
When these efforts failed, 575 plaintiffs from 341 families filed a suit
against JNR in March 1974. The suit sought monetary compensation
for the noise and vibration pollution suffered by the plaintiffs and an
injunction to slow the Shinkansen trains in Nagoya in order to
reduce the pollution. The court case became the focus of the citizens'
movement in Nagoya. Although the courts awarded the plaintiffs
compensation, the demand for an injunction was rejected by both the
Nagoya District Court in 1980 and the Nagoya High Court in 1985.

The movement enjoyed the cooperation of Dōrō and Kokurō,
JNR's two major labor unions. During the period 1974–1983, Dōrō
defied JNR and slowed down the Shinkansen trains in Nagoya.
Occasionally Kokurō also slowed down the trains, and both unions
provided witnesses to testify in court on behalf of the citizens'
movement.[17]

After the court case began in 1974, JNR offered to negotiate with
affected residents in Nagoya on an individual basis to buy residential property within twenty meters of the Shinkansen and to provide
some sound- and vibration-proofing for the homes most affected.
The lawyers and most of the leaders regarded JNR's proposal as an
attempt to break up the movement's solidarity. And, indeed, several
leaders did negotiate deals with JNR in the mid-1970s and then
dropped out of the movement. However, after the Nagoya district
court announced its decision in 1980, the leaders neither encouraged
nor opposed individual negotiations with JNR. Of the 391 plaintiffs
who appealed the verdict of the district court, the majority were

from families that eventually negotiated individual deals with JNR for reconstruction of their homes or resettlement away from the Shinkansen.[18]

In Tokyo's Kita Ward and in Saitama Prefecture, the Shinkansen citizens' movements initially worked with local governments and neighborhood associations to oppose the construction of the Shinkansen in these areas. During 1978–1980, however, the local governments and many neighborhood associations approved the national government's Shinkansen policies, even though the citizens' movements had organized sit-ins at city halls and ward halls in an attempt to prevent the local governments from changing their positions. By early 1982 the citizens' movements in Kita Ward and most parts of Saitama had changed their own official positions, from absolute opposition to conditional approval. Before the Shinkansen was built in northern Tokyo and southern Saitama, the citizens' movements demanded that JNR provide generous compensation *and* alternate sites of land for residents who faced eviction, and develop a means to reduce Shinkansen noise and vibration to tolerable levels.[19] Regardless of official policies, however, until the mid-1980s some members of the citizens' movements continued to advocate opposition to the construction of the Shinkansen in their neighborhoods.

Between 1980 and 1982, negotiation, court cases, and mass mobilization were the most important strategies of the Shinkansen citizens' movements. During my field research I was able to attend almost all the executive meetings for the leaders of the citizens' movement in Kita Ward. The leaders convened special meetings to discuss the court case, negotiations with JNR, and the mobilization of members and supporters for particular activities. Media issues arose periodically, but no executive meetings were devoted specifically to this topic.

The mass media represented both a resource and a constraint, but the media were not unique in this regard. All the strategies were hard to control because they were based on exchange relationships with third parties. Court cases, for example, meant dependence on lawyers, who often had political objectives somewhat different from those of the victims of the Shinkansen project and tried to exert control over many facets of the citizens' movements. Negotiations required the services of Diet politicians to arrange meetings, and, of course, the politicians expected favors in return.

In developing media strategies, the leaders of the Shinkansen citizens' movements dealt with six major types of media: (1) national daily newspapers, such as *Asahi, Mainichi,* and *Yomiuri,* all of which publish local editions or local supplements; (2) local (region, prefecture, or city) newspapers;[20] (3) NHK (Nippon Hōsō Kyōkai, "Japan Broadcasting Corporation"), the national public service broadcasting network;[21] (4) private, commercial broadcasting networks; (5) the media network of the JCP, which includes a national newspaper, *Akahata* (Red Flag), and several local newspapers, such as *Atarashii Kita Ku* (New Kita Ward); and (6) mini-media developed by the citizens' movements, including newspapers, publicity pamphlets, and handouts.

Media strategies tended to be ad hoc in nature, and controversies periodically arose involving both the mass media and the mini-media. Some participants advocated standard repertoires of action involving the mini-media—for example, publishing an article in the movement's newspaper or distributing handouts at local train stations—for practically any problem that arose. For citizens' movements and other would-be users of the media, an inverse relationship appears to exist between two key criteria, scope of impact and degree of control: as audience size increases, control diminishes. The movement has the greatest control over its own mini-media, less control over local papers, and less still over the national mainstream newspapers and television channels.

Importance of the Mass Media for a Protest Movement

Despite the inherent problems in control of the national mass media, they present tantalizing opportunities. Several scholars have emphasized the value of the mass media as a resource by which protest movements can transform their concerns into part of the agenda of decision makers.[22] The mass media enable protest movements to draw support from third parties having the political resources to pressure government officials.[23] Roger Cobb and Charles Elder have argued that protest movements must "put the appeal in a symbolic context that will have a maximum impact on followers, potential supporters, the opposition, or the decision makers. Each strategy is dependent to some extent on the amount of attention that is provided by the mass media."[24] This view, of course, overlooks the potentially detrimental consequences of media attention. It also neglects the importance of the movements' own mini-media.

The leaders of the Shinkansen citizens' movements disagreed about the role of the mass media in their struggle. Opinions ranged from utter contempt to great expectations. One leader in Kita Ward argued that the support of "public opinion" determined the success of a political movement and that the use of the mass media was essential in winning this support. He thought that even the judges of court cases would be influenced by what they read in the news-papers. Other leaders disagreed, claiming that the judges had avoided reading media reports about the Shinkansen when they made their decision about the Nagoya Shinkansen pollution case. Some leaders saw the mass media as a fickle and unreliable ally at best and a destructive force at worse. One leader in Saitama held that *Yomiuri* editors and reporters had tried to undermine the local movement by continuing to treat an expelled leader as the move-ment's spokesperson. She claimed that only one journalist in all Japan, Yoshihito Homma of *Mainichi,* had been supportive of the movement, but leaders of the citizens' movement in Nagoya dis-agreed about the degree to which even Homma's work had bene-fited their movement.[25]

Most leaders thought that the mass media could be used as a resource to gain the support of "public opinion"—but only if the leaders exercised extreme caution. They believed that the mass media often misunderstood the citizens' movements and failed to perform an adequate "watchdog" role over the national ministries and public corporations. Consequently, the leaders themselves had to assume a watchdog role over the media. Although debates over policies regarding the media continued within the citizens' movements, the basic media strategy of the movements had several important fea-tures: to exert as much influence over the mass media as possible to obtain favorable coverage, to try to avert negative coverage, and to use the movements' own mini-media as an alternative communica-tion network.

The Mass Media as a Two-edged Sword

The diversity of opinions about the mass media within the leadership of the citizens' movements reflected the mass media's potential both to help and to hurt the Shinkansen citizens' movements.

Japanese newspapers have given extensive coverage to pollution issues since the early 1970s.[26] Articles sympathetic toward citizens' movements dealing with environmental issues are not difficult to find in newspapers such as *Asahi* or *Mainichi.* Indeed, sympathetic articles from national newspapers, as well as from regional papers, such as *Tokyo Shimbun* or the Nagoya-based *Chūnichi Shimbun,* have been reprinted in the movements' own papers and pamphlets.[27] In its letters to the editor section *Asahi* printed many letters by Giju Hibino, a leader of the Nagoya citizens' movement, concerning Shinkansen pollution. *Asahi* thus allowed a leader of the citizens' movement to use the mass media to disseminate his ideas.[28]

How the media dealt with issues central to the movement is seen in their coverage of the Nagoya District Court's 1980 decision to reject the plaintiffs' request for an injunction to modify the operation of the Shinkansen in Nagoya, on grounds that an injunction would trigger similar demands throughout the Shinkansen system and thus be detrimental to the "public good." All major Japanese newspapers published detailed articles about the decision. *Mainichi* journalist Homma has characterized the mass media's coverage of the decision as generally sympathetic toward the Nagoya citizens' movement.[29] *Yomiuri,* for example, published an interview with a legal scholar who condemned the decision as equivalent to the denial of personal rights.[30] An article in *Mainichi* endorsed the plaintiffs' demands, questioned a notion of "the public good" that required local residents to suffer, and noted that the JNR unions' slowdown of the Shinkansen in Nagoya on the day of the decision had not disrupted the Shinkansen's schedule.[31]

Not all media reports were favorable, however. *Nihon Keizai Shimbun* (Japan Economic Newspaper) provided sympathetic coverage of JNR's viewpoint.[32] A front-page article in *Yomiuri* portrayed the central issue in the Nagoya Shinkansen pollution case as a choice between the residents' health or "the public good."[33] Even articles sympathetic to the plaintiffs' position contained passages that showed the movement in an unfavorable light. For example, one article in *Mainichi* described the suffering caused by the Shinkansen in Nagoya but also reported contention among the plaintiffs, noting the split between those who had accepted JNR's offers for resettlement and had left the movement and those who wanted to continue the legal battle.[34]

Three newspaper articles in particular suggest the dimensions of the movements' problems with media control. First, several months after the Kita Ward assembly approved the construction of the Shinkansen in the ward, *Yomiuri* ran an article suggesting that the citizens' movement represented a distinctly minority opinion.[35] The report stated that residents in Kita Ward were divided into three factions: opponents, proponents, and conditional proponents (the condition being that the Shinkansen stop at Akabane, the largest JNR station in Kita Ward). The article quoted Kita Ward mayor Masachiyo Kobayashi's endorsement of JNR's claim that the Shinkansen would not cause any environmental problems in the ward.[36] It concluded by noting that while the movement had just begun a petition campaign, those demanding a Shinkansen station at Akabane had already collected 60,000 signatures on their petition.

Second, an article published in *Asahi* in 1978 concerning Susumu Nambara, president of the Shinkansen movement in Kita Ward during the late 1970s, permitted him to clarify the movement's goals and to describe its growing membership, but overall the article was rather negative.[37] The article questioned whether the movement remained a viable organization and reported significant strife among its leadership. It noted, for example, that one group of leaders had been expelled for approving local construction of the Shinkansen project and that the movement had abolished its system of multiple vice presidents and had designated Nambara as its president because of difficulties in formulating policies.

Third, an article published in *Sankei* in September 1980 portrayed the Shinkansen citizens' movement in southern Saitama as floundering.[38] The article focused on its problems, ignored signs of revitalization, and quoted a Ministry of Transportation official, who suggested that residents who refused to sell land condemned for the Shinkansen project would be forcibly evicted. The piece also resorted to the tactic most despised by the leaders: treating a leader who had been expelled from the movement as its spokesperson. The article identified Kotarō Koike as the representative of Yono Anti-Shinkansen Alliance and discussed his meeting with the minister of transportation to approve the Shinkansen project. In fact, Koike had been expelled from the Yono movement because of this very meeting. His defection and later cooperation with JNR and the Ministry of Transportation were major blows to the anti-Shinkansen citizens' movement in Saitama and Tokyo. Consequently, the media's portrayal of Koike as the representative of the citizens' movement enraged the leaders.[39]

Each of these cases illustrates the volatile nature of media. In a news account one favorable sentence can be followed by another undermining its good effect. By their very nature, social movements made up of volunteers regularly gain and lose leaders and followers. This makes it hard for the media to identify appropriate spokespersons and equally hard for the movement to control what its representatives—much less its detractors—say. It is little wonder that leaders of protest movements face the media with a strange mix of hope and fear.

Attempts to Influence the Mass Media

During interviews, major concerns about the coverage of the Shinkansen citizens' movements were expressed by the leaders. They wanted their movements to be portrayed as powerful, united, committed to the public good, and having the support of many organizations. They noted, however, that some media reports described the citizens' movements as weak, factionalized, obstructionist, and interested in narrow goals. The leaders thus adopted various strategies to manipulate the media or at least to contain the damage that the media could cause. Major strategies included limiting the media's access to the members and activities of the citizens' movements; attacking hostile media organizations; coordinating media strategy with other strategies; creating media events; and developing the minimedia as an alternative to the mass media.

Limiting Access

The leaders' principal form of control over the mass media was the power to limit access to the members and activities of their movements. The leaders tried to get the mass media to interview only officially designated representatives, and in Nagoya and Kita Ward they specifically instructed members to avoid independent contact with the mass media.

These policies served several purposes. First, the leaders wanted to ensure that only official policies were communicated and to prevent self-designated spokespersons from disseminating potentially embarrassing independent ideas. Behind their façades of unity, all the citizens' movements had members who disagreed with official policies.[40] Second, the leaders hoped to prevent former leaders who had defected or been expelled from being treated as representatives of the movements. Unfortunately, some former leaders wanted to present their own interpretations, and the mass media provided them a forum.

The leaders also barred the mass media from certain movement activities. The Nagoya movement initially opened its meetings to everyone. After the hearings of the court case began, however, the leaders feared that open meetings would provide enemies with access to sensitive information. Consequently, all outsiders, especially representatives of the mass media, were explicitly excluded from many meetings. The mass media were allowed to cover only certain rallies for which the leadership sought publicity. When publicly confronted, however, they occasionally relented. After the Nagoya district court issued its verdict on the Shinkansen pollution case in September 1980, the Nagoya movement discussed strategy in a series of meetings, culminating in a general assembly for all members. When several reporters showed up and protested their exclusion, the leaders reluctantly allowed them to attend.[41]

Not all movement leaders agreed with the policy of excluding the mass media from certain activities. During one executive meeting in Kita Ward, the leaders discussed plans for a tour of Shinkansen pollution in Nagoya, and one leader announced that a reporter wanted to accompany the leaders on the chartered bus to Nagoya. The president argued that all activities should be open and that the movement must avoid the tactics of JNR, which denied the public access to information. Most leaders, however, wanted to exclude the reporter, noting that the mass media could be briefed in Nagoya.

Attacking Hostile Media Organizations

The citizens' movements did not remain passive victims of media criticism. Movement leaders in Kita Ward and Saitama organized protests directed at media organizations that they regarded as hostile, particularly if they could find some point of media vulnerability. Targets were typically local, as opposed to national, media organizations, but NHK also came in for retaliatory action. NHK was vulnerable because all television owners are supposed to pay a nominal monthly fee for its support. One leader in Kita Ward contacted the headquarters of NHK and threatened to organize a boycott against payment of these fees unless NHK presented the citizens' movement's position in addition to JNR's in its coverage of Shinkansen issues. She claimed that as a result of her actions, NHK sent a reporter to interview her, and NHK's coverage of Shinkansen issues in Kita Ward became somewhat more balanced.[42]

The citizens' movements in Saitama used *oshikake* (perhaps best translated as "mob action at the doorsteps") against media organizations that had portrayed the movement unfavorably. The Yono Anti-Shinkansen Alliance, for example, organized an *oshikake* against *Saitama Shimbun,* which had run articles critical of it. The alliance mobilized several hundred people for a demonstration and picket against the newspaper in April 1979. Several movement leaders later claimed that after this show of strength, the newspaper gave them no major problems.[43]

Coordinating Media Strategy with Other Strategies

Since the late 1960s, court cases have been a major tactic of Japanese citizens' movements opposing pollution and an integral part of what Charles Tilly has called the "repertoire of collective action"—the types of political protest that people engage in within a particular society at a specific historical time.[44] In fact, leaders of the Shinkansen citizens' movements admitted that they had been naive in their hopes for resolving problems through the judicial system. Some leaders regarded court cases as the only solution to pollution during the 1970s; they began to realize the limitations of litigation only after the Nagoya district court rejected the plaintiffs' demand for an injunction in 1980.[45]

It became imperative to find ways to shape media coverage because activities related to court cases attracted the most attention. The ultimate example of media attention to the Shinkansen citizens' movements occurred on September 11, 1980, when the Nagoya District Court announced its decision on the Nagoya Shinkansen Pollution Court Case. All the major newspapers and television networks in Japan sent representatives to cover the event, and parts of the rally that the citizens' movement organized in front of the courthouse were broadcast live throughout Japan. A rally to celebrate the start of the Shinkansen court case in Kita Ward attracted more media attention than any other movement event in Tokyo, and media people outnumbered plaintiffs at the initial procedures at the Tokyo district court.

The leaders coordinated their use of the courts with their attempts to influence the mass media, especially in Saitama and Kita Ward. The lawyers and plaintiffs in Saitama argued that an important goal of their case was to obtain favorable coverage from the mass media. The Saitama Shinkansen court case, which was begun by eighty-nine plaintiffs in April 1980, boldly challenged the policy-making processes of the Ministry of Transportation as undemocratic and unconstitutional and demanded that the court revoke approval that the ministry had granted JNR to build the Shinkansen in southern Saitama. Although the case was eventually dismissed, the lawyers and plaintiffs did not regard it as a failure because they had been able to attract favorable media coverage. The formal hearings of the case usually lasted only about thirty minutes and involved tedious legal arguments that even the plaintiffs found excruciatingly boring and, at times, incomprehensible.[46] After the hearings, however, the lawyers and the leaders held press conferences, usually attended by about five to ten journalists, which gave them opportunities to defend the citizens' movement. The more articulate plaintiffs actively participated in the discussions, and the lawyer in charge of the case mesmerized the press.

The lawyers and plaintiffs in Kita Ward also worked to coordinate their legal and media strategies. In their suit against JNR, 203 plaintiffs sought an injunction against the construction of the Shinkansen in their ward. The case was begun in September 1980 specifically to take advantage of the wave of publicity surrounding the decision of the Nagoya District Court concerning Shinkansen pollution. When media attention waned after the early hearings, the lawyers had twenty-eight additional plaintiffs join the case in February 1982, in part to have an opportunity for a press conference to revive media attention.

Creating Media Events

Movement leaders organized activities to attract media attention and project desired messages. In effect, the leaders tried to create the news. Nagoya leaders, for example, organized several *arigatō undō* (thank-you activities) with the ostensible purpose of thanking Shinkansen drivers for slowing down the trains as they ran through Nagoya but with the ulterior motive of providing shows for the media. The most important of these occurred on September 10, 1980, the day before the Nagoya District Court announced its verdict, when the two major labor unions of JNR, Dōrō and Kokurō, both reduced the speed of all the Shinkansen trains in Nagoya to seventy kilometers per hour. In the afternoon dozens of old people, plus a few housewives and children, climbed onto rooftops along the Shinkansen lines to wave and cheer at the drivers. The *arigatō undō* was an attempt to get sympathetic coverage from the mass media. Who, after all, could be hostile toward old people up on a roof on a hot summer day? In staging the event, the movement also saw a way to communicate major themes: first, the movement did not oppose the Shinkansen itself; second, unions and other groups supported the demands of the citizens' movement; third, JNR could reduce noise and vibration pollution by slowing down the trains; and fourth, a slowdown in Nagoya did not disrupt the Shinkansen system.

The Shinkansen citizens' movements also created some media events that backfired. The Japanese mass media have a special interest in activities that involve not only the courts but also high-ranking officials from the national bureaucracies and public corporations.

Consequently, when the leaders of the Nagoya movement met with JNR president Fumio Takagi shortly after the Nagoya District Court ruling in September 1980, hundreds of media people covered the event. The Nagoya leaders sought additional publicity for their movement by demanding that Takagi visit Nagoya to investigate Shinkansen pollution. Scores of media people accompanied Takagi in June 1981 when he finally visited Nagoya. Television cameras filmed his every move, and Nagoya Television made a special documentary, which showed his visits to homes near the Shinkansen line, his discussions with local residents, and his heated exchanges with movement leaders.

JNR benefited more from the publicity thus obtained than the citizens' movement did. JNR, which set the conditions for the visit, refused to allow lawyers and union officials supporting the movement to participate. Thus, several articulate spokespersons for the movement could not be filmed. JNR also controlled the timing; the visit occurred when media attention again focused on Shinkansen issues, shortly before the hearings of the Nagoya case began at the high court level. JNR always argued that it had done everything possible to deal with "inconveniences" caused by the Shinkansen, and a visit by Takagi to Nagoya tended to substantiate these claims.

The visit also caused conflict within the movement's leadership. Takagi had wanted to visit a home in which JNR had installed sound- and vibration-proofing. Officials from JNR thus contacted a couple, whom I shall call the Tadas, who were the only leaders who had had their home reconstructed with JNR money. The couple wanted to receive Takagi and the media entourage in their home. However, the other leaders balked because they did not want the couple to address the media or to focus any attention on the reconstruction of homes, JNR's principal means to deal with Shinkansen pollution.

Mrs. Tada later explained what she had hoped to achieve. She insisted that because she was a member of the ruling LDP and an associate of a former prime minister, she knew how to influence the power hierarchy of Japan. She had wanted to show Takagi how the insulation JNR provided did not solve the sound and vibration problems. Then, crying a few tears for dramatic effect, she would have pleaded for a comprehensive solution to the problems caused by the Shinkansen. Mrs. Tada argued that the mass media would have loved to film an old lady and her disabled husband begging Takagi and that through the media she could have communicated with the people of Japan.

The controversy involved different images that the leaders hoped to project through the media. Mrs. Tada wanted the movement to be portrayed as an organization cooperating to the extent possible with the government and humbly seeking a solution. Other leaders wanted to be portrayed as boldly asserting their right to eliminate Shinkansen pollution. Mrs. Tada claimed that the tears of a grandmother would have had more appeal to the media and a greater impact on public opinion than the defiant shouts of the other leaders.[47]

Developing the Mini-Media

In analyzing the relationship between the media and political protest, it is essential to analyze not only the *mass* media but also the *mini-media* that protest movements develop. The leaders of the Shinkansen citizens' movements realized that the mass media were not always supportive and that they did not meet the needs of the movement. Consequently, they created their own alternative communication network. Because of the importance of the mini-media to the citizens' movements, members with media skills (printers, writers, or photographers) were able to attain leadership positions.[48]

These mini-media were of several kinds: newspapers, pamphlets, and other publications; mobile street broadcasting from speaker trucks, including day-long "caravans" throughout Kita Ward; *bira maki,* the distribution of printed statements at railroad and subway stations during rush hours, accompanied by speeches over loudspeaker systems; documentary films and slide shows about Shinkansen pollution and the activities of the citizens' movements; and even songs for "Karaoke Days."[49] One leader of the anti-Shinkansen citizens' movement in Yono City, Saitama, was a professional song lyricist. He collaborated with another leader, an amateur composer, to produce several anti-Shinkansen songs. Aping a custom popular in the bars of Japan, the Yono Anti-Shinkansen League hosted "Karaoke Days," in which the participants sang the songs through a microphone to a tape-recorded accompaniment. It might be added that all these mini-media, with the exception of "Karaoke Days," are standard tactics used by a wide variety of groups in Japan, including labor unions, student movements, and pacifist groups.

Because of the diversity of the Shinkansen citizens' movements and the mini-media that they created, it is difficult to generalize about the functions of the mini-media. In Nagoya the newspaper of the movement, *Shizukesa e no Tatakai* (The Fight for Tranquility) played a pivotal role in developing the movement. About ten people wrote the original issue (October 12, 1971), had 3,000 copies printed, and distributed them in mailboxes along the Shinkansen route in Nagoya. A meeting announced in the paper drew about seventy people, and many leaders regarded this meeting as the beginning of the mass movement. Early issues of the newspaper helped to mobilize participants for various activities and built support for the boycott movement against paying NHK fees.[50] The seventh issue (April 25, 1973) mobilized participants for the first important negotiating session with officials from JNR, the Ministry of Transportation, and EA on April 29, 1973. The eighth issue (September 20, 1973) announced the start of the court case and began the process of recruiting plaintiffs.

In contrast to the situation in Nagoya, newspapers in Saitama and Kita Ward played no role in recruiting plaintiffs for the court cases. The Shinkansen citizens' movement in Kita Ward did not even have a regular newspaper until *after* the court case had begun. In Kita Ward plaintiffs were recruited through neighborhood associations, political parties, labor unions, and personal relations with the leaders. Not all the leaders of the various Shinkansen citizens' movements in Saitama supported the decision to start a court case, so only a few leaders assumed the responsibility to recruit plaintiffs in Saitama.

A major function of the mini-media in Yono City, Saitama, was to condemn "betrayers" of the citizens' movement. Corruption was such a major problem for the Yono Anti-Shinkansen Alliance that over about a decade several sets of leaders were expelled from the alliance after allegedly accepting bribes from pro-Shinkansen forces. Leaders who dropped out of the movement and negotiated privately with officials from JNR faced not only demonstrations and pickets at their doorsteps but also photographers making movies of such events for the movement to show to its members.[51] The annual reports and publicity pamphlets of the anti-Shinkansen citizens' movement in Yono, which were distributed at mass rallies, included long denunciations of former leaders.[52]

Acrimonious fights also occurred within the leadership of the Shinkansen citizens' movements in Nagoya and Kita Ward, and several leaders were expelled in both areas. In contrast to the situation in Yono, however, the mini-media of these movements avoided mention of the controversies. For example, in explaining the departure of the Nagoya Shinkansen Alliance's first president, who had negotiated privately with JNR, the movement's official newspaper merely announced that he had resigned because of poor health and old age.[53]

The leaders of the citizens' movements never carefully analyzed what they were trying to achieve through some of their mini-media. In Kita Ward a proposal made by a lawyer to have a monthly *bira maki* was perfunctorily adopted at an executive meeting of movement leaders without discussion, and the monthly *bira maki* became a standard operating procedure of the movement. The most important *bira maki* occurred at JNR's largest station in Kita Ward, Akabane, which is near a sleazy area full of brothels and cabarets. Commuters there generally refused the handouts or tossed them in the garbage. Yet each month members of the citizens' movement continued to compete with pimps and missionaries for commuters' attention.

Conclusions

The leaders of the Shinkansen citizens' movements never achieved more than limited influence over the mass media. Yet their movements were transformed by the media, with three main effects: the media exacerbated conflicts within the movements; they increased the power of leaders, lawyers, and any others who became media spokespersons; and they influenced the movements' strategies and choice of activities.

Exacerbating Internal Conflicts

Control of the media represents power, and thus it is perhaps inevitable that any conflict among members of a movement—contests over policy, ideological differences, and competing outside allegiances—becomes magnified in the race to represent the movement and its positions before the mass media. How conflicts become magnified because of the media is illustrated by the relations between supporters and opponents of the Japan Communist Party within the Shinkansen citizens' movement.

Both fervent supporters and bitter opponents of the JCP held leadership positions. Of the sixty-one leaders that I interviewed, nearly one-fourth (23 percent) were members or supporters of the JCP; these included such prominent figures as the executive directors of the movements in Kita Ward and Nagoya and the president of the plaintiffs' association in Saitama, all of whom were JCP members. From 1980 the movement in Kita Ward had a formal affiliation with the JCP through Kuminren (Federation of Ward Residents), an organization sponsored by local labor unions, various citizens' movements, and the local branches of the socialist and communist parties to oppose the Shinkansen policies of the national government. On the other hand, however, some leaders of the Shinkansen citizens' movements were critics of the JCP. These included members and supporters of the LDP (18 percent of those interviewed) and the JSP (13 percent); anti-JCP "new left" radicals (8 percent, all in the citizens' movement in Urawa, Saitama); and several leaders who had been expelled from the JCP or had dropped out (see table 7.1). The stage was thus set for conflict.

The JCP has developed an extensive print media. According to official statements, the party aspired in 1981 to achieve a membership of 500,000 and to increase the circulation of its national daily newspaper, *Akahata* (Red Flag), to 4 million.[54] (The JCP claimed that the Sunday edition of *Akahata* had a circulation of more than 3.5 million in February 1980.)[55] The JCP also publishes local newspapers in three areas of Japan, including *Atarashii Kita Ku* (New Kita Ward), which had a circulation of about 10,000 in 1982.[56] The JCP's official introduction states that party members have an obligation to promote *Akahata* and other party publications.[57]

The national JCP media treated the Shinkansen citizens' movements gingerly to avoid offending pro-Shinkansen forces throughout Japan. The local JCP newspaper in Kita Ward, however, provided extensive coverage during 1980–1982 of the Shinkansen citizens' movement in Kita Ward. It ran several interviews with the movement's president and sympathetic articles on all its major activities, often stressing how local JCP politicians had helped the movement.

As could be expected, opinions about the JCP media efforts were divided along party lines. One leader in Kita Ward argued that the coverage of the citizens' movement by the local JCP newspaper linked the movement too closely with the party and inclined the communist readers of *Atarashii Kita Ku* to regard the Shinkansen citizens' movement as their own. Opponents of the JCP within Kita Ward also complained that the JCP had too much control over parts of the movement's mini-media, especially the distribution of handouts at stations. The *bira maki* were directed by the Federation of Ward Residents, and JCP politicians from the Kita Ward and Tokyo Metropolitan assemblies actively participated and wore armbands identifying their party affiliation. Moreover, during the *bira maki* JCP politicians gave speeches from a speaker truck with *Akahata* clearly written on the side. Several members of the citizens' move-

**Table 7.1   Parties Supported by Leaders of Shinkansen Citizens'
Movements (Percentages; N = 61)**

MEMBERS OR SUPPORTERS OF SPECIFIC PARTIES			
	MEMBERS	SUPPORTERS	TOTAL
LDP (Liberal Democratic Party)	4.9	13.1	18.0
JSP (Japan Socialist Party)	3.3	9.8	13.1
JCP (Japan Communist Party)	13.1	9.8	23.0
Kōmeitō (Clean Government Party)		1.6	1.6
Total members	21.3		
OTHER CATEGORIES			
Supported either JCP or JSP, but neither in particular			18.0
Leftist, but anti-JCP			8.2
Had supported various opposition parties			1.6
Supported no party			11.5
Unknown, refused to answer			4.9
Total			99.9

Source: David Earl Groth, "Biting the Bullet: The Politics of Grass-Roots Protest in Contemporary Japan," Ph.D. diss., Stanford University, 1987, p. 140. My categories are the descriptions of my informants rather than a mere listing of the major political parties in Japan. For example, several leaders defined themselves as leftist but definitely opposed to the JCP. Other leaders described themselves as supporters of either the JSP or the JCP depending upon various circumstances, such as which candidates were running or which party the members of their families were supporting.

ment in Kita Ward argued that the *bira maki* at Akabane, Kita Ward's largest train station, hurt the movement by giving the impression that it was subordinate to the JCP.

Increasing the Power of Leaders and Lawyers

Media strategies enhanced the power of the leaders. The leaders increased their power by determining which members would address the mass media and what images they would try to project. Some leaders tried to stifle dissent by preventing members from freely discussing their ideas with reporters.

Control over media issues also augmented the lawyers' power, especially in Nagoya. The more the court case became the focus of the citizens' movement in Nagoya, the more power the lawyers gained. The expansion of the lawyers' power is well illustrated through the Nagoya movement's newspaper, *Shizukesa e no Tatakai.* From October 1971 to April 1974 the movement's leaders wrote and edited the first nine issues that appeared. The court case was formally begun in March 1974, and the lawyers assumed control of the news-paper from the tenth issue (June 1974). The eleventh issue (July 25, 1974) printed a new contact number for the movement—the tele-phone number of the lawyers' office rather than the leaders' home telephone numbers.

The lawyers in Nagoya also tried to control the contents of speeches that the leaders made at rallies exposed to the mass media. Several Nagoya leaders noted that the lawyers wanted all speeches to be shown to them beforehand, and one leader reported that even the speech about Shinkansen pollution that a fifth-grader made at a rally had been submitted to the lawyers for review. Only two leaders said that they refused to allow the lawyers to review their speeches in advance. At the press conference that the Nagoya movement held immediately after the Nagoya District Court announced its verdict, a "representative of the plaintiffs" delivered a speech that attracted much media attention. She later admitted to me that the speech had been written by the lawyers.

In contrast to the situation in Nagoya, the leaders of the citizens' movements in Kita Ward and Saitama vied with their lawyers for control of media strategies. The leaders in Saitama simply ignored a request that their lawyers had made at an executive meeting to change the format and contents of the newsletter of the plaintiffs' association. Despite the misgivings of their lawyers, the leaders in Kita Ward appeared on a live broadcast when the Tōhoku Shin-kansen began operation in 1982 from Ōmiya, Saitama, and briefly discussed their movement.

Skewing the Repertoire of Activities

The media influenced the leaders' choice of tactics. Activities such as court cases and meetings with high-ranking JNR officials and gov-ernment bureaucrats gained importance because they attracted media attention but did not lead to media condemnation. Conversely, the specter of media opprobrium loomed over discussions of more con-troversial tactics.

Activists in Kita Ward debated whether to engage in confrontational tactics and whether media coverage of such events would benefit or hurt the movement. A typical confrontation between the citizens' movement and its opponents occurred in October 1980 when the citizens' movement disrupted the opening ceremony for the construction of the Shinkansen in Kita Ward. About one hundred members formed human barricades in front of the ceremony and prevented the mayor of Kita Ward from entering. The citizens' movement also organized vigils and sit-ins at a construction site for the Shinkansen in July 1981 and January–February 1982. The most ardent proponents of such confrontations had experience in labor movements and supported leftist factions of the JSP. These leaders thought that confrontations helped the movement not only to achieve political goals but also to gain media coverage. They argued that the media would certainly want to cover a good fight. Other leaders and especially several lawyers of the movement believed that media coverage of "radical" activities harmed the citizens' movement. For example, at one study meeting for a group of plaintiffs in Kita Ward, the lawyer in charge noted that major newspapers had published articles about the three-story protest tower that the movement had built in Akabane. He thought that the coverage had hurt the movement because the articles had compared the protest tower in Kita Ward to those in Narita and had thus implicitly associated the citizens' movement with the violent protest against the Narita Airport.

Regardless of what the mass media might say or imply, however, the leaders in Kita Ward maintained the tower as a symbol of their movement. Some leaders favored having the protest tower precisely because it attracted media attention. At one executive meeting in 1981, several leaders argued that the movement should appropriate money to rebuild the tower: they had seen it on television, and it had looked shabby.[58]

Media as Trickster?

Legitimation and mobilization are among the services that the mass media can perform not only for the state but also for protest movements. The Shinkansen citizens' movements experienced success and failure in securing these services. The movements attracted media attention and influenced segments of the media, but the leaders were never more than moderately satisfied with the mass media's coverage and knew that some reports caused misunderstanding and even hostility. Although the leaders tried to be watchdogs of the media, they realized the narrow scope of their influence over the media.

The Shinkansen citizens' movements developed mini-media as alternatives to the mass media. The Nagoya movement's newspaper, for example, played a crucial role in mobilizing participants. This suggests that the basic media strategy of a protest movement, at least in Japan, must include the development of mini-media geared to its needs. To do so, however, requires resources: money, personnel with media skills, significant time and effort from many participants, and access to expensive equipment.

At times, however, the mini-media backfire. The pamphlets of the Yono citizens' movement, for example, horrified members and supporters by revealing the corruption of former leaders; the noisy street broadcasts protesting noise pollution in Kita Ward inadvertently satirized the citizens' movement. During the distribution of handouts at Akabane station, the Kita Ward movement created a bizarre vision of movement activists clamoring for attention alongside gangsters, pimps, and missionaries.

The leaders faced formidable challenges in using the media as a resource. Strife and diversity within the Shinkansen movements precluded a united effort to deal with the media. The membership and leadership of the movements fluctuated, and the participants included members and opponents of the JCP, plaintiffs in the court cases and skeptics of the litigation, victims of the Shinkansen, and those who were not directly affected by the project, such as the lawyers. In developing any strategy, the leaders had to address diverse needs and affiliations while sustaining solidarity and momentum.

In chapter 1 of this volume Susan Pharr offered the "trickster" metaphor, a concept borrowed from structural anthropology, that provides a way to illuminate the contradictory roles of the media, which allow them to serve alternately the interest of the state and the interest of society. The mass media occupy an ambiguous insider-outsider role with regard to various political forces—politicians, bureaucrats, average citizens, and protest movements—and offer a mosaic of ideas and images. The media elude control by any group. The mass media encourage, support, applaud, and endorse, but they also badger, ridicule, embarrass, and challenge. They played both roles in their treatment of the Shinkansen citizens' movements. Both the mass media and the mini-media presented tantalizing opportunities for the movements, but the consequences of the media coverage were difficult to manage and even to predict.

Notes

I would like to thank the members of the project on media and politics in Japan for comments and suggestions. I am especially grateful to Susan Pharr and John Campbell for written critiques. I would also like to thank the Japan Foundation, the Danforth Foundation, and the Fulbright-Hayes program for funding that made possible my research in Japan.

1. Todd Gitlin, *The Whole World is Watching: Mass Media in the Making and Unmaking of the New Left* (Berkeley: University of California Press, 1980), p. 1.
2. Ibid., pp. 243–244.
3. Ibid., p. 5.
4. For material on the Shinkansen citizens' movements, see David Earl Groth, "Biting the Bullet: The Politics of Grass-Roots Protest in Contemporary Japan," Ph.D. diss., Stanford University, 1987. The author is now completing a book about the Shinkansen citizens' movements.
5. Chalmers Johnson, *MITI and the Japanese Miracle* (Stanford, Calif.: Stanford University Press, 1982), pp. 19–20, 315.
6. For a discussion of Japan's public corporations, see Chalmers Johnson, *Japan's Public Policy Companies* (Washington, D.C.: American Enterprise Institute, 1978). For a review of Japanese National Railroads on the eve of privatization, see Paul H. Noguchi, *Delayed Departures, Overdue Arrivals: Industrial Familialism and the Japanese National Railroads* (Honolulu: University of Hawai'i Press, 1990).
7. Kakuei Tanaka, *Building a New Japan: A Plan for Remodeling the Japanese Archipelago* (Tokyo: Simul Press, 1972), pp. 114–125. According to Ezra Vogel, this work was actually written by MITI bureaucrats. Ezra Vogel, *Japan as Number One* (New York: Harper and Row, 1985), p. 91.
8. Margaret McKean, *Environmental Protest and Citizen Politics in Japan* (Berkeley: University of California Press, 1981), p. 1.
9. *Zenkoku shimin undō dantai meibo, 1979–1980* (National Directory of Citizens' Movements) (Tokyo: Kōgai Mondai Kenkyūkai, 1980).
10. *Zenkoku jūmin dantai meibo* (National Directory of Residents' Movements) (Tokyo: Chihō Jichi Sōgō Kenkyūkai, 1974).
11. Ryōhei Kakumoto, *Tōkaidō Shinkansen* (The Tōkaidō Shinkansen) (Tokyo: Chūōkōronsha, 1964), p. 123.
12. Harutoshi Funabashi, Kōichi Hasegawa, Munekazu Hatanaka, and Harumi Katsuta, *Shinkansen kōgai: kōsoku bummei no shakai mondai* (Shinkansen Pollution: Social Problems of a High-Speed Civilization) (Tokyo: Yūhikaku, 1985), p.i.
13. The complaints about noise and vibration pollution might seem exaggerated, but in its decision of 11 September 1980 on the Nagoya Shinkansen Pollution Case, the Nagoya District Court recognized that the Shinkansen caused such pollution in Nagoya. However, the court rejected the plaintiffs' claim that the Shinkansen pollution caused physiological damage.

14. For example, most leaders of the Toda Anti-Shinkansen Alliance Saitama Prefecture owned significant tracts of land condemned for the Shinkansen project. Several Toda leaders estimated that they would have to pay taxes equivalent to 70–80 percent of the money they would receive in compensation. The leaders also noted that very little land was available for sale in the Toda area at practically any price.

15. John McCarthy and Mayer Zald, "Resource Mobilization and Social Movements: A Partial Theory," *American Journal of Sociology* 82, no. 6 (May 1977): 1213. The argument is also developed in Mayer Zald and John McCarthy, eds., *The Dynamics of Social Movements: Resource Mobilization, Social Control, and Tactics* (Cambridge, Mass.: Winthrop Publishers, 1979).

16. The leaders of the citizens' movements generally referred to the meetings with officials from JNR, the Ministry of Transportation, and EA as *chokusetsu kōshō* (direct negotiations), but the officials themselves referred to them as *setsumeikai* (explanatory sessions) or *hanashiai* (discussions).

17. The drivers of the Shinkansen trains belong to two unions: Dōrō and Kokurō. During my field research the Dōrō drivers regularly slowed the Shinkansen trains in Nagoya to 110 kilometers per hour to reduce the pollution, but Kokurō drivers did so only on particular occasions. Neither union, however, slowed the trains to speeds that would reduce the pollution to the levels demanded by the Nagoya citizens' movement in its lawsuit against JNR.

18. The leaders, however, generally refused individual negotiations with JNR. Of the eleven men designated in mid-1982 as the leaders of both the Nagoya citizens' movement and the plaintiffs' association, only one had negotiated with JNR to obtain individual benefits.

19. The priority given to these two demands varied. For example, the citizens' movement in Toda City, Saitama Prefecture, emphasized the first demand, but the citizens' movement in Tokyo's Kita Ward, after changing its policy to conditional approval, focused on the second.

20. One source puts the number of local newspapers in Japan in 1972 at 1,122, including 220 daily papers. Norio Tamura, "Mass/Miniature Communications and Citizen Participation," *Local Government Review* [Tokyo] 4 (1976): 10.

21. NHK is analyzed by Ellis Krauss in this volume, chapter 3.

22. Roger W. Cobb and Charles D. Elder, *Participation in American Politics: The Dynamics of Agenda-Building* (Baltimore: Johns Hopkins University Press, 1972), chaps. 9 and 10.

23. Michael Lipsky, *Protest in City Politics: Rent Strikes, Housing, and the Power of the Poor* (Chicago: Rand McNally, 1970).

24. Cobb and Elder, *Participation in American Politics,* p. 150.

25. Homma has written many articles and two books about the Shinkansen project and the problems it has caused. One book examines the Shinkansen court case in Nagoya: Yoshihito Homma, *Shinkansen saiban* (The Shinkansen Court Case) (Tokyo: Gendai Hyōron Sha, 1980). One leader of

the citizens' movement in Nagoya said that he had made a special trip to Tokyo to thank Homma. Other leaders in Nagoya, however, criticized parts of Homma's work.

26. Noted by Hiraku Shōji and Ken'ichi Miyamoto, *Nihon no kōgai* (Pollution in Japan) (Tokyo: Iwanami, 1975), p. 1.

27. For example, in his *Chihō kara no sakebi* (The Cry from the Local Area), no. 1 (Nagoya: independently published and distributed, no date [1975?]), Giju Hibino, a leader of the Shinkansen citizens' movement in Nagoya, used both his own essays and reprints of newspapers articles, such as the following: "Rōjin no chōsen" (The Defiance of an Old Man), *Asahi Shimbun,* 21 July 1971; " 'Tatakai wa korekara,' kōgi jūnen, Hibino san" ("The Fight Is from Now On": The Ten Years of Protest of Mr. Hibino), *Mainichi Shimbun,* 3 February 1974; and "Umi wo wataru Shinkansen kōgai: BBC hōsō ga shuzai" (Shinkansen Pollution Goes Overseas: BBC Provides Coverage), *Chūnichi Shimbun,* 14 April 1975. The citizens' movement in Nagoya published sixty-three issues of its newspaper *Shizukesa e no Tatakai* (The Fight for Tranquility) between October 1971 and November 1982. Two issues (no. 6, 25 October 1972, and no. 7, 25 April 1973) reprinted articles from *Mainichi, Asahi,* or *Chūnichi.* The citizens' movement in Kita Ward, Tokyo, published eleven issues of its newspaper *Tōhoku Shinkansen sashitome genkokudan nyūsu* (News of the Association of Plaintiffs Seeking an Injunction against the Tōhoku Shinkansen) between October 1980 and September 1982. One issue (no. 4, 14 February 1981) reprinted an article from *Tokyo Shimbun.* In the later issues of their newspapers and publicity pamphlets, the movements did not reprint articles from mainstream newspapers. Perhaps as the leaders gained experience in producing their minimedia, they did not need to rely on articles from the mass media for fillers.

28. In his publicity pamphlet, Hibino reprinted letters that *Asahi Shimbun* (Nagoya edition) had published on 4 February and 14 and 27 September 1973; 19 February, 3 April, 8 May, and 22 November 1974; and 14 March, 14 April, 29 June, and 29 July 1975.

29. Homma, *Shinkansen saiban,* p. 272.

30. " 'Jinkakuken' hitei ni hitoshii" (Equivalent to the Denial of "Personal Rights"), *Yomiuri Shimbun,* 11 September 1980 (evening), p. 2.

31. Riichirō Amiya, "Kōkyōsei to wa nani ka?" (What Is the Public Good?), *Mainichi Shimbun,* 12 September 1980, p. 2.

32. "Shinkansen soshō: jūmin, jitsujō no haiso" (The Shinkansen Lawsuit: In Effect, the Residents Have Lost), *Nihon Keizai Shimbun,* 11 September 1980 (evening), p. 1; and " 'Gensoku nashi' ni hotto" (No Slowdown—A Great Relief), *Nihon Keizai Shimbun,* 11 September 1980 (evening).

33. "Shinkansen soshō, jūmin gawa ga haiso" (The Shinkansen Lawsuit—The Residents Lost), *Yomiuri Shimbun,* 11 September 1980 (evening), p. 1. The Nagoya movement has always insisted that there was no conflict between its goals and "the public good."

34. Yoshihito Homma, "Shizukana seikatsu wa modoru no ka" (Will the Tranquil Way of Life Return?), *Mainichi Shimbun,* 24 March 1980, p. 3.

35. "San iken tairitsu kukkiri" (A Clear Clash of Three Opinions), *Yomiuri Shimbun,* 1 September 1978, p. 20.

36. Each of the twenty-three wards of Tokyo has an elected unicameral assembly *(kugikai)* and an elected head of the ward *(kugichō).* I use the term *mayor* for *kugichō.*

37. "Higai bōshi e—oi shiranu ichinen" ("In Preventing the Damage— One Year in Which an Old Man Forgot His Age), *Asahi Shimbun,* 15 May 1978, p. 21.

38. "Hantai undō ni dōyō" (Confusion in the Opposition Movement), *Sankei Shimbun* (Saitama edition), 4 September 1980, p. 1.

39. Misidentification of representatives in news reports should not necessarily be regarded as deliberate. The media were used to dealing with Koike, who, until his expulsion in late 1979, had long been the official representative of the Yono Anti-Shinkansen Alliance. Both the mass media and the leaders of the citizens' movements in Saitama and Tokyo had regarded him as an articulate spokesperson. All the Shinkansen movements I studied experienced serious leadership problems and had important leaders who dropped out, defected, or were expelled. Consequently, it was difficult to keep track of exactly who represented the various Shinkansen citizens' movements at a particular time. Even the National Organization of Victims of Pollution, a federation of antipollution citizens' movements, made mistakes. The brochure for the 1981 "Environmental Week" listed a former president of the Kita Ward movement who had defected. The error was discussed at an executive meeting of the Kita Ward movement, and the decision was made not to distribute the brochure in Kita Ward.

40. For example, during 1981–1982, the official policy of the citizens' movement in Kita Ward was to oppose Shinkansen pollution, but a few participants continued to advocate absolute opposition to the construction of the Shinkansen in their neighborhoods.

41. This incident was reported to me by several leaders of the Nagoya movement.

42. The leader in Kita Ward was able to draw on the experience of the Shinkansen citizens' movements in dealing with NHK. In fact, the Shinkansen citizens' movement in Nagoya initially developed strength in 1971 as an organization of several thousand families who refused to pay NHK user fees. Since the electrical currents of the Shinkansen sometimes cause poor television reception, the leaders of the citizens' movement demanded that NHK negotiate with JNR to resolve the problem, threatening that if NHK did not comply, they would expand the nonpayment movement. According to one former leader in Nagoya, residents along the entire Tōkaidō Shinkansen corridor were eager to join, because it offered an excuse not to pay NHK user fees.

43. The photographer of the Yono Anti-Shinkansen Alliance called my attention to this *oshikake* and showed me a film that he had made documenting it. Exactly what triggered the action is unclear. One leader claimed that the newspaper had printed an article implying that a situation similar to

the radical protest movement against the Narita International Airport would develop in Yono City if the Shinkansen movement were not destroyed.

44. Charles Tilly, *From Mobilization to Revolution* (New York: Random House, 1978), pp. 143–159.

45. In its 1982 decision on the Osaka International Airport Pollution Case, the Japanese Supreme Court further dampened enthusiasm for court cases by rejecting the plaintiffs' demand for an injunction to modify the operation of the Osaka International Airport. The Osaka High Court had granted the injunction in 1975, but the defendant (the minister of transportation) appealed the decision.

46. See the account by Kyōko Asai, "Shinkansen hantai no oni onna" (Resolute Woman Opposing the Shinkansen), *Gungun* 11 (July 1982): 9.

47. The Nagoya movement might have missed a rare opportunity for effective publicity. Because of her oratorical skills, Mrs. Tada was chosen as the principal speaker for a movement rally on the night before the Nagoya District Court announced its verdict. During a visit of Kita Ward activists to Nagoya, she made people cry with her descriptions of Shinkansen pollution. For an intriguing discussion of the portrayal of suffering mothers in Japan's popular media, see Ian Buruma, *Behind the Mask: On Sexual Demons, Sacred Mothers, Transvestites, Gangsters, and Other Japanese Cultural Heroes* (New York: New American Library, 1984), chap. 2.

48. The Shinkansen citizens' movements occurred before the popularization of personal computers and word processing in Japan. Someone adept with a word processor can now prepare an edition of a movement newspaper in a few hours, but in the early 1980s the skills of printers were crucial for producing attractive mini-media publications. At least three leaders of the citizens' movements had some experience working as printers. One activist in Yono, for example, had helped produce documents for the Japanese army at her father's printing company as a young woman, and she had an almost encyclopedic knowledge of typefaces, paper, and ink. Her expertise, however, would be almost irrelevant to the production of mini-media in the 1990s.

49. It is ironic that the citizens' movements used noisy speaker trucks to protest the noise pollution of the Shinkansen. In effect, the citizens' movement itself became a cause of noise pollution.

50. As noted earlier, the Shinkansen interferes with the transmission of electrical currents and thus causes poor television reception. The leaders of the early Nagoya movement felt that NHK had an obligation to force JNR to deal not only with this problem but also with Shinkansen pollution in general.

51. The photographer of the Yono Anti-Shinkansen Alliance kindly showed me such a movie in October 1982.

52. For example, Yono Shi Shinkansen Hantai Dōmei Kyōgikai (Yono City Anti-Shinkansen League), "Dai hakkai teiki sōkai gian" (Draft Resolution of the Eighth Regular General Meeting) (Yono, Saitama: 10 May 1981), pp. 3–4.

53. *Shizukesa e no Tatakai* 25 (25 September 1975): 1.

54. Central Committee of the Japan Communist Party, *Nihon kyōsantō shōkai* (Introduction to the Japan Communist Party) (Tokyo: Central Committee of the Japan Communist Party, 1981), p. 120.

55. Ibid., p. 121.

56. Information about the local newspapers of the JCP was supplied by the editor of *Atarashii Kita Ku.*

57. Central Committee of JCP, *Nihon kyōsantō shōkai,* p. 89.

58. JNR also treated the symbolism of the protest tower seriously. It filed a suit against the president of the citizens' movement to have the protest tower dismantled, alleging that the tower was on JNR's land. The citizens' movement and its lawyers countered that it was on the "public" land of a local Shintō shrine.

8

Media Coverage of U.S.–Japanese Relations

ELLIS S. KRAUSS

UNTIL recently one of the important factors in the U.S.–Japanese relationship received little attention: the role of the mass media. Are the media merely the "messenger," objectively reporting events that take place without making an independent contribution to the relationship? Or do the mass media make major independent contributions in determining the nature of the bilateral linkage? The answers to these questions are almost impossible to ascertain, but in this chapter I will argue that because the media *are* the medium, they affect the message, and because they *are* the channel, they affect the conflict. The structure and process of print and television news gathering and editing inevitably affect the presentation and content of news that each country receives about the other. Therefore, for better or worse, mass media are one of the major contributors to friction between the United States and Japan, and to its management. The main purpose of this chapter, then, will be to analyze how the structural differences between mass media in Japan and the United States affect the kind of news the two countries receive about each other and thus the relationship between them.

The Medium Molds the Message

Mass media perform two crucial functions in modern democracies such as Japan and the United States. First, they are part of the communication process among and between political elites. We often underestimate the extent to which political elites in a particular nation actually derive their information from the mass media and send (intentional and unintentional) signals through them to other elites.[1] Certainly the same is true, probably more so, when it comes to the elites of two different nations. Thus in addition to the actual process of negotiation between the two countries, the mass media are another important channel by which Japanese and American elites communicate with each other.

The second major function the mass media perform in these democracies is to help shape the images of mass publics, including the popular images of other nations. These may not derive solely from the mass media, but undoubtedly the media contribute to the process of image formation by providing information and symbols that can be used to form images and/or to reinforce or disconfirm images derived from other sources. Although there are other sources of elite communication, such as personal contacts, and of mass image formation, such as family and school, the mass media are an increasingly important contributor, particularly in these media-saturated democracies.

If this is the case, then the question of whether the mass media are merely a channel or an independent source of trade friction between the United States and Japan is moot: as an important channel of communication between and among political elites and as a major factor in the image formation process of mass publics, the mass media are automatically a major determinant of the relationship, because there is no such thing as a perfectly neutral and objective communication channel. Whatever the intent of the communicators, it is impossible for some form of bias not to enter into mass media news because the organization and process of selection, editing, and presentation of the news will affect the type of news that is presented.

The media are neither the neutral messenger they claim to be nor the politicized, partisan, and ideologically biased force politicians often claim them to be. First, as discussed in chapter 3 of this volume, the selection, processing, and transmission that inevitably are part of the journalistic process are shaped first by the characteristics of the news organization, which in turn are influenced by the environment—legal, financial, commercial, and so forth—in which the organization operates. Thus, simply put, organization influences process, which shapes content. Second, far more important than personal political biases are the shared professional biases that derive from professional norms. These include the collective definitions of what "news" is and what it means to be "objective" and "professional," and beliefs about the proper relationship with a source, standards for good journalism, and the way to perform the technical aspects of one's job. The different political and ideological biases of reporters, editors, and publishers may cancel each other out within the same media organization or across various media organizations. The *shared* organizational forms and professional norms of various media within a particular country, however, can most consistently shape the media product within a nation.

While the structural aspects of the media are not the sole determinant of what is transmitted, as the basic organizational and motivational framework within which media elites operate, they provide fundamental and predictable explanations for why the patterns of media products in different countries may vary. The differences in structure and process of the mass media organizations in Japan and the United States therefore affect the pattern of information and images that elites and mass audiences on both sides of the Pacific receive about each other, and thus they fundamentally influence the relationship between the two countries.

Concentration and Coverage

Concentration

The Japanese and American societies are among the most media-influenced in the world. The United States has had nearly three times the number of newspapers of any other developed country and about ten times the number in Japan, but the circulation per capita in Japan has been more than double that of the United States and greater than that of any other major advanced industrialized country. Circulation in Japan is more than one copy per household (1.22).[2] In other words, the U.S. newspaper distribution system is much more decentralized than Japan's and thus larger, but Japan's more concentrated system saturates its readership more.

The concentration of newspaper distribution in Japan is further reinforced by the existence of true national newspapers with nation-wide distribution systems and huge circulations. The circulation of each of these dwarfs those of the few newspapers, such as *USA Today*, the *New York Times*, or the *Christian Science Monitor*, that have pretenses to being "national" papers in the United States.[3]

The characteristic of greater diversity and decentralization in the United States but greater concentration and saturation in Japan also extends to television news in the two countries. America's three national television networks must compete with independent channels and the Cable News Network (CNN) for daily visual news coverage of national events. In Japan the public broadcasting service NHK until recently dominated news coverage. With greater news programming and audience, and far greater reportorial staffs, NHK was at the center of the broadcast information system in Japan. The commercial stations were unable legally to enter into exclusive programming contracts and derived much of their national news from Tokyo stations partially owned by the giant national papers and relied to some extent on their news staffs for discovering stories; they also depended heavily on the giant national newspapers for their news. Only in the late 1980s did the commercial stations mount a real challenge to NHK in the news field and undermine NHK's dominance (see chapter 5).

The combination of a dominant public network and commercial stations dependent on the national newspapers for much of their news gathering has made both Japanese television news gathering and distribution more heavily centralized than has been the case in the United States for most of the postwar period.

The Basic Disparity of Coverage

One of the most striking differences in the coverage of each country by the other is the sheer difference in amount of information. The United States plays a much larger role in the news from abroad in Japan than Japan does in the United States. This fact is obvious to anyone who reads the newspapers or watches television news in both countries, but few realize how great that disparity is. As one astute American journalist observed, for the United States to match the coverage that Japan gives the United States, "we'd have to be at war with them."[4] Yet there are actually few data measuring the degree of that difference. One rough and admittedly incomplete indicator is a small experiment I conducted, in which I analyzed the content of one week of news in the *New York Times* and *Asahi Shimbun* (morning edition only), each recognized as the leading newspapers "of record" in their respective countries.[5] The results confirmed the subjective impression of far greater attention to news of the United States in Japan than of Japan in the United States. Thus, there were only six articles in the *New York Times* about Japan that week. Half of these articles were on page 1, the other half in the business section. Further, of these articles, two were actually about Japanese transplant factories or about Detroit emulating Japanese production technology, and two were about West German chancellor Helmut Kohl's speech urging Japan to do more to aid Eastern Europe. Only two articles all week were actually about Japan, properly speaking.

By contrast, the same week there were nineteen *New York Times* articles on the former Soviet Union (excluding Eastern Europe), all but four (two in business, one in sports, and one editorial) in the main news section of the paper. Further, there was a different pattern to the coverage of Japan and the former Soviet Union. A full half of the articles on Japan that week appeared on one day (Tuesday), and there were three days in the week when no Japan-related article at all was published in that day's edition. The articles on the former Soviet Union appeared every day but one during that week, and although seven articles appeared on one day (Monday), on every day that week (except the one day with no article) there were at least two articles. In other words, compared to news about the former Soviet Union, news about Japan received much less coverage, and that coverage was more erratic.

As for Japanese newspaper coverage of the United States during a similar one-week period, *Asahi* ran forty articles on the United States, of which three were on the first page. Thus, although the attention paid to each country on the first page was similar during this week, inside the newspaper the extent of difference in coverage was striking. Instead of the *New York Times'* average of less than one article per day, *Asahi* averaged nearly six articles per day. Further, the coverage was more consistent: there was no day on which fewer than three articles about the United States appeared, and on most days there were at least six.

Despite the continued difference in the amount of coverage the two countries give each other, the imbalance is not as great as it once was: the amount of American coverage of Japan has been increasing consistently over the past three decades. Most observers would agree that coverage of Japan has increased substantially in the elite U.S. press so that few days go by without at least one or a few stories about Japan in at least one, if not more, of the major American "national" newspapers.

Again, there is systematic evidence confirming subjective impressions. The number of articles about Japan in the *New York Times* increased nearly fivefold from 1966 to 1986.[6] Interestingly, however, when broken down by type of content that large increase was mostly in articles about the economy. Articles about the economy as a percentage of the total tripled from 1966 to 1986, while the percentage of articles about politics, defense, international relations, welfare, or social and cultural matters decreased or remained the same as a percentage of the total, even though the actual number of articles may have increased in some cases during those two decades.[7] In other words, while Americans were able to read a great deal more about Japan by the 1980s, what they read primarily concerned business and economics, not Japanese politics, foreign policy, culture, or society. Further, one analysis of placement of articles on several friction issues—such as the FSX fighter plane, Japanese purchases of Columbia Pictures and Rockefeller Center, and the Structural Impediments Initiative (SII) issues—found that on the first two issues about 40 percent, and on SII about two-thirds, of articles were on the first page of the business section rather than the first page of the news section.[8]

During the 1980s the trend toward more information about Japan continued, as can be seen in table 8.1, which shows the number of articles containing the word *Japan* that appeared during the whole of the years indicated.

As can be seen, the number of articles published in which Japan played a role more than doubled in each of the two U.S. newspapers. Undoubtedly, the strong interest in Japan on the West Coast accounts for the fact that the *Los Angeles Times* had twice as many articles concerning Japan as the *Washington Post*. Coverage in the *Financial Times* of London is given to provide a comparison. Although there was an increase in articles referring to Japan, the British paper's increase was not as great as that of the American papers. However, the *Financial Times* began the decade with substantially more focus on Japan than either American newspaper. The American press, then, has begun to catch up with or, in the case of the *Los Angeles Times,* even surpass the coverage the London paper has always given Japan. That the increase in American attention to Japan is not merely a function of broader coverage of other countries, or of Asia more generally, is shown by the fact that the number of articles referring to

Table 8.1 Number of Times "Japan" Mentioned in Newspapers (1984 and 1990)

	1984	1990
Washington Post	1,646	3,124
Los Angeles Times	3,548	7,472
Financial Times (London)	5,864	6,425

Source: Adapted from data presented in "Datagraph: American Press's Interest in Japan," *Journal of Japanese Trade and Industry* 6 (1991): 52.

China shows no comparable increase except during 1989, the year of the Tiananmen uprising.[9] Nevertheless, Japan's press coverage of the United States remains overwhelmingly larger.

Similarly, in Japanese television coverage the United States looms extraordinarily large. In a content analysis done in 1983 of three weeks of the NHK main evening news show, I found that approximately 60 percent of the foreign news items concerned the United States.[10] Another study of NHK and the American network CBS over a four-month period in 1987 found that although CBS carried almost double the international and foreign items carried by NHK, NHK broadcast two and a half times as many items about Japanese–U.S. relations as CBS.[11] A third study found that 45 percent of the foreign news and 30 percent of all foreign scenes in documentaries on Japanese television were about the United States.[12]

Perhaps the most recent and systematic evidence of an "information gap" in television news between the two countries is an analysis of the content of the major television evening news programs in each country and how they portray the other nation in their news coverage.[13] During the seven months of coverage in late 1992 and early 1993 analyzed by the project, there were more than 1,100 separate items about the United States on Japan's television news, but only 92 segments about Japan on American television news. The ratio of more than ten to one in Japan's favor was equally true of the actual amount of time devoted to such coverage. Although the first few months of the study encompassed the U.S. presidential election and inauguration, which undoubtedly diminished the amount of other news coverage and thus contributed to the size of the "gap," clearly there is a large disparity in the amount of news that the citizens of the two nations receive about each other.

Equally striking is the difference in priorities given to the different regions of the world in each country's television news coverage, as table 8.2 shows. While a full third of Japan's international news focused on the United States, all of Asia ranked only third in U.S. news coverage of the regions of the world, equal to the Middle East. More than half of all international news stories concerned Eastern (including Russia) and Western Europe. Not shown is the fact, from the same study, that Japan receives less coverage on U.S. television news than Britain, France, or Germany individually, despite having an economy almost as large as all three combined.

Finally, as in newspaper coverage, Japan as presented in U.S. television news is primarily a matter of business, economics, or U.S.–Japanese relations. More than 68 percent of the American television

Table 8.2   Japan and the United States: Television News Coverage
of World Regions (Percentages)

JAPAN	UNITED STATES
1. U.S. (33)	1. Eastern Europe (34)
2. Asia (30)	2. Western Europe (21)
3. Western Europe (14)	3. Middle East (13); Asia (13)
4. Eastern Europe (12)	4. Africa (11)
	5. Central and South America (6)

Source: Kensuke Kōno, Yumiko Hara, and Kensaku Saitō, "Terebi wa aitekoku wo dō tsutaete iru ka (2)," *Hōso Kenkyū to Chōsa,* July 1994, table 3, p. 7.

news segments dealt with international relations, led by U.S.–Japanese relations, and 59 percent related to economics or business. On the other hand, about 46 percent focused on government and politics, while fewer than 40 percent each portrayed culture, social issues, or daily life (percentages total more than 100 percent because items could be classified in more than one category). In Japan, conversely, the United States is more a cultural and social story than an economic or international one: more than 45 percent of Japanese television news segments on the United States involved social problems, another 34 percent concerned culture, and only 20 percent related to economics. Less than one-third (between 28 percent and 31 percent each) involved international relations, social life, daily life, or politics and government. Clearly, while Japan tends to be a matter of economics, business, trade friction, or government and politics to American news executives, the United States is more a societal and cultural story to Japan's television networks.[14] Further, Japan's U.S. coverage, more than America's Japan coverage, tends to emphasize problems and manmade troubles (such as violence) and natural disasters.[15]

Some causes of the disparity obviously are not media-related: for the United States, after all, Japan is just one, though an important one, of many key relationships, while for Japan the United States is its single most crucial economic, political, and military relationship. Further, Japan's wartime defeat by the United States and the subsequent American Occupation of Japan gave the United States an overwhelming presence in the Japanese consciousness. For its part, the United States has a greater consciousness of Europe than of Asia as a legacy of immigration patterns. Nevertheless, the size of the disparity argues that more is at work here than differences in history and global role.

Structure and Coverage

The structure of the media and journalistic norms in the two countries have reinforced the differences in history and global role to produce more news about the United States in Japan and less about Japan in the United States. First, there is simply more news coverage of all kinds in Japan than in the United States. While U.S. newspapers publish one edition per day and the television networks have only one major news program per day (the evening news), the Japanese major newspapers have both morning and afternoon editions and networks like NHK have continuous news programs throughout the day—fifteen in all.

Second, American newspapers tend to be relatively unspecialized in their formats, making almost no distinctions among types of news except for sports and sometimes business and finance. On the other hand, Japanese major newspapers are specialized by page. Thus after the first page, which has the major news stories of the day whatever their type, there usually follows a political page, international page(s), economic pages, and so forth. Thus in American newspapers international news competes with domestic news for space, and if there seems to be a lot of interesting domestic news, foreign news will get less space that day. In Japanese newspapers the space for foreign news is always the same so that foreign news does not compete with domestic news for space.

In part because of the large number of countries competing for the attention of editors in American papers to fill a relatively small (and daily fluctuating) foreign "news hole," foreign stories must be particularly dramatic—usually "coups and earthquakes"[16]—to make the news pages. Japan's long-term political stability has helped to discount its value as a news story. As one journalist put it, Japan is a "high significance/low drama" story for American media.[17] Generally lacking dramatic news and also dynamic and memorable personalities as political leaders, Japan does not fit easily into U.S. journalists' definitions of what constitutes "news." This may be especially true of television news, where dramatic images conveyed by video or live visuals often are favored in coverage and in determining what stories go on the air.[18] Japan thus does not make the news as often as its significance warrants.

When Japan does gain coverge in American newspapers or network news, the item rarely features the society, culture, or daily life of its people. Instead, Japan is defined primarily as an economic or trade-friction story. Stories about business, economics, or trade and diplomacy are abstract stories, not the kind of items that involve the daily life of individuals. As a consequence, U.S. news audiences do not receive a clear and complete image of the people and nation of Japan, giving Japan a "faceless" image to Americans.[19]

With its larger number of news outlets and fixed newspaper space reserved for foreign news, Japan offers a greater potential for stories about the United States. Another factor is that the foreign desk of a Japanese media organization considers any information about the United States relevant to Japan as "news." While in the United States Japan must meet criteria of drama and importance to compete for limited space with other foreign and domestic stories, in Japan stories about the United States seem to be defined as news and are used to fill a constant and larger amount of foreign news space.

Finally, time is an important factor in the decisions of television news organizations leading to disparities of coverage. Tokyo is fourteen hours ahead of the eastern United States where most U.S. political and economic news takes place. This means that when it is 4 P.M. in Washington, it is 6 A.M. the next day in Tokyo; the end of a news day in the United States is thus the start of a news day in Japan. On the other hand, when it is 4 P.M. in Tokyo, it is 2 A.M. in New York, so that the end of a news day in Japan falls in the middle of the night in the United States. These simple temporal facts make a difference for the news process. The accumulation of events that have taken place in the United States that day can be reported on the long morning news shows of Japanese television and then fed into the other news programs throughout the day. The major news events in Japan, however, tend to take place after the network evening news programs in the United States, and are already almost stale news by the time the major noon and evening news broadcasts come around again. This increases the likelihood that events from elsewhere may supplant news from Japan in the limited time available. Although CNN can incorporate any major stories from Japan at any time, the lack of drama in Japanese news items and the small number of people watching the news in the middle of the night still keep to a minimum the incorporation of Japanese stories and their audience impact.

Time enters into the coverage of U.S. news by Japanese newspapers in a slightly different way than for television, but with the same result—more coverage. Japan's major national newspapers publish a completely separate afternoon edition *(yūkan)* daily, in addition to their main morning *(chōkan)* edition. The afternoon editions need "new" news to differentiate themselves from the morning editions. Because the end of the news day in the United States fits nicely with the 10 A.M. Tokyo deadline for the afternoon editions, stories about the United States find their way easily and in large numbers into these editions. One Japanese journalist who has served as a Washington correspondent calls the afternoon editions "the root of the various evils" that, when combined with the time difference, force Japanese newspaper reporters in the United States to produce twice as many articles as domestic reporters and lead to the excessive news about the United States in Japanese papers.[20] Even U.S. news that the foreign desk considers relatively unimportant will be included by the editors because of the need to fill space in the afternoon editions and the traditional conception that American news is inherently more important than other foreign news.[21]

On television many of the main evening news programs are an hour long, and even shorter ones may contain far more news items than the typical American news program. Here, too, the structural dimension of the comparative size of the "news hole" works together with the historical American focus of Japan's news and the Eurocentrism of U.S. news to create the large "information gap" between the two countries.

Newspaper "Balance" and the Relationship to Domestic Sources

United States and Japan: Different Types of "Balance"

The structure of television news organizations also makes the quality of news about each other different in the two countries. A quantitative study of three cases of U.S.–Japanese friction—conducted by the Mansfield Center for Pacific Affairs and the Dentsū Institute for Humanistic Studies—included measures of "balance" (defined as roughly equal representation of both sides) in analyzing the major newspaper coverage in the two countries. The results showed a fair amount of "balance" in both U.S. and Japanese newspaper coverage; the two sides, however, attained that balance in different ways. American newspapers tended to give arguments and rebuttals of arguments on both sides of an issue in most articles. Even in articles where only one side's argument was given, there generally was not a great deal of disparity between the proportion of articles favoring one side and the proportion of articles favoring the other.[22]

In the Japanese case, however, balance was attained mainly by a larger proportion of articles that presented no arguments for either side. In the FSX and SII disputes, for example, three out of every five Japanese articles presented no arguments for either side. Instead, they tended to give factual descriptions of events. Of the remainder, a greater number of Japanese articles presented only one side's point of view, and the overwhelming proportion of these favored the Japanese position.[23] Thus, although American newspaper articles about U.S.–Japanese friction were more interpretive and the Japanese articles tended to be more descriptive, when the latter did take sides they tended to favor their own country's viewpoint.

Evidence for such "journalistic nationalism" among Japanese reporters comes from a survey of reporters conducted by the East-West Center at the University of Hawai'i. This survey asked Japanese reporters stationed in Washington and Western (mostly American but a few European) correspondents in Tokyo to rate each other's press on such dimensions as seriousness/shallowness, objectivity/nonobjectivity, balance/imbalance, and so forth. Consistently, Tokyo-based Western correspondents rated the Japanese press as more nonobjective, imbalanced, and incomplete than the ratings given by Washington-based Japanese reporters to American newspapers.[24]

What might account for Japanese newspapers' tendency to be more factual but also more one-sided, while American newspapers are more interpretive but also more evenhanded? One of the major causes of these differences is probably the contrast in the organization of reporter-source relations and journalist norms of "objectivity" that derive from a different historical tradition of relationship to authority. Newspapers in the United States, as in Western Europe, originally developed as partisan mouthpieces for particular political parties and ideologies. Only in the mid-twentieth century did norms of "objective" news reporting become dominant. American newspaper norms thus still call for an interpretive style—"good" journalism presents different arguments and points of view—but have incorporated the notion that subjective arguments must be "balanced" by giving space to both sides of an issue.

In contrast, Japanese journalism before 1945 developed with greater official restrictions. For a brief period after the 1868 Meiji Restoration, newspapers were an important part of the movement for a constitution and expansion of Western-style democratic rights, but thereafter Japan's modernizing elite asserted greater control over the press. Japanese newspapers had to operate under a variety of official and unofficial restrictions and finally, during the repressive military-dominated period from the 1930s to 1945, came to be primarily transmitters of official policy perspectives and ideology. With the greater freedom of the press after the American Occupation (1945–1952), Japanese newspapers became institutionally independent and often quite critical of government in their editorial and editing perspectives.[25] As in the West, providing "objective news" and separating fact from opinion became institutionalized in newspapers, but in the Japanese case, this was seen to mean providing confirmed factual accounts rather than balanced but interpretive accounts. More often than not, facts supplied by official sources, such as the bureaucracy, easily fit the definition of confirmed description and are used extensively by Japanese reporters. Thus, modern norms of journalistic responsibility have combined with the different historical legacies in the two countries to produce two different concepts of "balance."

Reporters' Clubs and Official Sources

How news gathering is organized reflects such differences. In the United States newspaper reporters are assigned to specific "beats," but their relationships with their sources (including those outside of government in "think tanks," policy institutes, academia, interest groups, or other political parties) are relatively informal and wide-ranging. Television correspondents—with the exception of those covering the White House, the Pentagon, and the State Department, for example—are not assigned to specialized institutions at all; instead, they cover all news in a particular region. Whether or not they are assigned to a specific "beat," U.S. reporters' modus operandi is to try to balance a story by seeking an opposing point of view and to check out the "facts" and viewpoints of official sources obtained in press releases and briefings by going to others in different organizations and institutions.[26]

The organization of relationships between reporters and sources is different in Japan. As described in chapters 3 and 4, national newspaper reporters and NHK correspondents are generally assigned to a reporters' club *(kisha kurabu)* affiliated with a specific institution or organization in Japanese government and society. Regional or local journalists and all magazine reporters are excluded.[27]

In Japan the overwhelming amount of basic news originates with the reporters stationed in these clubs. Indeed, Japanese media as a matter of organizational practice separate reporters engaged in gathering news from those who write more interpretive and investigative articles. Those journalists who are not attached to a reporters' club are called *yūgun* (originally a military term whose best translation in this context is probably something like "troubleshooter"). The *yūgun* reporters write Japanese newspapers' in-depth series, which constitute the closest thing to Western-style news analysis, interpretation, and investigative reporting one finds in Japan.[28] Thus, separating interpretation and description in the news is mirrored in role distinctions between types of reporters.

Reporters' clubs have important consequences for the news in Japan. They foster conformity among the national newspapers in news selection and presentation, despite the newspapers' ostensibly different editorial stances.[29] They represent an "early warning" system for both NHK television news and—through their affiliated major newspapers—the commercial stations and promote a reporter's dependence on official sources. Reporters at these clubs are kept so busy with the innumerable press releases and the daily activities of the officials they cover that they have little time for investigative journalism or checking independent sources.[30] Further, the clubs' rules keep many kinds of information given by officials off the record.[31]

In the course of covering their agency's top officials, reporters are expected to go on *yomawari*, "night rounds" (also called *yo-uchi*, or "night attack"). They drop in on the officials' homes late at night, where they are served food and drink by the official and where they get an informal and off-the-record background briefing of sorts.[32] It is here that reporters learn what is really going on behind the press releases and formal statements. Yet they often cannot or do not report these out of deference to the honesty and openness of the official.

This type of reporter dependence can only result in a relationship with a source in which the reporter has difficulty writing independently or critically. In addition, the incestuous, closed, and intensive relationship gives officials the opportunity to manipulate the news in a one-sided fashion,[33] confident that their reporters' dependence on them for information and lack of a wide range of alternative sources will deter contradiction in the news reports.

Until recently foreign correspondents were barred from the reporters' clubs. Today their admission and any limitations on what activities they may participate in are left to the discretion of the particular club and its members.[34] Ironically, after their struggle for the right to be included, few correspondents choose to participate even when a particular club allows them to do so. Some may make this decision because of the barrier of language, while others may be uncomfortable with the operating style of the Japanese reporters' clubs. Whatever the reason, the lack of foreign correspondents in these clubs as regular members probably has certain unintended consequences for Japanese media coverage of the U.S.–Japanese relationship. Japanese reporters, already tied to the officials they cover and who feed them the official version of stories, are structurally hampered from checking out the American perspective by talking with their U.S. correspondents on a daily basis.

Thus, reporters' clubs and different journalistic norms regarding what constitutes news result in a large number of factual and noninterpretive stories in Japanese coverage of U.S.–Japanese relations, stories based on Japanese and official sources of information. Given the specialized dependence of Japanese reporters on officials and their isolation from American correspondents, it is no surprise that even when they do write interpretive pieces, they naturally tend to represent the Japanese perspective.

Foreign Correspondents

Further evidence of the importance of the domestic structure of news gathering and processing is found in stories filed by Japanese reporters in the United States. In the United States, where the reporters' club system does not operate and journalists come into frequent contact with their American counterparts, articles by Japanese journalists do not fit the pattern described above. The Mansfield study cited earlier indicated that in both countries, reports from abroad were less likely to blame the other side than stories filed at home. Thus, "Japanese stories with a U.S. dateline were much less likely to ascribe blame to the United States than those with a Japanese dateline. Similarly, American stories with a Japanese dateline were less likely to ascribe blame to Japan than those with a U.S. dateline. In other words, journalists based in a foreign country seem to be less critical of that country than their colleagues at home writing on the same issue."[35]

Systematic exposure to the other side's point of view obviously leads to a more evenhanded approach to the issues. In other respects, however, foreign correspondents face problems of news gathering in the other country that can exacerbate national differences in media organizations and styles, and can affect coverage of Japanese–U.S. friction.

American Reporters in Tokyo: The "Feedback Effect" and the "Revisionist" Trend

By the late 1980s there were more than 75 U.S. companies employing more than 250 reporters (of whom 100 were Japanese nationals) covering Japan, an increase of more than 60 percent compared to the decade before.³⁶ As compared to the past, many more Tokyo-based American reporters now speak and read Japanese and have studied Japanese history and culture.

This fact alone has had profound consequences for coverage of U.S.–Japanese relations. The 1991 example of the Speaker of Japan's upper house calling American workers "lazy"—a statement that still reverberates in American public opinion—is one case in point. Japanese public officials used to feel able to say one thing to domestic reporters and to take a more careful, polite, and conciliatory approach to foreign journalists. Now that more American journalists have better Japanese-language skills, they are able to read the Japanese papers and talk to their Japanese counterparts, making it much more difficult for officials to segment their audiences. Attempts to do so cause a "feedback effect": the statement intended for domestic consumption is reported in the Japanese press and then is picked up by the U.S. press, triggering an American reaction, which itself becomes a new incident in friction. Such an effect is increasingly common as a result of the changing composition of the American press corps in Tokyo.

Despite the fair degree of balance achieved in American coverage of Japan and the tendency of both countries' foreign correspondents not to ascribe blame to their host country, the Mansfield Center study found that American reporters in Tokyo were more parochial than Japanese reporters in at least one important respect: Tokyo-based American reporters tended to use Japanese sources for their stories even less than Japanese correspondents in Washington used American sources. The explanation for this finding is not far to seek. One factor is the reporters' club system, which keeps most foreign journalists from daily, institutionalized contact with Japanese officials. Although foreign reporters have access to officials at some levels, it is difficult for them to gain access at the highest levels.

But even if American reporters could join reporters' clubs freely, as may happen in the future, or could gain easier access to higher officials, it is questionable whether they would do so. American reporters equate the reporters' club system with "spoonfeeding" and consider it at variance with their own norms about what constitutes good reporting. Further, at least one reporter I spoke to said that high-ranking Japanese officials rarely say anything of value to foreign journalists anyway. He gave the example of the bureau chief of an elite American newspaper, who interviewed the then prime minister three times but failed to use the material because the leader had said nothing useful or newsworthy.³⁷

A recent trend in coverage by American foreign correspondents in Tokyo is for their stories to reflect the "revisionist" point of view or assumptions. "Revisionism" is the school of thought that finds Japanese institutions unique and fundamentally different from both American institutions and economic theory, and thus sees them to be a major source of the bilateral trade friction. An interview with a knowledgeable American correspondent for a news magazine revealed much about this development and about the nature of American reporting on Japan.[38] According to this correspondent, Ezra Vogel's *Japan as Number One* (1979) offered the most influential view, which shaped reporting about Japan for almost a decade. But by the late 1980s it had been replaced by the revisionist view. " 'The rules of engagement'—the 'agenda' "—is now set by the revisionists with "the other side shooting blanks." Revisionism became "the conventional wisdom."

There are several reasons for this, the reporter said. One is that "the official reality" of the U.S. government and classical economics is "so completely out of step with what's going on here." During the Bush administration, for example, there were too many discrepancies between the views and explanations of the U.S. executive branch, on the one hand, and what reporters themselves experienced in Japan, on the other. In contrast, most of what the revisionists say "jibes with what journalists see and what journalists hear in Japan"—in other words, fits with a perspective that treats Japan as unique.

Second, the "visceral reaction" of the Tokyo government in attacking the revisionist view was "a 'red flag' to journalists." It did not undercut the influence of revisionism but instead drew attention to it and spurred American journalists' interest in it. Finally, the reporter noted how *Atlantic Monthly* editor James Fallows, formerly based in Tokyo, helped popularize and legitimize revisionism in the journalistic community. As a "god of journalism" with "unassailable liberal credentials," Fallows, in supporting the revisionist line, guaranteed that revisionism could no longer be accused of being motivated by racism or "Japan bashing."

Revisionist voices are by no means the only ones heard in the coverage of Japan. Establishment papers, such as the *Wall Street Journal* or the *New York Times,* typically reflect the assumptions of classical economics that all economies work according to the same universal principles, or that the U.S. and Japanese economies are converging.[39] Some observers attribute the spread of the revisionist perspective more to its popularity among editors in the United States than to its adoption by reporters abroad.[40] Nevertheless, the views of the American magazine correspondent presented here are interesting not only for what they reveal about the origins of the revisionist tendency among Tokyo-based American correspondents but also for what they suggest about those correspondents themselves. They reveal the iconoclastic norms of the reporters who are wary of both their own government's official orthodoxy as well as the Japanese government's official "line," and the prestige hierarchy in American journalism, whereby norms set by fellow professionals can dominate those set by news organizations. Finally, they reinforce the view of America's Japan coverage as giving equal importance to conveying viewpoints and "facts."

The Japanese Correspondent in Washington

Each major Japanese news organization stations several reporters in the United States, usually most of them (four or five persons) in Washington, somewhat fewer (one to three) in New York, and one on the West Coast, usually in Los Angeles. This in itself represents a structural problem: the news from the United States is heavily oriented toward political news from Washington. The same might be said about American news from Japan, as most U.S. correspondents are based in Tokyo; the contexts, however, are different. The Tokyo region contains almost one-quarter of the country's population, most of the corporate headquarters, and a concentration of educational and cultural institutions. It is thus more than the political and administrative center of Japan; it plays a very different role in Japanese society than does Washington in American society. Only if Washington, New York, Boston, and Los Angeles were merged would there be an equivalent American city.[41]

The different roles of Washington and Tokyo in their respective societies, and the greater diversity and size of the United States in comparison to Japan mean that news from Washington does not necessarily reflect the entire society as well as it is presented as doing. The problem, according to former Japanese correspondents in Washington whom I interviewed, is that "the beltway mentality"—that distinctive Washington form of parochialism that obsessively attributes importance to the smallest national political event or gossip—soon affects Japanese reporters as well.[42]

This is one reason why the Japanese press often tends to overreact to bills—however minor or however unlikely their passage—that might be hostile to Japan. There are other reasons for this syndrome as well. One is the failure to understand the congressional process, in which less than 5 percent of the bills introduced into Congress each session pass. Another is the problem of access to sources. While gaining access to the White House is difficult for Japanese reporters, they can easily gain access to members of Congress and their staffs.[43] Congressional activities and views may therefore take on a greater role in news reporting from the United States than they warrant. Perhaps this explains the tendency of the Japanese press to see "Japan bashing" everywhere in the United States. It is interesting to note that the Mansfield Center study found very few instances of genuine "Japan bashing" in articles about Japan in the U.S. press (or of "America bashing" in the Japanese press, for that matter), but found far more numerous references to "Japan bashing" in the Japanese press![44]

One major access problem for Japanese journalists in Washington springs from limited language ability. If this problem has lessened among American correspondents in Tokyo—although it has by no means disappeared—Japanese reporters in Washington still see it as a major problem for them. A survey of Japanese reporters in the United States, conducted by the East-West Center in Honolulu, revealed that inability to use the spoken English language freely was considered to be the major problem facing the journalists.[45] In the past this has sometimes led to such phenomena as the "*yokotate* [horizontal-vertical] reporter," referring to the Japanese correspondent who performed his job by reading the (horizontal) print in American newspaper stories and translating it into (vertically printed) Japanese reports for his newspaper.[46]

Although the *yokotate* reporter is found less these days among Japanese correspondents in Washington, the problem of spoken-language ability often induces them to use more Japanese sources, especially embassy personnel, than they otherwise might.[47] From interviews with foreign correspondents I formed the impression that while American reporters tend to use their embassy to establish their government's "official line" before moving on to alternative sources, the Japanese reporter is more likely to use the embassy as a final source.[48] Indeed, it is not uncommon for Japanese reporters to exchange information with embassy personnel, involving the reporter in a closer relationship with government officials abroad than an American reporter would condone.

Finally, the norms of Japanese journalism that constrain reporters at home also constrain those abroad. Asked which type of articles easily win editors' approval, one Washington-based journalist I interviewed said that stories about friction were easy to gain approval for, but those about culture and society more difficult; "straight news" was easy, but "analysis" was likely to be "sunk" *(botsu)*.[49]

The Different Worlds of Television News

Kristin Kyoko Altman has graphically described the changing role of television news in recent domestic politics in Japan (see chapter 5). NHK's neutral and factual style of news and its dominance in Japan's television news market have now been overtaken by the commercial stations' more freewheeling approach. Popular programs like Hiroshi Kume's *News Station,* with its willingness to indulge in controversy, have been emulated by many of the other flagship commercial stations in Japan. How will commercial television's new influence and style of coverage affect the image of U.S.–Japanese relations that the average Japanese citizen receives? As a result of these trends, are Japanese and U.S. news coverage converging, if not in amount of coverage, then in how the relationship is covered? What are the consequences?

In one respect, U.S. and Japanese television news coverage of the two countries' relationship may be becoming more similar: its focus on the personality of the national executive. American coverage of foreign affairs has long revolved around the personal accomplishments and foibles of the president. But in Japan, although individual prime ministers have been expected to make their pilgrimages to Washington and bring back an *omiyage* (souvenir) demonstrating the continued U.S. commitment to Japan, television coverage has not focused on the personalities of Japan's leaders.

During the tenure of Prime Minister Yasuhiro Nakasone (1982–1987), this situation began to change. Tall in stature and "presidential" in bearing, Nakasone was very aware of the new importance of television coverage. At summit meetings he was fully conscious of the contrast he made to previous Japanese leaders who had seemed somehow to be the odd man out when photo opportunities came. He skillfully used his television image at Group of Seven and U.S.–Japanese summit meetings to increase his personal popularity with the Japanese public and thus his political clout in the LDP. Less photogenic and less skillful at media manipulation, Nakasone's successors seemed to return the coverage of U.S.–Japanese relations to its orientation toward fact and substance.[50]

But the 1993 election broke this pattern once again, and this time the change may be more permanent. For example, during the summit meeting of February 1994 between President Bill Clinton and Prime Minister Morihiro Hosokawa, in which the two leaders failed to reach any agreement to ease trade friction and when relations between the countries were at a low ebb, much coverage focused on Hosokawa's dashing dress and his ability to stand up to the United States. The rising importance of television in news coverage and increased attention in Japan to the executive's personal leadership image in foreign affairs could presage a more personality-centered era of coverage of U.S.–Japanese relations.

For the present, differences in U.S. and Japanese television coverage of the relationship continue to stand out. In the Mansfield study cited earlier, television news images of each country were similar to those found in newspapers, in terms of both balance and objectivity. Japanese stories about the United States were more likely (90 percent) to be rated as balanced and objective than American stories about Japan (57 percent), but Japanese stories that did deviate from balance and objectivity were more likely to be negative than positive about the United States, while American stories that deviated were slightly more likely to be positive about Japan. Thus although individual Japanese news segments about the United States are more likely to be balanced and objective than those in the United States, overall American coverage may be more so than Japanese.[51]

There may be a major difference between television and newspapers, however, in how these similar results are achieved. Recall that in the case of Japanese newspapers, factual news dominated but was derived primarily from Japanese official sources; this seemed to account for the observed patterns of balance and objectivity. In the case of television, however, there is no dearth of opinionated reporting. Although no overt expression of personal opinion or commentary by the anchor or journalist was found in American television news about Japan, more than one-quarter of all Japanese television news items about the United States—especially those of the commercial networks—contained such opinion.[52] Clearly, the "Kume style" of opinionated journalism and its emulation by many commercial stations' news anchors and reporters, as described in chapter 5, also affects reporting about the United States.

Some evidence indicates that opinionated reporting may contribute to a negative view of the United States. News items in which the anchor or journalist expressed an opinion were seven times more likely to be critical of the United States, six times more likely to contain an unfavorable bias, and three times more likely to see the United States as flawed than items when no anchor or journalist

opinion was expressed.[53] The relationship between opinionated television journalism and the view transmitted of the other nation, however, may be more complicated. First, American anchors and
reporters, even if they refrain from voicing opinions, can convey a
negative view of the other country through more subtle means of
communication, such as facial expression, body language, or tone of
voice.[54] Second, U.S. television news items are more likely (53 percent) than Japanese television news items (33 percent) to contain
opinions expressed by other people than an anchor or journalist.
And in Japan newscasters and reporters are more likely to express
their opinion when others appearing in the news segment also did so
than when they did not (45 percent to 20 percent).[55] In other words,
expressions of overt opinion about the other country are by no
means lacking on American television news, but they tend to be
expressed by persons appearing in the segment rather than by the station's news staff. When Japanese anchors or reporters express their
opinions, there are likely to be others also expressing theirs, making
it difficult to say which opinion may carry more weight in transmitting critical views of the United States. Also muddying the waters is
the fact that anchors and journalists tend to express their opinions on
items whose subjects also have an independent relationship to a negative image of the United States on Japanese television.[56]

All that can be said at this point, therefore, is that the Japanese
style of television journalism in recent years differs both from American television and from Japanese newspapers. Instead of the neutral
and factual style of Japanese newspapers or the neutral tone of the
American anchor and correspondent, the anchors and correspondents of Japanese commercial stations provide much of the personal
commentary and opinion about the other country, and not all of this
commentary is positive.

Differences were also observed in the overall image of the other
country portrayed. Although the overwhelming number of items in
both countries did not provide either a positive or negative image of
the other nation, when items deviated from the norm, they were in a
more negative direction for Japanese television news coverage of the
United States than vice versa. Thus, an almost equal percentage (14–
15 percent) of items were rated by American coders as being positive, negative, or mixed in their overall image of Japan, while Japanese coders were more likely to rate an item as negative (14 percent)
than positive (4 percent) or mixed (3 percent) in its portrayal of the
United States.[57]

The negative images, incidentally, were related to different types of news story in each country. American items were more likely to convey a positive image of Japan if they were about education, science, and culture, and a negative image if they were about economics and business. Japanese television news, however, did not show a similar relationship. It seems that the trade friction of recent years is finding a reflection in the images American television news conveys, but not necessarily on Japanese television news. On the other hand, Japanese television news stories suggesting flaws in the United States, a conflict within or involving the United States, or differences between the two countries were more likely to be related to negative than positive images of the United States. Interestingly, American news stories about possible flaws in Japan, conflict within Japan or between it and another country, or differences between the two countries were equally likely to be associated with a positive as with a negative image of Japan.[58]

As Japan's commercial television networks attempted to challenge NHK's dominance of the news market, they adopted a style of journalism in which anchors and correspondents more freely expressed their own opinions about the subject of the story. As Altman points out in chapter 5, the new style not only has had an impact on ratings, it also has left its mark on domestic politics. The admittedly preliminary and tentative discussion here suggests that it may also have some impact on the coverage of U.S.–Japanese relations. Further analysis is needed to explore whether there is a convergence between the United States and Japan toward a personal leadership focus of coverage of the relationship and whether the opinionated style of journalism itself makes for negative coverage of the United States in Japan.

More certain is that Japan's television news today clearly differs from the more neutral, factual orientation of both NHK and Japanese newspaper news and also differs from American television news in the role of its anchors and reporters. American and Japanese television news also differ in the kind of stories they carry that are associated with positive and negative images of the other country.

Mass Media and the U.S.–Japanese Relationship

Differences in media systems and their effects on coverage of U.S.–Japanese relations provoke thought on how the mass media contribute to U.S.–Japanese friction. Measuring the exact contribution of media coverage to friction is nearly impossible. Such differences do lead, however, to characteristic strengths and weakness in the type of information the citizens in the two countries receive about each other and about the tensions between their governments.

Japan's media system provides its citizens with a consistently high *density* of concrete information about the relationship with the United States. The pattern shows a constant barrage of fact and detail about actions of the U.S. government and industry as related to Japan. The advantage of this density of concrete information is that Japanese citizens, who also have received an excellent fact-oriented education, are kept remarkably well informed about American behavior and trends that affect their country.

Ironically, they may be too well informed about the United States, especially American political life in Washington. If we drew a cognitive map of a Japanese citizen's view of the world based solely on the information provided by the mass media, the United States would probably occupy a large proportion of the globe. This alone is an unhealthy dimension to media reporting in Japan; it overestimates U.S. impact on Japan and feeds the intensity of Japanese reactions to even the most trivial or ephemeral events. This is especially true because political events and "friction-related" incidents receive more coverage than background analysis or stories about U.S. society outside Washington. The smashing of a Toshiba radio by a few grandstanding members of Congress or a soon-to-be-doomed bill introduced by an unimportant representative or senator to shut off Japan's imports, however striking a media image they may convey, hardly constitute epoch-making events in U.S.–Japanese relations. They do, however, constitute important aspects of the perceptual "reality" of those relations, in part because they assume untoward importance in the totality of information about foreign affairs the average Japanese citizen receives, and in part because they are conveyed without context.

Lack of context is the second disadvantage of the large amount of information conveyed. The short, fact-based nature of information about U.S.–Japanese relations does not provide a "filter" to order those facts, assign them priority, and relate them to each other in order to gain an understanding of events. The lack of opinions from diverse sources to give alternative views of facts and thus alternative "realities" deprives those facts of meaning or assigns them invalid or partial meanings. In this sense, the new, more opinionated journalistic style of television news may be filling a void and serving a useful function in the Japanese media system.

A third disadvantage is that when meanings are assigned to facts in newspapers, they are usually those assigned by the Japanese government because the reporters' club system induces a dependence on official sources. Even when they are posted abroad, Japanese reporters rely on their government's embassy staff more than one would expect. Thus, when opinions or interpretations of fact are conveyed in the print media, they represent the official Japanese viewpoint. When the American side does manage to get through, its point of view can come across as groundless complaining or unsubstantiated scapegoating and "Japan bashing" because readers know little about the assumptions of the U.S. side and the context from which those complaints emerge. The opinions expressed frequently on television news by anchors and reporters, if they are also unbalanced in terms of negative commentary about the United States, clearly exacerbate this problem. Whether the new commercial television journalism in Japan provides a helpful counterpoint to newspaper treatment will depend on whether the opinions presented are balanced.

A final, related problem on the Japanese side is the relative imbalance that occurs in mutual criticism. As we have seen, Japan's media are willing to criticize and more likely to blame the United States, but not very willing to critique their own government's policies and actions. The U.S. media are relatively evenhanded in criticizing both Japan and their own country's policy and behavior. When citizens of one country are exposed to opinions critical of both countries, but citizens of the other hear little in the way of national self-criticism, what are the consequences of such an imbalance in media criticism for the relationship between the two countries?

On the American side, as a result of their media systems U.S. citizens receive much less news about Japan than its international importance warrants. When news about Japan is covered, it often includes opinion and debate about Japan (not necessarily by journalists themselves, but by others who are quoted in the press or who appear on television news). Such reports, however, lack sufficient hard facts to substantiate those views and thus to allow the audience to make informed decisions and choices among the competing views of what the Japanese government, industry, and people are actually doing. While Japanese citizens tend to receive facts without viewpoints, Americans tend to be given opinions and interpretations without many facts.

Despite the appearance of varied opinions in American articles about Japan, there is an increasing tendency for the information to be fitted into two formulas: that Japan is primarily a matter of economic news and that Japan is unique. In part because Japan has not been a major military or political power in the postwar world, its main impact on the American consciousness and reality has been economic. The predominantly economic image of Japan, however, is no more complete than the image the Japanese press often offers of the United States as predominantly militaristic, racist, and violent.

The problem of uniqueness is more complicated. The revisionist view that Japan's institutions are different from those of the United States may have a great deal of validity. Indeed, this essay itself may be considered "revisionist" in its view that media institutions in Japan and the United States fundamentally differ. The problem is that insofar as the American media compare Japan only to the United States, they may also be giving a false impression of both nations: the former as deviant and the latter as the norm. Many institutions and practices that American reporters find "unique" about Japan resemble those found in Europe. Frequently it is the United States that is "unique" and not Japan, but because American-centered and bilateral comparisons dominate the perspective of reporters and editors of the American press and television, this understanding is rarely conveyed by the media.[59]

Finally, there is the problem, noted earlier, that when Japanese television news items reveal possible flaws in the United States, the existence of conflict within it or with other countries, and differences between the two countries, they tend to be associated with a more negative than positive overall image of the United States; however, this is not true in the case of comparable items on American television. One plausible explanation of the asymmetrical findings is that differences, conflicts, and flaws as conveyed by the media are filtered through preexisting expectations and perceptions of the audience. Japan, after all, has been portrayed to Americans by its politicians and media as an unstoppable economic juggernaut, superior and threatening to the United States; against that background, U.S. news portrayal of conflict and flaws in Japan becomes reassuring (and thus a less negative image) to Americans; it means either that Japan is not invulnerable as expected or that the United States is finally taking action against Japan.

Conversely, during the earlier postwar period, Japanese looked to the United States as a model and protector, but lately Japan has been the target of constant American criticism and demands to open its markets and reduce its trade deficits. In this case, emphasis on flaws in, conflicts concerning, and differences with the other country may be seen in a more negative light. The relationship between prior relationship and image, conflict and threat, and current media image needs further exploration if we are to understand how the same type of media portrayal can be invested with such different symbolism in the two countries.

These results serve to remind us that as much as media structure and process affect the news coverage the audience in each country receives about the other country and thus the bilateral relationship, the bilateral relationship itself—its history and the coverage it has received through the years—also can affect the meaning the audience attributes to the coverage.

Notes

I would like to thank Kiyofuku Chūma of *Asahi Shimbun* and Mikio Arai, formerly of the NHK News Division, for their generous help in arranging interviews with former Japanese correspondents in Washington during my research trip to Tokyo in December 1991. I am grateful to these journalists, including Hiroshi Andō, himself the author of an excellent recent book on media and U.S.–Japanese friction, for sharing their knowledge and experiences with me so freely. Portions of this article also appear in my "Structure of U.S.–Japan Friction" in a book resulting from a research project, "The Domestic Sources of U.S.–Japan Friction," funded by the U.S.–Japan Foundation, or in the conference project reports of the Mansfield Center for Pacific Affairs (see notes 8 and 13 below). I am grateful to the U.S.–Japan Foundation for funding for my research trip to Tokyo and to the members of the "U.S.–Japan Friction" project for their comments and suggestions on my research. Also, I am grateful to Tovah LaDier of the Mansfield Center for Pacific Affairs and to Stanley Budner, whose conference projects and data analysis provided the opportunity to pursue the subject and use the data analyzed in the Mansfield Center projects. My thanks also go to Glen Fukushima; discussions with him back in 1983 when we were both Fulbright scholars first stimulated my interest in media coverage of U.S.–Japanese relations.

1. Ofer Feldman, *Politics and the News Media in Japan* (Ann Arbor: University of Michigan Press, 1993), especially pp. 177–185.

2. Nihon Shimbun Kyōkai (Japanese Newspaper Publishers and Editors Association), *The Japanese Press 1993* (Tokyo: Nihon Shimbun Kyōkai, 1993), pp. 86–87. In 1988 the United States had 1,657 newspapers compared to Japan's 124, but Japan had a circulation of 580 copies per 1,000 inhabitants compared to a U.S. figure of 259 per 1,000. In 1992 the per-capita circulation rate in Japan was still 580 per 1,000 inhabitants, with almost 52 million newspapers sold each morning (over 71 million per day, if morning and afternoon editions are counted).

3. I say "pretensions" to being national papers because in addition to

having small per-capita circulation, these papers lack true nationwide distribution systems (except by mail), and it is frequently difficult to have one of them delivered if one lives outside the major cities on the two coasts. It is also difficult to find them at newsstands in many parts of the United States. In contrast, it is possible to have the national Japanese papers delivered or to find them at the newsstand in almost every nook and cranny of Japan.

4. James Impocco, *U.S. News and World Report* bureau chief in Tokyo, interview, 20 December 1991.

5. The week was that of Monday 4 May to and including Sunday 10 May 1992. Because of time differences, of course, the actual content of the news would be one day "off" between the two newspapers' editions.

6. Shigehiko Tōgō and Atsushi Kuse, *"Nihon mondai" Amerika de wa dō hōdōsarete iru ka* ("Japan Problem": How Is It Being Reported in America?) (Tokyo: Kanki Shuppan, 1988), pp. 189–190 and chart 1, p. 191.

7. Ibid.

8. Stanley Budner, "United States and Japanese Media Coverage of Frictions between the Two Countries," in *Communicating across the Pacific,* (Missoula, Mont.: Mansfield Center for Pacific Affairs, 1993), p. 19. The percentage calculation of proportion of articles in the business section is mine.

9. "Datagraph: American Press's Interest in Japan," *Journal of Japanese Trade and Industry* 6 (1991): 52.

10. Data from fifteen weekday evening (7 P.M.) news programs over a three-week period in 1983. Sample, methodology, and other results of this analysis are described in chapter 3 of this volume.

11. Jack Lyle and John Davidson Thomas, "Japanese-American Relations: What Viewers See on Television News in Each Nation," unpublished report of a study funded by the Hōsō Bunka Foundation, Boston, October 1987, pp. 23 and 8.

12. *A Report on Television Stereotypes of Three Nations—France, U.S. and Japan* (Tokyo: International News Flow Project—Japan, 1988), p. IV-7.

13. The study was sponsored by the Mansfield Center for Pacific Affairs in the United States and the NHK Broadcasting Culture Research Institute, among others. The analysis included the main news programs on NHK and the leading Tokyo flagship stations of the commercial networks in Japan and those on the three national networks, PBS, and CNN in the United States for the periods 14 September–11 December 1992 and 1 February–31 May 1993. Descriptions of the project and resulting conference, along with the preliminary data results and analysis, have been published in *Creating Images: American and Japanese Television News Coverage of the Other— Summary of Conference and Research* (Missoula, Mont.: Mansfield Center for Pacific Affairs, 1994); in an article by Isao Kawasaki and Masahiko Kōno, "Nichibei terebi nyūsu no hikaku" (A Comparison of US and Japanese Television News), *Hōsō Kenkyū to Chōsa* (Broadcasting Studies and Surveys), June 1994, pp. 2–17; and in an article by Kensuke Kōno, Yumiko Hara, and Kensaku Saitō, "Terebi wa aitekoku wo dō tsutaete iru ka (2)" (How Is Television Portraying the Other Country?), *Hōsō Kenkyū to Chōsa*, July 1994,

pp. 2–25. I served on the advisory committee and the research team for this project.

14. Kōno et al., "Terebi wa aitekoku," table 5, p. 11, and chart 2, p. 12.

15. Stanley Budner, "Summary of Research Results," in *Creating Images*, p. 6.

16. Morton Rosenbloom, *Coups and Earthquakes: Reporting the World for America* (New York: Harper and Row, 1979).

17. Remark made by James Impocco, Tokyo bureau chief, *U.S. News and World Report*, at the conference, "Japanese and American Media Coverage of Friction between Two Nations," sponsored by the Mansfield Center for Pacific Affairs and the Dentsū Institute for Humanistic Studies, Honolulu, Hawai'i, 28 April–1 May 1991 (hereafter cited as Conference on Japanese and American Media).

18. For a more extensive discussion of this phenomenon, see this volume, chapter 3.

19. This was one of the conclusions of many of the working journalists at the Conference on Japanese and American Media.

20. See Hiroshi Andō, *Nichibei jōhō masatsu* (Japanese–U.S. News Friction) (Tokyo: Iwanami Shinsho, 1991), pp. 210–211 n.9. Also Andō, interview, Tokyo, 21 December 1991. Andō is a former *Asahi* newspaper correspondent in Washington.

21. Andō interview.

22. Budner, "United States and Japanese Newspaper Coverage," table 3, p. 11, table G, p. 3, and table J, p. 33. On the binational newspaper data discussed below and their possible consequences, also see Stanley Budner and Ellis S. Krauss, "Newspaper Coverage of U.S.–Japan Frictions: Balance and Objectivity in the American and Japanese Press," *Asian Survey* 35(4) (April, 1995).

23. Budner, "United States and Japanese Newspaper Coverage," table 3, p. 11, table G, p.3, and table J., p.33; Budner and Krauss, "Newspaper Coverage of U.S.–Japan Frictions: Balance and Objectivity in the American and Japanese Press."

24. The results are in Robert Hewitt, "Correspondents Give Their Views on Japan–U.S. News Coverage," special report (Honolulu: East West Center, 1991), originally presented at the Conference on Japanese and American Media; also cited in Andō, *Nichi-bei jōhō masatsu,* charts 2 and 3, p. 163.

25. On these historical developments, see this volume, chapter 1. By "editing perspectives" I mean the selection and placement of articles on the front page.

26. An extreme example of the lengths to which reporters can go to confirm a story when they are under great challenges to their credibility is illustrated in the Watergate news digging of Bob Woodward and Carl Bernstein, *All the President's Men* (New York: Simon and Schuster, 1974), passim.

27. See Yuri Ōiwa, "Nihon no kisha kurabu ankēto: gaikokujin kisha no kaiken shusseki jōken" (Japan Reporters' Club Survey: The Press Confer-

ence Attendance Conditions of Foreign Reporters), *Asahi Shimbun Weekly AERA*, 1 October 1991, p. 28. The Japan Newspaper Association recently decided to allow foreign reporters to join reporters' clubs, but whether they actually can do so or not is still left up to the individual clubs.

28. For a description of the life of the *yūgun* reporter and how it differs from that of the reporters' club correspondent, see Kiyoshi Kuroda, *Shimbun kisha no genba* (On the Scene with Newspaper Reporters) (Tokyo: Kōdansha Gendai Shinsho, 1985), chap. 5. Many Japanese reporters prefer the assignment of *yūgun* to that of reporters' club correspondent exactly because of its lack of specialization and the freedom it provides to choose one's own topics and to offer more interpretation.

29. Nathaniel Thayer, "Competition and Conformity: An Inquiry into the Structure of Japanese Newspapers," in *Modern Japanese Organization and Decision-Making*, ed. Ezra Vogel (Berkeley: University of California Press, 1975), pp. 284–303. Table 3, p. 288, contains a breakdown of the page subjects discussed above; table 5, p. 292, has a list of the assignments of political reporters in *Asahi Shimbun*. Feldman, *Politics and the News Media in Japan*, table 4-2, pp. 70–71, has a list of the reporters' clubs in Tokyo by type of organization to which they are attached.

30. Taketoshi Yamamoto, "The Press Clubs of Japan," *Journal of Japanese Studies* 15, no. 2 (Summer 1989): 374.

31. Jung Bock Lee, *The Political Character of the Japanese Press* (Seoul: Seoul National University Press, 1985), p. 65.

32. See Thayer, "Competition and Conformity," p. 294. Also, Young C. Kim, *Japanese Journalists and Their World* (Charlottesville: University Press of Virginia, 1981), pp. 51–54.

33. See this point and the specific examples as given by Lee, *The Political Character of the Japanese Press*, pp. 65–67.

34. See note 27 above.

35. Budner, "United States and Japanese Newspaper Coverage," p. 18.

36. Ibid., charts 2 and 3, pp. 192–193. The data cited are for 1988. In 1976 there were only 46 companies with 158 reporters.

37. American journalist in Tokyo, interview, 20 December 1992. Interviewees were promised anonymity to promote frank and open discussion.

38. Ibid.

39. For a devastating critique of this view, see Chalmers Johnson, "Studies of Japanese Political Economy: A Crisis in Theory," *Japan Foundation Newsletter* 16, no. 3 (December 1988), pp. 1–11. Johnson is the leading academic revisionist.

40. Ronald Morse, an expert on Japan and a veteran observer of U.S.–Japanese relations, personal communication, 3 March 1994.

41. In Europe, of course, capital cities such as Paris and London play roles much more similar to that of Tokyo in the lives of their respective nations.

42. NHK former correspondent in Washington, interview, Tokyo, 18 December 1991.

43. Ibid.; former *Asahi* Washington correspondent, interview, Tokyo, 16 December 1991.

44. Budner, "United States and Japanese Newspaper Coverage," p. 14.

45. Robert Hewitt, "Correspondents Give Their Views," pp. 14 and 24, for example.

46. Andō, *Nichibei jōhō masatsu,* pp. 127–131.

47. Ibid., p. 128.

48. Former *Asahi* Washington correspondent interview.

49. Ibid.

50. See Ellis S. Krauss, "Japan," in *Mass Media and Democracy,* ed. Anthony Mughan, Richard Gunther, and Paul Beck (forthcoming).

51. For the Mansfield study, see note 13 above. Budner, "Summary of Research Results," in *Creating Images,* pp. 6–7.

52. Ibid., p. 7; Kōno et al., "Terebi wa aitekoku," p. 17.

53. Ellis S. Krauss, "Explaining American and Japanese Coverage of the Other Nation," in *Creating Images,* p. 18. These relationships were part of the preliminary analysis of the data, before more complicated analysis revealing some of the possible caveats given here.

54. Kōno et.al., "Terebi wa aitekoku," p. 17.

55. Ibid., p. 18.

56. Budner, "Summary of Research Results."

57. Ibid., p.7.

58. Ibid., p. 9.

59. On this point about Japanese similarity to Europe and the artificiality of many U.S.–Japanese comparisons, see Steven R. Reed, *Making Common Sense of Japan* (Pittsburgh: University of Pittsburgh Press, 1993), chaps. 1 and 2.

PART IV

Media and the Public

9

Media Exposure and the Quality of Political Participation in Japan

SCOTT C. FLANAGAN

THE growth of the mass media throughout the twentieth century has profoundly altered our world. It has expanded our horizons and changed the very nature of mass electorates, particularly in the media-intensive advanced industrial democracies. In particular, the mass media have helped to make possible the process of cognitive mobilization described by Ronald Inglehart, by which people become sufficiently informed about and interested in policy and politics to take part in political life.[1] A highly educated, politically savvy citizen behaves very differently in the political arena than does an uneducated, ill-informed citizen. A high concentration of the latter type of citizen gives rise to an elitist and hierarchic patron-client type of political system, while a high concentration of the former leads to a more pluralistic and participatory democracy. Growing up in postindustrial "information societies" has its own transforming effects on citizens. These result in electoral realignments, the rise of citizen movements, new forms of direct democracy such as citizen initiatives and referendums, and the decline of parties and party identifications.[2]

Most studies of the role of the media do not focus on these broader effects, largely because the processes of change involved are so complex and interactive that isolating and measuring any independent media effect is difficult. Instead, scholars have tried to show the direct effect of the media on politics, for example, on the political attitudes and behavior of mass electorates. But this effort, too, has foundered, leading to the conclusion—seemingly belied by the reality all around us in media-saturated societies—that the media have limited effects on politics. Some even argue that with the rise of television, any media influence on mass political behavior must be a negative one.

This chapter takes issue with these conclusions. At least in the Japanese case, the media appear to have played a positive transforming role in improving the quality of mass political participation over the postwar period. The progressive saturation of society with print and electronic media has helped create a more knowledgeable electorate, one that is better equipped to translate its political preferences into appropriate voting choices. The media have made the electorate more aware of and interested in national politics and issues. Voters have thereby become more likely to engage in political activities requiring more commitment, and they do so voluntarily, not because they are pressured to participate by the state or by authority figures in their lives.

Media Effects: An Overview

In the early decades of media research, efforts focused on the question of the role of the media in changing opinions. George Orwell's *1984* and similar works had long raised the specter of media-delivery technology that would arm governments and other elites with the means to manipulate people and mold their attitudes. However, little evidence of direct media effect on attitudes was found in several decades of research, beginning in the 1940s with the advent of mass opinion studies. The concepts of perceptual screening, selective perception, and cognitive dissonance, among others, helped explain why. It was found that individuals tend to gravitate to media that reflect long-held political dispositions and preferences, thus producing a conundrum for researchers: do liberals seek out the *New York Times* (or its Japanese equivalent, *Asahi*), or do people become liberal *because* they read the *Times* (or *Asahi*)?[3] Similarly, people screen information, retaining incoming information that fits their preexisting perceptions and discounting information when it challenges their beliefs.[4] Indeed, research has stood Orwell on his head by finding that not only is there no relationship between level of media exposure and attitude change, but also, remarkably, the greater the individual's level of exposure to political information in the media, the more stable his or her political attitudes, issue positions, partisanship, and voting behavior.[5] The consistency with which these perplexing correlations were found gave rise to the minimal effects hypothesis, which holds that if the media have any effect on attitude change, it is only on those citizens who have little or no prior information or opinions.

Beginning in the 1960s, however, this view came to be challenged. There has been a search for more refined methods of measurement.[6] Scholars have also sought to identify more localized impacts in response to specific, perhaps unique, events or impacts on special subgroups of media users.[7] Two studies pertaining to Japan demonstrate that the media can and do play an important role in attitude formation for subpopulations that are just developing attitudes in a given area. A study of lifestyles of university students found that among youths who are in the process of being socialized into adult roles and political values, the media play a politicizing role in Japan. While the media do not appear to affect the individual's direction of party support, those with broader media exposure are likely to develop a party identification earlier in life.[8] A second study focused on the media coverage of the Lockheed scandal, to measure any impact on political attitudes and vote choice in the 1976 lower house election.[9] It found that the media exerted a substantial effect on voting behavior, but only for a small subgroup of the electorate that met all the following criteria: high levels of media exposure, a strong conviction that corruption was a serious problem, no party identification, and high level of education. Those with established partisan ties were apparently not moved by the media coverage of the scandal to change them; those respondents with low levels of education had greater difficulty in making the appropriate linkage between being concerned about the corruption issues and voting against the Liberal Democratic Party (LDP). While the shift in voting behavior within the subpopulation meeting all four of these criteria was striking, it constituted only about 5–10 percent of the electorate.[10]

Another approach in exploring the media's impact has been to concede that the media do not play a large, audience-wide role in changing viewers' ideology or issue preferences. Instead, it is argued that the media exert other kinds of direct effects, less obvious but still important, for example, on agenda setting and political mobilization. In this chapter I will pursue this second revisionist tack, looking at several broad, blanket effects of the media on the Japanese population beyond attitude change—specifically, effects on the quality, levels, and context of participation within the mass electorate.[11]

It may seem paradoxical to be asserting a primarily positive role for the Japanese media in these areas at a time when much of the American literature is arguing just the opposite—namely, that the media are *undermining* the quality, levels, and context of participation. Such arguments are supported by research that has shown that Americans increasingly rely on television rather than the print media for their political information and that the growing exposure to this medium is eroding the intellectual content of political discourse. Television communicates images rather than facts, turns politics into stories and personalities, and captures its audience through the entertainment value of visual action shots. Viewers learn little and remember less—only images and vague impressions that leave one less able to discriminate among candidates on the issues and to understand one's own political behavior. Many assign to television the blame for erosion of partisanship, increased voter volatility, shallow political thinking, and waning interest in politics.[12] Add to this the recent spate of negative advertisements in U.S. election campaigns, which are believed to confuse and disgust voters and to turn them away from the polls. The composite picture of the media's impact on the quality, levels, and campaign context of participation in the United States is negative indeed.

Such blanket conclusions are suspect, however. Many of them are based on research findings that contrast the knowledge or behavior of persons relying on television for their political information with the knowledge or behavior of those who rely on print media, or else compare heavy and light viewers. Yet perhaps there is something intrinsic in the kinds of people who subject themselves to long hours of television that might explain some of the differences found. Television may be less effective in communicating hard news and candidate issue positions, but does this mean that television is playing a negative role? It might be argued that television provides enough information to encourage viewers to turn to the print media to seek a better understanding of the facts underlying the issues. Television can alert individuals to the key stories of the day and lead to sufficient understanding for viewers to decide what merits more attention and what can be ignored. Such viewers can thus employ print media more efficiently. Those who are not encouraged by television to look for further information in the print media, it might be argued, are likely to be marginal participants or apoliticals who would not have been reached by the print media anyway, even in the absence of television.

These counterarguments are merely conjectural. It is clear in the Japanese case, however, that there is no pretelevision era to which one can nostalgically appeal—an era in which the politically informed, involved, and participant citizen is supposed to have existed. In the pre–World War II period, even at the height of the short period of "party government," citizen participation at the local level was more mobilized than autonomous in nature, and patron-client politics prevailed. The average Japanese citizen today is more informed and sophisticated about politics than ever before; I suspect the same could be said for the populations of every other advanced industrial democracy.

To question whether democracy can survive television[13] or to argue that television in particular or the media in general are lowering the quality and level of participation, one would have to demonstrate that the average citizen would be more informed and involved with politics in the absence of television or of all the media. Surely it is closer to the truth to argue that the advent of the mass media has transformed politics, moving it decisively closer to the democratic ideal. The rise of the mass media can be credited with undermining the mobilized, patron-client mode of politics, which was based in part on the monopoly of political information by the few, and with eroding elitism by shining light on the secret world in which politics was traditionally conducted. Diffusion of the media has permitted citizens to better understand the issues of the day, to recognize when and how their self-interest is involved, and to communicate their preferences to political leaders through opinion polls, letters to the editor, and demonstrations and other political events staged for the media.

This chapter explores several identifiable positive effects of exposure to the media—effects on the quality, levels, and context of political participation within the Japanese electorate. Four different kinds of media effects are examined, associated with (1) improving citizens' ability to appropriately link their political attitudes and preferences with their voting choice; (2) enhancing their awareness and concern regarding the issues of the day; (3) raising their involvement and participation in politics beyond the simple act of voting; and (4) shifting the issue context and the role of candidate images in ways that have both depolarized political competition and enhanced the potential for electoral change. The data presented throughout the analysis are taken from the 1976 JABISS Election Study.[14]

Demographic Profile of Media Consumers

Japan ranks high in media consumption, but media use varies widely across society. According to the 1976 JABISS survey, 34 percent of the public watch television three or more hours a day, 30 percent watch it for two to three hours, and 35 percent watch for less than two hours. Only 1 percent do not watch at all. Newspaper readership also distributes widely, with only 6 percent of people reporting that they do not read a paper. Some are quite avid readers; even though most major dailies deliver both morning and evening editions to subscribers, 13 percent of the respondents report reading two different papers, and an additional 3 percent read three or more papers. Two-thirds of the readers read at least one national paper; the rest read a regional, sports, or religious paper.[15] Magazine reading appears to be a much more limited activity, since only 45 percent of people report reading weekly magazines at least occasionally and only 8 percent read at least one a week.[16]

The JABISS survey included four items pertaining to exposure to political information in the media. Viewing of television news and political programming distributed as follows: daily, 62 percent; a few times a week, 22 percent; once weekly or never, 16 percent. Regarding frequency of watching election-related programs or reading election articles before the 1976 general election, 14–15 percent watched or read none, while 16–21 percent watched or read ten or more programs and/or articles; the remainder fell between those two extremes. Exposure to election coverage in weekly magazines is more limited: 51 percent read no such articles, 15 percent read three or more, and the remainder fit in between those extremes.

Table 9.1 provides a demographic profile of high consumers of media in Japan. Some of the relationships shown are not statistically significant, suggesting a rather broad and even distribution across several demographic attributes. The important exceptions, however, are socioeconomic status (SES) and sex. The SES variable is a scale that combines and equally weights respondents' educational level, household income, and occupational status of head of the household. As might be expected, better-off, well-educated people were the heaviest consumers of newspapers and magazines, while less educated, poorer people watched television more. The number of papers read, the type of paper (national vs. regional or sports papers), and the frequency of magazine reading all exhibit a substantial relationship to high socioeconomic status. The same pattern emerges with sex, with males the more frequent consumers of the print media and women spending more time watching television. On two of the media variables in table 9.1 the full set of demographic attributes comes into play. Those who read magazines frequently and those who relied on newspapers rather than television (as their major source of information about the Lockheed scandal) tended to be younger, male, urban, employed in modern occupational environments (blue- and white-collar wage earners in large enterprises), and of higher SES.

Table 9.1   Association between Various Demographic Attributes and Media Exposure

	Frequency of TV Viewing	Number of Papers Read	Type of Papers Read	Frequency of Magazine Reading	Reliance on Print Media	Exposure to Political Information
Socioeconomic status (SES)	-.11	.22	.22	.22	.17	.16
Age	(.02)	(-.02)	(-.03)	-.29	-.07	.05*
Sex (M)	-.14	.13	.05*	.13	.22	.24
Urbanization	(.03)	.05*	.13	.13	.08	.06*
Modern occupational environment	(.04)	(.00)	.10	.08	.10	.05*

Note: All correlations are significant at the .01 level, except those marked by an asterisk, which are significant at the .05 level, and those in parentheses, which are not significant even at the .05 level. Modern occupational environments are those blue- and white-collar wage-earning jobs in large enterprises, while, at the other end of the continuum, traditional occupational environments refer to farming and old middle-class positions in small enterprises.

These findings are not surprising. Reading, after all, demands concentration, comprehension, and a certain level of motivating interest. The less familiar the individual is with the subject matter, the greater the effort that is required for comprehension. Low education increases the difficulty encountered in reading political articles in newspapers and magazines; low incomes may also discourage exposure, since the cost of newspapers, magazines, and books presents more of a hurdle for the poor than the rich. In rural areas the availability of print media may limit exposure compared to urban areas where newsstands are ubiquitous. Finally, women and the elderly, who are more likely to spend much time at home, have fewer opportunities than men and younger people to purchase newspapers and magazines.

When it comes to acquiring information about politics, it is striking that television may play an important equalizing role by making such information readily available to those who would otherwise have less access to it. For example, rural respondents, who are less likely to read magazines or national papers, are not substantially disadvantaged with regard to media exposure to political information (see table 9.1).[17] Also older respondents, who read few magazines and rely less on the print media, nevertheless report marginally higher levels of exposure to political information through the media.

Television, however, does not play an equalizing role for women in relation to men. Although women spend more hours every day watching television than men, their exposure to political information is much less, even if we restrict our attention to those items in the index that refer only to television. Undoubtedly, this is a reflection of traditional cultural norms in Japan, according to which politics is an inappropriate activity for women.[18] Where these cultural norms remain widespread, especially among older women in rural areas and among those low in education, women are evidently inhibited from following politics in the media.

Media Exposure and People's Patterns of Association

The literature on Japanese mass political behavior often divides Japanese political culture into two contrasting ideal types. One picture is of a Japanese citizenry that is parochial, deferential, conformist, and heavily enmeshed in personalistic, patron-client networks. In contrast, the modern cultural type is viewed as being more cosmopolitan, self-assertive, and independent and hence less likely to relate to politics through personalistic social networks. We would thus expect "modern" Japanese citizens to rely more on the media for the political information needed to form opinions and make voting and other political decisions, and the "traditionals" to turn to patrons, local people of influence, or other persons within their immediate interpersonal networks.

But are "traditional versus modern" value orientations really associated with reliance on social networks versus reliance on the media as a primary source of political information? After all, educational levels are exceptionally high in Japan, where the literacy rate is very close to 100 percent, and both television and print media have virtually saturated Japanese society. Previous tests have found no association between type of values and reliance on personal networks rather than on the media for political information.[19]

In a separate analysis using the 1976 JABISS data, I tested for the convergence of values type and network involvement. The findings support the notion that higher levels of network involvement are associated with traditional values. However, the associations are rather modest and do not hold for all demographic categories within the electorate. Evidently, many respondents with modern values are also heavily involved in social networks.

While there is some linkage between values and network involvement, the further expectation that "traditionals" rely on social networks rather than on the media as a source of political information is not confirmed by the data. Indeed, rather than showing a dichotomy between turning to the media or to social networks for information, the data presented in table 9.2 demonstrate conclusively that there is a strong positive relationship between social network involvement and exposure to political information in the media. Instead of providing an alternate source that obviates the need to turn to the media, social network involvement evidently stimulates higher levels of attentiveness to following politics in the media.

Table 9.2 furthermore reveals that there is, if anything, a slight negative relationship between frequency of watching television and social network involvement, and no meaningful relationship between network involvement and the type of newspaper (national/regional) people read. In addition, general exposure to the print media yields only modest associations with network involvement. Correlations become quite substantial, however, for exposure to political information in the media index, reaching .31 with the combined network involvement scale. Moreover, these strong correlations hold up rather well when we control the relationships by sex and SES. In

Table 9.2 Media Exposure and Associativeness (Pearson's *r*)

	Frequency of TV Viewing	Number of Papers Read	Type of Papers Read	Frequency of Magazine Reading	Exposure to Political Information	Partial Controlling for Sex and SES
Informal associations	−.06*	.09	(.03)	.10	.23	.17
Formal associations	(−.04)	.15	(.03)	(.04)	.24	.22
Candidate networks	(−.01)	.12	−.05*	(.02)	.17	.17
Combined network involvement index	−.05*	.17	(−.01)	.09	.31	.26

Note: The informal associations scale measures the respondent's number of friends in neighborhood, work place, and other settings and frequency of talking with them. The formal associations scale taps the number of memberships and the level of active involvement across three kinds of community-based organizations and five extra-community organizations, such as trade and professional associations, unions, religious organizations, and sports and hobby groups. The candidate networks scale was based on four items: whether the respondent knew a candidate who sent them postcards, had done some special favor for them, had done something for the people of their area, or had a deep relationship with their area. Since all three scales loaded heavily on a single unrotated factor, they were also combined into a single "combined network involvement index." All correlations are significant at the .01 level, except those marked by an asterisk, which are significant at the .05 level, and those in parentheses, which are not significant even at the .05 level. The partial correlations are for the Media Exposure to Political Information Scale.

other words, it is not demographic attributes that lead those who are highly involved in social networks also to seek political information from the media.

Organizational involvement and, more broadly, network involvement stimulate interest in politics by bringing political issues affecting a group to the attention of its members and often by providing members with the means to become more actively involved in politics.[20] Thus, network involvement can overcome the inherent biases that incline citizens of high SES toward more active political involvement—biases such as having more knowledge and sophistication about politics, greater stakes in political outcomes, and more leisure time. Involvement in social networks, then, may provide Japanese citizens of low SES with both the motivation and the resources to become more active in politics.[21] In any case, network involvement does appear to stimulate higher levels of attentiveness to politics in the media. There is, then, no dichotomy between the media and personalistic networks as sources of political information. Rather, higher levels of involvement in social networks encourage higher levels of selective exposure to media with an explicitly political content.

As noted above, the direction of causality is often difficult to ascertain in these kinds of analyses. It has been suggested, for instance, that the direction of the relationships between social network involvement and media exposure may differ for different kinds of citizens.[22] For the traditional citizen, involvement in a social network would be expected to precede attentiveness to politics in the media and psychological involvement. For some modern types, media exposure and/or psychological involvement might precede network involvement and stimulate the individual to join an organization to further his or her political interests. However, in our study, the indexes for both formal and informal associations measure involvement in basically nonpolitical associations, some of which are not really "voluntary" organizations and nearly all of which are organizations one does not typically join for political reasons (see note to table 9.2).

Our conclusion is that for the great majority of Japanese, involvement in most kinds of social networks precedes and serves to stimulate media exposure and psychological involvement rather than the reverse. Still, we must also recognize that once a person has joined an organization or taken up residence in a community, higher levels of media exposure or psychological involvement in politics may induce him or her to take a more active role in networks.

Having identified the role that demographic attributes and social network involvement play in media exposure, we will now investigate three different identifiable effects of the media on the quality and levels of participation within the Japanese electorate: the electorate's understanding of politics, agenda setting, and political involvement.

Media Effects

Knowledge and Issue Constraints

Perhaps the information-transmission role of the media is played nowhere more effectively than in Japan. The JABISS findings show high levels of trust in the media. When asked which media they trusted the most, only 3 percent of the respondents said they did not trust any, while 65 percent selected television or the newspapers and 30 percent could not say. Conversely, when asked which media they trusted the least, only 3 percent mentioned television or the press, while 52 percent said weekly magazines and 40 percent could not say. Only 19–22 percent perceived any partisan bias on the part of television or the press, and these perceptions of bias were nearly balanced: only slightly higher percentages felt that television favored the LDP (11 percent vs. 8 percent) and that the press favored the opposition parties (10 percent vs. 12 percent). Most important, these perceptions of bias were not associated with cynicism; there was a slight tendency for respondents to perceive the bias as favoring their own side of the political spectrum.

Those who follow politics in the media tend to be more knowledgeable about politics. In a separate analysis I combined three component scales into a political knowledge index.[23] Correlations between all four scales and media exposure were quite high, reaching .37 on the combined knowledge index. They held up well when controlled for SES and sex, and remained significant when a third control variable, level of psychological involvement in politics, was added.[24] Table 9.3 seeks to convey some sense of what these correlations mean in percentage terms by dichotomizing the political knowledge index into high and low categories, and the media exposure index into five high/low groups. Only 29 percent of those in the low-exposure category rank high on knowledge, compared to 72 percent in the high-exposure category. Clearly, then, exposure to politics in the media enhances one's knowledge about politics.

A second issue we will consider here is whether media exposure has any effect on issue constraint. Over the last two decades there

Table 9.3   Association between Media Exposure and Political Knowledge

LEVEL OF POLITICAL KNOWLEDGE	LEVELS OF EXPOSURE TO POLITICS IN THE MEDIA (PERCENTAGES)				
	LOW	MEDIUM LOW	MEDIUM	MEDIUM HIGH	HIGH
High	29	38	50	60	72
Low	71	62	50	40	28
Total percentage	100	100	100	100	100
N of cases	304	205	452	295	285

has been a lively debate in the American literature over the degree of consistency of political attitudes within the American electorate and the extent to which it has increased over time.[25] This work stems from Philip Converse's seminal article on the nature of mass belief systems. Converse found that the consistency of relationships across domestic issues in his elite sample was more than twice as great as in his mass sample. He argued that only those with high cognitive abilities could effectively comprehend and order political phenomena consistently, for example, within overarching ideological frameworks of liberal-conservative or left-right. Such ideological frameworks enable individuals effectively to sort out political phenomena and to link their positions on one issue with their positions on others.[26] Building on that work, James Stimpson found that respondents with higher levels of cognitive ability, as measured by education and political knowledge, have a more consistent issue-attitude structure, which in turn is more strongly related to party identification, candidate affect, and the vote. Stimpson's factor-analysis approach also found that for higher cognitive ability groups, fewer factors explain more of their differences on issues.[27]

What about Japan? Table 9.4 divides the Japanese sample into four paired groups, which are high or low on levels of education and media exposure, and shows their responses to questions testing issue awareness. The table enables us to see whether media exposure and education are associated with issue consistency. A positive result would support the conclusion that media exposure not only increases the citizen's knowledge about politics but aids in his or her ability to assimilate political information in a more complex and sophisticated manner and to link political phenomena in a more meaningful way.[28]

The table shows a high level (41 percent) of "don't know" re-

Table 9.4   Issue Awareness by Media Exposure and Education Level
Groups (Percentages)

	HAVE CLEAR ISSUE POSITIONS	CAN'T SAY	DON'T KNOW	TOTAL PERCENTAGE
Low education, low exposure	46	13	41	100
High education, low exposure	58	17	25	100
Low education, high exposure	67	15	18	100
High education, high exposure	84	2	14	100

sponses among the low education/low media exposure group, compared with only 14 percent for the high/high group. In the two mixed middle categories, it appears that media exposure is somewhat more important than education in aiding respondents in forming issue opinions. Interestingly, the high education/low media exposure group emerges as the one most likely to respond with a neutral, "can't say" reply. This may be a way of avoiding commitment on an issue about which one has not formed any opinion, without seeming to be ignorant about it. Only 2 percent of the high/high group on average selected the "can't say" response.

There is also the broader question of attitude constraint. If people's attitudes are truly consistent, then their issue positions should be linked with other kinds of attitudes and behaviors, including such important political decisions as vote choice. The citizen with a more integrated belief system should not only hold more consistent issue positions, but also should be better able to link those issue positions and other associated attitudes to his or her electoral choices.

Table 9.5 presents the results of this test. Issue positions and several other kinds of attitudes are correlated with vote choice for each of the four education and media exposure categories. To simplify presentation, the items in each of three major factor domains (political morality, foreign relations, and cultural politics) are combined into single issue-area scales, except for the strike and economy items, which did not load on those factors and hence appear as separate items (see table 9.9).

In addition, affect thermometers, tapping the respondent's positive or negative feelings toward various social and political groups,

Table 9.5 Political Attitude Constraint: Simple and Multiple Correlations between Various Attitude Dimensions and the 1976 Vote by Media Exposure and Education Level Groups

	Low Education, Low Exposure	High Education, Low Exposure	Low Education, High Exposure	High Education, High Exposure
Valence issues				
Political morality issues scale	.17	.22	.11*	.24
Foreign relations scale	(.04)	.12*	(.09)	.10*
Position issues				
1950s cultural politics issue scale	.38	.34	.27	.46
Right to strike issue item	.35	.30	.42	.39
Need to stimulate business item	−.11*	(.03)	.18	.14
Affect				
Left/right party affect	.46	.30	.56	.53
Left/right group affect	.32	.27	.33	.41
Establishment/ antiestablishment group affect	.14*	.11*	.22	.24
Subjective class identification	(.07)	.14*	.22	.24
Multiple correlation	.478	.420	.570	.602

Note: All correlations are significant at the .01 level, except those marked by an asterisk, which are significant at the .05 level, and those in parentheses, which are not significant even at the .05 level.

political figures, organizations, and institutions, are used to construct three additional scales. The first is a left/right party affect scale, which we would expect to correlate most strongly with vote choice.[29] A second, left/right group affect scale matches feelings toward two closely identified leftist groups, unions, and the student movement against those for two closely associated conservative groups, big business, and the bureaucracy. The third affect scale is more of an establishment/antiestablishment scale, pitting citizen movements and radicals against the courts and police. Each of these scales has a clear, logical association with vote choice, although as we move from parties to party-aligned groups to unaligned groups, we should expect to find that it is increasingly difficult for the electorate to make the appropriate connection with their voting choice. A final variable in table 9.5 is the respondent's subjective class identification. Although class is not a very salient concept in Japanese culture, it nevertheless has a logical association with left/right vote choice.

Looking first at the simple correlations between the variables shown in table 9.5 and the vote, we find that for the two valence issue scales, the correlations are relatively low and reveal inconsistent patterns. What association exists between the morality scale and the vote is attributable to the corruption issues rather than the welfare issue. Following a yearlong campaign in the press against the Lockheed scandal and money politics associated with the ruling party, it is not surprising to find that those who were more strongly opposed to political corruption would be somewhat more likely to vote against the ruling party.

When we look beyond the valence issue scales and turn to the other variables in the table, however, in virtually every case, the two high media exposure groups capture both the highest and second highest correlations. On these seven variables, the high/high group is first four times and second three, and the high media exposure/low education group is first three times and second three times. Even in the case of the economy item, which exhibits rather modest correlations with the vote, it is interesting to note that the low/low group completely misses the linkage, associating the left with stimulating business, while the associations for the two high media exposure groups, though modest, are at least logical. The final test in table 9.5 computed the multiple correlation of the principal variables in table 9.5 with vote by combining the position issue and affect items into single scales and regressing the resultant position issues and left-right affect scales along with subjective class identification on vote. As expected, the high/high group yields the highest multiple *r*, but it is interesting to note that the high media exposure/low education group is strongly second.[30]

It cannot be claimed that the results shown in table 9.5 are definitive, because not all attitude dimensions that can be logically linked to the vote have been investigated. Nevertheless, it does appear from these findings that media exposure has a significant effect on a voter's ability to perform the "good citizen" role in a democratic polity. Even when we control for the effects of education or raw cognitive ability, the high media exposure/low education citizen appears to do significantly better than his or her high education/low media exposure counterpart in making the appropriate connections between issue preferences and other relevant political attitudes and voting choice.

Agenda Setting

The media can also have the effect of increasing the electorate's awareness and concern about the issues of the day. Indeed, this is the message of the literature on agenda setting, which holds that media coverage of an issue is directly related to the awareness and salience of that issue among the public. For instance, respondents in panel studies tend to give similar rankings to the importance of current issues, and their rankings reflect cues that they are receiving from news stories.[31] While the media may not be very successful in telling people what to think, they are extremely successful in telling people what to think about.[32]

From the JABISS battery of twelve issue items (identified in table 9.9), I constructed an issue salience and issue position scale for three issue areas: 1950s cultural politics, corruption, and Soviet and Chinese relations.[33]

Not surprisingly, media exposure is related to the salience attached to the three corruption-related issues, given the enormous play those issues received in the media for nearly the entire year before the survey, as a result of the Lockheed scandal and Prime Minister Takeo Miki's struggle to reform the ruling party from within. Also, although the cultural politics issues were certainly not as salient in the mid-1970s as they had been in the mid-1950s, these were still the issues on which the parties were most divided. Hence, these issues continued to play an important role in structuring political competition in Japan, and increased media exposure and knowledge about politics should be related to a recognition of their enduring importance. Finally, exposure to the media has an effect of broadening one's horizons and enhancing one's knowledge and interest in foreign affairs. Apparently those with higher media exposure attach greater salience to important foreign policy issues.

Table 9.6 presents the partial correlations, which have already been controlled for the effects of SES and sex. So it is not higher edu-

Table 9.6 Association between Media Exposure and Issue Salience
and Position (Partial *r*)

	1950S CULTURAL POLITICS ISSUES	CORRUPTION ISSUES	SOVIET & CHINESE RELATIONS
	Issue Salience Scales		
Media exposure to politics	.16	.15	.16
	Issue Position Scales		
Media exposure to politics	(–.00)	.14	.16

Note: The reported statistics are the partial correlations controlled by sex and SES. All partials are significant at the .001 level, except for the one in parentheses.

cation or income or sex roles that explain the reported relationships. Nor do any other demographic attributes account for the findings, and no clear demographic profile emerges for respondents ranking high on issue salience.

The most interesting finding in the table, however, is the association between media exposure and the respondents' positions on the issue items. No association exists in the case of the cultural politics issues, but in the case of the corruption and Soviet and Chinese relations items, significant relationships are found. Those with high levels of media exposure are more likely to take a strong anticorruption position and pro-Chinese and anti-Soviet stands. Is this evidence of a media effect on attitude change? Once it is recognized that these are valence issues, with virtually the entire population lined up on one side, rather than position issues that divide the population, it becomes clear that it is not attitude change but attitude mobilization that is occurring here. By stimulating greater interest in and awareness of an issue, media exposure increases the likelihood that people will move from a noncommittal to an "agree" or an "agree to strongly agree" position on a valence issue. There is no question here of what side of the issue people are on; rather, it is a question of how strong a stand people take on the issue. What we are seeing here, then, is the mobilization of opinion. This mobilizing effect on citizen attitudes and behaviors is a very important role that the media play. For this reason, we will now turn to a more detailed analysis of the impact of the media in enhancing psychological involvement and political participation.

Political Involvement

The mobilizing effect of the media on increasing citizen interest and political involvement has been known for some time. Indeed, the early Columbia University studies found a complex interactive relationship between media exposure and psychological involvement in politics.[34] Through an elaborate panel survey design, Paul Lazarsfeld and his group were able to show that the media stimulated interest in election campaigns and that this heightened interest was associated with increased information seeking and attentiveness to the media.

Numerous other studies in the United States and elsewhere have since reported strong relationships between media exposure and both interest in politics and various modes of political participation, such as voting turnout and campaign participation. Although most of the more recent studies have not had the luxury of an extensive panel design with which to test for the direction of causation between media exposure and political involvement, it seems reasonable to assume that Lazarsfeld's findings can be generalized. In other words, exposure to politics in the media does play an important role in stimulating interest and participation. The reverse direction of causation undoubtedly also plays an important role. Those with higher levels of interest and involvement in politics are more likely to turn to the media in search of more political information.

Although these interactive effects cannot be easily distinguished with the JABISS data, there is evidence to suggest that the media play a very important, even central, role in stimulating interest in politics. Respondents who reported that they had discussed the election on at least one occasion before voting day were asked if they had ever had a political discussion prompted by something they had seen on television or read in the newspapers. In each case 62 percent of those responding to the question answered in the affirmative. If we cross-tabulate the two questions, a full 71 percent had had a conversation prompted by one or the other medium. Moreover, those who had been stimulated by the media in this way exhibited higher levels of political interest and were more likely to have engaged in active forms of political participation beyond voting, such as attending campaign meetings, soliciting the votes of others, and engaging in other kinds of campaign- and noncampaign-related activities.

Table 9.7 reports very strong relationships between level of media exposure and political involvement in terms of interest in, discussion of, and participation in politics.[35]

Table 9.7 Media Exposure and Political Involvement

	Levels of Exposure to Politics in the Media (Percentage of Respondents)				
	Low	Medium Low	Medium	Medium High	High
High levels of interest in politics	11	24	36	56	74
High levels of discussing politics	31	39	52	70	75
High levels of political participation	34	33	47	61	67
Range of Ns	(277–301)	(191–204)	(416–449)	(269–294)	(259–283)

Table 9.7 shows that for those at the low end of the exposure scale only 11 percent fall into the high-interest category, 31 percent are high in frequency of discussing politics, and 34 percent have high levels of participation. In contrast, among those at the high end of the media exposure scale, 74 percent, 75 percent, and 67 percent, respectively, have high levels of interest, discussion, and participation. I also found, incidentally, strong bivariate correlations, which ranged from .54 to .31, and little attenuation in the relationships when they were controlled by sex and SES.

The path analysis diagram shown in the figure demonstrates the interrelationships of ten important variables in mobilizing political involvement. The variables have been ordered in the sequence that is believed to portray the primary direction of causal influence, but interactive effects cannot be ruled out in many cases, and thus the magnitude of the path coefficients should be treated cautiously. The variables include a new psychological involvement scale derived by combining the highly interrelated interest and discussion scales, as well as a tenth variable, strength of partisanship, which is also added

Path analytical model of the role of media exposure in the political involvement process

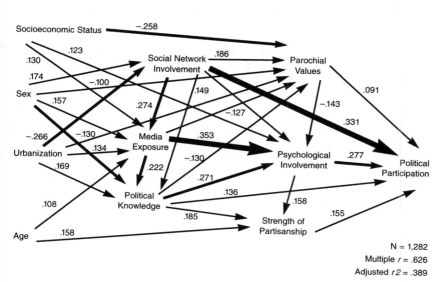

N = 1,282
Multiple *r* = .626
Adjusted *r*2 = .389

Note: The stronger path coefficients, those above .200 and .300, have been represented by thicker lines.

to the analysis because of its well-established associations with participation. These ten variables were then regressed on the political participation scale.

As shown in the figure and table 9.8, the four most important variables in explaining levels of political participation are, in order of importance, social network involvement, psychological involvement, political knowledge, and strength of partisanship, all of which have strong direct effects. Although media exposure to politics has no direct relationship with participation, of all the variables it has the strongest indirect relationships, which are exerted by stimulating higher levels of psychological involvement and political knowledge. Right behind media exposure in strength of impact on participation levels is sex. Sex is related to participation as a result of the fact that men have more political knowledge, are more attentive to politics in the media, and are more heavily involved in social networks.

The remaining three demographic variables have little net effect on participation, but some interesting relationships emerge. First, when the effects of network involvement are controlled, urbanization has a significant positive relationship with media exposure. Second, when the effects of SES are controlled, which has a strong inverse relationship with age (−.22), age also comes in as positively related to media exposure. (These are relationships we might have expected, but in the bivariate relationships presented in table 9.1, these associations appeared to be too marginal to merit comment.) Finally, urban-

Table 9.8 **Direct and Indirect Effects of All Independent Variables in Path Analysis Model on Political Participation Levels**

INDEPENDENT VARIABLES	DIRECT EFFECTS	INDIRECT EFFECTS	TOTAL EFFECTS
Social network involvement	.331	.134	.465
Psychological involvement	.277	.024	.301
Political knowledge	.136	.104	.240
Strength of partisanship	.155	0	.155
Media exposure to politics	0	.154	.154
Sex	0	.146	.146
Urbanization	0	−.051	−.051
Parochial values	.091	−.043	.048
Socioeconomic status	0	.040	.040
Age	0	.039	.039

ization has some complex and offsetting relationships with participation. Urbanization enhances participation levels through its association with higher levels of media exposure and political knowledge. At the same time, however, urbanization reduces participation levels by eroding network involvement and parochial loyalties.[36]

Although the pattern of relationships shown in the figure is complex, it does enable us to summarize the role of media exposure. We find both a picture of those citizen attributes associated with higher levels of media exposure and a picture of the media's role in the process of mobilizing political involvement. Older urban males of high SES, who are integrated into various kinds of formal and informal nonpolitical social networks, are more likely to be high consumers of political information in the media. In turn, media exposure, through its direct impact on political knowledge and psychological involvement, emerges as a key element in stimulating higher levels of political involvement and participation.

Media Effects and Electoral Campaigns

The media's agenda-setting effects in Japan go beyond alerting the electorate to the issues of the day; the media also tell the electorate what *kind* of issues to think about. If the media are the message, then the media source affects the types of messages that can be effectively communicated. As television has come increasingly to dominate perceptions of politics, it has altered the kinds of issues that dominate the political agenda.

Through the postwar period there has been a dramatic shift in the type of issues voters care about. In the 1950s constitutional and other issues—such as the role of the emperor, the status of the military, Japan's alignment with the United States, and the legitimacy of dissent and protest activities—deeply divided the population, polarizing the political system into conservative and progressive camps. These "cultural politics" issues held less importance in the 1960s, but by that time a second set of "position issues" had arisen that pitted the conservatives' growth-at-any-cost economic policies against growing concerns about pollution, environmental degradation, and other quality-of-life concerns. Disagreements over these issues, while not as intense as those over the cultural politics questions of the 1950s, tended to divide the electorate along similar lines, thereby reinforcing the conservative-progressive split.

Since the 1970s—and, indeed, into the 1990s—political debate in

Japan has progressively shifted from position issues to valence issues, which tend to be shortlived and do not divide the electorate in meaningful ways. By posing good against bad, right against wrong, valence issues align the entire electorate on the same side (e.g., against crime or corruption). Valence issues can have a stronger impact on electoral outcomes than position issues, but the effects are ephemeral, particularly in the voter's mind. Unlike position issues, which evoke a confrontation between vested interests, valence issues depend on public outrage and emotion for their salience and therefore tend to dissipate with time. The shift from position to valence issues, therefore, has tended to transform electoral decisions in Japan into referenda on the quality of the incumbent regime's performance.

Much of this shift in the issue agenda has stemmed from changing political events and party positions, but the media too have played a subtle but significant role. Politicians in all the advanced industrial democracies have increasingly tailored their message to what can be effectively communicated through television: images, personalities, symbols, and emotions. Because television does not effectively communicate hard information, the ideological rationale and logical arguments that buttress issue positions on the left or right are largely lost.

These effects of television have been reinforced by the nature of its audiences. Print media tend to have more specialized audiences, while television reaches the entire population, not just certain special interests or social strata. Politicians, therefore, tailor their television messages so as to appeal to the entire population and offend no potential supporters. The safest avenue, then, is a basic emotional appeal to ethics, morality, personality, patriotism, and whatever is held in common. Commentators and reporters for the electronic media carefully avoid controversy and labor to appear neutral to a national audience, thereby reinforcing this bland projection of the issue agenda. It is no coincidence that as television has increasingly replaced print media as the principal source of political information and images, valence issues have increasingly replaced position issues in importance to the mass publics in advanced industrial democracies.

In some European democracies, this effect of television has been somewhat offset by a strongly partisan press that presents a particular party's ideology and arguments pertaining to key position issues. A partisan press may not change many opinions, given the self-selection of media sources referred to earlier. But it does serve daily to rehearse ideological arguments and the rationales derived from them for supporting one or another side of current issues, thereby pushing position issues to the fore in public debates. However, the print media, and especially the influential national dailies, have been scrupulously neutral in Japan. Indeed, Japanese newspapers often seem so eager to avoid controversy that they go beyond neutrality. Not only do they rigidly avoid partisan advocacy and candidate endorsements, they also occasionally censor newsworthy items that might be seen as favoring or disfavoring one party or another. Instances have been reported in which the major dailies refused to print advertisements of one party that were directly critical of another, omitted or downplayed stories or incidents that cast one of the political parties in a bad light, and suppressed their own preelection polls because they feared that the one-sided findings might influence voter behavior.[37] Moreover, as Young C. Kim has observed, Japanese newspaper editorials "are unusually ambiguous, making it difficult to ascertain the position of a newspaper on a given issue."[38] The Japanese press thus plays a role in enhancing the salience of valence relative to position issues.

In the United States scholars have been arguing for the last two decades that the growing reliance on television for political information and the kinds of messages it conveys are trivializing politics.[39] The rise of negative campaigning has prompted the complaint that election outcomes increasingly hinge on candidates' character defects, not on their positions on issues. Although strict laws on media use in elections have deterred the rise of negative campaign advertisements in Japan, the media frenzy that accompanied revelations of Prime Minster Sōsuke Uno's relationships with his mistresses just before the 1989 upper house election suggests that change may be afoot. Previously, the private, personal activities of prime ministers had not been viewed as newsworthy.

While the kinds of media influences examined here may be viewed as largely negative in the West, in the Japanese case they have paradoxically played three positive roles in changing the context of political competition. First, by underplaying divisive ideological issues, the media have helped to quiet the extremely contentious, position-issue politics of the 1950s and 1960s, in which the electorate was locked in polarized camps. The media have subtly depolarized the political debate. Second, by contributing to the shift from position to valence issues, the media have enhanced electoral volatility. The rise of a new position issue may not alter party fortunes greatly, especially if the issue cuts across the major issue cleavages that originally defined the party system. In such cases, whichever side of the issue a party takes is likely to repel as many old supporters as it attracts new ones. In contrast, a new valence issue supported by the entire electorate could have a substantial impact on support for a party, assuming the party is clearly identified in the voters' minds with either the positive or the negative side of the issue. At the same time, because valence issues are inherently short-term in nature, their rise and fall can shift votes back and forth between parties from election to election. In the Japanese case, the shift from position to valence issues in the early 1970s is clearly associated with a rise in interelection volatility rates.[40]

The media's increasing impact on electoral outcomes is apparent in the three postwar elections before 1990 in which they sought to make corruption the top issue: the Black Mist scandals of 1967, the Lockheed scandal of 1976, and the Recruit scandal of 1989. In each election associated with one of these scandals, volatility rose and LDP support fell (the LDP being the primary media target in all three cases). In 1967 the LDP share of the vote fell by 5.9 percentage points from the previous election. Nonmedia factors may have been at work then, including demographic changes that were reducing population in conservative constituencies and increasing it in more urban constituencies where progressive or mixed influences predominated. Those demographic shifts had largely worked themselves out by 1976, when the LDP share still fell by 5.1 percentage points, again well above the period average. And in the 1989 upper house election, the average LDP decline was an enormous 12.8 percentage points. The Recruit scandal was not the sole factor at work here; nonetheless, electoral results in these key years suggest the growing power of the media to set the agenda and temporarily reduce electoral support for the ruling party.

The growing volatility of the electorate demonstrated in these trends increased the viability of defections from the LDP, defections that ultimately drove the party from power in 1993. There were major defections from both the LDP and the JSP in the 1970s, but in the context of a politics that was still largely shaped by the cultural politics position issues of the 1950s, the electorate did not reward those defections. By the 1990s the growing volatility of the electorate meant that defections were no longer equivalent to electoral suicide. Once Morihiro Hosokawa had demonstrated the viability of his Japan New Party—a party with a clean, fresh media image—in the 1992 upper house election, several LDP factional groups were emboldened to launch their own independent parties, a development that was the primary cause of the LDP defeat in the 1993 lower house election. Although the LDP returned to power in June 1994 in coalition with the JSP, the changes in the electoral system made while the

LDP was out of power have virtually ensured that the major realignment of the party system already under way will bring a permanent end to the four-decade pattern of one-party dominance. Thus the media's role in diminishing ideological cleavages and fixing the voters' attention on the issues of political corruption and reform has contributed to this major political transformation.

A third positive role played by the media involves drawing attention to candidates' images. Restrictions on candidates' use of the media have prevented the emergence of anything like the extraordinary personalization of campaigns seen in the United States. Nonetheless, the growing dominance of television in a context of restricted media access for candidates puts party leaders in the spotlight, in what might be called the prime-ministerization of election campaigns. Beginning with Prime Minister Yasuhiro Nakasone in the mid-1980s and continuing with such leaders as Takako Doi of the JSP, Toshiki Kaifu of the LDP, and the Japan New Party's Hosokawa in the late 1980s and early 1990s, we see popular leaders enhancing their parties' support in the polls. We also see the effects of unpopular leaders, such as Noboru Takeshita and Sōsuke Uno (and behind-the-scenes leaders, such as Kakuei Tanaka and Shin Kanemaru), in lowering party support.

The growing media focus on party leaders may yield two additional benefits, both related to the electorate's remarkable inattention to national politics compared to local candidates and the local benefits they can bring. These effects are, first, to further nationalize the criteria upon which voters base their electoral decisions and, second, to affect the selection of party leaders and their power within their parties. Increasingly, party leaders have to be people who project a popular, responsive image in the media, rather than simply good fund raisers and faction builders. Uno and Kaifu were the first prime ministers who were not faction leaders. Their ascendance to the prime ministership, however brief, suggests that party leaders must increasingly look to the public rather than just to intraparty factional politics for the support needed to rise to the top.

Conclusion

In the process of investigating the role of the media in Japan, we have been able to construct a profile of the high media consumer. All else being equal, those who invest more in following politics in the media are likely to be older, urban, male, and high in socioeconomic status.

There are, then, certain expected biases in patterns of media consumption. In the Japanese case, however, the inequalities associated with urbanization and socioeconomic status are partially offset by the large and somewhat unexpected role played by social network involvement. There is not a dichotomy, as has sometimes been posited in the literature, between citizens who turn to the media for political information and those who rely on personalistic networks. Rather, involvement in social networks stimulates more attentiveness to politics in the media. Those respondents who are highly involved in social networks are unusually high consumers of political information in the media. Being a part of formal and informal associations stimulates political interest and awareness. Because network involvement is higher in rural areas and largely unrelated to socioeconomic status in Japan, it plays an important role in equalizing media exposure.

Beyond profiling media exposure, this analysis has demonstrated five important kinds of media effects associated with improving the quality, levels, and context of political participation in Japan. First, media exposure not only increases the citizen's political knowledge, it also enhances a person's ability to translate issue preferences into electoral choices. Second, media exposure tends to increase political knowledge, issue awareness, and issue salience. Third, media exposure increases people's interest in politics and their proclivity to discuss politics with others. Through these and other relationships, media exposure plays an important role in a mobilization process at the psychological level, which leads to higher levels of political involvement and participation. Fourth, through their influence in shifting the issue agenda from position to valence issues, the media have helped to depolarize political competition, enhance electoral volatility, and move Japan toward a pattern of regular party turnover. Finally, by increasing the effect of party leaders' images on the fortunes of their parties, the media bring national issues to the fore in electoral campaigns and weaken the power of party factions. In short, the media have enhanced the quality, levels, and context of political participation in Japan over the postwar period.

A word of caution is in order regarding the conclusions that should be drawn from this chapter. Some readers may feel somewhat puzzled by the overall positive tone of this analysis. The findings presented here should not be construed as a ringing endorsement of the performance of the Japanese media. I am well aware of the many deficiencies of the Japanese media, deficiencies that have been most ably detailed by Kim, Ofer Feldman, and others, including the authors of some chapters in this volume.[41] Readers should recall that, in this chapter, we have not been analyzing the performance of the media—what reporters, newscasters, editors, and the media as an institution *do*—but rather its consequences: the *effects* of the media on mass political behavior. In that light, surely an additional contributing reason for the overall positive effects of the media must be the

Table 9.9 Factor Loadings of 12 Issue Items on 4 Principal Factors (Oblique Rotation)

Issue Items	Factor 1	Factor 2	Factor 3	Factor 4
Political morality factor				
Reform money power politics	.753	−.020	−.010	−.058
Prohibit political donations by corporations	.745	−.080	.044	−.074
Protect public interests against big business	.638	.020	−.175	−.057
Increase welfare even at cost of tax hike	.624	.079	−.041	.183
1950s cultural politics factor				
Strengthen Japanese–U.S. security ties	−.078	.826	−.042	.073
Strengthen defense forces	−.043	.782	−.062	.048
Increase emperor's power	.106	.703	.164	.079
Foreign relations factor				
Conclude Sino–Japanese peace treaty	.119	.038	−.822	−.045
Improve Japanese–North Korean relations	−.104	−.178	−.764	.146
Demand Soviet return of northern territories	.196	.144	−.671	−.087
Economy factor				
Stimulate business even at risk of inflation	−.076	.177	−.064	.890
Multiple factor loading items				
Legalize public employees' right to strike	.265	−.493	.067	.393

Note: The above factor loadings are for the full sample. An identical factor structure emerged for each of the four media exposure and education level groups.

context of politics and the nature of the political culture from the early 1950s onward. In Japan—a country emerging from a prewar authoritarian tradition, where politics had been the preserve of men of influence, where decisions regularly had been made in secret, where money politics and corruption had been woven deeply into the structure of the everyday conduct of politics—the media have exercised and continue to exercise a beneficial democratizing role.

Notes

1. Ronald Inglehart, *The Silent Revolution* (Princeton, N.J.: Princeton University Press, 1977).
2. Russell Dalton, Scott Flanagan, and Paul Beck, eds., *Electoral Change in Advanced Industrial Democracies* (Princeton, N.J.: Princeton University Press, 1984).
3. See, for example, the case of Britain, where the media biases of the press are easily identified. David Butler and Donald Stokes, *Political Change in Britain* (New York: St. Martin's Press, 1976).
4. Ole Holsti, "Cognitive Dynamics and Images of the Enemy," in David Finlay et al., *Enemies in Politics* (Chicago: Rand McNally, 1976); Alexander George, *Presidential Decisionmaking in Foreign Policy* (Boulder, Colo.: Westview Press, 1980).
5. A popular explanation for this seemingly paradoxical finding is that the relationship between, for example, media exposure and voting stability is essentially spurious and that levels of both media exposure and voting stability are influenced by the same third variable: strength of partisanship. Helmut Norpoth and Kenneth Baker, "Mass Media Use and Electoral Choice in West Germany," *Comparative Politics* 13 (October 1980): 1–14. This explanation is clearly consistent with and reinforces the minimal effects view.
6. Joseph Wagner, "Media Do Make a Difference: The Differential Impact of Mass Media in the 1976 Presidential Race," *American Journal of Political Science* 27 (August 1983): 407–430.
7. Denis McQuail, "The Influence and Effects of Mass Media," in *Mass Communication and Society,* ed. James Curran, Michael Gurevitch, and Janet Woollacott (Beverly Hills, Calif.: Sage Publications, 1979), pp. 70–93.
8. Hiroshi Akuto, Toshiharu Mikami, Hirosuke Mizuno, Ryō Makita, Eiji Takagi, and Jun Saitō, "Gendai daigakusei no seikatsu to iken: masu media kōdō, seiji iken oyobi kachikan wo chūshin ni" (Lifestyles and Opinions of Contemporary University Students: Their Mass Media Behavior, Political Opinions, and Values), *Tokyo Shimbun Kenkyūjo Kiyō* (Tokyo Shimbun Research Institute Journal) 26 (1978): 31–109.
9. Scott C. Flanagan, "Media Influences and Voting Behavior," in Scott Flanagan, Ichirō Miyake, Shinsaku Kōhei, Bradley Richardson, and Jōji Watanuki, *The Japanese Voter* (New Haven: Yale University Press, 1991).

10. Several studies have argued that the media do exert some kinds of measurable blanket effects, often unintended, on attitudes. For example, one study found that heavy viewers of American television entertainment programs, reflecting these programs' subtle message, develop more hard-line attitudes on civil rights issues than do light viewers. See George Gerbner, Larry Gross, Michael Morgan, and Nancy Signorielli, "Charting the Mainstream: Television's Contributions to Political Orientations," *Journal of Communication* 32 (1982): 100–127. Another study argued that the print and television media, because of their different characteristics and treatments, often differentially favor one or another of the presidential candidates in measurable ways that are then reflected in the different voting choices of those respondents who rely on newspapers versus those relying on television. William C. Adams, "Media Power in Presidential Elections: An Exploratory Analysis, 1960–1980," in *Media Power in Politics*, ed. Doris Graber (Washington: CQ Press, 1984), pp. 175–185. While these studies are intriguing, the apparent blanket effects on attitude change demonstrated are still rather small and are not definitive.

11. Media studies on change of political attitudes tend to have very short-term perspectives, such as a single election campaign. The problem is that few people may change their attitudes based on what they have read or seen in the media over the past few weeks. In a society undergoing a long-term shift in basic social and political values, however, the media undoubtedly play a central role in the dissemination and cultivation of new values.

If long-term longitudinal data were available across the postwar period, the Japanese case might prove to be a fruitful setting in which to study the impact of the media on attitude change. It exhibits several conditions that should enhance the impact of the media on changing political attitudes: uniformity of the media's message, a comparatively high level of public trust in the media, and rapid growth of the media at a time of unprecedented change in political institutions and cultural values. It might be argued that these conditions enabled the media to exercise an important vanguard role in the transformation of Japan's political culture by building support for Japan's new political institutions, diffusing new social norms and values, and stimulating new modes and styles of citizen participation.

12. Jarol B. Manheim, "Can Democracy Survive Television?" *Journal of Communication* 26 (1976): 84–90; Anthony Smith, "Mass Communications," in *Democracy at the Polls*, ed. David Butler, Howard R. Penniman, and Austin Ranney (Washington, D.C.: American Enterprise Institute, 1981), pp. 173–195; and Wagner, "Media."

13. Manheim, "Can Democracy Survive Television?"

14. The 1976 JABISS Japanese Election Study was conducted at the time of the December 1976 lower house election in Japan. It comprised pre- and postelection panel surveys fielded in the period 20–28 November (1,796 completed interviews, completion rate 72 percent) and 11–19 December (1,556 interviews, completion rate 74 percent). The survey contained more than 400 items. Findings are presented in Flanagan et al., *The Japanese Voter.*

15. Six papers were coded as national. The percentage reporting reading each was: *Asahi,* 26 percent; *Yomiuri,* 23 percent; *Mainichi,* 16 percent; *Sankei,* 4 percent; *Nihon Keizai,* 4 percent; and *Akahata,* 2 percent. In contrast, the percentages for those coded regional or other were as follows: regional and sports papers, 41 percent; religious papers, 2 percent.

16. See note 17 below on the special characteristics of weekly magazines.

17. Of four items related to following politics in the media, only three loaded on the same factor, as can be seen by the unrotated factor loadings reported below:

Number of special election programs watched: .806
Number of newspaper election articles read: .788
Frequency of watching TV news: .604
Number of magazine election articles read: .378

As a result only the first three were included in the index of exposure to political information in the media.

A word of caution is in order concerning the conclusion one might draw from the failure of the fourth item to load heavily on the exposure index. Reasons for its poor performance may derive not only from the limited nature of magazine reading, relative to newspaper reading or television viewing, but also from the nature of weekly magazines themselves. In contrast with the more staid and respected monthly magazines, weekly magazines generally tend toward sensationalism, with heavy doses of sex, scandal, and gossip. They may therefore attract a different kind of readership than the other print media. Some evidence to support this hypothesis can be found in table 9.1. While the demographic profile of the weekly magazine readers does not differ significantly in most cases from that of the other print media variables, one glaring exception emerges: readers of weekly magazines are far younger than consumers of all other media categories. Perhaps a more general magazine-reading item would have been preferable, but in any case it seems appropriate to drop the magazine item from the index of exposure to political information.

18. See Susan Pharr, *Political Women in Japan* (Berkeley: University of California Press, 1981).

19. One of the items asked by Robert Ward and Akira Kubota in their 1967 Japanese Election Study was, "Do you feel that you found out more about the campaign from talking to other people or from newspapers and TV?" My secondary analysis found no correlation between this item and a traditional/modern attitude scale, and to the best of my knowledge, no study has been able to substantiate a correlation between this kind of question and traditional values.

20. Sidney Verba, Norman H. Nie, and Jae-on Kim, *Participation and Political Equality* (London: Cambridge University Press, 1978).

21. Actually, while there is a fairly substantial correlation between membership in nontraditional, non–community-based organizations and SES,

when we add in community organizations and the other elements in the social network index, the correlation almost disappears (r = .06). This explains in large part the comparatively low correlation reported by Verba, Nie, and Kim between socioeconomic resources and political participation in Japan (Verba et al., *Participation*, p. 64). See Scott Flanagan and Steven Renten, "Social Networks and Political Participation in Japan," paper presented at the annual meeting of the American Political Science Association, New York, 1981.

22. I am indebted to Hiroshi Akuto for this suggestion.

23. The first scale is a count of the number of times the respondent had sufficient knowledge to report a clear agree or disagree position on each of twelve issues. The second scale is a count of the number of times the respondent could name the party whose position was closest to his or her own for each of the same twelve issues. The last component was a measure of the richness of the respondent's images of the parties, counting the number of separate things he or she had to say about three of the most important parties.

The loadings on the first unrotated factor of the three component scales in the knowledge index were:

Have clear issue positions: .851
Can name closest party: .814
Depth of party image: .700

While there was no check on the accuracy of the respondent's perceptions as to which party was closest to his or her position on an issue, in general it can be expected that those who are willing to name a specific party have more information about party positions than those who are not willing to do so.

24. The index of psychological involvement was derived from two scales measuring the respondent's level of interest in politics and frequency of discussing politics with family, friends, neighbors, and colleagues. Control variables are assumed to be antecedent to both variables in the bivariate relationship being tested. This is clearly not the case here, since both media exposure and knowledge about politics can be expected to increase psychological involvement as well as the reverse. Hence, not all of the shared variance in these relationships should be attributed to the prior effects of psychological involvement. Nevertheless, what the partials demonstrate is that even in the worst-case scenario, among those respondents of the same sex and SES who have the same levels of psychological involvement, higher levels of media exposure are still associated with higher levels of knowledge.

25. See Gerald Pomper, "From Confusion to Clarity: Issues and American Voters," *American Political Science Review* 66 (June 1972): 415–428; Norman Nie and Kristi Anderson, "Mass Belief Systems Revisited: Political Change and Attitude Structure," *Journal of Politics* 36 (August 1974): 541–591. See also the following articles in the *American Journal of Political Science:* John Sullivan, James E. Pierson, and George E. Marcus, "Ideological

Constraint in the Mass Public," 22 (May 1978): 233–249; John Sullivan, James E. Pierson, George E. Marcus, and Stanley Feldman, "The More Things Change, the More They Stay the Same: The Stability of Mass Belief Systems," 23 (February 1979): 176–186; George F. Bishop, Alfred J. Tuchfarber, and Robert W. Oldendick, "Change in the Structure of American Political Attitudes," 22 (May 1978): 250–269; George F. Bishop, Alfred J. Tuchfarber, Robert W. Oldendick, and Stephen E. Bennett, "Questions about Question Wording: A Rejoinder to 'Revisiting Mass Belief Systems Revisited,'" 23 (February 1979): 187–192; and Norman Nie and James Rabjohn, "Revisiting Mass Belief Systems Revisited," 23 (February 1979); 139–175.

26. Philip Converse, "The Nature of Belief Systems in Mass Publics," in *Ideology and Discontent,* ed. David Apter (New York: Macmillan, 1964): 206–261.

27. James Stimpson, "Belief Systems: Constraint, Complexity and the 1972 Election," *American Journal of Political Science* 19 (August 1975): 393–417. See also Norman Luttbeg, "The Structure of Beliefs among Leaders and the Public," *Public Opinion Quarterly* 32 (1968): 398–409.

28. I am not suggesting that Japan is experiencing a phenomenon similar to that which has been argued by some for the United States: that with the weakening of party identifications in America, issue voting is on the upswing. Issue voting has never been particularly strong in Japan and does not appear to be increasing. The set of cultural politics issues discussed in this section has consistently yielded fairly strong correlations with the vote across the postwar period, but other kinds of issues that are important predictors in the American context—such as welfare, redistributive tax and spending policies, and the size and role of the government—have not been strongly related to partisanship or the vote in Japan. Thus, while I am not arguing that there is a discernible trend toward issue voting in Japan, I do suggest that those with higher levels of media exposure are better equipped to make the appropriate linkages between their issue preferences and vote choice.

29. To yield the highest scores on this scale, one would have had to match positive feelings toward the LDP and its faction leader Takeo Fukuda with negative feelings for the socialist (JSP) and communist (JCP) parties.

30. The problem of nonopinions and other sources of error in survey research is chronic and one of the major reasons why correlations in the .30–.40 range are considered to be very high and evidence of a strong relationship.

In the multiple correlation analysis at the bottom of table 9.5, it is somewhat surprising to find that the high education/low media exposure group ranks lower than even the low/low group. It may be that those with high education and low knowledge are more apt to give some response to a question, no matter how ill considered, rather than remove themselves from the sample, when in doubt, with the "don't know" response, as the low/low group does in large numbers. If that category's responses were sprinkled with a higher frequency of nonopinions, it would account for the lower multiple *r* that we encounter.

31. See Doris Graber, *Mass Media and American Politics* (Washington, D.C.: Congressional Quarterly Press, 1980), pp. 132–134; also, Donald Shaw and Maxwell McCombs, *The Emergence of American Political Issues: The Agenda Setting Function of the Press* (St. Paul: West Publishing, 1977).

32. B. C. Cohen, *The Press, the Public and Foreign Policy* (Princeton, N.J.: Princeton University Press, 1963).

33. To simplify presentation, the findings in table 9.6 are reported for the issue area scales, rather than for the individual issue items. For this purpose, the welfare issue is dropped from the political morality scale, yielding a three-item corruption scale, and the North Korean item is dropped from the foreign relations scale, leaving a Soviet and Chinese relations scale. The 1950s cultural politics issues scale remains unchanged. The two dropped items did not discriminate the population on issue salience, as almost everyone thought that the welfare issue was important and hardly anyone thought that the North Korean issue was important.

34. Paul F. Lazarsfeld, Bernard Berelson, and Hazel Gaudet, *The People's Choice* (New York: Columbia University Press, 1948).

35. The political interest scale was derived from four items: on level of interest in politics in general, the Lockheed incident, the election campaign, and the election outcome. The discussion scale was based on eight items concerning the frequency of discussing politics with family, neighbors, friends, and colleagues. The conventional participation scale placed in the bottom category those who voted only infrequently or never and did nothing else, placed in the next category those who only voted regularly, and distributed the rest of the sample by the number of political activities they had engaged in beyond voting (counting the number of activities they reported doing across thirteen conventional participation items).

36. Note also the unusual role that parochial values play here. While social network involvement reinforces parochial values, political knowledge, psychological involvement, and strength of partisanship are all negatively related to parochialism. When the effects of knowledge, psychological involvement, and partisanship on participation levels are controlled, however, it is those with parochial values, rather than those with cosmopolitan values, who are found to participate at higher levels. Undoubtedly, this has something to do with the relationship between parochial values and network involvement. Community solidarity and loyalty to one's district are traditional norms typically invoked in Japan to mobilize participation. This direct effect of parochial values, however, is virtually canceled out by its indirect effects, which lower participation levels through the association of parochial values with lower levels of political knowledge, psychological involvement, and strength of partisanship. As a result, the uncontrolled, simple bivariate correlation between parochial values and participation is insignificant.

37. Hajime Shinohara, "Kokumin no 'shiru kenri' to shimbun" (Citizens' "Right to Know" and Newspapers), *Shimbun Kenkyū* (Newspaper Studies) 227 (June 1970): 7–14; Michio Yanai, "Tokyoto chiji senkyo ni okeru masu media no taiō" (The Mass Media's Response to the Tokyo Mayoral Elec-

tions), *Shimbungaku Hyōron* (Journalism Review) 21 (1972): 36–54; and Young C. Kim, *Japanese Journalists and Their World* (Charlottesville: University Press of Virginia, 1981). These omissions in news reporting do not tend to favor one party or to bear any relationship to the ideological leanings of a paper's editorial staff. Indeed, the beneficiaries have often been the smaller fringe parties, such as the JCP and Kōmeito.

38. Kim, *Japanese Journalists,* p. 107.

39. Manheim, "Can Democracy Survive?"; Smith, "Mass Communications"; and Wagner, "Media Do Make a Difference."

40. The average change in the LDP vote share between each pair of succeeding elections across the six lower house elections from the late 1950s to the early 1970s was 2.2 percentage points, versus an average change of 3.4 percentage points for the seven lower house elections from the early 1970s through the 1990 election. A similar calculation for the upper house contests averaged across the two constituency races yields average changes of 2.3 points in the early period and 5.8 in the second (or 4.1 if the unusually volatile 1989 contest is excluded).

41. Kim, *Japanese Journalists;* Ofer Feldman, *Politics and the News Media in Japan* (Ann Arbor: University of Michigan Press, 1993).

10

Media in Electoral Campaigning in Japan and the United States

HIROSHI AKUTO

T H E growing importance of mass media in American political culture in the 1990s has thrown into question a vast body of descriptive and theoretical work in the areas of voting and mass communications dating back to the 1950s. Much of that work maintained that the key determinants of voting behavior were political party loyalty and the candidate's image. Issues were thought to be secondary, and the mass media were viewed as far less important to decision making than was personal communication.[1] Since the 1960s the supposed universality of those theories has been discredited; they were found to be rooted in a particular setting (America) at a particular time. Voters came to be seen as voting less for their party and more on issues. Furthermore, television essentially invalidated the "two-step flow model" emphasizing personal communications about the candidates and politics transmitted through opinion leaders.

Some, but not all, of these changes in American political culture have parallels or analogues in developments in Japan and other advanced industrial democracies. This chapter seeks to determine parallels and differences, particularly with regard to the impact of mass media on voter behavior in Japan and the United States. It is my view that despite various similarities, the differences are quite pronounced. They are rooted in both the regulatory frameworks and the political cultures of the two countries, and manifest themselves in profoundly different styles and methods of election campaigning. Three key differences stand out:

1. In election campaigns, mass media play a far more significant role in the United States than in Japan; personal connections and organizations are more important in Japan.
2. In characterizing the role of the mass media in the electoral pro-

cess, the hypothesis of "strong effect" appears to best match the U.S. situation, while the "limited effect" theory best matches the Japanese case.

3. Among the media, television plays the more important role in affecting voter attitudes in the United States, while newspapers continue to be more important in Japan.

A case study that forms the second part of this chapter investigates media bias and its effect on voters' attitudes. The study is limited to a 1986 mayoral election in Machida City, a suburb of Tokyo, and to newspaper coverage of the election (which was ignored by television). Among the questions investigated are the following: Did newspaper articles emphasize the "game" or, conversely, the "substance" aspects of the campaign? Did the newspapers exhibit systematic bias by devoting more coverage to the front-runner? Did they show any ideological bias? Japanese political news is found to focus more on substance than on the "contest" aspects of political races, to be more evenhanded in its coverage of the various candidates than the U.S. media, and—contrary to what many Japanese and foreign observers have said about Japanese newspapers—to exhibit remarkably little ideological or structural bias.

The Media and Political Culture in the United States

The U.S. electoral process underwent tremendous change in the 1970s, particularly the presidential contest. Primaries came to have unprecedented importance, and party conventions assumed new roles and grew in influence. It is a legacy of the "New Politics" of this era that Americans in the 1980s and 1990s are more interested in politics and wish to participate more directly in the political process. In the "old" days, state party leaders chose delegates to the national conventions behind closed doors. Before 1968 only one-third of the delegates were elected by primaries, but in 1980 three-quarters were so elected.[2] Other significant reforms were introduced through adoption of the "proportional allocation system" and the "winner-take-all system."[3] In short, the delegate election process was made more visible and less arbitrary.

Because of the increased importance of the primaries, the nomination game is often over long before the national convention opens. Conventions no longer function to select presidential candidates; rather, they are media events designed to introduce the party and its preselected candidates to the voters through live television. This could be seen, for example, in the convention extravaganzas produced in New York and Houston in the summer of 1992. Some 32 million voters participate in the primaries, whose season stretches from the New Hampshire primary in February to the party conventions in July and August. Because television covers both the primaries and the conventions, the impact on voters is immense. The equal-time provision of the 1934 Communication Act was progressively diluted in 1957, 1959, 1964, and 1976. The requirement that candidates be allotted the same amount of time was ended for broadcasts, where the forum was sponsored by an outside group. This paved the way for prime-time television debates between presidential candidates that have become watershed events in the campaign. These and later revisions made spot advertisements and political programs easier to produce and more riveting for viewers.[4]

In the mid-1970s Sidney Kraus and Denis Davis described some changes associated with television coverage of politics: (1) frequent coverage of primaries; (2) detailed coverage of national conventions of both parties; (3) the rise of television debates between presidential candidates; (4) prevalence of public opinion polls and regular television coverage of results; (5) increased political programming and improved quality; (6) spread of political advertisements; and (7) changes in newspaper coverage.[5]

These scholars' predictions that the hypothesis of limited effect was losing validity and that mass media would exert greater influence on politics proved correct. The trend continues to intensify as television and politics exploit each other for mutual profit. The growing use of television and other mass media to appeal directly to voters has transformed campaigning; events are staged for television, and communication is by image and sound bite. Other factors, too, are at work, including the reduced role of the parties and dysfunctional party machines. Ultimate causes are hard to pinpoint, but it seems clear that factors such as these are combining to achieve a complex result. The most notable changes are the centrality of polls, constant evidence of mass media manipulation, and the increasingly sophisticated and professionalized nature of campaign operations.

Polls became an essential tool to try to grasp the volatile and capricious shifts in opinion among the general public and to appeal to potential voters. In campaigning at all levels—presidential, senate and congressional, gubernatorial and mayoral—polls are the first step to learning the dissatisfactions and demands of voters. Results are scientifically analyzed to design election strategies tailored to pinpoint demographics. Candidates recruit pollsters, media specialists, and, at the top, election strategists.

Election coverage in the United States has evolved with these developments. Coverage has vastly increased, political programs have become spectacles, and television anchors are now celebrities far more famous than many politicians. The mass media's impact on voters has become more pronounced.[6] Television has become the stage for "media events."[7] Coverage in newspapers has also expanded in volume and changed in substance. To compete with television, newspaper coverage has become more sensational, featuring exposés, and also offering analysis and op-ed pieces written by popular writers and star reporters. Inside stories of presidential campaigns continue to demonstrate that print journalists are increasingly conscious of their roles and of the need to compete with television; their writing has become far more intent upon entertaining the reader. And in a fascinating parallel development, distrust of politicians and of the political process generally has grown.

Media and Campaigning, Japanese Style

In Japan, too, loyalty to political parties has eroded. As disaffection with the ruling Liberal Democratic Party (LDP) and the leading opposition party, the Japan Socialist Party (JSP), grew before the collapse of one-party LDP rule in the summer of 1993, the number of people who did not support any political party increased. This development promoted the trend toward multiparties, which continues today. An overall trend in the United States and many other advanced industrial societies toward greater distrust of government and of politicians can also be found in Japan. In addition, since the summer of 1993 there are signs of increased use of television—especially the talk-show format—by politicians, as shown in chapter 5. Overall, however, there continue to be profound differences in how the media are used in electoral campaigning in Japan, as compared to the United States, as a result of three factors. First, because of the nature of a parliamentary system, there is no nationwide electoral campaigning in Japan. This rules out any possibility of the kind of high-tech television saturation coverage of a central political drama that has paved the way for television's rise in U.S. presidential electoral campaigning. Second, regulations—which have remained largely unchanged over the postwar era—governing media coverage (for example, with regard to political advertising and the use of surveys) set limits on the role of the print media in campaigning and involve such severe restrictions on the use of television by candidates as to make Japan an entirely different case from the United States with regard to the media's role in election campaigning. Third, the nature of Japan's print media, which is profoundly different from that in the United States, gives Japanese newspapers, with their dense coverage of political races, the potential for playing a far more powerful role in electoral campaigning than is the case in the United States.

Perhaps the most significant difference is the absence in Japan of a single, central race to galvanize public and media attention. The main elections in Japan, which are for Diet members and thus are equivalent to the election of senators and representatives in the United States, are mostly local contests in diverse constituencies.

Only the elections of Tokyo's governor or of mayors of large cities seem even remotely analogous to U.S. presidential contests. These elections arouse public interest, they are usually fought one-on-one, and policies and personalities play an important part. However, voter interest, even in these more analogous elections, appears to be much lower than in the United States for the nationwide presidential campaign.

Severe limits on the role of the media in campaigning also play a major part in shaping the nature of campaigning, independent of these differences between the political systems. The restrictions on media use in Japanese general elections are far-reaching. Political candidates are not permitted to buy time on television or radio, or advertising space in newspapers or magazines. Instead, the government pays for and supervises political advertisements for all the candidates; only five newspaper advertisements are permitted, and they must be of a specified length. Candidates are permitted only four television and two radio appearances; two of the television appearances are on the public broadcasting system, NHK, and two are on the private channel of the candidate's choice; in both cases the appearances are government-sponsored. Television and radio appearances can be no longer than five and a half minutes each, and they are meticulously monitored to make sure that no candidate gains a visual image advantage over another. Even these brief appearances are available only to candidates running for Diet seats; they are unavailable to candidates running in local elections (of the kind discussed below) for mayors and governors.[8] Politicians increasingly have used appearances on talk shows to create the media image they cannot obtain through the highly regulated and equal media time provided by advertisements.

The effects of campaigning restrictions of this kind make Japan a very different electoral setting from the United States. Virtually none of the factors that have enhanced the media's impact on elections in the United States is found in Japan. Despite much fanfare over Japanese television's higher profile in political events in the summer of 1993 and certain seeming changes in candidates' strategies on media use (see chapter 5), the basic pattern of media coverage in Japan has not altered in profound ways. There are no television spots focusing on candidates, no candidate-created television shorts of the kind used in the United States, poring over the personal history of the candidates—displays of their courage, their personal triumphs. In Japan political parties hold conventions, but television coverage is not permitted. Though interest in the television-debate format is increasing, the format has been relatively little used so far. Japanese television gives fleeting exposure to candidates, except in the limited coverage of electoral contests for Diet seats, which means that, for the most part, television has relatively little effect. Moreover—and this is relevant to the study discussed below—because 95 percent of all television programming is generated by nationwide networks, gubernatorial and mayoral elections are slighted.

Under these conditions it is no wonder that the media in Japan exert not the "strong effect" found in the United States, but rather a "limited effect."[9] Not surprisingly, Japanese candidates rely heavily on the traditional campaign mode of cultivating and banking on personal relationships. Electoral campaigns are local and continue to be driven for the most part by the personal support organizations built up by individual politicians.[10]

Over the longer term, there is evidence that the election roles of television and other mass media are gradually changing. The election rules for the upper house, the House of Councillors, have been revised to provide for party-list voting for the national constituency. This has made it possible to pool the time slots allocated to a party's different candidates in order to allow party presidents to deliver keynote addresses lasting ten to twenty minutes on the air. A televised debate of party leaders took place in 1990, the first since the early 1960s. Meanwhile, the volume of political advertisements for elections at various levels has increased steadily in the three major national newspapers. One candidate for election to the Tokyo Metropolitan Assembly not so long ago ran an advertisement in the nationwide daily press. Network news operations are recruiting newscasters of the American type, and more time is being blocked out for political news and related programming. These trends are likely to continue and to strengthen. But the severe restrictions on media use, which are unlikely to undergo fundamental change, make Japanese electoral campaigning very different from its American counterpart and likely to remain so in the future.

So far, this discussion has stressed constraints that operate on media use in Japan, and especially those that limit the use of television in campaigning. But other factors hold the potential of promoting more active media use in Japanese campaigning. One of these is the sheer size and scope of the print media in Japan. Japan's five major newspapers (*Asahi, Mainichi, Yomiuri, Sankei,* and *Nikkei)* are all national, utterly unlike the U.S. situation, in which only a few newspapers, such as the *New York Times* and *Wall Street Journal,* even aspire to a broader audience. Because Japan's national newspapers—in local editions published throughout the country—all zero in on campaigns for Diet members, mayors, and governors, the print media are a far more powerful force in Japan than in the United States. Even if political advertising is itself restricted, Japanese newspapers' political reporting provides a great deal of information about the candidates and disseminates it to a broad readership.

Another possible source of print media influence in Japan is ideological. Austin Ranney and others have argued that American journalists demonstrate little ideologically motivated "political" bias, but that the news media themselves show substantial "structural" bias as private companies in pursuit of profit.[11] With regard to bias, the Japanese media industry overall is similar to its American counterpart in structured bias, and television, as in the American case, has been thought until recently to be free of political bias.[12] But Japan's newspapers, at least as they are perceived by the public, are a different matter. It is widely believed in Japan that *Asahi* and *Mainichi* are antigovernment, proliberal, and even proradical, while *Yomiuri, Sankei,* and *Nikkei* are more conservative. If popular perceptions of political bias among newspapers are correct, then the potential for newspapers to play a leading role in swaying electoral opinion in campaigning in Japan is far greater than this discussion so far—with its emphasis on the legal restrictions and structural constraints on media use—would suggest. The issue of political bias, little researched in Japan until recently, is thus included in our study.

To explore the role of the newspapers in electoral campaigning, the key issues to be taken up here are the agenda-setting capability of the media and the issue of media bias. According to Thomas Patterson, biased news coverage by the media will significantly affect voters' evaluations of issue salience—that is, the voters' political consciousness or judgment as to which political issues are important.[13] Biased news coverage also can influence the public's evaluation of candidates and issues. Patterson employed content analysis to prove the existence of such bias in U.S. media coverage and developed several explanations of why such coverage operates that way. His work focused on television, but the distinctions he makes among types of coverage that lead to bias obviously apply to the print media as well. He showed that bias is more likely to result when the media act in one of the following ways:

Treat the campaign as a "game" (involving winning or losing, tactics, a candidate's personal appearance, hoopla) rather than focusing on "substance" (issues, policies, traits, records, endorsements)

Eschew "descriptive" coverage in favor of a more interpretive approach and seek to be entertaining

Avoid "diffuse type" issues for "clear-cut type" issues and policy issues for "campaign" issues

Report whether or not a candidate is winning, rather than discussing a candidate's "issues" and "policies" or even "performance"

Emphasize campaign pledges, events, strategy, styles, and organizational activities rather than more substantive but less flashy aspects of the campaign, such as demographic characteristics of the electorate, and so on

Conducting a true U.S.–Japanese comparative study is exceedingly difficult because, as noted, Japan has no equivalent to a nationwide presidential election, and even legislative elections are quite different, given the nature of Japan's multimember-district electoral system. This system underwent reform in 1994, but as it has operated in the postwar era, it has produced not one winner but several from each district. Media coverage inevitably is more complex in this situation; for example, a one-on-one or "horse race" approach is hardly a possibility in such a context. The nearest things to the much studied U.S. presidential elections have been Japanese mayoral and gubernatorial elections. In such elections, at least, an analogous potential for horse-race coverage and for other "biasing" types of coverage in one-on-one contests exists. We fully recognize the limits of such a comparison: U.S. presidential races are likely to involve far higher levels of voter interest, vastly more media coverage, extraordinary amounts of television use, a much larger and more diverse constituency, and so on. The comparisons, at this preliminary stage of research, are meant mainly to be suggestive and to pave the way for future research.

The University of Tokyo's Media and Politics Study Group conducted a case study of media bias and agenda setting for a mayoral election that took place in Machida City in suburban Tokyo in February 1986. The first part of our research sought, by content analysis, to determine whether the media exhibited any of three biases suggested by Patterson: (1) an inclination (structural bias) to emphasize the "game" aspect of the election over political "substance"; (2) an inclination (structural bias) to devote more coverage to the leading candidate or "front-runner"; and (3) an ideological (political) bias toward right or left, liberal or conservative (which Patterson found not to exist in the United States). The second part of the research consisted of surveys of voter attitudes, to determine whether such attitudes were influenced by any media biases—to assess, in other words, whether agenda setting occurred.

Mayoral Election in Machida City, Suburban Tokyo

Machida is a fast-growing city whose population of 320,000 makes it the second largest city in Tokyo's Tama ward, after Hachiōji. More important, at the time of the 1986 mayoral election we studied, it was also one of a few of Tama's twenty-six cities headed by progressive mayors. The incumbent, Katsumasa Ōshita, was first elected in February 1970 when, as a secretary to the then chairman of the JSP, Mosaburō Suzuki, he beat a conservative newcomer by a margin of approximately 5,000 votes. Now, sixteen years later, Ōshita was trying to extend his administration to a fifth term with the support of the JSP, the Japan Communist Party (JCP), the Democratic Socialist Party, and Kakujiren, a new and minor progressive party. His opponents were Masao Obara, president of the Machida Medical Association, whose candidacy was advanced by the LDP to stop Ōshita from winning a fifth term, and Seitoku Iino, who had narrowly lost to Ōshita in the preceding election. Iino, who earlier had enjoyed the support of the LDP, was now running as a candidate of the Salaryman New Party (Sarariiman Shintō), a minor party. The election appeared to be a close contest among the three candidates.

The official campaign began on February 16, with the election set for February 23, seven days later, in accordance with national law on local elections. Content analysis was conducted of newspaper coverage of the election appearing over a three-week period before the actual election. A public opinion survey was conducted three days before election day.

Bias in Coverage by the Mass Media: A Content Analysis

Findings for each of the three investigations are shown in table 10.1.[14] Shown with the data for the Machida mayoral election are data from a similar study conducted for the 1979 Tokyo gubernatorial election and for U.S. newspapers in the 1976 American presidential primary, as reported by Patterson.[15]

Game versus Substance

Table 10.1 measures emphasis on "game" versus "substance" aspects of election campaigns as reflected in U.S. and Japanese mass media. Television is shown for the United States only, given the absence of comparable coverage in Japan. Codings for the U.S. and Japanese data do not precisely correspond, but they have been reconciled as far as possible. The Japanese newspapers, at least for the nonnational elections that were the focus of our study, consistently contained more "substance" coverage than their American counterparts. "Game" coverage in the Japanese case would likely have been higher had the elections been for the Diet, rather than for mayor of a small city or for governor of Tokyo. The greater obscurity of the Machida mayoral and Tokyo gubernatorial candidates relative to U.S. presidential candidates may well have translated into greater media coverage focused on "substance." However, the much greater Japanese media emphasis on "substance" merits further research and invites future comparative research on media coverage of subnational elections in the United States. For both the Machida and Tokyo elections, *Asahi* and *Mainichi* carried higher ratios of "substance" reporting than did *Yomiuri* and *Sankei*.

Structural Bias

In the Machida race, the four newspapers surveyed devoted a disproportionate amount of their election coverage (about 40 percent) to the incumbent, Ōshita (table 10.2). This finding was not consistent with the situation in the 1979 election for Tokyo governor. In that race newspaper coverage was quite evenly balanced between Suzuki and Ōta, and did not entirely neglect Asō, the distant third. This may be because, in contrast to the Machida case, all the Tokyo gubernatorial candidates were relatively obscure, and the race between the two front-runners was quite close.[16] From a comparative standpoint, however, it is quite striking that for both the Machida and Tokyo

	UNITED STATES					JAPAN						
						MACHIDA				TOKYO		
SUBJECT OF COVERAGE	NETWORK EVENING NEWSCASTS	ERIE TIMES/NEWS	L.A. HERALD EXAMINER	L.A. TIMES	TIME/NEWSWEEK	ASAHI	MAINICHI	YOMIURI	SANKEI	ASAHI	MAINICHI	YOMIURI
Winning & losing	24	26	25	20	23	6	5	14	4	6	4	6
Strategy, logistics	17	19	18	19	22	7	4	9	3	4	5	6
Appearances	17	14	14	12	9	8	6	9	6	7	4	4
Character						7	6	11	6	12	12	7
Hoopla & others						7	3	4	7	9	10	13
Subtotal	58	59	57	51	54	35	24	47	27	39	36	36
Issues, policies	18	19	18	21	17	11	14	8	18	13	17	6
Ideology, coalition						26	23	10	16	27	27	31
Campaign issues						4	2	2	1	0	0	0
Traits, records	7	6	5	8	11	5	5	4	3	2	5	1
Endorsement	4	4	5	6	4	0	0	0	0	0	0	0
Subtotal	29	29	28	35	32	45	44	24	38	43	49	39
Others	13	12	15	14	14	19	31	29	35	18	15	25
Total	100	100	100	100	100	100	100	100	100	100	100	100

Note: Data on Japan in this and all subsequent tables in this chapter are from the 1986 Machida mayoral election and the 1979 Tokyo gubernatorial election; U.S. data are derived from a reanalysis of the data presented in Patterson's 1980 study of the 1976 U.S. presidential election (Thomas E. Patterson, *The Mass Media Election: How Americans Choose Their President* [New York: Praeger, 1980]). Table based on a random sample of the election news coverage provided by each news source. The U.S. network figures are combined averages for the ABC, NBC, and CBS evening news programs. The figures for the *Erie Times* and *Erie News*, and those in *Time* and *Newsweek*, also have been combined because the separate figures were substantially the same.

Table 10.2 News Coverage of the Candidates (Japan) (Percentages)

	MACHIDA				TOKYO			
	ASAHI	MAINICHI	YOMIURI	SANKEI	ASAHI	MAINICHI	YOMIURI	
First place (Ōshita)	38	42	35	40	31	34	35	Election winner (Suzuki)
Second place (Obara)	28	38	32	29	40	38	35	Second place (Ōta)
Third place (Iino)	34	31	33	31	29	28	29	Third place (Asō)
Total	100	100	100	100	100	100	100	

Table 10.3 News Coverage of the Candidates (United States) (Percentages)

POSITION CANDIDATE FINISHED IN	NETWORK EVENING NEWSCASTS	ERIE TIME/NEWS	L.A. HERALD-EXAMINER	L.A. TIMES	TIME/NEWSWEEK
First place	59	58	52	60	62
Second place	17	18	29	19	14
Third place	16	16	17	15	13
Fourth place	8	8	2	6	11
Total	100	100	100	100	100

Note: Percentage of week's coverage devoted to each candidate, according to how the candidate ultimately fared in the upcoming primary election. Based on average for the 13 U.S. presidential primary weeks in 1976.

elections, media coverage was far less biased in the direction of front-running candidates than was true for media coverage, either by newspapers or television, in the United States (see table 10.3).

Political Bias

Despite widespread Japanese public perceptions of ideological bias among newspapers, we found no real evidence of it. Little ideological bias was observed in newspaper coverage of either the Machida mayoral or Tokyo gubernatorial elections. Coverage was predominantly (70–80 percent) neutral and objective (tables 10.4 and 10.5). Articles whose analysis was slanted either in favor of or against a candidate accounted for 20–30 percent of the total. But political bias (for or against liberals or conservatives) was largely absent, and candidates in both camps received positive comment. In the Machida race, Ōshita was subject to some critical comment, but an incumbent of sixteen years can expect his administration to receive critical attention. Negative comments accounted for 11–13 percent of coverage of Ōshita but were outweighed by positive comments. Negative references to both Obara and Iino were rare (1–5 percent).[17]

Voters' Evaluation of News Coverage by Mass Media

As noted previously, local elections are slighted by television news except for those in the largest cities or those involving some hint of political scandal. Newspapers are far more influential than television at the local level. Voter exposure to political coverage in newspapers and television is largely the same in the United States and Japan (table 10.6). In the Machida mayoral race, voters indicated a relatively low reliance on the mass media for information about the candidates (table 10.7). Not surprisingly for a local election largely ignored by television, that source was of negligible importance. Yet even newspapers were of little importance; they were identified as the most relied-upon source by only 8 percent of the respondents. Far more important than the mass media, particularly in small communities, are candidates' personal support organizations, whose glue consists of family ties, geography, or common interests. Thirty-three percent of those surveyed mentioned personal information from acquaintances and friends, and personal connections with a candidate, supporting organizations, and campaigners as their information source. Such a skewing would not be found in the United States.

Table 10.4 Political Bias of News Reporting, Machida Mayoral Election (Percentages)

	ŌSHITA (LIBERAL)			OBARA (CONSERVATIVE)			IINO (CONSERVATIVE & CENTER)		
	PRO-LIBERAL	NEUTRAL	PRO-CONSERVATIVE	PRO-LIBERAL	NEUTRAL	PRO-CONSERVATIVE	PRO-LIBERAL	NEUTRAL	PRO-CONSERVATIVE
Asahi	10	79	11	1	83	16	1	81	18
Mainichi	20	69	11	4	74	23	2	78	20
Yomiuri	19	73	7	5	79	17	3	79	18
Sankei	18	89	13		76	24		77	23

Table 10.5 Political Bias of News Reporting, Tokyo Gubernatorial Election (Percentages)

	ŌTA (LIBERAL)			SUZUKI (CONSERVATIVE)			ASŌ (MIDDLE OF THE ROAD)		
	PRO-LIBERAL	NEUTRAL	PRO-CONSERVATIVE	PRO-LIBERAL	NEUTRAL	PRO-CONSERVATIVE	PRO-LIBERAL	NEUTRAL	PRO-CONSERVATIVE
Asahi	9	84	6	5	80	15	14	83	3
Mainichi	13	81	5	5	76	18	17	78	5
Yomiuri	6	85	8	7	81	11	12	86	2

Table 10.6 Exposure to the Daily Paper's Political News and Network Newscasts (Percentages)

	ERIE		LOS ANGELES		JAPAN	
	NEWSPAPER	TV	NEWSPAPER	TV	NEWSPAPER	TV
Regularly	48	34	33	24	34	46
Somewhat often	21	30	15	27	29	23
Once in a while	11	23	10	30	16	18
Infrequently	7	12	15	16	16	11
Never	13	1	27	3	4	2
Total	100	100	100	100	100	100

Table 10.7 Most Influential News Sources in Japan (Percentages)

Newspapers	8.1[a]
Television	0.2[a]
Radio	0.2[a]
Ordinary magazines	0.3[a]
Bulletins of political parties/groups	4.3
Official election bulletins (kōhō)	22.0
Leaflets/handbills	4.6
Posters	2.9
Discussions with friends, acquaintances, and neighbors	12.0[b]
Messages/requests from candidates/campaigners (irai)	10.8[b]
Mail/telephone calls/addresses from campaigners (irai)	7.1[b]
Recommendation by labor unions and other groups	2.4[b]
Results of public opinion polls	3.3
Other	17.2
Total	100.0

[a] Mass communication.
[b] Personal communication.

Machida voters were exposed to surprisingly little "game" information in the mass media (newspapers). Their exposure to "substance," including policy, ideology-party, and campaign issues, was much higher. Table 10.8 analyzes respondents who first came in contact with various topics in the mass media (column 1), "on the street" (column 2), and in discussions with others (column 3).[18] Respondents learned most from the media about candidates' careers and abilities ("traits"). Of their initial exposure to election topics in the media, fully 59 percent was related to "substance." Only about 10 percent of the initial exposure was related to "game" topics, such as predictions, campaign tactics, or the personal appearance of the candidate.[19] High exposure to newspapers (55 percent) relative to television (4 percent) for information about the candidates might

Table 10.8   Topics Encountered and Discussed during the Campaign (Japan) (Percentages)

	THROUGH MASS MEDIA	ON THE STREET	DISCUSSED WITH OTHERS
Game			
Winning and losing	3		15
Strategy	2	1	9
Appearances	1	6	
Hoopla and others	3	4	
Subtotal	10	11	25
Substance			
Policy issues	19	9	13
Ideology, party, program-conservative	3	3	7
Campaign promises, slogans	3	2	2
Campaign issues		2	3
Candidates' traits	28	3	14
Other	7	3	
Subtotal	59	21	39
Other	4	50	18
"Don't know," "not applicable"	39	33	34
Total	100	100	100
N	582	582	582

explain voters' high reliance on mass media for "substance" (table 10.9). Domination of the media by television (as in the United States) might incline that reliance toward "game" news.

Machida voters derived more of their information on game aspects of the election from personal discussions (25 percent, versus 10 percent from mass media). Yet even in private discussions, "substance" accounted for 39 percent of the total. (See table 10.8.) Game aspects form a much larger part of the personal discussions voters have in conjunction with elections in the United States.[20]

"On the street" refers to voters' passive exposure to information, for example, through telephone canvassing, posters, and street oratory. Here, topics to which respondents were exposed fell largely into the hard-to-identify category of "other," at 50 percent. This category includes campaigning through personal connections via support organizations, which plays an important role in the process.

Voters' exposure to mass media and personal communication naturally influences their attitudes toward elections and candidates. Subjects of the Machida survey were asked to identify the "most important issues" in the election and also to identify "highlights" of the election. The second question was an attempt to get around the tendency of the first question to induce answers emphasizing substance over game aspects. Results are shown in table 10.10. The two

Table 10.9   Candidates' Campaign Exposure from Media and Direct Sources (Japan) (Percentages)

	MASS MEDIA	SAW & HEARD DIRECTLY
Newspaper, newspaper ads	55	1
Television	4	
Radio		
Telephone		39
Election bulletins	2	15
Posters	1	29
Leaflets, handbills	8	3
Street oratory	1	7
Candidates		2
Campaign, visit, election cars	1	16
Direct mail, postcards		3
"Don't know," "not applicable," unknown	32	21

questions netted quite different sets of answers: 65 percent of the
respondents identified "substance" issues as having top "importance," but 61 percent identified "game" aspects as being the "highlight" of the election.

For the "importance" question, "substance" issues topped the poll
at 65 percent, headed by policy issues at 41 percent. Indeed, many
issues were in dispute in the election, including welfare (12 percent),
taxes (8 percent), road construction (6 percent), and the number and
salaries of public servants. Also significant as an issue was whether
the incumbent should serve a fifth term, which was connected to
whether a conservative was to recapture the seat from a progressive.
The qualifications (traits) of candidates were also identified as
important by respondents.

**Table 10.10 Perceptions of Election's Most Important Aspect
(Japan) (Percentages)**

	IMPORTANT ISSUES	HIGHLIGHTS	PEOPLE'S INTERESTS
Game			
Winning and losing	13	53	25
Strategy	1	7	3
Appearances			
Hoopla and others		1	
Subtotal	14	61	28
Substance			
Policy issues	41	8	38
Ideology, party, program-conservative	6	14	11
Campaign promises, slogans	3	1	1
Campaign issues	7	2	5
Candidates' traits	7	4	2
Other			
Subtotal	65	30	56
Other	5	3	3
"Don't know," "not applicable"	28	25	30
Total	100	100	100
N	582	582	582

On the "highlight" question, however, respondents ranked game factors highest at 61 percent, headed by speculation about winners and losers at 53 percent. The power struggle between progressives and conservatives was identified by 14 percent of the respondents. The last column of table 10.10 indicates "perceived agenda setting," that is, respondents' perceptions of how the "general public" viewed the issues. Results on this question fell roughly between those for the "importance" and "highlight" questions, with game aspects identified by 28 percent of the respondents and substance aspects by 56 percent. Answers to this question suggest that voters (here, off their guard) regarded game aspects as more important than they admitted for the "importance" question; nonetheless, substance continued to top their perception of the public's view of the issues.

Comparative Analysis

Results of the content analysis and voter attitudes can be usefully compared with the work of Patterson regarding bias in U.S. media coverage of elections (see table 10.14).[21] Patterson's results and our findings (adjusted for the purposes of comparison) are shown in table 10.11. Patterson surveyed voter attitudes about the "most important" issues of the then current election five times during the campaign season, beginning in February with the start of the primaries, through the conventions in July and August, and up to the climax of campaigning in October. The "importance" question in the Machida survey sought comparable data, absent the longer time dimension (the campaign season lasted only seven days).

Patterson's data show that early in the campaign, American voters placed greater importance on substance, and notably on candidates' policies. Thereafter, until the poll in August, voters were inclined to view the contest as a horse race. But as the campaign season drew to a close in October, interest returned to substance questions, although in a different way from eight months earlier. At this point, voters were more interested in campaign issues or how candidates had maneuvered through the campaign period, rather than in policy issues. "Events" were cited as important by many voters in August and October, reflecting the significance of the national conventions and nationally televised debates during those months.

The Machida data, in contrast, indicate a greater attention to substance, at 56 percent, with policy and the conservative/progressive contest ranking high. Not surprisingly in view of the absence of

Table 10.11   Perceptions of Election's Most Important Aspect
              (United States and Japan) (Percentages)

	UNITED STATES					JAPAN
	FEBRUARY	APRIL	JUNE	AUGUST	OCTOBER	
Game	56	85	81	72	22	17
Substance						
Policy issues[a]	24	7	9	6	10	56
Campaign issues[b]	2	3	1	1	13	12
Candidates' traits	3	2	2	2	3	6
Subtotal	29	12	12	9	26	77
Events	8	1	1	16	44	
Others	7	2	6	3	8	9
Total	100	100	100	100	100	100
N	212	520	585	610	550	582

[a] Policy issues and ideology were combined in Japan.
[b] Campaign issues and campaign promises and slogans were combined in Japan.

debates and conventions, "events" were mentioned by no respondent.[22] It is conceivable that the Machida voters' emphasis on substance over game aspects stems in part from the relative absence of a structural bias favoring front-runners. Media concentration on front-runners is common in the United States. The smaller field of candidates typically seen in Japanese local races (in contrast to the U.S. presidential primary) makes it easier for the media to devote more attention to the second- and third-runners than it could if there were, say, fourth and fifth candidates.

Conclusion

This chapter has explored a few of the many ways in which the media operate differently in politics in Japan and the United States. The study reported here supports the utility of an agenda-setting approach to studying media bias and its effect on voters' attitudes. We have seen that Japanese newspapers, at least in the mayoral and gubernatorial elections studied here, devoted more attention to "substance" aspects of political campaigns; this attitude toward elections is reflected in voters' own claims about what are the "important" issues in their own and others' views. We have also seen far less structural bias in coverage of candidates than is claimed for the United States, at least in the 1976 presidential election for which data are available.

The Machida and Tokyo case studies will need to be supplemented by additional studies of local elections, including elections for Diet seats, if comparisons with American data are to yield more than tentative results. Data on the role of the media in U.S. mayoral, gubernatorial, and legislative elections would also be exceedingly valuable for comparative purposes. Moreover, the absence of television coverage of the Machida election campaign has meant a large gap in an area of critical theoretical importance. The gap is especially troubling in view of evidence that television may become more important in Japanese electoral campaigning and may exert greater influence on voters' decision making in the future than is the case today. Future studies in Japan must seek to fill that gap and test the hypothesis that television exerts a strong effect on elections. That hypothesis has not yet won general acceptance even in the United States, where it has been argued that while television offers information, it is unable to induce changes in voters' opinions and attitudes.[23]

At the present time, however, despite the advanced state of the media technology in Japan and the reality that Japan is a media-saturated society, the media play a far more limited role in elections in Japan than in the United States. At least in the local Japanese elections we studied, the media were far less biased than their American counterparts: more evenhanded in their amount of coverage of various candidates, more attentive to substance over the game aspects of the campaign, and also (like their American counterparts) relatively lacking in ideological bias (despite what the Japanese public often assumes about Japan's newspapers). At the same time, the Japanese media effects on agenda setting—again, at least in the local elections we studied—were rather marginal, supporting a "limited effects" interpretation for Japan. Studies conducted since the tumultuous 1993 general election suggest that while there have been major changes in political parties and party coalition strategy since then, the basic characteristics of the relation between media and politics have not altered.[24] In a larger sense, these various findings about Japan point to the need to take into account regulatory structure and media industry differences, along with electoral and political system differences, in building theories about the role of the media in industrial societies.

Notes

1. Several works seemed progressively to be perfecting the theory and methodology of voting studies: Paul F. Lazarsfeld, Bernard Berelson, and Hazel Gaudet, *The People's Choice* (New York: Columbia University Press, 1948); Bernard Berelson, Paul F. Lazarsfeld, and William McPhee, *Voting: A Study of Opinion Formation in a Presidential Campaign* (Chicago: University of Chicago Press, 1954); Angus Campbell, Gerald Gurin, and Warren E. Miller, *The Voter Decides* (Evanston, Ill.: Row, Peterson, 1954); and Angus Campbell, Philip E. Converse, Warren E. Miller, and Donald E. Stokes, *The American Voter* (New York: John Wiley, 1960).

2. Discussed by Austin Ranney, *Channels of Power: The Impact of Television on American Politics* (New York: Basic Books, 1983).

3. See Richard Joslyn, *Mass Media and Elections* (Reading, Mass.: Addison-Wesley, 1984).

4. Ibid.

5. Sidney Kraus and Denis Davis, *The Effects of Mass Communication on Political Behavior* (University Park: Pennsylvania State University Press, 1976).

6. Hiroshi Akuto, "Media and Politics in the United States," *Studies of Broadcasting* 24 (1988): 25–58.

7. See Dan D. Ninmo and Keith R. Sanders, eds., *Handbook of Political Communication* (Beverly Hills, Calif.: Sage Publications, 1981); Larry J. Sabato, *The Rise of Political Consultants: New Ways of Winning Elections* (New York: Basic Books, 1981); Christopher F. Arterton, *Media Politics: The News Strategies of Presidential Campaigns* (Lexington, Mass.: Lexington Books, 1984).

8. For a discussion of Japan's restrictions on media use, see Gerald L. Curtis, *The Japanese Way of Politics* (New York: Columbia University Press, 1988), pp. 166–169; Curtis, *Election Campaigning, Japanese Style* (New York: Columbia University Press, 1971), pp. 153–158; and Scott Flanagan, Ichirō Miyake, Shinsaku Kohei, Bradley Richardson, and Jōji Watanuki, *The Japanese Voter* (New Haven: Yale University Press, 1991), pp. 302–303.

9. Despite the limited formal role of television in Japanese elections, it has certainly had an impact on its audience's perception of political developments. Television has afforded opportunities to watch and reflect on events such as the emperor's visit to the United States, U.S. presidents' visits to Japan, and prime ministers' attendance at Group of Seven summits.

10. See Curtis, *Election Campaigning*.

11. Differences between the media environments of the two countries must be borne in mind. Because they have national circulation, major Japanese newspapers, far more than their American peers, emphasize national and international news, allocating only limited space to local (regional) news. The top five Japanese papers account for 52 percent of total circulation nationwide. In the United States, virtually all quality papers are local. A

similar distinction holds for television news. Japanese local stations originate very little (less than 5 percent) programming about local events or news, relying instead on programming from the networks (NHK, TBS, Fuji, Asahi, and others). American local broadcasters originate coverage of local events. See Ranney, *Channels of Power.*

12. The question of "structural bias" in Japanese television news needs to be further investigated. See this volume, chapter 3.

13. Thomas E. Patterson, *The Mass Media Election: How Americans Choose Their President* (New York: Praeger, 1980).

14. Coding used in the two studies is shown in tables 10.12 and 10.13 (page 336).

15. Patterson, *The Mass Media Election,* conducted several surveys over a nine-month campaign period, versus the seven-day campaign period in Machida. Our media survey ignored television, which scarcely covered the Machida election.

16. *Mainichi* and *Yomiuri* devoted about equal coverage to Suzuki and Ōta; *Asahi* gave slightly more coverage to Ōta.

17. For both the Machida and the Tokyo elections, a slight conservative bias was seen for *Sankei;* not conspicuous was any liberal orientation of *Asahi* and *Mainichi,* or conservative orientation for *Yomiuri.*

18. Respondents were requested to answer open-ended questions freely; their responses were later coded for substance and game categories.

19. This was far lower than expected by the investigators.

20. According to data on national elections in the United States, 37–69 percent of Americans tend to discuss the "game" aspects of elections, depending on the time period in the campaign.

21. Patterson, *The Mass Media Election.*

22. Table 10.14 (page 337) shows the comparison of the contents of personal communication in the United States and Japan. For this question, too, it became clear that the Japanese discuss more "substance" matters, such as policy issues and the candidate's career or past record, rather than topics in the "game" category.

23. Among the skeptics are Edwin Diamond, *Good News, Bad News* (Cambridge: MIT Press, 1978); and Thomas E. Patterson and Robert D. McClure, *The Unseeing Eye: The Myth of Television Power in National Politics* (New York: Putnam, 1976).

24. See Hiroshi Akuto, "Dealignment and the Consciousness of the Electorate in Japan—Analysis of the 1993 General Election of Japan," paper presented at the 1994 Annual Meeting of the American Political Science Association, New York, September 1994; "U.S.–Japan Communication Gap and the Role of TV News," paper presented at the 20th Anniversary International Symposium: "Communication between Diverse Cultures through Broadcasting," Tokyo, May 1994; and "International Understanding, International Misunderstanding, and the Communication Gap," paper presented at the International Symposium on "Creating Images: American and Japanese Television News Coverage of the Other," Tokyo, March 1994.

Table 10.12 Number of News Stories Analyzed (United States)

Code Type	ABC News	CBS News	NBC News	Erie Times	Erie News	L.A. Times	L.A. Herald	Time	Newsweek
Political story	1,137	1,254	1,074	633	653	580	245	502	489
Candidate story	351	329	308	166	216	361	232	58	56

Note: Description of code types is in text. News days were randomly selected for analysis. For these days all appropriate network evening news and newsmagazine stories were coded using the two codes. For newspapers the political story code was applied only to front-page stories and stories on the first page of the inside section. The candidate story code, however, was applied to all newspaper stories about the campaign, regardless of where they were located in the newspaper.

Table 10.13 Number of News Stories Analyzed (Japan)

Code Type	Machida (Mayor)				Tokyo (Governor)		
	Asahi	Mainichi	Yomiuri	Sankei	Asahi	Mainichi	Yomiuri
Political story	1,773	1,243	1,073	967	10,446	9,473	9,714
Candidate story	488	311	347	220	2,893	2,610	1,395

Note: Both political and candidate stories were counted by lines for all newspaper stories about the elections.

Table 10.14 Topics of Election Conversation during Campaign (Percentages)

	UNITED STATES					JAPAN
	FEBRUARY	APRIL	JUNE	AUGUST	OCTOBER	
Game	45	64	69	32	37	31
Substance						
Policy issues	5	12	11	31	19	25
Campaign issues	3	1	1	4	8	5
Candidates' traits	15	8	6	16	16	17
Subtotal	23	21	18	51	43	48
Events	12	3	5	10	15	
Others	20	12	8	7	5	21
Total	100	100	100	100	100	100
N	40	128	81	108	161	471

11

Media Agenda Setting in a Local Election: The Japanese Case

TOSHIO TAKESHITA AND IKUO TAKEUCHI

THE news and other mass media are said to serve as "gate-keepers" for information in society. The assumption is that by selecting and emphasizing issues or topics, the media ensure that the public will come to regard them as important or worthy of attention. Simply put, the media can set the public agenda and determine what people think about.[1] By setting the agenda, they play an important role in constructing social reality. In contemporary societies, most important social, political, and economic events occur beyond the immediate reach of our senses. We depend on media portrayals of reality to understand the "unseen environment." The mass media's definition of reality becomes the public's to a large extent.

While political scientists use the term *agenda setting* to describe the process by which some issues come to be adopted for policy consideration, scholars whose work focuses on the media apply the term to the cognitive effects of the media in defining the set of political issues that engage the interests of individual members of the public. Agenda-setting research attempts to investigate empirically some aspects of the reality-constructing function of mass media. To explore agenda setting in such a context, this study examines the roles the mass media play in a local election campaign in Japan, in terms of the media agenda-setting theory. The study measures correlations between political issues as defined by the media and issues as identified by voters, shortly before a mayoral election in Machida, a suburb of Tokyo, in 1986. On the whole, the results suggest that mass media do influence agendas, at least for some types of people in the audience. The findings are consistent with the observations that Japanese tend to be anxious to know what others think of a problem and that they often employ an out-group as a reference group. That cultural tendency would help explain the generally stronger media effect at the perceived salience level than at the personal level. We assume this to be characteristic of media agenda setting in Japan.

Agenda Setting in Elections in Japan

The seminal study of the media's ability to set the political agenda was published by Maxwell McCombs and Donald Shaw in 1972.[2] They tested the hypothesis by comparing issue emphasis in the media, as measured by content analysis, with voter's issue salience, as measured by polls, during the 1968 presidential campaign in Chapel Hill, North Carolina. Strong positive correlations were found between the two measures, which suggested that there were media agenda-setting effects. By the mid-1980s, more than 150 agenda-setting studies had appeared in the United States and Europe.[3]

Agenda setting has become an important subject in Japan as well.[4] Most studies conducted in Japan have dealt with media influence in the context of national politics or with politics in the Tokyo metropolitan area, which receives about as much media attention as national politics. Political scientists at Keiō University conducted a series of agenda-setting tests as part of a larger study of the political behavior of Tokyo residents.[5] Their research focused on "perceived media issue emphasis"—that is, the impressions of ordinary people as to which issues were most emphasized by the media.[6] They found that the agreement between perceived media issue emphasis and voter's issue salience was generally low, and quite low between the media's emphasis, as measured objectively, and voter's salience. However, when demographic attributes such as sex, age, level of education, and occupation and factors such as levels of reliance on the press, interest in politics, and party support were taken into account, certain voters were far more susceptible to media effects than others.[7]

Toshio Takeshita tested the agenda-setting hypothesis in Wakayama City, the capital of Wakayama prefecture, during an off-election period.[8] Content analysis was performed on television network news and national daily newspapers that aired or appeared in the six weeks before interviews to determine what issues were emphasized in media treatment.[9] Interviews were then conducted to determine which issues mattered to the public. Takeshita found that agenda-setting influence was positively correlated with the level of news exposure: as people's level of exposure to the news increased, the congruence between the media's emphasis and the public agenda became closer. When "interest in national politics" was taken into account, the stronger a subject's interest in politics, the stronger the agenda-setting effects. The relation between the subject's communications with others, on the one hand, and his or her adoption of the media's issue agenda was more complex, however. Essentially the relationship was curvilinear: moderate levels of interpersonal communication resulted in the strongest correlation between the media's emphasis and those issues most salient for voters. One possible explanation for this curvilinear relationship may be that while interpersonal communication generally boosts the agenda-setting effects, people who are extremely active communicators are the kind of people who are apt to have independent views, and who thus are somewhat less reliant on the media's definition of what matters. Newspapers, Takeshita found, exerted stronger agenda-setting influence than did television news.

In another study, this time focusing on a single issue, tax reform, Takeshita found that "attentiveness to the election" was the factor that most significantly correlated with the top ranking accorded the tax issue by voters.[10] Again the relationship was curvilinear: voters with a moderate level of attentiveness showed the strongest agenda-setting effects.

Research in Japan thus tends to support the view that agenda setting by the media does not occur for all groups and under all circumstances. But when factors such as level of media use or political interest, which affect receptivity to media stimuli, are weighed, there is much to support the agenda-setting hypothesis. These findings suggest the potential for media influence even on those members of the audience who at the time of the study seemed to be impervious to media effects.

Agenda Setting on Local Issues in Japan

It is often suggested that mass media effects are more difficult to detect when it comes to local as opposed to national news.[11] We assume that this tendency is also true in Japan, especially in metropolitan areas. Residents of Tokyo and Osaka live in rich media environments. Tokyo offers seven television stations, five AM and three FM stations, five national newspapers, and a vast selection of nationally circulated magazines. However, national and international news dominates news coverage in these media, and relatively limited time and space are allotted to local community affairs. Ironically, metropolitan residents in today's Japan are less informed about their local community than about national and international events. Hence, the media's agenda-setting influence is likely to be weaker on affairs at the local than at the national level.

However, because people have to turn to the media for local news and information, there is no reason to expect automatically that the media's agenda-setting influence is weak. As in other industrial countries, increased urbanization has encouraged geographical mobility and hindered the development of elaborate and intense social networks within the community that might function as personal channels for local information.[12] Given these contrary considerations, it is worth investigating the extent to which local news content in the mass media plays an agenda-setting role in a highly urbanized community.

Our study was conducted in February 1986 in Machida City, a suburb in the western part of the Tokyo metropolitan area, with a population of 320,000. During February 20–21, before the 1986 mayoral election (on February 23), personal interviews were obtained from a random sample of 800 residents (twenty years of age and older); of these, 582 interviews (73 percent) were successfully completed.

For the voter's issue salience, three kinds of measures—each corresponding to a different concept—were prepared:[13]

Personal issue salience. Issues regarded as personally most important to respondent. The relevant question was, "What do you think is the most important issue of this election?" (open-ended).

Perceived issue salience. Respondent's perception of other voters' issue salience. The measure was "What do you think most interests people in this city in this election?" (open-ended).

Interpersonal issue salience. The most frequently cited topic in conversations with family or friends. "Did you discuss something about this election with your family or friends in the past week? If you did, what kind of topics did you discuss and with whom?" (open-ended).

After the field survey, a list of issues nominated by the respondents was compressed into seven general issue categories (see table 11.1).

In the absence of a local newspaper, the local news sections of national dailies were the main source of information about the local campaign for Machida residents. We conducted content analysis of local news pages of four national dailies *(Asahi, Mainichi, Yomiuri,* and *Sankei)* for a three-week period (February 2–23). Excluded from the analysis were *Nihon Keizai Shimbun* (a national business paper) and television and radio news, whose coverage of the election was negligible.

For all stories covering the election, each column line referring to any issue was coded into one of several preliminary issue categories. The preliminary categories were later compressed into the same general categories as for the voter's issue salience.

Findings

Issue Emphasis by the Media

Content analysis reveals that issue emphasis in *Asahi, Mainichi,* and *Yomiuri* was quite similar (Spearman's Rhos = 0.70–0.85), with the correlation between those three and *Sankei* being slightly weaker (Rhos = 0.39–0.64). (See table 11.1.) Figures for the four newspapers were combined after weighting according to distribution rates in Machida, as determined by the Japan Audit Bureau of Circulation:

Table 11.1   Selected Issues Emphasized by 4 Newspapers during Machida Election Campaign (Media's Issue Emphasis)

ISSUE	PERCENTAGE	RANK
Provisions for urban facilities (e.g., roads and sewers)	21.6	1
Welfare (e.g., for aged, handicapped)	16.5	2
Administrative reform (e.g., streamlining of services and personnel)	13.1	3
Education (e.g., build more municipal high schools)	8.1	4
Connection with higher levels of government (e.g., leader's ability to get projects for local area)	5.4	5
Another term for the incumbent (e.g., had he been in office too long?)	2.2	6
Taxes (e.g., reducing local tax)	1.5	7
(N = 1,308)		

Note: The unit of analysis is the line of article. Figures for the 4 papers were combined after being weighted according to each distribution rate in Machida city, so that the N in this table is not the same as the actual total.

Asahi, 30.7 percent; *Mainichi,* 10.2 percent; *Yomiuri,* 44.0 percent; and *Sankei,* 2.1 percent. Inclusion of *Sankei* in the combined measure caused almost no problems, given its lower correlation together with a low circulation rate.

The top issues in the campaign coverage were "provision for urban facilities," followed by "welfare" and "administrative reform." Three candidates were running for mayor: the liberal incumbent Katsumasa Ōshita, and Masao Obara and Seitoku Iino, both conservatives. All candidates, and particularly Ōshita and Obara, made campaign pledges regarding urban facilities. Ōshita also stressed welfare, while the two conservatives criticized the incumbent on issues of administrative reform. The top issues for both the liberal and the conservative parties were also prominently treated in the media. (The issue of another term for the incumbent was not very salient in the media coverage.)

Voter's Issue Salience

Of the three types of issue salience listed above (personal, perceived, and interpersonal), interpersonal issue salience proved irrelevant: few people talked about election issues in their conversations with others. For personal issue salience, only 46.6 percent (271) of the respondents named an issue or issues of personal concern. The rest referred to other aspects of the campaign (such as "game" or "ideology") or fell into the "don't know" group, and appeared to pay little attention to issues in the campaign. The investigation focused on respondents who mentioned issues of concern in order to investigate agenda setting at the individual level in terms of the salience model. The same step was taken in processing perceived issue salience.

Are there any differences between the "issue" and "no issue" groups? The "issue" group includes a larger proportion of voters who are very interested in local politics and in the election. But with regard to the respondent's support of a party, there is little significant difference between the two groups. It might be concluded that the "issue" group contains more politically active voters than the "no issue" group, without ideological bias being evident either way. (Virtually the same differences are seen with regard to perceived issue salience.) (See table 11.2.)

At the personal level, "welfare" was cited as most important by the largest proportion of voters, followed by "provision for urban facilities" (see table 11.3). As for perceived issue salience, "provision

Table 11.2   Comparison of Voters Who Mentioned Some Issue and Those Who Didn't (Percentages)

Voter Characteristics	Mentioned	Did Not Mention	Total
Interest in local politics			
Very interested (N = 227)	52.0	48.0	100.0
Somewhat interested (N = 229)	48.0	52.0	100.0
Little/not at all (N = 125)	33.6	66.4	100.0
Interest in this election			
Very interested (N = 273)	53.5	46.5	100.0
Somewhat interested (N = 167)	47.3	52.7	100.0
Little/not at all (N = 142)	32.4	67.6	100.0
Party support[a]			
Conservative parties (N = 254)	50.0	50.0	100.0
Liberal parties (N = 75)	52.0	48.0	100.0
Independents (N = 204)	41.7	58.3	100.0

Note: This comparison was of the personal salience measure. The same pattern was observed in regard to the perceived salience measure.

Upper section: χ^2 = 11.3, d.f. = 2, p < .01
Middle section: χ^2 = 16.7, d.f. = 2, p < .001
Lower section: χ^2 = 4.0, d.f. = 2, nonsignificant
Missing cases were excluded from the analyses.

[a] Conservative parties include the Liberal Democratic Party, the Clean Government Party, the Democratic Socialist Party, and a few miniparties. Liberal parties include the Japan Socialist Party (presently the Social Democratic Party of Japan) and the Japan Communist Party.

Table 11.3   Voter's Personal Issue Salience during Machida Election Campaign

Issues	Percentage	Rank
Provisions for urban facilities	21.8	2
Welfare	24.7	1
Administrative reform	15.1	5
Education	11.4	6
Connection with higher levels of government	2.2	7
Another term for the incumbent	15.9	4
Taxes	16.2	3
(N = 271)		

Note: Total exceeds 100 percent because some respondents gave more than one issue.

for urban facilities" ranked highest, followed by "welfare" (see table 11.4). Patterns were similar, but not identical, for both types of issue salience.

Correspondence between Media Emphasis and Voter's Salience

The agenda-setting hypothesis of the salience model postulates that increased media emphasis on an issue leads to increased salience of that issue among the audience. Thus, if agenda setting occurs at all, there will likely be similar rankings for media emphasis on various issues and for the proportion of voters who perceive each of the same issues as most salient. The degree of association between both rankings therefore can be regarded as an indicator of the agenda-setting effects.

These rank-order correlations are shown in table 11.5. For all respondents (in the "issue" group), the correlation coefficient (Spearman's Rho) between the media's emphasis and the voter's salience is 0.39 at the personal salience level, and 0.68 at the perceived salience level. Correlations are also shown for respondents disaggregated by gender, age, education, and party support. None of the correlations in the table is statistically significant except for a few cases, and non-systematic differences are found across the categories, which might be difficult to explain. It is noteworthy, however, that the media/perceived salience correlations are generally stronger than the media/personal salience correlations. This implies that mass media exert

Table 11.4 **Voter's Perception of Other Machida Voters' Issue Salience (Perceived Issue Salience)**

ISSUES	PERCENTAGE	RANK
Provisions for urban facilities	26.9	1
Welfare	23.1	2
Administrative reform	14.1	5
Education	17.5	3
Connection with higher levels of government	6.4	7
Another term for the incumbent	12.0	6
Taxes	16.7	4
(N = 234)		

Note: Total exceeds 100 percent since some respondents gave more than one issue.

Table 11.5 Spearman's Rank-Order Correlations between Media's Emphasis and Voter's Salience (N = 7), by Demographic Variables of the Respondents

	PERSONAL SALIENCE	PERCEIVED SALIENCE
All respondents (N = 144; 123)	.39	.68
Sex		
Male (N = 144; 123)	.36	.81[a]
Female (N = 127; 111)	.36	.57
Age		
20s (N = 21; 33)	.32	.45
30s (N = 44; 44)	.36	.79[a]
40s (N = 80; 68)	.44	.58
50s (N = 66; 48)	.43	.51
60 and over (N = 60; 41)	.43	.40
Education (graduation)		
Junior high school (N = 47; 30)	.34	.40
High school (N = 139; 134)	.40	.57
College (N = 85; 70)	.27	.64
Party support		
Conservative parties (N = 127; 113)	.43	.52
Liberal parties (N = 39; 38)	.57	.82[a]
Independents (N = 85; 67)	.61	.40

Note: Of the numbers in parentheses, the first shows the number of cases for the personal-salience analysis; the second, the number of cases for the perceived-salience analysis. Missing cases were excluded from the analyses.

[a] $p < .05$ (one-tailed test).

more influence on what people think about the climate of opinion than on their personal views on the issues.

Media Use and Political Interest as Contingent Conditions

Results were then subjected to contingent-condition analysis, using three variables: (1) exposure to political content in newspapers; (2) interest in local politics; and (3) interest in the approaching election. Increased levels for each variable should lead to increased correlation between media emphasis and voter salience. That is, respondents using the media more heavily, and having greater interest in local politics and the election, should show stronger agenda-setting effects.

On the whole, the results shown in table 11.6 support the predic-

Table 11.6   Spearman's Rank-Order Correlations between Media's
             Emphasis and Voter's Salience (N = 7), by Contingent
             Variables: Media Exposure and Political Interests

	PERSONAL SALIENCE	PERCEIVED SALIENCE
All respondents (N = 271; 234)	.39	.68
Political use of newspapers		
Read always (N = 96; 84)	.59	.75a
Read sometimes (N = 90; 73)	.32	.41
Read rarely/not at all (N = 85; 77)	.39	.61
Interest in local politics		
Very interested (N = 118; 105)	.79a	.82a
Somewhat interested (N = 110; 93)	.43	.29
Little/not at all (N = 46; 45)	.20	.59
Interest in this election		
Very interested (N = 146; 119)	.83a	.82a
Somewhat interested (N = 79; 70)	.46	.57
Little/not at all (N = 46; 45)	.29	.57

Note: Of the numbers in parentheses, the first shows the number of cases for the personal-salience analysis; the second, the number of cases for the perceived-salience analysis. Missing cases were excluded from the analyses.

a $p < .05$ (one-tailed test).

tion: the highest level respondents for each contingent variable show the highest correlation both at the personal salience level and at the perceived salience level in all six comparisons, although the contingent variables are not always linearly related with the correlations. Evidently, some behavioral variables account better than do demographic variables for susceptibility to media influence, which is consistent with Takeshita's findings.[14]

Conclusion

The results of our study offer considerable support for the agenda-setting hypothesis. Media agenda-setting effects tend to register on a relatively limited range of people, but those who are most susceptible to the agenda-setting effects are less partisan and are among the most active voters. They might determine a close race. For this reason, the social consequences of media agenda setting should not be underestimated.

We have seen (table 11.5) that agenda-setting effects are generally more pronounced at the perceived salience level than at the personal salience level. How can we explain this finding in the Japanese setting? It has been observed that in deciding how to act in public, Japanese are often concerned with the expected responses of people outside their circle of acquaintance—that is, Japanese employ an out-group as a reference. These reference out-groups are called *seken,* which translates roughly as "the public," although the nuance is different.[15] Supposing the theory is more or less valid, it follows that Japanese will have a strong need to know the climate of opinion—stronger than that felt by persons living in many other cultures. This informational need will incline Japanese to interpret the media's issue emphasis as an indicator of public opinion. This might explain the generally stronger media effect at the perceived salience level than at the personal level. We assume this to be one of the characteristics of media agenda setting in Japan.

Notes

1. Bernard C. Cohen, *The Press and Foreign Policy* (Princeton, N.J.: Princeton University Press, 1963).

2. Maxwell McCombs and Donald Shaw, "The Agenda-Setting Function of Mass Media," *Public Opinion Quarterly* 36 (Spring 1972): 176–187.

3. For a comprehensive review, see Everett M. Rogers and James W. Dearing, "Agenda-Setting Research: Where Has It Been, Where Is It Going?" in *Communication Yearbook 11,* ed. J. A. Anderson (Newbury Park, Calif.: Sage Publications, 1988), pp. 555–594.

4. See Toshio Takeshita, "Masu media no gidai settei kinō" (The Agenda-Setting Function of Mass Media: Present State of Research and Associated Problems), *Shimbungaku Hyōron* (Japanese Journalism Review) 30 (1981): 203–218; Kazuto Kojima, "Seiji katei to masu komyunikēshon" (Political Process and Mass Communication), in *Gendai masukomyunikēshon-ron* (Mass Communication Theories Today), ed. Ikuo Takeuchi and Kazuto Kojima (Tokyo: Yūhikaku, 1982), pp. 218–245; Ikuo Takeuchi, "Juyō katei no kenkyū" (Study on Mass Media Uses and Effects), in *Gendai masukomyunikēshon-ron,* pp. 44–79; Toshio Takeshita, "Gidai settei kenkyū no shikaku" (The Perspective of Agenda-Setting Research: Theory and Verification in Mass Communication Effects Studies), *Hōsōgaku Kenkyū* (Broadcasting Studies) 34 (1984): 81–116; Naoyuki Okada, "Ajenda settei kenkyū no gaikan to kadai" (A Review and Research Agenda of Agenda-Setting Research), in *Bunka to gendai shakai* (Culture and Modern Society), ed. Munesuke Mita and Takashi Miyajima (Tokyo: University of Tokyo Press, 1987), pp. 175–207.

5. Toshikazu Maeda, "Kōdokushi to seiji ishiki" (Subscription Papers and Political Consciousness), *Hōgaku Kenkyū* (Keiō University Journal of Law, Politics, and Sociology) 51–55 (1987): 311–338; Fukashi Horie, "Taishū shakai to masu demokurashii" (Mass Society and Mass Democracy), in Fukashi Horie, Yasushi Haga, Shūjirō Katō, and Tomoaki Iwai, *Gendai no seiji to shakai* (Politics and Society of Our Time) (Tokyo: Hokuju Shuppan, 1982), pp. 30–42; Yoshiaki Kobayashi, "Jōhō to masu media" (Information and Mass Media), in *Jōhō to demokurashii* (Information and Democracy), ed. Nobuo Tomita and Norio Okazawa (Tokyo: Gakuyō Shobō, 1983), pp. 167–193; Yoshikatsu Iwabuchi, "Masu media no jōhō to sōten sentaku" (Mass Media Information and Issue Choice), in *Tōhyō kōdō to seiji ishiki* (Voting Behavior and Political Attitudes), ed. Fukashi Horie and Mitsuhiro Umemura (Tokyo: Keiō Tsūshin, 1986), pp. 181–195; Yoshikatsu Iwabuchi, "Sōten hōdō to sōten sentaku" (Study of Agenda-Setting in the 1986 Election), *Shimbun Kenkyūjo Nenpō* (Bulletin of the Institute for Communication Research, Keiō University) 33 (September 1989): 75–94; Yoshiaki Kobayashi, "Masu media to seiji ishiki" (Mass Media and Political Attitudes in Japan), *Leviathan* 7 (Fall 1990): 97–114.

6. The concept is used independently by Tony Atwater, Michael B. Salwen, and Ronald B. Anderson, "Media Agenda-Setting with Environmental Issues," *Journalism Quarterly* 62 (Summer 1985): 393–397. Theoretically speaking, perceived media issue emphasis is an intervening variable, situated between the media's issue emphasis (independent variable) and the voter's issue salience (dependent variable). However, the Keiō group have used it as a substitute for the independent variable in their analyses.

7. Kobayashi, "Masu-media to seiji-ishiki."

8. Toshio Takeshita, "Media gidai settei kasetsu no jisshōteki-kentō" (An Empirical Examination of the Media Agenda-Setting Hypothesis), *Tōdai Shimbun Kenkyūjo Kiyo* (Bulletin of the Institute of Journalism and Communication Studies, University of Tokyo) 31 (1983): 101–143.

9. Takeshita used the McCombs measurement method; see Donald Shaw and Maxwell McCombs, eds., *The Emergence of American Political Issues: The Agenda-Setting Function of the Press* (St. Paul: West Publishing, 1977).

10. Toshio Takeshita, "Sōten hōdō to gidai settei kasetsu" (Issue Reporting and the Agenda-Setting Hypothesis), in *Senkyo hōdō to tōhyō kōdō* (Election Coverage and Voting Behavior), ed. Institute of Journalism and Communication Studies, University of Tokyo (Tokyo: University of Tokyo Press, 1988), pp. 157–196. This study used a panel design and was conducted during the 1986 national election campaign.

11. Palmgreen and Clarke hypothesize that agenda-setting power is weaker at the local than at the national political level, naming three contributing factors: "(1) the greater ability of individuals personally to observe local political problems; (2) the nature and strength of local interpersonal political communication network; and (3) the relatively heavier media coverage of national political issues." Philip Palmgreen and Peter Clarke, "Agenda-Setting with Local and National Issues," *Communication Research*

4 (October 1977): 438. Their hypothesis is supported by data gathered in Toledo.

12. Many Japanese urban sociologists have argued that Japan experienced rapid and radical industrialization and urbanization during the 1960s and early 1970s, which facilitated disorganization of traditional communities all over the country. See, for example, Yuetsu Takahashi, "Nihon shakai no hendō to komyunityi" (Change of Japanese Society and Community), in *Gendai Nihon no komyunityi* (Community in Contemporary Japan), ed. Kokumin Seikatsu Center (Tokyo: Kawashima Shoten, 1975), pp. 37–54. This argument, the authors assume, applies to Machida City as a satellite city of Tokyo. According to the census data, the population of this city grew from 58,324 in 1955 to 255,305 in 1975.

13. Jack McLeod, Lee B. Becker, and James E. Byrnes, "Another Look at the Agenda-Setting Function of the Press," *Communication Research* 1 (April 1974): 131–166.

14. Takeshita, "Media gidai settei kasetsu no jisshōteki kentō."

15. Tadashi Inoue, *Sekentei no kōzō* (The Structure of *Sekentei*) (Tokyo: NHK Books, 1977).

PART V

Media and Politics

12

The Mass Media and Japanese Politics: Effects and Consequences

ELLIS S. KRAUSS

WHAT role do the mass media play in Japan's political democracy? As in all less-than-ideal democracies—which is to say, all existing ones—the question may be better phrased as, To what extent do the media play a democratic role, and how, and to what extent do they not, and why? The stereotype of Japan views it as a coherent, consensual society with a powerful state, ruled by a single party for most of the postwar period. How are the media helping to create pluralism, conflict, and diversity in Japan, and how are they reinforcing the homogeneity, consensus, and maintenance of authority? Another way of phrasing that question is to ask how the "trickster" role of the media, as outlined by Susan Pharr in chapter 1, actually works in the context of Japanese democracy.

Related to these questions of the media's role in Japanese politics are questions about how universal or variant the media's impact is in different societies. The question of whether the media make a great difference anywhere probably has elicited as much contradictory argument and evidence in academic research and in everyday political conversation as any other intellectual issue. In our daily conversations about politics, it seems that everyone has an opinion about what and how much the media have done to the political quality of life in the United States, usually attributing to them great, and negative, effects.

As Pharr points out, however, when academic research on politics has not ignored the media completely, it has tended to minimize the media's power to affect the polities in which we live. As several of the authors in this volume indicate, the "minimal effects" model of media such as television has been particularly dominant in the study of American politics; little evidence has been offered of the media's ability to change citizens' basic political attitudes and beliefs, and

therefore their behavior. Lately, there has been a scholarly reevalua-
tion of the media's role in politics, as social scientists use more
sophisticated conceptual approaches to the media.

Does the nature of technology drive process and outcomes so that
the roles, behavior, and effects of mass media in relation to politics
are the same everywhere? Or is the effect of the technology subject to
the intervening factors of different journalistic organizations and the
institutions of society, economy, and polity?

Japan is a particularly good context to try to answer these questions of the universality or difference in the impact of the media. It is
the society most similar to the United States in media use, but most
different from Western democracies in societal, political, and journalistic institutional arrangements. Japan thus provides an especially
interesting laboratory for evaluating the universal or variant consequences of the media on politics.

The authors of this volume cannot answer all these questions, nor
can they answer any definitively. They do, however, take the first step
toward evaluating the role and impact of the mass media in Japanese
political life. Let us look more specifically at what they have found in
relation to these questions about media's role in, and effect on,
Japan's political democracy.[1] We will consider first the structure and
autonomy of the mass media in Japan; second, the role the media
play in elite politics in Japan, including an evaluation of how the
"trickster" personae of the mass media may affect democratic politics; and finally, how media messages affect the social life and democratic participation of the average citizen.

Japan's Media Structure: How Independent? How Diverse?

American scholars and journalists writing about Japan have presented contradictory images of Japan as a society and polity, and of
the relationship between the state and society in Japan. Some observers have emphasized the coherent, consensual, and controlled aspects
of Japanese life; others, the more pluralist, conflictual, and democratic nature of that social and political system. The various views of
Japanese politics include the following:

An autonomous and powerful bureaucracy at the heart of a central-
    ized Japanese state[2]
A more or less unique "elusive state" because power is diffused
    among the many power centers that make up public-private rela-

tionships in Japan but that do not operate according to democratic law or process and instead repress or coopt opposition[3]

A system that operates by "reciprocal consent" between the public and private sectors with big business being especially powerful[4]

A system that has democratic, pluralist elements despite, or even because of, the importance of state bureaucratic jurisdictions and long-term, one-party dominance that distinguish it from classical pluralism[5]

A system with fragmented interest-group politics that makes it somewhat similar to a classically pluralist system like the United States[6]

Given these often contradictory models of the extent of cohesion and democratic pluralism in Japan, what does the evidence of our authors indicate about Japan's media system and the extent of its controlled and controlling dimensions versus its independent and democratic elements?

The evidence seems to demonstrate that Japan has an interesting pattern of control and independence, conformity and competition in its media. On the one hand, as Eleanor Westney describes (chapter 2), Japanese citizens enjoy a highly plural structure of media in which national, regional, and local papers compete; diverse editorial positions are represented among the papers; and there is a public broadcasting system and commercial competition in television and radio. Media firms tend to be independently and usually internally owned, ostensibly providing even greater autonomy. Further, competition among national newspapers is fierce, as is also the case in broadcasting, and the legal framework guarantees freedom of the press and prevents concentration of ownership in the media industry. Structurally, at least, the Japanese media appear to be exceedingly diverse, independent, and accessible to many social groups and voices. They are lively and have often pursued government corruption and wrongdoing.

When one looks beyond structure and surface impressions, however, contrary elements appear. Newspapers are highly integrated with the business world through nonownership connections. The oligarchy of national newspapers not only dominates the press but also has close connections with and influence over broadcasting. As Westney further points out, structural diversity seems to result not in a great variety of information and opinion, but in conformity in content. When we look at the collection of information in Japan, we see further evidence of centralization and concentration rather than diversity. The public broadcaster, NHK, and the commercial stations and national newspapers primarily rely for their information on the reporters' club system. This system, as chapters 3 and 4 argue, tends to breed conformity and also dependence on official sources, particularly in the national bureaucracy. When one adds in the nearly draconian restrictions on campaign advertising and use of television in election campaigns, described in the introduction and chapter 10, we find a very mixed picture of restriction and independence, cohesion and diversity in the Japanese media.

We need to remember, of course, that other media, such as book and magazine publishing, contribute great diversity to the system, as Westney points out. The nonmainstream press, such as *Akahata* (Red Flag), the mass-circulation daily of the Japan Communist Party, and the mini-media, as discussed in chapter 7, give voice to highly critical views of prevailing social and political arrangements, and further broaden the spectrum of opinion that gets represented in the media. We also should recall that no country has a perfectly diverse and unrestricted media system. Concentration of ownership in the American press and the importance of the wire services as a source of news for both local papers and television news, the politico-media subcultures of many European countries, the kind of conformity described by Timothy Crouse[7] in American journalists' coverage of presidential election campaigns and the White House press corps, and the "lobby system" in Great Britain that regulates relations between officials and reporters:[8] all these should make us chary of seeing the concentrated, nonindependent, and conformist elements in Japan as a unique characteristic of Japanese journalism. What may be distinctive about the media system in Japan is not that nonpluralist and controlled elements exist—they do in all democracies—but rather that in Japan the institutions of newspaper and broadcast journalism, business, and the state connect in such a way that their informal processes have often wound up limiting the pluralism and autonomy that the formal structures should provide.

Media and Politics in Japan: What Roles?

The question of the role the mass media have played in Japan's politics and democracy takes on more salience when we realize that less than a half-century ago, the nascent Japanese democracy of the prewar period had been repressed by the military, and Japanese lived under an authoritarian regime with severe restrictions on press freedom. As Susan Pharr points out in the introduction, the American Occupation saw the media as a major tool and component in the democratization of Japan.

There is no question that many of the Occupation's goals for Japan have been realized: the ideal of democracy, support for democratic institutions, and responsiveness to the people have been accepted by the vast majority of the Japanese people and elites. Chapter 9 makes abundantly clear the role the media have played in stimulating interest in politics and political participation by the average citizen. Also, the media have played a major role in transmitting and representing the popular will. Indeed, some of our authors indicate that Japanese citizens and elites may be *more* attuned to public opinion as indicated by the media than is the case in other societies. In chapter 11 Toshio Takeshita and Ikuo Takeuchi, for example, speculate that the agenda-setting effects of the media that they found in election campaigns might be due partly to the Japanese citizens' cultural proclivity to refer to the "public opinion" about an issue. Similarly, in chapter 6 John Campbell notes the Japanese political elite's extraordinary attentiveness to the state of public opinion as reflected in the press.

One hypothesis is that, as Takeshita and Takeuchi imply, this exceptional interest in public opinion can best be explained by the group-centered nature of Japanese culture, which translates into acute sensitivity to what others think. One can also suggest a less cultural and more sociological hypothesis: that Japan's media-saturated and densely crowded society itself has produced this effect. Finally, I might offer a third hypothesis that is more politically based. In all democratic political systems, norms of legitimation based on the "will of the people" have become accepted, but some forms of democratic government make it easier than others to determine what that will is. Japan has had a parliamentary form of government (that is, no direct election of chief executive) with an electoral system of multimember representative constituencies at the national level (in other words, not a proportional representation system) that made it difficult to determine what the "mandate" of general elections was. Further, only one party was in power for thirty-eight years, which means that the opposition parties were poor conveyors of minority public opinion. Perhaps with this combination of political institutions, the media by default came to be perceived as performing the function of representing the general "public" more than in other democracies.

Whatever the reason, clearly the media have played an important part in conveying public opinion to political elites and helping to keep them responsive. This is particularly important in a regime with formal democratic institutions but with no alternation in power for so long. While in many other parliamentary governments, opposition parties—by embarrassing the government, uncovering malfeasance, and proposing policy alternatives—usually have had a chance to take power and throw out their rivals, this had not happened in Japan since the formation of the Liberal Democratic Party (LDP) in 1955. Indeed, if one includes participation by smaller conservative parties in government before the LDP's formation, the conservatives actually had ruled or shared in the ruling of Japan from 1945 to 1993.[9]

Because opposition parties had little prospect of taking power, their sniping seemed fruitless and ineffective, and thus the perceived role played by the media in pursuing scandal and transmitting public reaction and opinion became even more important. This is not an unusual role for the media in any democracy, but this aspect of the media role took on increasing importance in the context of a one-party-dominant political system.

Much change has taken place since 1993. The LDP over the summer of that year lost power to a multiparty coalition including most of its former opposition parties, then in 1994 it returned to power, but in coalition with its former ideological rival, the Japan Socialist Party. An overhaul of the electoral system has now been completed. It is possible that the entire "game of politics," and with it the media's role, may be transformed. Now that there are multiple, viable opposition parties and fluid coalition politics, the media's role as the primary effective "opposition" of those perennially in power may diminish. The media may become more what they tend to be in other democracies that have alternation of parties in power: a more neutral critic of both government and opposition, capable of abusing, but also of being used by, all parties. In chapter 5, Kristin Altman discusses the fluid conditions in the last months of LDP rule and the media's contribution to them, which may presage a more multifaceted media role of the future.

In terms of nonelite opposition, by being available to protest movements as a tool, as David Groth describes in chapter 7, the mass media in Japan have given those with little influence through the normal channels of politics the possibility of at least having their voices heard and perhaps their concerns addressed by the powerful. Again, this occurs elsewhere, but given a one-party democratic regime with highly institutionalized connections to a specific range of supporting interest groups, those outside the coalition of the LDP and government may have a particular need for an alternative channel for having their demands raised.

The media's role in Japanese politics and democracy has not been only on the side of stimulating the "inputs" of the political system: facilitating political participation and demands, checking the abuses of those in power, and providing a potential channel of influence for those less powerful. It has also contributed to maintaining those in power. The discussion in chapter 3 of how NHK news portrays the bureaucracy, especially the public bureaucracy, makes clear that television probably has been a conservative force in legitimizing the Japanese state. The reporters' club system also provides Japanese politicians and officials with a mechanism for transmitting their messages to the public to an extent probably unparalleled in other democracies. These have undoubtedly contributed to the continuity of state, especially bureaucratic, power in postwar Japan.

Further, even the role of the media in keeping government responsive also ultimately helped the powerful. It has been said of Japan's conservative, perennial ruling party, the LDP, that it practiced "creative conservatism"[10] for the pragmatic and—though sometimes belatedly—responsive way it reacted to the public and to changes in the salience and content of issues that the public perceived as important. One pillar of this responsiveness was the attention the media give to public sentiment and the attention the political elite in turn give to the media's representation of public sentiment, all helping to keep the LDP in power for so long.

The media indirectly may have helped to maintain the LDP in power in a different way through their lack of presence, rather than their presence. Although the press was important in Japanese elections, we should note that the media might have been more influential in Japanese election campaigns if not for the restrictions and regulations governing their use, as described in chapters 1 and 10. The extreme Japanese restrictions on electoral campaigning, which prevented more than a minimum amount of advertising for individual candidates either in newspapers or on television, and the completely equal access given to all candidates meant that, despite political party access to the media, no candidate could really use the media to gain an advantage over any other. In effect, this gave a de facto advantage to incumbents rather than challengers. However, as chapter 5 indicates, both the media and the political elite have lately found creative ways of getting around these restrictions—for example, by the use of talk shows, as in the United States. Under the new electoral system—which includes both single-member and regional proportional representation districts, though with the same media campaign restrictions—it is possible that these practices will become even more prevalent. The parties may endeavor to gain points, especially in the proportional representation districts, by creating party image through similar "end runs" around media restrictions.

Given these important roles for the media in Japan's postwar political system, where have their roles and effects been minimal? One weakness of the media, perhaps in all countries, is that they direct attention to problems but often can impede finding solutions to them, as Campbell argues in chapter 6. This duality, which is the focus of chapter 1, perhaps helps illuminate the sometimes contradictory findings on the media's role: when Japanese elites are asked to name the most influential group in Japanese society, all but the media elites choose the media.[11] In other surveys when elites are asked to name the group most influential in *policy making,* the media are seen as less influential than bureaucrats, politicians, or big business.[12]

Although the media can be important agenda setters under some circumstances, they do indeed play a more limited role in policy making. Because of strict legal rules on their use, they have also played a more limited role in elections in Japan than in the United States and some other democracies. They have been an important force in democratizing Japan and in checking and limiting governmental power under long-term LDP rule. In other ways, however, they have also helped maintain the Japanese state and the LDP in power. This brings us to the metaphor of the media as "trickster."

Media as Trickster?

Chapter 1 provides an intriguing proposition to resolve the disparity of evidence and argument in the literature, which holds that the media have limited impact on the policy agenda *or* are a determining influence on it and that they support authority and community and induce quiescence *but* are an independent watchdog of government, limiting authority and stimulating reform. Pharr argues persuasively that the media do all these things simultaneously in a cumulative sense in any given society. She uses the metaphor of the media as the modern "trickster"—a role outside the established order that mediates between that order and the realm of *chaos* (the unknown) and also the realm of *cosmos* (values and meaning). The media perform the role of evaluator of the established order, and thus of critic and provider of alternative perception and meaning to the way the state—and its opposition—says things should be. Simultaneously, however, the media—by providing an outlet for frustration, sending positive messages about authority, and binding people to the existing community—also reinforce fundamental arrangements and the established order. The riddle of divergent findings on media impact thus is no enigma but rather lies at the core of the media's role in modern society: they can ignore issues or place them before the public, can bond society while alienating it, can create support for the state or its opposition but also undermine it, can reinforce the established order and also change it. It is the unpredictability of the media's role, in a cumulative sense, that accounts for their great power.

The "trickster" duality of the media in Japan is especially well revealed in chapters 5, 6, and 7. In chapter 6 Campbell shows clearly how in the late 1960s entrepreneurs in the social welfare policy community who wanted to mobilize support behind a range of policy proposals concerning the elderly mounted a media campaign to draw attention to their issue. They successfully used the strategy to draw public attention to the problem, but the media failed to support the bureaucrats' desired solutions. In the attempt to cut back on burgeoning welfare expansion, the bureaucrats' first attempt to use the media failed miserably because of media resistance. In a second attempt five years later, the media took the bait, but the ironic net result was public support not for retrenchment but for yet more welfare expansion. Handmaidens to the bureaucracy in one instance and "watchdogs" resisting state plans the next, helping officials achieve their general "agenda setting" goals at first but ultimately not their specific policy aims: thus the media in Japan play their ambivalent trickster role.

Viewed from the perspective of the opposition, it is tempting to think of the media as always the "watchdog" ally of those who wish to alter the existing order. This is especially the case in Japan, where opposition parties were long shut out of power but mass movements were often successful in gaining attention through the media. Certainly, governments and conservatives in Japan, as elsewhere, frequently criticize the media for this opposition "bias."

One salient example of pro-opposition media bias is the media's coverage of the 1960 anti–U.S.–Japan Mutual Security Treaty struggle, probably the greatest political crisis in postwar Japan. The conservative party and later U.S. analysts of the crisis blamed the media for their leftist bias in stimulating the massive protest against the government.[13] Yet a closer examination of the media's role has revealed much more ambivalence than the critics have alleged. Jung

Bock Lee's analysis of the role of the printed press concluded that the newspapers were "harshly critical" of the LDP government on many occasions during the crisis:

> Nevertheless, it is abundantly clear that the press did not support the leftwing opposition on this crucial issue. The press, despite its dissatisfaction with the terms of the revised Treaty, agreed with the conservative government, in a broad sense, that Japan should maintain a close relationship with the U.S. and the western bloc. . . .
>
> The press also came to condemn one-sidedly the violent student demonstrations. . . . Moreover, the press issued the joint declaration not only denouncing the student violence but also discrediting the tactics of the whole opposition movement.[14]

Hiroshi Matsuda's study of television's role in the crisis similarly argues that once the demonstrations resulted in some violence, television coverage joined the campaign of the printed press to defuse the crisis and turned the slogan "protect parliamentary democracy" against the left and the demonstrators.[15] Indeed, three major unions distributed 200,000 leaflets in the train stations and streets protesting the failure of the coverage of newspapers and television to transmit the truth about the violent incidents.[16] Japanese scholars associated with the left have discussed this contradictory behavior of the capitalist media—by which they advance with the masses, but then retreat to their basic posture of siding with authority—as the "boomerang locus" of the media.[17] Thus, the treaty crisis provides ample evidence that both faces of the "trickster" were at play.

The grass-roots movements against environmental pollution that arose in the late 1960s and early 1970s are cited as another classic case of media power to transform the state's agenda and serve as a force for reform on behalf of the opposition. From their extensive coverage of four court cases on behalf of pollution victims in specific locales, to the publicity they gave to leftist urban executives and to citizens' movements fighting for prevention of pollution,[18] the media helped propel the issue to the top of the public agenda and also create the support of "third parties" so crucial to success of a protest movement.[19]

In chapter 7, discussing one part of this antipollution protest—against the noise pollution of the *Shinkansen* "bullet trains"—Groth reminds us that there is another side to the media's role in these movements. His study shows how important to protest efforts the media have become in modern Japanese society—determining the movement's tactics to gain legitimation and carry out mobilization. Yet permeating his description of the movement in its relationship with the mass media is a sense of the leaders' wariness and distrust of the media. The media gave the movement coverage, but not to the extent desired by the movement, and the coverage was not necessarily of the kind the activists wanted. Groth reminds us that from the perspective of the source, in this case a protest movement, the "watchdogs" themselves need watchdogs, the evaluator evaluation. Because it could not control the "trickster" any more effectively than could government bureaucrats, the movement created its own information network of mini-media, which it *could* control. Yet such an effort requires a large investment of movement resources and, by definition, a media effort that cannot reach a mass audience.

Finally, events leading up to and following from the 1993 election, described in chapter 5, also show the "trickster" at work. Media talk shows helped undermine Kiichi Miyazawa's LDP government and to bring in the reformer Morihiro Hosokawa, himself a very "mediagenic" figure and highly skillful manipulator of the media. Hosokawa, however, was eventually forced to resign because of revelations of possible ethical violations in his past, in part pursued and in part disseminated by the media.

The "trickster" metaphor for the media in Japan, then, seems quite apt: the media may put new issues on the agenda or not, reinforce authority or undermine it, transmit information and images that support the state or its opponents—in short, help to change the established order and help to maintain it. If this is the case, then future research must focus on *when and under what conditions* the media play each of the dual trickster roles.

Do Different Media Play Different Tricks?

The question of when and under what conditions the media play each of their inherent roles in modern society draws attention to another possibility raised by the findings presented in this volume: different media may play *more* or *less* of each of the trickster roles. This proposition is consonant with media research that indicates that the structure of media organizations determines the kind of news and information the public receives.[20] Each country may have a different pattern of organizations playing varying "trickster" roles, depending on the structure of media organizations and their connection to the state and society in each nation. Similarly, changes in media markets as well as in political processes can affect which media are more likely to play a particular role at any given time.

In Japan's case, the evidence presented in this volume gives a preliminary indication that the organization of the printed press has probably played both facets of the trickster, but that television until recently may have played mainly the role of reinforcing the established order. Westney's discussion of media organizations as business firms in chapter 2 illustrates that this duality in the trickster role of newspapers in Japan may have a basis in their ambivalent nature. On the one hand, each national newspaper is an independent, internally owned company with a heterogeneous audience, which induces the press to defend society and all substrata of the public; on the other hand, as organizations that are highly integrated into establishment business and governmental networks, the newspapers are an integral part and defender of the established order. I should also add that the particular bifurcation in the role of the professional journalist in Japan is part of this equation. This duality has its roots in their history, as described by Pharr: marginality in the prewar era laid the basis for modern norms casting journalists as independent "watchdogs" of democracy, while their current affluence and professionalism, and their dependence on official sources through the reporters' club system, create the basis for a "servant" role. The duality of pro- and anti-establishment attitudes runs deeply through the national newspapers as commercial and journalistic institutions.

Television's role seemingly has been less bifurcated and more heavily oriented toward supporting the established order. The nature of NHK's relationship to the state, combined with reporters' clubs' dependence in news gathering, led television news to portray the state bureaucracy more frequently and in a manner that reinforces state authority, as described in chapter 3. We would expect commercial broadcasters, given their financial and news "network" ties to newspapers, to be somewhat more dualistic. Indeed, recently the commercial stations seem to be playing their "trickster" evaluative role much more actively. For example, Asahi News Network's popular and iconoclastic newscaster Hiroshi Kume, with his focus on the scandal involving LDP powerbroker Shin Kanemaru, seems to have had as much responsibility as the newspapers for bringing about Kanemaru's resignation from the National Diet[21] and for undermining LDP credibility before and during the 1993 election.

Nevertheless, this is a new trend: NHK's dominance of news for most of the postwar period has meant that television has probably been more a bulwark of the established order than a force for change, especially when we take into account its quite limited impact on election campaigning and outcomes,[22] as described in chapter 10. The push by commercial networks to compete with NHK in the news field since the late 1980s and their success in doing so using more opinionated and controversial journalism, however, indicates that television may become the equal of the press in its multifaceted "trickster" manifestations.

Effects: Mass Media and Mass Society?

In evaluating the role of the media in Japan's democracy, in addition to their functions in elite politics, we must also analyze the extent to which media usage and messages have directly or indirectly affected society and the average citizen's ability to participate in politics.

One of the most powerful perspectives on the mass media is the notion that their impact is primarily to contribute to the breakdown and decline in importance of personal networks and established social relations and thus to undermine the societal bonds that underlie democratic life. William Kornhauser's influential concept of a "mass society"[23] is typical of the fears of postwar dystopian theorists reviewing the history and trends of the twentieth century. In such a society individuals are atomistic and anomistic, unintegrated into the secondary social groups that mediate between the state and the individual, and alienated from each other and the political units of which they are members. Such individuals are readily available for mobilization into mass movements or by the state, as in totalitarian regimes.

Powerful mass media technologies, such as radio and television, seemingly provide the tools for leaders of mass movements and the state to accomplish such mobilization. They also serve as a prime means by which the atomized and alienated individual would be created. Such technologies undermined the personal and social relationships underlying the participation in secondary institutions that protected the individual from the state and gave him or her a means of influencing it. They also provided elites with a powerful way to propagandize and influence the individual directly. The linkage between the development of the art of propaganda under Joseph Goebbels and the totalitarian Third Reich's "mass society" seemed to confirm the threat.

Early media research, however, mitigated such fears about the media's impact. The classic research of Paul Lazarsfeld and others in the 1940s led to the formulation of a "two-step flow hypothesis."[24] Few of the individuals whom Lazarsfeld studied were directly influenced by radio coverage of an election campaign. Rather, the information conveyed by the media was first translated and conveyed by "opinion leaders" through personal networks to the public. Personal networks of communication mediated between the media and individuals. This importance and resilience of personal social networks in the influence process was hardly the profile of a "mass society." Partly because of such research indicating that the media had minimal effects, the nightmare vision of the media creating a mass society of alienated individuals receded from social science literature.

The "two-step flow hypothesis," however, was conceived and tested in a pretelevision age. As television permeated societies like the United States and social science research became more sophisticated in its conceptualization, the idea of the importance of the media's impact in creating "mass society" effects returned. Social scientists began to realize that testing for direct change in basic attitudes and voting behavior was a simplistic model of media impact. More important might be the indirect effects—effects on how media information combined with that received from personal networks, on images, and on beliefs that indirectly affected behavior, such as cynicism and apathy. Some research conducted in the 1970s in the United States seemed to indicate that television news was creating "video-malaise," citizens cynical and apathetic toward politics and their political system.[25]

Japan, which is both media-saturated and small-group-oriented, offers an ideal setting for testing the universality of this kind of media impact. Have the availability of and exposure to mass media, especially television, helped break down those social networks and make citizens more apathetic toward political participation and their political system?

The evidence in this volume is that the media have not had those effects in Japan. Indeed, surprisingly, Flanagan's chapter on the effects of media exposure on political participation indicates the opposite: exposure to media and participation in social networks, political involvement, and support for the perennial ruling party go hand in hand. Although media exposure has no direct effects, it has the strongest indirect effects on political participation of any of the ten variables he tested (see chapter 9). Media exposure has relationships with more psychological involvement and political knowledge and through these with greater political participation. Takeshita and Takeuchi also find that in elections, agenda-setting influence by the media is strongest among those who are the most active voters, not the least active (see chapter 11).

Also interesting in this context is the finding that integration into formal and informal nonpolitical social networks is not negatively related to exposure to political information in the media—as we might expect if media and the breakdown of social group and personal communication networks were related—but rather, positively related. That males of higher socioeconomic status participate more in politics is not surprising; that this same substratum of the population also consumes political information from the media and is highly integrated into social networks is directly contrary to "mass society" expectations. Nor is the relationship of social network involvement confined to this higher status group: even Japanese citizens of lower socioeconomic status who are involved in organizational networks participate more. Flanagan concludes that this network involvement does seem to stimulate more attentiveness to politics in the media. He finds no dichotomy between the media and social networks as sources of political information. Indeed, he finds that greater involvement in social networks encourages exposure to politics in the media.

If this is the case, then neither the "mass society" nor the "two-step flow hypothesis" seems applicable to Japan. Rather than breaking down social networks and organizational involvement and thus creating a "mass society," the media seem to become a resource for those who are most stimulated to seek political information by their involvement in these groups. And this phenomenon is not confined to "opinion leaders" but rather characterizes everyone involved in those networks, even those of lower socioeconomic status. Further, Takeshita and Takeuchi found that few people talked about election issues in their conversations with others, and yet their data show media agenda-setting effects. None of this accords with the "two-step flow" model.

High rates of media saturation and exposure have not weakened the intermediary networks of Japanese society. There need not be a contradiction between having influential mass media effects and having dense personal groups and a rich network of intermediate associations that can underlie democratic political life.

Conclusion

Thus, although the mass media may perform universal functions in all democracies—communication between elites and the public, "trickster" roles of creating change and preserving order, and so forth—how the media perform those functions varies in different societies. As I have argued elsewhere,[26] institutions intervene between mass media and their consequences. The structures of organizations and "rules of the game" of mass media, along with social, economic, and political life, and the ways in which these are linked, result in different national patterns of media performance and varying consequences for politics. This volume has attempted only to begin the process of mapping that pattern in one country where this analysis has been neglected previously—Japan. Further research in a more comparative framework is necessary to understand how far Japan's pattern is unique or universal, and why.[27]

Notes

1. I also deal with many of these questions in Ellis S. Krauss, "Japan," in *Media Technologies and Democracy*, ed. Anthony Mughan, Richard Gunther, and Paul Beck (forthcoming).
2. Chalmers Johnson, *MITI and the Japanese Miracle* (Stanford, Calif.: Stanford University Press, 1982).
3. Karel van Wolferen, *The Enigma of Japanese Power* (New York: Alfred A. Knopf, 1989), pp. 25–49 and passim.
4. Richard J. Samuels, *The Business of the Japanese State* (Ithaca: Cornell University Press, 1987).
5. Michio Muramatsu and Ellis S. Krauss, "The Conservative Policy Line and the Development of 'Patterned Pluralism,' " in *The Political Economy of Japan,* ed. Kozo Yamamura and Yasukichi Yasuba, 3 vols. (Stanford: Stanford University Press, 1987), 1:516–554.
6. Samuel Kernell, ed., *Parallel Politics: Economic Policymaking in Japan and the United States* (Washington, D.C.: Brookings Institution, 1991).
7. Timothy Crouse, *The Boys on the Bus* (New York: Ballantine Books, 1972).
8. Michael Cockerell, Peter Hennessy, and David Walker, *Sources Close to the Prime Minister* (London: Macmillan, 1984).
9. This is similar to the Christian Democrats in Italy. For an analysis of the "uncommon democracies" of Japan, Italy, Sweden, and Israel, where one party has remained in power for more than twenty years, see T. J. Pempel, ed., *Uncommon Democracies* (Ithaca: Cornell University Press, 1990).

10. T. J. Pempel, *Policy and Politics in Japan: Creative Conservatism* (Philadelphia: Temple University Press, 1982).

11. Ikuo Kabashima and Jeffrey Broadbent, "Referent Pluralism: Mass Media and Politics in Japan," *Journal of Japanese Studies* 12, no. 2 (Summer 1986): 329–361.

12. Michio Muramatsu, *Sengo Nihon no kanryōsei* (Postwar Japan's Bureaucracy) (Tokyo: Tōyō Keizai Shimbunsha, 1981), chart 1-3, p. 27.

13. On the 1960 crisis and the media, see Jung Bock Lee, *The Political Character of the Japanese Press* (Seoul: Seoul National University Press, 1985), chap. 5; Hiroshi Matsuda, *Dokyumento—hōsō sengo-shi II: sasaku to jānarizumu* (Document—A Postwar History of Broadcasting, II: Manipulation and Journalism) (Kanagawa: Sōshisha, 1981), pp. 131–186; George R. Packard III, *Protest in Tokyo* (Princeton, N.J.: Princeton University Press, 1966), especially pp. 278–284; Edward P. Whittemore, *The Press in Japan Today: A Case Study* (Columbia: University of South Carolina Press, 1961).

14. Lee, *The Political Character of the Japanese Press,* p. 163.

15. Matsuda, *Dokyumento—hōsō sengoshi, II,* pp. 145–170.

16. Ibid., p. 173.

17. Ibid., p. 174.

18. On the phenomenon of pollution protests and leftist local executives, including the role of publicity, see Kurt Steiner, Ellis S. Krauss, and Scott C. Flanagan, *Political Opposition and Local Politics in Japan* (Princeton, N.J.: Princeton University Press, 1980).

19. Michael Lipsky, "Protest as a Political Resource," *American Political Science Review* 62, no. 4 (December 1968): 1144–1158. As James W. White has stated, discussing the attempt by protest movements to gain third-party support, "in any instance where a protest group can enlist the support or even the attention of the mass media, a powerful ally (at least as concerns getting their interests onto the public agenda) has been gained" ("Protest and Change in Contemporary Japan: An Overview," in *Institutions for Change in Japanese Society,* ed. George DeVos [Berkeley: Institute of East Asian Studies, University of California, 1984], pp. 75–76).

20. See, for example, Edward J. Epstein, *News from Nowhere: Television and the News* (New York: Vintage Books, 1973); Herbert J. Gans, *Deciding What's News: A Study of CBS Evening News, NBC Nightly News, Newsweek and Time* (New York: Vintage Books, 1980); Philip Schlesinger, *Putting Reality Together: BBC News* (Beverly Hills, Calif.: Sage Publications, 1979).

21. See Jacob M. Schlesinger and Masayoshi Kanabayashi, "TV Rabble-Rouser Helped to Topple One of Japan's Mightiest Politicians," *Wall Street Journal,* 16 October 1992, p. A10.

22. For a more detailed analysis of the differences between television and newspapers in political life in Japan, see Krauss, "Japan."

23. William Kornhauser, *The Politics of Mass Society* (Glencoe, Ill.: Free Press, 1961).

24. Paul F. Lazarsfeld, Bernard Berelson, and Hazel Gaudet, *The People's*

Choice: How the Voter Makes Up His Mind in a Presidential Campaign (New York: Columbia University Press, 1948); also see Elihu Katz and Paul F. Lazarsfeld, *Personal Influence: The Part Played by People in the Flow of Mass Communications* (Glencoe, Ill.: Free Press, 1955).

25. Michael Robinson, "Public Affairs Television and the Growth of Political Malaise: The Case of the 'Selling of the Pentagon,'" *American Political Science Review* 70 (June, 1976): 409–432.

26. Krauss, "Japan."

27. Such comparative analysis is the purpose of the project "Media Technologies and Democracy" organized by Paul Beck, Anthony Mughan, and Richard Gunther and to be published as a book.

CONTRIBUTORS

Hiroshi Akuto is professor of social psychology at Tōyō Eiwa Women's University and professor emeritus of the University of Tokyo, where he was professor of social psychology. He has written numerous books and articles on electoral campaigning in Japan and the United States, the role of the media, and other topics relating to society and culture.

Kristin Kyoko Altman is a political reporter and anchor for *News Station* on TV Asahi. During the 1993–1994 academic year, she was an associate of the Program on U.S.–Japan Relations, Harvard University.

John Creighton Campbell, professor of political science at the University of Michigan, Ann Arbor, is the author of *Contemporary Japanese Budget Politics* (1977) and *How Policies Change: The Japanese Government and the Aging Society* (1992). He is currently working on a book about the Japanese health care system.

Maggie Farley is a correspondent for the *Boston Globe* based in Hong Kong. Formerly she worked for Fuji Television in Tokyo. She received her M.A. in East Asian regional studies at Harvard University in 1992.

Scott C. Flanagan, director of Asian studies and professor of political science at Florida State University, Tallahassee, is the author or coauthor of numerous works, including *Politics in Japan* (1984) and *The Japanese Voter* (1991).

David Earl Groth has taught at the University of Hawai'i-Hilo, Leiden National University in the Netherlands, and the University of California Irvine and Santa Cruz campuses. He is the author of *Biting the Bullet: The Politics of Grass-Roots Protest in Japan* (forthcoming) and is currently writing a book on foreign workers in Japan.

Ellis S. Krauss, professor in the Graduate School of International Relations and Pacific Studies at the University of California, San Diego, is the author of *Japanese Radicals Revisited* (1974) and co-editor of *Political Opposition and Local Politics in Japan* (1980), *Conflict in Japan* (1984), and *Democracy in Japan* (1989). He is currently completing a book on television news and politics in Japan.

Susan J. Pharr is Edwin O. Reischauer Professor of Japanese Politics at Harvard University and director of the Program on U.S.–Japan Relations. She is the author of numerous works on Japanese politics and society, including *Political Women in Japan* (1981) and *Losing Face: Status Politics in Japan* (1990).

Toshio Takeshita, associate professor of communication studies at the University of Tsukuba, formerly was affiliated with the Institute of Journalism and Communication Studies at the University of Tokyo. He has conducted several studies on media and agenda setting in Japan.

Ikuo Takeuchi is professor of sociology at Tōyō University and professor emeritus at the University of Tokyo, where formerly he was director of the Institute of Journalism and Communication Studies. He is the author of numerous works on mass communication effects and public opinion.

D. Eleanor Westney is associate professor of management at the Sloan School of Management, Massachusetts Institute of Technology. She is the author of many works on organizational behavior and business culture in Japan and the United States, including *Imitation and Innovation: The Transfer of Western Organizational Patterns to Meiji Japan* (1987).

INDEX

ABC News, 99, 107
Abe, Shintarō, 148
advertising: as constraint on news coverage, 116, 139, 171; expenditures, 54; industry in United States, 54; magazine, 81; newspaper, 62, 64, 67, 81; political, 7, 317, 318, 361–362; radio, 72; television, 54–55, 72
agenda-setting role of media, 293–294, 339, 348–349; on environmental issues, 364; "limited effects" hypothesis, 314, 315, 318, 333; on local issues, 321, 341–342, 346–348, 350 n. 11; studies of, 340–341; two-step flow model, 313, 368, 369
aging-society problem, 203–206
Akahata (Red Flag) newspaper, 5, 24, 219, 231
alliances, in protest movements, 219
Andō, Hiroshi, 190
anthropology, symbolic, 24, 26
Ariyoshi, Sawako, 199
Arsenio Hall program, 178
Article 21, Japanese Constitution, 181–182
Asahi Journal, 148
Asahi News Network, 60, 71. *See also* TV Asahi
Asahi Newspaper (Shimbun): advertising revenue, 64; articles on United States, 246, 247; automotive safety issue, 190; circulation, 4–5; coral incident, 140; coverage of government and business, 31–32; diversification, 69; election coverage, 322, 323–324, 326, 335 n. 16; environmental issue coverage, 190, 206, 221; foreign operations, 76, 87 n. 59; history, 10–

11, 64; local news section, 86 n. 38, 342–344; Machida City election coverage, 322, 323–324, 326; new technology, 58; ownership, 84 n. 14; perceived political bias, 319, 335 n. 17; publishing activities, 59, 69; scandal coverage, 147, 148; Shinkansen protest coverage, 222; television involvement, 60, 61, 71
Atarashii Kita Ku Newspaper, 231
automotive safety issue, media coverage, 190

Babcock-Abrahams, Barbara, 25
background briefings *(kondan),* 168, 175
Bagdikian, Ben, 55
balance: in newspapers, 253–254; in television news, 263
ban-kisha, 168
Bank of Japan, 153, 155
banks: cooperative, 153; lending to media firms, 56, 65; shareholdings in media firms, 57; trust, 152–153
BBC (British Broadcasting Corporation), 90
Berger, Peter, 26
Bertelsmann, 76
bias: effects in election campaigns, 319–320; in Japanese coverage of U.S., 263–264; of journalists, 107–108, 117; perceived, of national newspapers, 22, 288, 319, 325, 326, 335 n. 17; research on, 321; of television news, 129 n. 64, 288; in U.S. media, 320
bira maki, 228, 230, 231–232
Boeing, 153
books. *See* publishing
Boyd, Richard, 191

Production Notes

Composition and paging were done in
FrameMaker software on an AGFA
AccuSet Postscript Imagesetter by the
design and production staff of
University of Hawai'i Press.

The text typeface is Sabon and the
display typeface is CG Jasper.

Offset presswork and binding were done
by The Maple-Vail Book Manufacturing
Group. Text paper is Glatfelter Smooth
Antique, basis 50.